Sovereign Lives

Sovereign Lives
Power in Global Politics

Edited by Jenny Edkins, Véronique Pin-Fat
and Michael J. Shapiro

ROUTLEDGE New York • London

Published in 2004 by
Routledge
270 Madison Avenue
New York, NY 10016
www.routledge-ny.com

Published in Great Britain by
Routledge
2 Park Square
Milton Park, Abingdon,
Oxon OX14 4RN, U.K.
www.routledge.co.uk

Routledge is an imprint of the Taylor and Francis Group.

Printed in the United States of America on acid-free paper.

10 9 8 7 6 5 4 3 2 1

Library of Congress Cataloging-In-Publication data:

Sovereign lives : power in global politics / Jenny Edkins, Véronique Pin-Fat, and Michael J. Shapiro, editors.
    p. cm.
Includes bibliographical references and index.
ISBN 0-415-94735-9 (cl : alk. paper) -- ISBN 0-415-94736-7 (pb : alk. paper)
1. Power (Social sciences) 2. Sovereignty. 3. Globalization. 4. International relations.
5. World politics--1989- I. Edkins, Jenny. II. Pin-Fat, Véronique, 1965- III. Shapiro, Michael J.
JC330.S68 2004
320'.01'1--dc22

2004003835

Contents

List of Illustrations

Contributors

William E. Connolly is the Eisenhower-Krieger Professor of political science at Johns Hopkins University. His book, *The Terms of Political Discourse,* recently won the Lippincott Award for being a book "of exceptional quality . . . still considered significant after a time span of at least 15 years." His recent books include *The Ethos of Pluralization* (1995), *Why I Am Not a Secularist* (1999) and *Neuropolitics: Thinking, Culture, Speed* (2002).

Michael Dillon is professor of politics at the University of Lancaster, UK. Co-editor of *The Journal for Cultural Research* (Routledge), he publishes extensively in international relations, and in political and cultural theory.

Jenny Edkins is professor of international politics at the University of Wales Aberystwyth. Her most recent book is *Trauma and the Memory of Politics* (Cambridge University Press, 2003). She is author of *Whose Hunger? Concepts of Famine, Practices of Aid* (Minnesota, 2000) and *Poststructuralism and International Relations: Bringing the Political Back in* (Lynne Rienner, 1999).

Jorge Fernandes is a researcher at the Globalization Research Center, University of Hawaii. He works on postcolonial migrancy and Creole formations.

Jasmina Husanović has a doctorate from the Department of International Politics, University of Wales, Aberystwyth. Her research interests span recent political theory, as well as the question of emancipatory political practice and the sovereign project, and Bosnian and Balkan themes in this regard. She has published in *Forum Bosnae, International Feminist Journal of Politics, International Journal of Human Rights,* and *Millennium* and has contributed a chapter in *The Kosovo Tragedy: The Human Rights Dimension*, ed. Ken Booth (London: Frank Cass, 2001). She is also involved in civil society activism in Bosnia.

Erin Manning is in the Fine Arts Faculty at Concordia University in Montreal, Canada. She also teaches in the Mel Hoppenheim School of Cinema at Concordia. She is assistant professor at Concordia University with a joint appointment in film studies and studio art. She has recently published *Ephemeral Territories: Representing Nation, Home and Identity in Canada* (Minneapolis: Minnesota UP, 2003). Her current book project is entitled *Transnational Movements of Desire and a Politics of Touch*.

Patricia Molloy has a doctorate in education from the University of Toronto, Canada. She has published extensively on the cultural study of international politics and ethics, and is the author of *From the Strategic Self to the Ethical Relation: Pedagogies of War and Peace*, which is forthcoming from the University of Minnesota Press.

Véronique Pin-Fat is Lecturer in International Relations and Director of the MA Human Rights in the Centre for International Politics, The University of Manchester. She publishes in international politics.

Guillermina Seri is a Ph.D. candidate from the Department of Political Science at the University of Florida, Gainesville. Her dissertation examines the relationships between policing and governance in both a theoretical and comparative perspective. Specifically, it explores the role of narratives in the prevalence of non-democratic policing (and exclusionary political) patterns.

Michael J. Shapiro is Professor of Political Science at the University of Hawaii. Among his recent publications are *Cinematic Political Thought* (University of Edinburgh Press, 1999) and *For Moral Ambiguity: National Culture and the Politics of the Family* (University of Minnesota Press, 2001). His most recent book is *Methods and Nations: Cultural Governance and the Indigenous Subject* (New York: Routledge, 2004).

Karena Shaw is particularly interested in the challenges posed by critical social movements to contemporary theories and practices of politics. She has written in the areas of feminist, environmental and indigenous politics, and co-edited *A Political Space: Reading the Global through Clayoquot Sound* (University of Minnesota Press, 2003). Her current research focuses on how the strategies and practices pursued by these movements are reformulating political possibility.

She is currently Assistant Professor in the School of Environmental Studies at the University of Victoria, Canada, and formerly taught at Keele University, UK.

Christine Sylvester is Professor of Women, Gender, Development at the Institute of Social Studies, The Hague. Author most recently of *Feminist International Relations: An Unfinished Journey* (Cambridge, 2002) and *Producing Women and Progress in Zimbabwe* (Heinemann, 2000), she has written on the arts and international relations/development in *Alternatives, Millennium, and the International Feminist Journal of Politics* and is editor of a special issue of the e-journal *Borderlands* on Dramaturgies of Violence (November 2003).

R. B. J. Walker is Professor of International Relations at the University of Keele and holds a chair at the University of Victoria, British Columbia. He has written extensively on the implications of contemporary global trans-formations for modern accounts of sovereignty, subjectivity and political practice. He is the editor of the journal *Alternatives: Global, Local, Political.* His best known work is *Inside/Outside: International Relations as Political Theory*, Cambridge University Press, 1993, and he is currently on the verge of completing a new book *After the Globe/Before the World.* His *publications* include numerous journal articles and books and book chapters.

CHAPTER 1

Introduction
Life, Power, Resistance
JENNY EDKINS AND VÉRONIQUE PIN-FAT

"In order to understand what power relations are about, perhaps we should investigate ... forms of resistance."

—*Michel Foucault*[1]

Introduction

Among the key questions for political and social theory at the beginning of the twenty-first century are those concerning forms of power in the global arena. These questions have been raised in a variety of ways. From one point of view, they appear as questions of the state and its purported or predicted disappearance as a sovereign political institution.[2] This change is often spoken of in terms of globalization, or in terms of the rise in importance of other centers of power: multinational corporations, international financial institutions, terrorist networks, international organizations like the United Nations, nongovernmental organizations, and so forth.[3] Borders are no longer as impervious as they once were, and neither finance nor challenges to security are great respecters of frontiers. From another perspective, the questions at stake depend upon a change in world system from a multipolar balance of power to a unipolar system comprising one superpower or, latterly, what has been called *hyperpouissance*—a hyperpower.[4] The risk, we are told, is a new medievalism where there is neither a balance between superpowers nor a single overall ruler.[5] From this position, a world ruled by a beneficent hyperpower or a society of states may seem to offer stability and order—though perhaps at the expense of justice.[6] And from yet a further point of view, what is to be examined is pictured in terms of the rise of new forms of imperialism, forms of power that are more than just the shadow of old empire or a form of cultural neocolonialism. Although there may be opportunities here for a form of revolutionary change, and new forms of "multitude,"[7] for the most part this description has little that appeals.[8]

However, none of these pictures adequately addresses the question of what form power takes in the contemporary world or considers afresh the way in which power relations themselves are understood. What counts as power? Does it make sense to talk of power as if it were something tangible that could be possessed by a central political institution such as a sovereign state or an imperial power? What produces or reinforces the appearance of domination?

The discussions of the changing forms of power in the contemporary global world sketched above do not examine the image of power to which they all subscribe: one that sees power as an imaginary entity or force that has an independent but intangible being, and can be collected, gathered, and harnessed to the will of a preexisting institution or collectivity. Writings in this volume begin from a different view, the view that power can more usefully be seen as dispersed, not centralized, as produced in social interaction, not possessed, and as productive of subjects, not merely controlling them.

This analysis of power leads to the first contention prompting this collection: that power cannot be grasped or satisfactorily understood as a top-down phenomenon. It is not something that is centralized and possessed, but rather something that is present in and formative of social relations, and it does not exist in advance of the entities to which it gives rise. According to Michel Foucault, it is more helpful to speak of power relations than power per se, and to emphasize the way in which power is produced in social interaction and is itself productive of social subjectivities. Furthermore, and importantly, power relations entail resistance. As this chapter will go on to emphasize, "there are no relations of power without resistances ... formed right at the point where relations of power are exercised." It is through the analysis and unpacking of these intricate relationships of power and resistance that forms of domination produced by sedimented power relations can be understood and vitally contested. Most studies of power relations on a world scale adopt a top-down approach. Such an approach starts from entities, be they individual subjects or institutional forms such as the state, that are assumed to possess power or "be" powerful. In this collection, the emphasis is very much the reverse. The focus is firmly on lives lived, hence the title Sovereign Lives. In our approach, day-to-day social interactions—lives—are examined as productive of both power and subjectivities. What is interesting to us is not the examination of power as something that already exists but the detailed study of power relations in both their productive and controlling aspects.

Because of the way in which they conceptualize power as an object to be possessed by someone or something, the traditional images of world politics that we started with focus on institutions that are assumed to be the holders of power: the sovereign state, international organizations, social movements perhaps, and multinational corporations. They are concerned to ask about the relative significance of these institutions in the contemporary world. In contrast, the contributors to this volume are not interested so much in institutions themselves as in what they see as the prior question of the forms of power relation that give rise to and sustain particular institutions in the first place. They seek to show in a very grounded, localized, and historically situated way how these forms of power relation work, and, most importantly, what forms of subjectivity and resistance they entail. What forms of life do particular power relations make possible? What does this mean for people caught up in these power relations? How does this change? Can subjects contest their subjectification, and if so, how? What counts as resistance? Is there any escape from power relations? Does that question even make sense?

The second claim motivating this collection is that sovereign power is far from dead. The notion of sovereign power as opposed to sovereignty is crucial here. The volume does not focus on the debate concerning the survival or otherwise of sovereign statehood, but rather traces the continuance of certain grammars of power and resistance, irrespective of the site or sites in which they are located. The interesting question is not whether a system or even a society of states has been replaced by an empire or by some other institutional configuration, but what relations or grammars of power persist and how they operate. Following Giorgio Agamben, we seek to extend a Foucauldian analysis to encompass an expansive and more thoroughly analytic view of what William Connolly calls the logic of sovereignty. We want to break away from a notion of "sovereignty" as synonymous with "sovereign statehood" that often appears at the center of analysis. Instead we want to insist upon an engagement with the term "sovereign power". Barry Hindess reminds us that it is high time that we in political theory "cut off the King's head" and follow Foucault's injunction to develop "a political philosophy that isn't erected around the problem of sovereignty." Foucault sees the notion of sovereignty as little more than a smoke screen concealing the operation of disciplinary practices. He argues that "the procedures of normalization" or discipline "come to be ever more constantly engaged in the colonization of those of law" such that "sovereignty and disciplinary mechanisms are two absolutely integral constituents of the general mechanism of power in our society." This "general mechanism of power" has been analyzed by Agamben as "sovereign power," and the essays in this volume trace ways in which this form of power is productive of particular forms of life (or lives lived) and crucially, their attendant forms of resistance.

Foucault argues that the best way to move toward a new economy of power relations "consists in taking the forms of resistance against different forms of power as a starting point [and] using this resistance ... to bring to light power relations, locate their position, find out their point of application and the methods used." This introductory chapter takes Foucault's suggestion on board and uses an analysis of forms of resistance to locate and differentiate forms of power relation. It argues, following Agamben, that the predominant form of power in the contemporary world remains sovereign power, and it examines how that form of power operates through the production of a form of life that Agamben calls "bare life." We argue that sovereign power in its current form needs to be seen not so much as a power relation but rather as a relationship of violence. The chapter locates examples of practical resistance to such a form of power in two practices or modes: first, in a refusal to "draw the line" or make distinctions between forms of life of the type upon which sovereign power relies, and, second, in what we call the assumption of bare life, that is, voluntarily taking on the very form of life that sovereign power seeks to impose. This assumption of bare life, in its very voluntarism, subverts the operation of sovereign power and reinstates properly political power relations.

Resistance, Power Relations, and Subjectivity in Foucault and Agamben

Before examining sovereign power and identifying two specific forms of resistance to it, two preliminary moves are necessary. First, we elaborate what might be meant by resistance, more generally in the context of a Foucauldian approach to power. Indeed, we go on to locate resistance as an inseparable part of power relations. Second, drawing on Agamben's work, we argue that sovereign power leads to a form of administration of bare life, exemplified in the concentration camp, which can no longer usefully be regarded as a power relation.

Power and Resistance

In the Foucauldian picture, power is relational, not an object: "power is neither given, nor exchanged, nor recovered, but rather exercised ... it only exists in action."[9] Power is not something that can be possessed or traded; it is something that is continually produced through or present in certain forms of social relationship. Not only is power produced in these social relations, power itself as a relation is "directly productive" not repressive.[10] Power is not to be seen as something that "subdues or crushes individuals." On the contrary, "it is one of the prime effects of power that certain bodies, certain gestures, certain discourses, certain desires, come to be identified and constituted as individuals."[11] In this relational view, power "is produced from one moment to the next, at every point, or rather in every relation from one point to another."[12]

Importantly, relations of power entail resistance: they would not count as relations of power were resistance not present. As Foucault puts it, "where there is power, there is resistance." In a sense, that is what a relation of power is. To complain that this means "there is no 'escaping' power," Foucault argues, would be simply mistaken. Such a comment "would be to misunderstand the strictly relational character of power relationships [whose] existence depends on a multiplicity of points of resistance . . . present everywhere in the power network."

What are the implications of this analysis? If resistance and power go hand in hand, then there is no possibility of a grand refusal overcoming power relations, since refusal is already part of what produces a power relation as such. What happens instead is that we have

> a plurality of resistances, each of them a special case: resistances that are possible, necessary, improbable; others that are spontaneous, savage, solitary, concerted, rampant, or violent; still others that are quick to compromise, interested, or sacrificial; by definition they can only exist in the strategic of field of power relations. But this does not mean that they are only a reaction or a rebound, forming with respect to the basic domination an underside that is in the end always passive, doomed to perpetual defeat.[13]

Pessimism is not justified, for just as relations of power can form a dense web that seems to solidify into institutions like the state and sediment into forms of domination, so points of resistance can come together to lead to revolution. However, "more often one is dealing with mobile and transitory points of resistance" that produce shifting cleavages and regroupings. These are the very fabric of political life.

Another way of putting it is to say that relations of power are "exercised only over free subjects and only insofar as they are 'free.'" Like power and resistance, "the power relationship and freedom's refusal to submit cannot be separated." What is meant by freedom here is "a field of possibilities in which several kinds of conduct, several ways of reacting and modes of behaviour are available." Freedom is the condition for the exercise of power: slavery, for example, is not a power relationship unless there is a chance of escape. Freedom and the power relation provoke each other; like power and resistance, they cannot be separated. If there were no relations of power in Foucauldian terms, then the notion of freedom would not arise.

As we have seen, foucault suggests that it is through the study of points of resistance or what he calls "antiauthority struggles" that we can come to understand better the operation of relations of power. He contends that the chief forms of resistance in contemporary society are all struggles that contest a certain form of subjectification. They all

> revolve around the question: Who are we? They are a refusal of ... abstractions [that] ignore who we are individually, and also a refusal of a scientific or administrative inquisition that determines who one is.[14]

In other words, Foucault argues, these practices of resistance both point to and contest the way in which contemporary power is at the same time "an individualizing and a totalizing form of power." In many ways, this bears a striking similarity to what Agamben calls sovereign power, and we turn to examine this notion next.

Sovereign Power and Bare Life

Agamben extends and elaborates Foucault's writings through the introduction of two notions: sovereign power and bare or naked life. Sovereign power remains a principal way in which power relationships are exercised in contemporary global society. Foucault tells us that although there cannot be a society without power relations, because "to live in society is ... to live in such a way that some act on the actions of others," it is nevertheless the case that established power relations are not the only ones possible.[15] They can be challenged in favor of other forms. Agamben takes Foucault's analysis further and argues that sovereign power has developed to an extent that the question has changed. It has become a question of whether any form of power relation is possible, or as he puts it "Is today a life of power available?"[16] In this section, we discuss how Agamben arrives at this formulation and ask what it means, especially for the notion of resistance.

Agamben's work enables us to establish what it is about sovereign power that makes it a distinct form of power relation: it is the way it operates through the sovereign ban, that is, through the making of distinctions, in particular distinctions between forms of life. In ancient Greek thought, there were two words for "life:" zoe, which meant the simple fact of living shared by all beings, and bios, which signified the particular way of life of an individual or group. Agamben argues that from the start, sovereign power relies on the separation of these two forms of life, which can be called politically qualified life (in the ancient world, the life appropriate to the public or political sphere) and bare or naked life (the life of the home or domestic sphere). In modern biopolitics, Agamben argues, bare life is politicized and political life disappears. Sovereign politics constitutes itself first by the exclusion of bare life or, more accurately, by the inclusion of bare life in the sovereign realm by virtue of its very exclusion from it. Bare life, included by exclusion, becomes sacred life—life that can be killed but not sacrificed, or homo sacer. The sovereign is the one who decides on the exception: in this sense, the sovereign is both inside and outside the law. What this logic of sovereignty produces is a zone of indistinction. The form of life that inhabits that zone is homo sacer: "Neither political bios nor natural zoe, sacred life is the zone of indistinction in which zoe and bios constitute each other in including and excluding each other."

In Agamben's analysis of sovereign power, the camp is the ultimate expression of the sovereign exception and the arena where life becomes nothing but bare life, life included by its exclusion:

> Inasmuch as its inhabitants have been stripped of every political status and reduced completely to naked life, the camp is also the most absolute biopolitical space that has ever been realised—a space in which power confronts nothing other than pure biological life without any mediation. The camp is the paradigm itself of political space at the point in which politics becomes biopolitics and the *homo sacer* becomes indistinguishable from the citizen.[17]

This leads him to the question with which we began this section: "Is today a life of power available?" For Agamben, such a life is not possible within present forms of sovereign power and their reliance on the division of forms of life from pure living itself. A life of power would mean an exodus from sovereign power, a nonstatist politics, and "the emancipation from such a division."

Bare Life as a Power-Less Life

In this section, we suggest that when the insights of Foucault and Agamben are combined, there are unexpected implications for the notion of resistance: implications that are to be found in the depoliticized and technologized administrative depths of the camp rather than outside it. We argue that both Foucault and Agamben are gesturing toward the conclusion that bare life is a power-less life and, correspondingly, that life constituted within biopolitics cannot be a political life. This moves us then toward the somewhat surprising conclusion that far from seeking to escape power relations, we should be attempting to reinstate them, and with them the possibility (and possibilities or potentialities) of politics.[18] Despite its name, sovereign power is not a properly political power relation, we will argue, but a relationship of violence.

Following Foucault, we have argued that power and freedom occupy the same moment of possibility. Resistance is inevitable whenever and wherever there are power relations. One implication is that without power relations there can be no subjectivities, whether collective or individual. As Foucault puts it,

> we must cease once and for all to describe the effects of power in negative terms: it "excludes," it "represses," it "censors," it "abstracts," it "masks," it "conceals.". In fact, power produces; it produces reality; it produces domains of objects and rituals of truth. The individual and the knowledge that may be gained of him belong to this production. [19]

The second simultaneous implication is that without power relations there is no possibility of resistance and no freedom. An undecidable and undetermined (i.e., free) subjectivity, in excess of power relations, cannot "be" in the absence of power. Freedom and resistance are found as part of power relations and such relations are productive of subjectivities.

Taking these two implications from Foucault, we can begin to ask what examples there might be in practice of a mode of being where there are no power relations and where resistance is impossible. It can be argued, following Agamben, that the concentration camp is such an example.

In the camp, the majority of the prisoners become what was termed "Muselmänner" in camp jargon. Primo Levi describes these as "the drowned:"

> Their life is short, but their number is endless; they…form the backbone of the camp, an anonymous mass, continually renewed and always identical, of non-men who march and labour in silence, the divine spark dead within them, already too empty to really suffer. One hesitates to call them living: one hesitates to call their death death, in the face of which they have no fear, as they are too tired to understand. [20]

The drowned are "bare life"—their concerns are limited to where the next mouthful of food is coming from—and they are also homines sacri, sacred men: they can be killed at will by the camp guards, without ceremony and without justification having to be offered or provocation demonstrated. More significantly for the argument here, they offer no resistance. Indeed, they are indifferent to their fate. They are reduced to a state where they are unable even to commit suicide: they do not have the possibility of killing themselves. In Foucault's terms, then, for the drowned of the concentration camp there are no relations of power, only relations of violence. Agamben insists, however, that despite their abjection, these prisoners, in many ways seemingly nonhuman, are potentially all the more fully human. As Levi tells us, in the camps the worst survived: those who stole, cheated, obtained favors, collaborated; the best all died. In such circumstances, who is the more human, the one who drowns or the one who survives? In other words, just because resistance is impossible, it does not mean that the person who has drowned has no worth. To be outside relations of power, to be beyond resistance, that is to be one of the drowned, is not to be without value: Levi shows us quite the reverse, Agamben argues. Levi's paradox is that the one who appears inhuman (the drowned) is perhaps the most human.

The camp then is an example of where power, at its zenith, disappears and becomes pure administration. What we have in the camps is not a power relation. Power is no longer necessary: it is no longer necessary, for example, in its role as constitutive of subjectivities, because there is no longer a subject—just bare life. But more to the point, if power relations are productive as Foucault tells us, there is no thing, no subject, no anything that is being produced in the camp. All we have is bare life being administered.

For Foucault, power relations are a very specific form of social relation: "power relations ... are distinct from objective capacities as well as from relations of communication." Power as a relation is distinct from "technical" or "objective" capacities. In other words, a power relation is to be seen as distinct from a relationship of violence. A relationship of violence acts "immediately and directly on others" whereas a relationship of power "acts upon their actions." Slaves in chains, for example, are not in a power relation but in a relationship of violence:

> Where the determining factors are exhaustive, there is no relationship of power: slavery is not a power relationship when a man is in chains, only when he has some possible mobility, even a chance of escape ... . At the very heart of the power relationship, and constantly provoking it, are the recalcitrance of the will and the intransigence of freedom.[21]

In the camps, for those inmates who reached the depths, who faced the Gorgon, there were no relations of power, only violence and constraint.

Agamben, of course, importantly argues that what took place in the camp as a zone of indistinction has extended in the contemporary world to encompass regions outside the camp as well. We have all become homines sacri or bare life in the face of a biopolitics that technologizes, administers and depoliticizes, and thereby renders the political and power relations irrelevant.

Sovereign Lives as Bare Lives

There are many examples outside the camp that demonstrate how in living our lives under sovereign power we have all become *homines sacri*. Contributions to this volume trace different ways in which sovereign power produces bare life and show how a zone of indistinction is becoming globalized.

A zone of indistinction can be understood quite literally as the demarcation of a specific topographical area. Seri, for example, concentrates on zoning as an activity that both reproduces and stablizes sovereign power. In particular, she traces the ways in which zones of exception are discursively, though differently, constituted by the United States and Argentina with reference to the "triple frontier" after September 11, 2001. The zoning of an area as one of exception where lawlessness, international crime, terrorism, and danger have their "natural home" so to speak, impacts on the lives of people who live there in a variety of ways. She argues that not only are inhabitants regarded with suspicion, but the constitution of the "triple frontier" as a zone of exception threatens to engulf Argentina and, indeed, the whole of South America with far-reaching political and economic consequences.

But borders can be other than this. Indeed, Molloy offers a reading of capital punishment as a biopolitical bordering—one where the very terms "life" and "death" become political rather than biological concepts and the very "threshold [border] of the exercise of sovereign power" is revealed. As such, Molloy argues that the death-row inmate is a prime exemplar of a life lived in a zone of indistinction between life and death. The inmate may indeed be in possession of her biological life as she awaits her execution/ death, but this form of life is a stark example of one that is barely so, for it is abandoned to a state of exception. Even while different sovereign authorities might fight over an inmate's future, whether "dead or alive" (e.g., in the case of Hiep and Faulder), what is clear is that sovereign power produces bare life whereby the taking of it is neither a crime nor is it the sacrifice of a fully "human" life. Similarly, Fernandes offers a "biological" example of political border-drawing in his analysis of sovereign responses to viruses. Fernandes shows how nation-states code bare life through the fear of viral pandemics, thereby not only providing a way of controlling flows of peoples, especially migrants, but also a way of reasserting and "safeguarding" politically qualified lives. By offering a biopolitical analysis, Fernandes demonstrates that the role a virus can play in the grammar of global public health is one that both draws and actively polices the boundaries of "imagined immunities" (pp. 225–226). Often this is at the expense of the recognition of the "humanity" of migrants whose subjectivity/life is reduced to a potential contagion of the body politic.

Such examples demonstrate how political life has vanished into little more than the technologization and administration of life as bare life, whether on death row exposed to the vagaries of contending sovereign jurisdictions or through the control of viral contagions. In the face of this, what possible responses can there be to the apparent ubiquity of sovereign power and its impact on lives lived? It is this which we will now begin to address.

Resistance to Sovereign Power

To summarize the argument so far, Agamben argues that the drawing of lines between *zoç* and *bios* constitutes "the fundamental activity of sovereign power [that] is the production of bare life as originary political element."[22] The problem with this, as he so powerfully demonstrates, is that "bare life remains included in politics in the form of the exception, that is, as something that is included solely through an exclusion."[23] It is this that leads us to the camps and to his disheartening declaration that "today … we are all virtually *homines sacri*."[24] Perhaps it is this conclusion that prompts William Connolly to say in Chapter 2 of this volume that Agamben proffers a "logic of sovereignty," that brings us to "a historical impasse" where no way out is disclosed.[25] The possibility of resistance then becomes questionable.

Against Connolly's reading, we would want to suggest that Agamben's contribution, when read alongside Foucault as we have done here, provides an insight into ways in which sovereign power can be resisted and indeed its "logic" or grammar refused. As we have pointed out, the possibility of resistance is in general not one that relies on an "escape" or "emancipation" from power relations. Indeed, we have argued that the logic of this leads us into the camps that are marked by such an absence of power relations. But equally, a resistance to sovereign power's creation of zones of indistinction (the camp being the paradigmatic example) cannot consist of a call for a reinstatement of classical politics either: of a reinstatement of the distinction between zoe and bios. Firstly, this is not a possibility because the very distinction itself, and the lines that it draws, is "the fundamental activity of sovereign power." Secondly, the classical distinction requires that bare life can only be included through an exclusion, that is, in the form of an exception. And thirdly, there cannot be a return to a politics that maintains the distinction between zoē and bios, or, in Agamben's words,

> There is no return from the camps to classical politics. In the camps, city and house became indistinguishable, and the possibility of differentiating between our biological body and our political body— between what is incommunicable and mute and what is communicable and sayable—was taken from us forever.[26]

Either way, whether through an emancipatory ideal or through a reinstatement of classical politics, we are all homines sacri or bare life. However, resistance may be possible not through emancipation or nostalgic return, but, as we will argue, through either of two other strategies: first through refusal and, second, through acceptance.

We have argued that Agamben's work demonstrates that sovereign power is no longer a form of power relation in Foucault's terms but a relationship of violence (as his discussion of the camp shows). Indeed, to understand sovereign power as such means that forms of resistance that simply call for an "end to violence" cannot succeed. Michael Shapiro's meditation on violence in this volume shows how violent such "endings" can be as enactments of imperial sovereignty themselves post-9/11. Since this is the case, then, however paradoxically, resistance to sovereign power takes place when there is a demand for a return to properly political power relations, and takes the form of such a demand.

Agamben's injunction is that we must find "a completely new politics— that is, a politics no longer founded on the exception of bare life." If the zone of indistinction has extended beyond the camp to embrace much of the rest of the world, then what we have is an extension of bare life, and its lack of relationalities of power: in other words, an impossibility of politics. The absence of a power relation is not desirable because there is then no possibility of resistance. We have nothing but a form of servitude or slavery. So, rephrasing in Foucauldian terms, Agamben is arguing that we have moved to a power-less relation, that is, to a relationship of violence. Let us remind ourselves how Foucault describes such a relationship and its contrast with a power relation:

> A relationship of violence acts upon a body or upon things; it forces, it bends, it breaks, it destroys, or it closes off all possibilities. Its opposite pole can only be passivity, and if it comes up against any resistance it has no other option but to try to break it down. A power relationship, on the other hand, can only be articulated on the basis of two elements that are indispensable if it is really to be a power relationship: that the "other" (the one over whom power is exercised) is recognised and maintained to the very end as a subject who acts; and that, faced with a relationship of power, a whole field of responses, reactions, results, and possible inventions may open up.[27]

In this context, it then makes sense when Agamben argues that the question we should be addressing is not "Is there any escape from power?" but, on the contrary, "Is today a life of power available?"[28]

Since sovereign power relies on two things—first, the drawing of lines between forms of life and, second, the production thereby of a generalized bare life—there are two ways in which the demand for a return to politics can be articulated: the refusal of sovereign distinctions and the acceptance of bare life. We elaborate what we mean by this in the remainder of this chapter.

Resistance as the Refusal of Sovereign Distinctions

One potential form of resistance to sovereign power consists of a refusal to draw any lines between *zoç* and *bios*, inside and outside, human and inhuman. As we have shown, sovereign power does not involve a power relation in Foucauldian terms. It is more appropriately considered to have become a form of governance or technique of administration through relationships of violence that reduce political subjects to mere bare or naked life. As Michael Dillon puts it, "Sovereign power [is] a form of rule gone global [that] has come to develop and deploy modes of destruction whose dissemination it finds increasingly impossible to control because these have become integral to its propagation and survival."[29]

In asking for a refusal to draw lines as a possibility of resistance, then, we are not asking for the elimination of power relations and, consequently, we are not asking for the erasure of the possibility of a mode of political being that is empowered and empowering, is free and that speaks: quite the opposite. Following Agamben, we are suggesting that it is only through a refusal to draw any lines at all (and, indeed, nothing less will do) that sovereign power (as a form of violence) can be contested and a properly political power relation can be reinstated.

We could call this escaping the logic of sovereign power. Our overall argument is that we can escape sovereign power and reinstate a form of power relation by contesting its assumption of the right to draw lines, that is, by contesting the sovereign ban. Any other resistance always inevitably remains within this relationship of violence. To move outside it (and return to a power relation), we need not only contest its right to draw lines in particular places, but also resist the call to draw any lines of the sort sovereign power demands.

The grammar of sovereign power cannot be resisted by challenging or fighting over where the lines are drawn. While, of course, this is a strategy that can be deployed as a form of resistance, it is not a resistance to sovereign power per se as it still tacitly or even explicitly accepts that lines must be drawn somewhere (and preferably more inclusively). Christine Sylvester's exploration of what she calls "fictional development sovereignties" in this volume can be read as testimony to this. Nevertheless, strategies that address where lines are drawn are, undoubtedly, crucially important and often seem the only possibility for resistance. Indeed, in Chapters 2 and 9 both William Connolly and Karena Shaw offer compelling arguments and illustrations as to how and why this can and should be done. For example, Connolly proposes the notion of an "ethos of sovereignty" by which he means "a modified ethos of constitutional action [that] would nonetheless incline the effective range of court decisions and popular responses in a different direction" such that, despite the paradoxes of sovereignty, such an ethos could alter its course. Furthermore, Shaw suggests that the discourses and practices of sovereignty that take the form of a sovereign state can be "a terrain of power and resistance" mobilized by "those seeking to resist or delegitimize assertions of sovereignty over them." Shaw unpicks the complex ways in which a Hobbesian grammar of a "shared ontology as the precondition for legitimate authority" is reproduced by indigenous peoples but yet offers (albeit precariously) possibilities of critically reconfiguring both what that shared ontology might be and the constitution of legitimate authority. The promise of the arguments both Connolly and Shaw make is an active demonstration that the grammar of sovereign statehood (distinct from sovereign power) is not fixed in a timeless configuration. As Connolly puts it, resistance is possible within a logic of state sovereignty transformed by an appropriate ethos such that "old ideas [old practices of sovereignty, territory, property, capital, mastery, nationhood, and faith] provide new sites for possible metamorphosis today."

However, while possible and sometimes desirable, these forms of resistance remain limited and constrained by the grammar of sovereign power, as there is no refusal here of its line-drawing "ethos" that engages with Agamben's conclusion that we are all now homines sacri or bare life. Although they contest the violence of sovereign power's drawing of the line, they risk their own violent relation in demanding that the line be drawn differently. In both cases, the drawing of the line represents a foreclosure of possibility and a denial of the properly political power relation. In what follows, we offer some suggestions for and examples of resistance that succeed in refusing the "paradox of sovereignty" that leads us all into zones of indistinction.

How might resistance as refusal be possible? The metaphysics of presence that sovereign power's founding and foundationalist drawing of a line presupposes (inside/outside, zoē/bios, universal/particular, members/ strangers, colonial/indigenous) can be challenged by examining the relationship between time and politics. In Chapter 4, Erin Manning argues that the possibility of resistance to the imperatives of sovereign statehood (in this case, federalist) lies in "taking time" and "making time" for politics. As she puts it, "Politics that takes time makes time to count those who are excluded, to disagree with those who otherwise have "no part." Politics is the discursive space where one contests and resists the way in which Hobbes's presupposed ontological "whole," around which the sovereign state is configured as a legitimate authority, is counted, and instead engages with miscounting through a dialogue of disagreement. The implications of Manning's position stretch beyond the sovereign state and speak to sovereign power. As she says pithily, "sovereign politics are a waste of time" because they constitute a failure to take the time to "miscount." We might say that "miscounting" is a refusal of, and resistance to, the grammar of sovereign power's drawing of lines between that which "counts" (bios) and that which does not (zoe). It is the refusal to play sovereign power's language-game and follow the rules of "counting" and as such, vitally, it defies and refuses its grammar.

Husanovic also proposes a form of resistance that refuses to draw biopolitical lines. In her examination of grassroots activism in Bosnia, she highlights how some forms of activism can be seen as a refusal of gendered ethnonationalist logics of identity and life. Aware that a refusal of one set of lines may, nonetheless, produce others in their wake, she asks how "emancipatory openings" themselves can resist the danger of foreclosure we described above. Her answer is a form of communitas that is "non-conventional, non-statist, non-sovereign, and non-biopolitical." Vitally, this communitas is not based on the presence of a shared identity, but rather a lack of identity within the institutionalized biopolitical framework. In short it is a form of community, albeit unstable and necessarily shifting, which is based on identification with what she calls the "excluded remainder of the social edifice."

Resistance as the Acceptance of Bare Life

Having demonstrated ways in which a *refusal* of the grammar of sovereign power is possible, we now turn to look at how the *acceptance* of bare life can produce forms of resistance. As we have sought to trace, the issue that needs to be addressed about sovereign power is its production of all life as bare life. Indeed, this is a central concern of Agamben's work. What cannot and must not be tolerated is bare life:

> This biopolitical body that is bare life must itself instead be transformed into the site for the constitution and installation of a form of life that is wholly exhausted in bare life and a bios that is only its own zoe⁻ ... . If we give the name form-of-life to this being that is only its own bare existence and to this life that, being its own form, remains inseparable from it [i.e., not included by exclusion and, therefore, only ever based on exclusion] we will witness the emergence of a field of research beyond the terrain defined by the intersection of politics and philosophy, medico-biological sciences and jurisprudence."[30]

In May 2003, Abbas Amini, an Iranian "seeking asylum" in the United Kingdom (U.K.), went on a hunger strike in protest against the U.K. government's treatment of asylum seekers. Apart from refusing food and water, he also sewed his own eyes, ears, and mouth with coarse thread. Of this he said, "I sewed my eyes so others could see, I sewed my ears so others could hear, I sewed my mouth to give others a voice." When he heard that the Home Office was challenging his successful asylum claim, Amini swore his friends and family to secrecy and began his action as a private protest. The Home Office's appeal was rejected by an independent appeals tribunal, but Amini did not stop his protest. On the contrary, he claimed that his action was not just on his own behalf, but for all asylum seekers. When he ended his action some days later, his words were: "I have ended this because I have come to re-alise that this is a very important struggle to be continued." In an interview with Tania Branigan of the Guardian, he revealed of his act, "Yes, it was po-litical … . Professional psychiatrists have all stated that I am not psycholog-ically damaged and have no mental illness. But the pressure on me was so huge that I got to the point where I thought there was no hope."

The present asylum policy of the UK government "justifies and ignores serious, systematic and gross violations of civil and human rights, legit-imises repressive laws, and rejects those fighting against them as lawbreak-ers. It denies people's rights to struggle for change, for an end to repression, and to exert their rights as human beings." In short, it produces asylum seekers as nothing more than bare life in the camps that house them while they wait to be processed. Then either their asylum claim is granted or they are deported as nothing more than economic migrants. It is yet another ex-ample of how sovereign power draws lines. Even when successful, however, immigrants remain without any genuine political voice: they become homines sacri, like the rest of us. Amini notes that many local people in Nottingham supported him: "A huge number of people fully understand us because they live in the same conditions we do."

An analysis of Amini's protest suggests that he is an example of someone who, through acceptance, has transformed his bare life into a "form-of-life" as Agamben suggests. While Amini's campaign is specific to his circumstances and the context within which it occurs, the political signifi-cance of this form of protest is far-reaching. Amini's political act viscerally reveals and draws attention to his own person as nothing but the bare life produced by sovereign power. When he sewed up his mouth to give others a voice, that is, to demand that others speak for him as one who cannot speak for himself, he used the very bare life that sovereign power imposes on him to unmask the relationship of violence in which he had been placed. Vitally, in doing so he claimed back the possibility of speaking politically.

This action is similar to that of the nonviolent protester who uses their own body to obstruct and draw attention to the violence of the state. The image of the lone demonstrator with his shopping bag standing in front of the tank in Tian an Men Square is iconic here. Faced with the naked life of the subject, sovereign power has a choice: it can either respond politically or it has to reveal the relations of violence on which it depends. Whichever route it takes, it can no longer conceal its violence under the pretence of politics.

Agamben has asked us to think of a nonsovereign power form-of-life where bare life is not included by exclusion—"the constitution and installation of a form of life that is wholly exhausted in bare life and a bios that is only its own zoē." Amini's ultimate success in being granted asylum in the U.K. does not mean that he becomes politically qualified life: he remains firmly within the grammar of sovereign power, where all life, we have argued, is produced as homines sacri or bare life. However, Amini's political act of resistance, using his own body, can be read as an act where, with all hope lost, the only site left for resistance is in complete embrace of bare life as a form-of-life that is its own bios and therefore, vice versa. Indeed, we might say that his sewn muteness, deafness, and blindness shows that our bare life or bodies are, indeed, all we have left and illustrates the way in which "the possibility of differentiating between our biological body and our political body—between what is incommunicable and mute and what is communicable and sayable—was taken from us forever." He continues his protest even after the success of his appeal.

It seems, then, that the asylum system attempts to remove the possibility of a properly political power relation. The refugee, fleeing persecution elsewhere and claiming a political right to asylum, clearly appears on the face of it as politically qualified. Once refugees enter the U.K., they are produced in the zone of indistinction of the camps as bare life, life that is not politically qualified. Even the successful are no longer a political voice telling of oppression and mistreatment, but only lives to be saved. By his actions, Amini demonstrates that this is the case, and in doing so claims back the possibility of speaking politically. Furthermore, when he sews up his mouth to give others a voice, that is, to demand that others speak for him, he is using the very bare life that sovereign power imposes on him to demonstrate the relationship of violence in which he has been placed. Like the nonviolent demonstrator who puts his body on the line, this strategy is particularly effective in showing clearly that sovereign power does not willingly enter into a power relation, but rather survives through relationships of violence.

Concluding Remarks

We have traced in this introductory chapter how sovereign power, that form of rule that today pervades the globe, produces bare life as the form of life under its sway. The contributions to this volume, in their various ways, trace such sovereign lives. They examine how they are lived, and how those lives at different times and in different places contest sovereign power.

We have argued here that sovereign power is not, despite appearances, a form of power relation but rather a relationship of violence. In that it seeks to refuse those whose lives it controls any politically valid response, it operates as a form of technologized administration. A power relation is one that is invariably accompanied by resistance: the subjects it produces are party to the relation, and their freedom to resist is a necessary component of what is happening. Sovereign power on the other hand, with the production of its subjects as bare life, attempts to rule out the possibility of resistance. A properly political power relation is not practicable in those circumstances.

What this tells us is that to contest sovereign power we need something different. In challenging sovereign power, we are not facing a power relation but a relationship of violence, one that denies a political voice to the form-of-life it has produced. Resistance such as would be possible from within a power relation, and indeed as an inherent part of it, cannot take place. Other forms of opposition must be found, forms that seek to reinstate a properly political relationship by producing sovereign power as a form of power relation. Two strategies of contestation were suggested: a refusal and an acceptance. First, the refusal. The abstract drawing of lines is the way in which sovereign power produces bare life. This drawing of lines must be refused, wherever the lines are drawn. Negotiating the precise location of the lines remains within the violence of sovereignty power. On the other hand, a refusal to draw any line takes away the ground upon which sovereign power is constituted. It insists instead on the politics of decisioning and particular distinctions and demands that specifics of time, place, and circumstance be attended to in each instance. Second, the acceptance. When life is produced as bare life, it is not helpful for that life to demand its reinstatement as politically qualified life. To do so would be to validate the very drawing of lines upon which sovereignty depends and which produces life as bare life in the first place. An alternative strategy is the acceptance or what we have called the assumption of bare life. Through this strategy, the subject at one and the same time both acknowledges its status as nothing but life and demands recognition as such. It refuses the distinction between bare life and politically qualified life and demands that all life as such is worthy of recognition.

As is apparent, the two strategies are the same at heart. Both seek to overturn the denial of politics that has taken place under biopolitics and to reinstate properly political power relations, with their accompanying freedoms and potentialities. We have discussed examples of what such contestation of sovereign power might look like. Practices that contest sovereign power are apparent in many places: whether in hunger strikes, grassroots communitas, or street demonstrations, creative ways of provoking sovereign power and embroiling it into a political or power relation have been and are being found.

Notes

1. Michel Foucault, "The Subject and Power." In *Michel Foucault: Power*, Vol. 3, Essential Works of Foucault 1954–1984, edited by James D. Faubion (New York: The New Press, 1994), pp.326–48, 329.
2. Richard Falk, *On Humane Governance: Toward a New Global Politics* (Cambridge: Polity, 1995); see also Richard Falk, *The Great Terror War* (New York: Arris Publishing, 2003).
3. See, for example, John G. Ikenberry, *After Victory: Institutions, Strategic Restraint, and the Rebuilding of Order After Major Wars* (Princeton, New Jersey: Princeton University Press, 2000).
4. See, for example, Robert D. Kaplan, *The Coming Anarchy: Shattering the Dreams of the Post Cold War* (New York: Vintage Books, 2001). The French use of this term became widespread in 2003 during disagreements over the U.S. policy with regard to Iraq.
5. See, for example, John J. Mearscheimer, *The Tragedy of Great Power Politics* (New York: W. W. Norton, 2001); Robert D. Kaplan, *The Coming Anarchy: Shattering the Dreams of the Post Cold War* (New York: Vintage Books, 2001).
6. Hedley Bull, *The Anarchical Society: A Study of Order in World Politics*, 2nd edition (London: Macmillan, 1995).
7. Michael Hardt and Antonio Negri, *Empire* (Cambridge, Massachusetts: Harvard University Press, 2000). See also, for example, Chalmers A. Johnson, *Blowback: The Costs and Consequences of American Empire* (New York: Owl Books, 2003).
8. For other recent attempts to delineate what power in global politics might involve, especially after September 11, see, for example, Robert Cooper, *The Postmodern State and the World Order* (London: Demos, 2000); Charles A. Kupchan, *The End of the American Era: US Foreign Policy and the Geopolitics of the Twenty-first Century* (New York: Alfred A. Knopf, 2002); and for one overview of the debates, Booth, Ken, and Tim Dunne (editors), *Worlds in Collision: Terror and the Future of Global Order* (London: Palgrave Macmillan, 2002).
9. This is a view that draws among others on the work of Michel Foucault, as we elaborate below.
10. Michel Foucault, *Power/Knowledge: Selected Interviews and Other Writings 1972–1977*, trans. by Colin Gordon (Brighton: Harvester Press, 1980) p. 142.
11. A clear exception would be Cynthia Enloe's work, which insists on attention to the detail and specifics of power relations to build the larger picture. Cynthia Enloe, *Bananas Beaches and Bases: Making Feminist Sense of International Politics* (Berkeley: University of California Press, 1990).
12. It is not impossible to analyze power relations in the Foucauldian sense by looking at institutions, but there are dangers in doing so. See Foucault, "The Subject and Power," pp. 342–343.
13. This is Agamben's term. Giorgio Agamben, *Homo Sacer: Sovereign Power and Bare Life*, trans. by Daniel Heller-Roazen (Stanford, California: Stanford University Press, 1998).
14. See Chapter 2. We would read Connolly's analysis there as focusing rather more on sovereignty than sovereign power.
15. Foucault, *Power/Knowledge* p. 121. Barry Hindess, *Discourses of Power: From Hobbes to Foucault* (Oxford: Blackwell, 1996).
16. Foucault, *Power/Knowledge*, pp. 105–106.
17. Foucault, "The Subject and Power," p. 329.
18. Michel Foucault,."Two Lectures," trans. by Leo Marshall, Colin Gordon, John Mepham, and Kate Soper. *Power/Knowledge: Selected Interviews and Other Writings 1972–1977*,. edited by Colin Gordon (Brighton: Harvester, 1980) pp. 78–108, 89.
19. Michel Foucault, *The History of Sexuality: Volume 1: An Introduction*, trans. by Robert Hurley (Harmondsworth: Penguin Books, 1990), p. 94.
20. Foucault, "Two Lectures," p. 98.
21. Foucault, *The History of Sexuality*, p. 93.
22. Foucault, *The History of Sexuality*, p. 95.
23. Foucault, *The History of Sexuality*, p. 95.
24. Foucault, *The History of Sexuality*, p. 95.
24. Foucault, *The History of Sexuality*, p. 95.
26. Foucault, "The Subject and Power," p. 342.
27. Foucault, "The Subject and Power," p. 342.
28. Our analysis differs from Michael Dillon's reading of Foucault in Chapter 3. Dillon sees power as "a force that circulates" and one that "only comes to presence in the context of the freedom

of human being acting in effect as a conducive material for power's very circulation and strategic organizing." (Michael Dillon, "Correlating Sovereign and Biopower," this volume, pp. 41–60. However, it is not so much that human being acts as a conducive material for the circulation of power but rather that human beings, in their social relations and interactions, produce the effect of power and are produced as subjects by it. Freedom then for Foucault is not an excess of being over power or indeed "possibility"; rather, what we call "freedom" is nothing but the necessary opposite and companion, if you like, of what is called "power."

29. Foucault, "The Subject and Power," p. 329.
30. Foucault, "The Subject and Power," p. 331.
31. Foucault, "The Subject and Power," p. 332.
32. Foucault, "The Subject and Power," p. 343.
33. Giorgio Agamben, *Means Without End: Notes on Politics*, trans. by Vincenzo Binetti and Cesare Casarino. Minneapolis: University of Minnesota Press, 2000, p. 9 [emphasis in original].
34. Agamben himself wants to retain a term form-of-life, by which he means "a life that can never be separated from its form, a life in which it is never possible to isolate something such as naked life" (Agamben, *Means Without End*," pp. 3–4.
34. Or, in Foucauldian terms, becomes the technologized subject of governance and discipline.
36. Agamben, *Homo Sacer*, pp. 80–86.
37. Agamben, *Homo Sacer*, p. 90.
38. Agamben, *Means Without End*, p. 41 [emphasis in original].
39. Agamben, *Means Without End*, p. 9 [emphasis in original].
40. Agamben, *Means Without End*, p. 8.
41. Politics, seen here as the realm of possibilities and power relations, is similar to what has been called elsewhere by Jenny Edkins "the political." Edkins has argued previously that the realm we call "politics" has been depoliticized, becoming nothing but administration (Jenny Edkins, *Poststructuralism and International Relations* (Boulder, Colorado: Lynne Rienner, 1999); she suggested, alongside other writers, using the notion of "the political." to indicate the sphere of repoliticization. The argument here extends and develops that made earlier.
42. Michel Foucault, *Discipline and Punish: The Birth of the Prison*, trans. by Alan Sheridan (London: Allen Lane, 1991), p. 194.
43. Primo Levi, *If This Is a Man and the Truce*, trans. by Stuart Woolf (London: Abacus, 1979), p. 96.
44. Giorgio Agamben, *Remnants of Auschwitz: The Witness and the Archive*, trans. by Daniel Heller-Roazen (New York: Zone Books, 1999).
45. When faced with a friend who tells him that he survived for a purpose, perhaps to write or to bear witness, Levi is appalled; he feels this implies he might be alive in the place of another. He reflects: "The 'saved' of the Lager were not the best, those predestined to good; the bearers of a message. What I had seen and lived through proved the exact contrary. Preferably the worst survived; the selfish, the violent, the insensitive, the collaborators of the 'grey zones', the spies. It was not a certain rule (there were none, nor are there certain rules in human matters), but it was, nevertheless, a rule. I felt innocent, yes, but enrolled among the saved and therefore in permanent search of a justification in my own eyes and those of others. The worst survived—that is, the fittest; the best all died" (Primo Levi, *The Drowned and the Saved*, trans. by Raymond Rosenthal (London: Abacus, 1989), p. 63). The survivors retained their dignity, their awareness, their "humanity," but at what cost?
46. Agamben, *Remnants of Auschwitz*.
47. Foucault, "The Subject and Power," p. 339.
48. Foucault, "The Subject and Power," p. 340.
49. Foucault, "The Subject and Power," p. 342.
50. Guillermina Seri, "On the 'Triple Frontier' and the 'Borderization' of Argentina: A Tale of Zones," this volume, pp. 79–100.
51. Patricia Molloy, "Killing Canadians: The International Politics of Capital Punishment," this volume, p. 136.
52. Patricia Molloy, "Killing Canadians: The International Politics of Capital Punishment," this volume, pp. 125–140.
53. These cases are discussed, among others, in Molloy, "Killing Canadians."
54. Jorge Fernandes, "Ebola Takes to the Road: Mobilizing Viruses in Defense of the Nation-State," this volume, pp. 189–210.
55. Agamben, *Homo Sacer*, p. 181.

56. Agamben, *Homo Sacer*, p. 11 [emphasis added].
57. Agamben, *Homo Sacer*, p. 115.
58. William E. Connolly, "The Complexity of Sovereignty," this volume, p. 27.
59. For an alternative understanding of emancipatory politics which draws upon the insights of Agamben, see Jasmina Husanović, "'In Search of Agency': Beyond the 'Old/New' Biopolitics of Sovereignty in Bosnia," this volume, pp. 211–238.
60. Agamben, *Homo Sacer*, p. 181.
61. Agamben, *Homo Sacer*, p. 188 [emphasis added].
62. Michael J. Shapiro, "'The Nation-State and Violence': Wim Wenders contra Imperial Sovereignty," this volume, pp. 101–124.
63. Agamben, *Homo Sacer*, p. 11.
64. Foucault, "The Subject and Power," p. 340.
65. Agamben, *Means without End*, p. 9 [additional emphasis added].
66. Dillon, "Correlating Sovereign and Biopower," this volume, p. 41.
67. Christine Sylvester, "Fictional Development Sovereignties," this volume, pp. 141–163.
68. Connolly, "The Complexity of Sovereignty," this volume, p. 33.
69. Karena Shaw, "Creating/Negotiating Interstices: Indigenous Sovereignties," this volume, pp. 165–187.
70. Shaw, "Creating/Negotiating Interstices," this volume, pp. 165–187.
71. Connolly, "The Complexity of Sovereignty," this volume, p. 39.
72. Connolly, "The Complexity of Sovereignty," this volume, p. 23. Our insertion is Agamben's phrase and what Connolly and others in the volume call either the "logic" or the "contradiction" of sovereignty.
73. Erin Manning, "Time for Politics," this volume, p. 62.
74. This resonates strongly with Shaw's account of a colonial and pan-Indian "counting" of aboriginal identity and its contestations.
75. Manning, "Time for Politics," this volume, p. 77.
76. Husanović, "In Search of Agency."
77. Husanović, "In Search of Agency", this volume, p. 223.
78. Husanović, "In Search of Agency", this volume, p. 224.
79. Husanović, "In Search of Agency", this volume, p. 224.
80. Agamben, *Homo Sacer*, p. 188.
81. Sam Azad, "Abbas Amini gets leave to remain but continues to protest," Independent Race and Refugee News Network, May 29, 2003. URL http://www.irr.org.uk/2003/may/ak000016. html. The spelling of Amini's first name varies.
82. Abbas Amini, BBC News, May 30, 2003. URL http://news.bbc.co.uk/1/hi/england/notting-hamshire/2949896.stm
83. Tania Branigan, "Kurdish Poet Finds his Voice," *Guardian*, May 31, 2003. URL http://www.guardian.co.uk/print/0,3858,4680738-103601,00.html
84. Maryam Namazie, Executive Director of the International Federation of Iranian Refugees, "Abas Amini is granted leave to remain in the UK," *Hambastegi: Paper of the International Federation of Iranian Refugees*, 156 (May 29, 2003): 2. URL http://www.rowzane.com/000_day-row/2305/230531156 hameng1.pdf
85. Azad, "Amini gets leave to remain."
86. Agamben, *Homo Sacer*, p. 188 [emphasis added].

CHAPTER 2

The Complexity of Sovereignty

WILLIAM E. CONNOLLY

The Persistence of Sovereignty

The fall of the Soviet Union, the breakup of Yugoslavia, the extension and intensification of global capital, the consolidation of the European Union, the NATO intervention in Kosovo to overturn ethnic cleansing of the region by Slobodan Milosevic, the trial of Milosevic by an international tribunal, lectures to George W. Bush by European and Japanese leaders about the importance of global action to reverse global warming, the attacks of 9/11 linked to a virtual network of terrorists definitively linked to no single state, the low-grade civil war between Israel and Palestinians—these are just a few events that pose the question: what is happening to state sovereignty today? Is it being overtaken by global capital, international humanism, a global ecological crisis? Or does it persist, while its terms and sites are changing? My sense is not only that sovereignty persists, but that it does so amidst an intensification of ambiguities and uncertainties that have inhabited it all along. Perhaps the first thing is to explore ambiguities and uncertainties that have haunted sovereignty since its inception.

The Paradox of Sovereignty

According to theorists from a variety of intellectual traditions, there is a fundamental paradox located at the center of the rule of law in democratic states. Jean Jacques Rousseau, Carl Schmitt, Franz Kafka, Paul Ricoeur, Hannah Arendt, Jacques Derrida, Gilles Deleuze, and Giorgio Agamben, while disagreeing on numerous other issues, concur in asserting that a democratic state seeking to honor the rule of law is also one with a sovereign power uncertainly situated within and above the law. The rule of law in a state is enabled by a practice of sovereignty that rises above the law. Often the paradox of sovereignty is asserted with respect to the founding of a state, but those who locate a paradox in the founding act typically discern its echoes and reverberations in the state that results as well.[1] Jean Jacques Rousseau, a founder of modern democratic theory, puts the paradox this way:

> In order for an emerging people to appreciate the healthy maxims of politics and follow the fundamental rules of statecraft, the effect would have to become the cause; the social spirit which should be the result of the institution, would have to preside over the founding of the institution itself; and men would have to be prior to the laws what they ought to become by means of laws.[2]

For a polity of self-rule through law to emerge out of a nondemocratic condition, "effect would have to become cause." This is so because the spirit needed to nourish democratic self-rule can only grow out of prior ethos of community already infused into the populace. The complication revolves around, first, whether these infusions exceed or express the self-rule of the people itself and, second, how to wheel either condition, which depends upon the other, into place without first installing the other that depends upon it. Rousseau "resolved" the paradox of sovereignty through recourse to the fiction of a wise legislator who imbues people with the spirit of self-rule before they begin to rule themselves. But he knew this fiction was insufficient to the actuality of any people already set in history. Moreover, well before Wittgenstein's account of how every rule and law encounters uncertainty and indeterminacy as it bumps into new and unforeseen circumstances, Rousseau understood that issue too. He knew that the paradox of founding returns as a recurring paradox of democratic sovereignty: if the populace is not infused by the right spirit of community, even a written constitution would be insufficient to guide it when new and unforeseen circumstances arise.

His response to the paradox is to reduce the arrival of new and unforeseen things to a minimum. Hence his portrayal of the kind of place where self-rule through law is possible: a small, isolated polity; a highly unified educational system; general festivals and rituals that instill common sentiments in all citizens; a national mode of dress that discourages amorous relations with people from other countries; tight rules of chastity for men and women to regulate and discipline the passions; the minimization of commerce through the regularity of self-subsistent family farms; the close regulation of commerce with foreigners; the regulation of theater; severe limits on economic inequality; a citizen militia; a nuclear family in which the male is supreme; and so on so forth. The objective of these institutions, disciplines, prohibitions, and injunctions is to instill the same sentiments, habits, and restraints in the citizenry. Self-rule, Rousseau thought, is circular when it works: its preconditions of possibility require citizen habitualization to common sentiments that they then express as their collective will. To be a sovereign, territorial people, it is necessary to become a highly unified nation.

Rousseau seems to have thought that if democratic sovereignty was to maintain itself, the element of arbitrariness in its formation and maintenance had to be obscure to those who were its objects. Why? Because to consent to being the object of sovereignty, it is best to see yourself as the subject or agent of sovereignty. So he invested a ruse in the Wise Legislator at the very founding of sovereignty: "It is this sublime reason, which rises above the grasp of common men, whose decisions the legislator places in the mouths of the immortals in order to convince by divine authority those who cannot be moved by human prudence."[3] The Legislator, by instilling the right sentiments into the populace and linking them to divine authority, forges them into a sovereign people. But this means that they are crafted by a sublime reason above their grasp into a form through which they rule, making that rule oscillate uncertainly between obedience to something prior to the people and the decisions of the people.

Perhaps no democrat has plumbed the paradox of sovereignty as deeply as Rousseau. He is wise in trying to negotiate its terms rather than simply transcend them. For the people to rule, it must be infused with an ethos that precedes and exceeds its rule; to make that rule legitimate to the people, it must interpret what it has already become as expressive of what divine authority calls upon it to be. Sometimes, a written constitution or the traditions of western civilization stand in for divine authority. But Rousseau's basic understanding of the paradox has withstood the test of numerous attempts to dissolve it into proceduralism, or narrow, prudential renderings of a social contract, or representation by a high court of the simple dictates of a written constitution. To negotiate the paradox is to somehow come to terms with the indispensability of a positive ethos to politics, sovereignty, and the democratic state.

But, for all that, the particular ethos of sovereignty that Rousseau embraces is so inconsonant with the defining features of the contemporary condition that the worst kind of nightmare would result were it to emerge as an active agenda today. The Serbian drive to create a state of ethnic purity approximates the sort of action that would have to be taken to try to forge a sovereign people today with the characteristics that Rousseau seeks. Thus, Rousseau helps us to appreciate the complexity of sovereignty, but not to negotiate a response through which democracy, law, state, and sovereignty speak affirmatively to each other.

Sovereignty and Biopolitics

Giorgio Agamben also finds a paradox within sovereignty. He thinks it has become stark in late-modernity as the state inserts itself more deeply into biological life, that is, as issues of biology become prominent in decisions regarding abortion, artificial insemination, the line between life and death, organ transplant, strategies of citizen induction, and standards of "racial" inclusion and exclusion. In a way that is reminiscent of Rousseau's myth of the Legislator, he also contends that the practice of sovereignty is tied to the sacred. The aura of sovereign authority is sustained through the mystique of the sacred.

For Agamben, the paradox of sovereignty resides in the fact that the state requires a final authority to resolve questions of law, while the final authority is insufficiently informed by any law that precedes it. Modern sovereignty carries forward, if implicitly, the pagan logic of *homo sacer*, or the sacred man. Homo Sacer is "the life that cannot be sacrificed and yet may be killed."[4] It is connected to sovereignty because the "sovereign sphere is the sphere in which it is permitted to kill without committing homicide and without celebrating a sacrifice."[5] This logic sinks more deeply into the world as the state increasingly participates in "biopolitics," penetrating more deeply into the biological depths of human life.

Agamben contends that the "logic" that binds sovereignty, the sacred, and biopolitics together leads (inexorably?) to a state in which a supreme power can annihilate a whole minority in the name of national unity. It is the nexus between the paradox of sovereignty, the sacred, and biopolitics that makes the concentration camp the paradigm of modern politics, with the German Nazi regime expressing its outer limit. If Agamben is right, the emergence of biopolitics plunges the paradox of sovereignty beyond constitutional disputes over democratic rule into the very logic of the Nazi Holocaust.

It is because he finds this logic so compelling and disastrous that Agamben insists that it must be overcome entirely. Here are two formulations in which he announces this necessity:

> And only if it is possible to think the relation between potentiality and actuality differently—and even to think beyond this relation—will it be possible to think a constituting power wholly released from the sovereign ban. Until [this happens] a political theory freed from the aporias of sovereignty remains unthinkable.
>
> Only if it is possible to think the Being of abandonment beyond every idea of law will we have moved out of the paradox of sovereignty toward a politics of freedom from every ban.[6]

Nowhere in his book, however, is a way out of the logic actually disclosed. The response of Hannah Arendt—to pull the state out of biopolitics—is considered and appropriately rejected as unviable. But nothing else is offered to replace it. Agamben thus carries us through the conjunction of sovereignty, the sacred, and biopolitics to a historical impasse. This combination is almost enough to make you return to Rousseau. Indeed, Agamben helps us to see the persistent attraction to the Rousseauian idea of the nation, in a world where its preconditions of attainment are even less propitious than that in Rousseau's day. For Rousseau tried to conceal from many the paradox he encounters, while Agamben's analysis exacerbates a paradox that he cannot imagine how to transcend.

Perhaps it is possible both to resist the fantasy to return to a past that never was and to slip past Agamben's insistence that the paradox must be overcome in a new way. At any rate, I want to suggest that while Agamben's analysis is insightful in identifying three critical elements in the paradox and in pointing to dangers that flow from it, the formalism of his analysis disarms the most promising ways to negotiate it. To show this, I reconsider three key elements in his account: the meaning and role of the sacred, the relation between biopolitics and sovereignty, and the "logic" of sovereignty.

(1) *The sacred*: Agamben's account of the sacred, drawing its credibility from one statement written in the early days of the Roman Empire, needs to be revised. I concur that sovereignty and the sacred touch one another historically. Rousseau's invocation of the Legislator expresses this connection. Sovereignty and the sacred are connected historically, partly because kings have linked their rule to divinity and partly because the persistence of a political regime sometimes imparts the ability to locate a single body powerful enough to resolve key issues of governance. But the sacred is not well defined as that which is both the highest and the most susceptible to annihilation. Rather, the sacred is said to deserve awe because it is thought to be closest to the divine, or at least to touch the highest concerns of human existence.

Something might be sacred because it represents or symbolizes a divine law, because it is a book that is divinely inspired, because it is a ruler divinely authorized, or because it is a set of rituals expressive of the highest human relation to the divine. Those who defile these things are said to be worthy of punishment, or even death, not because they touch the sacred, but because they do so in a blasphemous manner. They translate a divine being into an idol; or ridicule a sacred text; or disrespect an authoritative priesthood; or question the connection between sovereignty and the sacred. When Spinoza challenged the faith of the Elders in the beleaguered Hebrew community of Amsterdam in the seventeenth century, the Elders accused him of defiling their faith. He was officially cursed and banned. This action fits Agamben's model of one who is "included while being excluded," but it does fit that of one who is to be killed without being sacrificed because he participates *in* the sacred. Spinoza was banned (*included* as a pariah through enforced exclusion) because he defiled the sacred. When the Khomeini of Iran offered a reward for the execution of Salman Rushdie, the latter became a target of annihilation. Again, not because he was part of the sacred, but because he defiled it. When I call the majority of the American Supreme Court that decided the 2000 election in favor of a candidate from the political party they already supported "The Gang of Five", some take that to show lack of awe for a body that stands at that point where sovereignty and the sacred touch.

Agamben's attempt to fold a double sense into the logic of the sacred should be rejected in favor of the conventional rendering he seeks to overturn. The sacred is that which is to be approached with awe. There might well be ambivalence in people's orientation to the sacred, one they do not themselves acknowledge because of the fear of divine or human retribution. Those most punitive toward others who criticize or "defile" what they consider to be sacred often enough harbor such ambivalence. The intensity of their drive to punish is a displacement of that ambivalence. That is familiar enough. Spinoza, Nietzsche, and Freud, among others, read narrow definitions and harsh punishments of blasphemy this way.

To construe the sacred in the more conventional way is to pave the way to relax the demands of those who seek to impose their understandings of the sacred upon others in a culture with a plurality of renderings of the divine and the sacred. It sets the stage for a more public and active pluralization of the sacred. Thereby, it identifies one (among several others to be pursued) precondition to renegotiate the ethos of sovereignty to mesh more smoothly with a culture of deep pluralism. At this point, I merely suggest that a return to the conventional idea of the sacred can help to loosen the nexus between sovereignty and the sacred without eliminating presumptive respect for sovereign decisions.

(2) *Biopolitics and sovereignty*: Agamben contends that biopolitics has become intensified today. This intensification translates the paradox of sovereignty into a potential disaster. The analysis that he offers at this point seems not so much wrong to me as overly formal. It reflects a classical liberal and Arendtian assumption that there was a time when politics was restricted to public life, and biocultural life was kept in the private realm. What a joke. Every way of life involves the infusion of norms, judgments, and standards into the affective life of participants at both private and public levels. Every way of life is biocultural and biopolitical. Aristotle, Epicurus, Lucretius, Augustine, Spinoza, Rousseau, and Hegel, writing during different periods, all appreciate the layering of culture into different layers of biological life and the concomitant mixing of biology into culture. They treat the biological not as merely the genetic or fixed, but as zones of corporeality infused with cultural habits, dispositions, sentiments, and norms.

Biocultural life has been intensified today with the emergence of new technologies of infusion. But the shift is not as radical as Agamben makes it out to be. In late-modern life, new technologies enable physicians, biologists, geneticists, prison systems, advertisers, media talking-heads, and psychiatrists to sink deeply into human biology. They help to shape the cultural being of biology, although not always as they intend to do. Agamben's review of new medical technologies to keep people breathing after their brains have stopped functioning captures something of this change, showing why a sovereign authority now has to *decide* when death has arrived rather than letting that outcome *express* the slow play of biocultural tradition. Numerous such judgments, previously left to religious tradition in predominantly Christian cultures, have now become explicit issues of technology and sovereignty in religiously diverse states.

Agamben tends to describe the state as the "nation-state." He does not ask whether disturbing developments in the logic of sovereignty are bound not merely to a conjunction between biopolitics and sovereignty, *but to a conjunction between them and renewed attempts to consolidate the spirituality of the nation during a time when it is even more difficult to do so.* If and as the reactive drive to restore the fictive unity of a nation is relaxed, it becomes more possible to negotiate a generous ethos of pluralism that copes in more inclusive ways with the nexus between biology, politics, and sovereignty. More than anything else, the dubious drive to translate deep plurality into nationhood translates sovereignty into a punitive, corrective, exclusionary, and marginalizing practice.[7] The shape of the ethos infusing the practice of sovereignty is therefore critical, and not a mere conjugation of sovereignty and biopolitics.

(3) *The "logic" of sovereignty*: Agamben retains one habit of several theorists that he criticizes: he acts as if an account of the "logic of sovereignty" reveals ironclad paradoxes, paradoxes that could be resolved only by transcending that logic altogether. His mode of analysis engenders the eschatological gesture through which it closes. I doubt, however, that politics or culture possesses as tight a logic as Agamben delineates. If I am right, biocultural life displays neither the close coherence that many theorists seek nor the tight paradox that Agamben and others discern. Biocultural life exceeds any textbook logic because of the nonlogical character of its materiality. It is more messy, layered, and complex than any logical analysis can capture. The very illogicalness of its materiality ensures that it corresponds entirely to no design, no simple causal pattern, or no simple set of paradoxes. Agamben displays the hubris of academic intellectualism when he encloses political culture within a tightly defined logic.

Some social theorists, again, express this hubris by presenting a tight model of causal explanation, others by displaying a closed model of historical realization, and others by dissolving the first two images into tightly defined paradoxes. All three stances overstate the extent to which the complexity of biopolitical culture is resolvable into a consummate logic. The attraction of these perspectives of coherence, realization, and tight paradox is that, if accepted, they allow social and cultural theorists to assume the role that ecclesiastical authorities once played in Christian states: that of definitive public visionaries who articulate the larger picture of the actual, the possible, and the desirable in which sovereignty, law, and politics are encased. Kant, for example, participated in such a political drive. He sought to replace ecclesiological authority with the public authority of academic (Kantian) philosophers who continued the Christian tradition by other means. The continuing attraction of the Kantian problematic in academic philosophy is bound to the authoritative standing that it bestows upon academic philosophers in biocultural life. Agamben, of course, translates Kantian antinomies into paradoxes. But just below that facelift beats the heart of another scholar who reduces cultural life to a logic.

If you loosen the logic that Agamben articulates, you may both express more appreciation for the materialization of culture and locate more space for maneuver within the paradoxes that he delineates. There is a paradox of sovereignty, but it is a social or cultural paradox, one with more room for negotiation, adjustment, and honing than Agamben suggests. The best way to pursue this issue is to delineate two ambiguities residing in sovereignty that escape Agamben's attention.

The first ambiguity, almost detected by Agamben, is an equivocation in the idea of sovereignty between acting with final authority and acting with irresistible power. This finds expression in the *Oxford English Dictionary*, in the definition of sovereignty as "supremacy in respect of power, domination, or rank; supreme dominion, authority or rule." The idea of finality flows through these terms, but in some it expresses final authority and in others an irresistible effect. Both dimensions find presence in the terms "rank" and "rule." Agamben senses this difference, in his assertion that the sovereign decides the exception. But, within the idea of the exception "decided" by sovereignty, an oscillation flows between a juridically established authority that authoritatively decides the exception and social powers that assert themselves irresistibly in and around the decision.

This ambivalence within sovereign finality finds expression in Christian theology as well as human law. The point of the nominalist critique of those scholastics who had projected an immanent purpose into the world is that this traditional projection implicitly undermines the very idea of God's omnipotence. A sovereign God, they contended, is One governed by no prior purpose implicitly limiting His power. So they attacked the doctrine of an expressive or enchanted world through which traditional theology had bestowed meaning and direction upon human life. They expanded the human experience of contingency in nature by subtracting purpose, belonging, and intrinsic meaning from it, in the interests of honoring a God of absolute sovereign power over being. They increased God's sovereign power by depleting the sovereign purpose to which He conformed. Their opponents, of course, said that in doing so they subtracted meaning and purpose from the world over which God presided. Today, they would be called theological nihilists.

The theological oscillation and debate subsists within the contemporary language of state sovereignty, as the finality of sovereignty circulates uncertainly between authoritativeness and irresistibility. The practice of sovereignty thrives on this instability.

The significance of the dissonant conjunction between effective and expressive sovereignty becomes apparent when linked to a second oscillation. Alexis de Tocqueville captured much of it in his exploration of nineteenth-century American democracy. "The principle of sovereignty of the people," he says, "which is always to be found, more or less, at the bottom of almost all human institutions, usually remains buried there."[8] In European societies, Divine Right invested sovereign authority in the King, but below that authority, enabling and confining it, were specific traditions already infused into the multitude. This underground interplay between the multitude, tradition, and official sovereignty supported some initiatives by the official or positional sovereign, resisted others, and rendered others barely thinkable. Think of a monarch who commanded the people to convert from Christianity to Buddhism in one generation. He might face the fate that met Pharaoh Ikhaneton when he converted Egyptians to a new, austere faith. They barely conformed to its external dictates for a generation and then reverted aggressively to the old rituals upon his death.

The multitude, already infused with tradition, comes even more into the fore in a democratic, constitutional regime. It helps to set the ethos in which official sovereignty is set. Better put, in democratic constitutionalism, sovereignty circulates uncertainly between the multitude, the traditions it embodies, constitutionally sanctioned authorities and, where operative, the written constitution that the authorities interpret. The relative weight of each element can be specified more closely, although never completely, according to need and context. The police in American cities thus both express and help to shape the ethos of sovereignty. They can find evidence or plant it, follow the spirit of Miranda or render it ineffective, intimidate a section of the populace or act evenhandedly, depending upon the unstable confluence of legal rulings given to them, the larger ethos in which they participate, and the professional police ethos carved out of dangers, ethnic loyalties and hostilities in the city. What would happen to a court that "decides" that cops must walk without guns? Or that they are free to shoot at any citizen? An unconscious context of the thinkable and the unthinkable, the habitually expected and the impermissible, would enter into readings of constitutional texts and sovereign decisions.

According to Tocqueville, the tradition that infused the ethos of sovereignty in nineteenth-century America was, above all, Christianity. This was the main reason why Amerindians could not be included in the polity. They lacked Christianity. So when a Supreme Court decision supported the autonomy of the Cherokee in Southeastern United States, the sovereign ethos of a superior Christian civilization overturned that mere legality, even though a minority of Christians protested such a rendering of the Christian spirit. Tocqueville saw how this slippery circulation of sovereign power/authority operated. Here is what he says about how the "American government" and "the white population" enter into asymmetrical relations each time a new area is reserved by treaty for the "Indians":

> Who can guarantee that they will be able to remain in peace in their new asylum? The United States pledges itself to maintain them there, but the territory they now occupy was formerly secured to them by the most solemn oaths. Now, the American government does not, it is true, take their land from them, but it allows encroachments on it. No doubt within a few years the same white population which is now pressing around them will again be on their tracks in the solitudes of Arkansas; then they will suffer again from the same ills without the same remedies; and because sooner or later there will be no land left for them, their only refuge will be the grave."[9]

A sovereign majority of the white population, infused with a generic sense of Christian superiority, defined and decided the exception in this case. Was any court going to decide with effective finality against the population that it recognized to be legitimate citizens? Would it, for instance, order all Christian whites in and around Georgia to march north and west instead of allowing *them* to drive the Cherokee west to Oklahoma in the march of tears? Tocqueville himself had regrets about this result. But he did not dissent from it because of his view that sovereignty circulates between the people, the highest court, and a Christendom that forms the first "political institution" of American civilization. Lacking Christianity, Amerindians became the sovereign exception, the (non)people to be excluded from the territory that they occupied first. In every territorial civilization, Tocqueville says, "there are certain great social principles which a people either introduces everywhere or tolerates nowhere."[10] Strict constructionists in the United States understand this equation at a visceral level, concurring with Tocqueville that Christianity, which exercises no explicit power over the state, functions as the first political institution in imparting specific meaning and weight to the porous words of the Constitution.

The process that Tocqueville describes is already invested in the fateful conjunction between biopolitics and sovereignty. The living space available to Amerindians was squeezed by the effective sovereignty of Euro-American Christians. But the circulation that Tocqueville charts does not conform to the airtight logic of sovereignty that Agamben characterizes. *If* a political movement had successfully changed the cultural ethos in which Presidents governed, courts decided, and the Christian populace set the context and reception of decisions, the paradox of sovereignty would still remain, biopolitics would still operate, and the relevant constitutional language would still be insufficient to determine judicial decisions. *But a modified ethos of constitutional action would nonetheless incline the effective range of court decisions and popular responses in a different direction.* A change in ethos, which forms a critical component in the complexity of sovereignty, alters the course of sovereignty.

The contemporary relevance of this point is underlined by saying that the conjunction of biopolitics and Article 48 of the Weimar Republic did not alone generate the Nazi Holocaust against Jews, the Romana, and homosexuals. A series of intense relays between these forces and a political culture infused with anti-Semitism and resentment against defeat in World War I generated the devastating result. Without the last element—the element I call an ethos of sovereignty—the conjunction between biopolitics and Article 48 might have proceeded in a different direction. The point is to see that, given the paradox that helps to constitute it, an ethos of sovereignty is both external to sovereignty and internal to it, both part of it and one of its cultural conditions of possibility.

Gilles Deleuze and Felix Guattari concur with the perspective adopted here. Agreeing that there is a paradox at the center of sovereignty, they nonetheless find the most powerful sources of fascism to flow from a series of "resonances" between state sovereignty, fascist gangs, and a larger populace ripe for the micropolitics of fascism.

> But fascism is inseparable from the proliferation of molecular focuses in interaction, which skip from point to point to point, *before* beginning to resonate together in the National Socialist State. Rural fascism and city or neighborhood fascism, youth fascism and war veteran's fascism, fascism of the Left and fascism of the Right, fascism of the couple, family, school, and office: every fascism is defined by a micro-black hole that stands on its own and communicates with the others, before resonating in a great, generalized, central black hole . . . Even after the National Socialist State had been established, microfascisms persisted that gave it unequaled ability to act upon the "masses."[11]

Sovereignty and Empire

While attending to the modern intensification of biopolitics, Agamben pays little heed to the changed global context in which sovereignty is set. Once you acknowledge that an ethos is internal as well as external to sovereignty, you appreciate that territorial sovereignty has always operated within a global as well as an internal context. Hegel saw this, saying that in the modern world there is always only one real sovereign state. The World Historical State exercises sovereignty by maintaining the international order as it governs its internal populace. Such a state is contained and restrained, when the world is lucky, within the world historical pull of Geist. Other states, ranged around it as satellites, are contained and restrained by it, making theirs a subordinate sovereignty.

In *Empire* Michael Hardt and Antonio Negri attend to the changing global context of sovereignty.[12] They claim that with the acceleration and expansion of capital into something approaching a global system, the context of sovereignty has changed dramatically. They describe the nineteenth century idealized by Hegel as the era of Imperialism, presided over by a dominant state. But Imperialism today gives way to Empire.

Empire is a worldwide assemblage, an assemblage in which some states have much more priority than others, but one marked above all by the migration of sovereignty toward global structures that exceed the power or control of any single state. Here are some of their descriptions of the emerging condition:

> Empire can only be conceived as a universal republic, a network of powers and counterpowers structured in a boundless and inclusive architecture. (p. 166)
>
> The recognition of the rise of transnational corporations above … the constitutional command of the nation-states should not … lead us to think constitutional mechanisms and controls as such have declined.… Instead, the constitutional functions have been displaced to another level. (pp. 308–309)
>
> The fundamental principle of Empire … is that its power has no actual and localizable terrain or center. Imperial power is distributed … through mobile and articulated mechanisms of control. (p. 384)

So not only is the global context of state sovereignty shifting, but also sovereignty is migrating from states—where it was never entirely anchored—to a loosely assembled global system. Let me say a couple of words on behalf of the Hardt–Negri analysis before proposing some modifications in it.

The idea of Empire—as a loose assemblage of differentiated powers not entirely under the thumb of a dominant state or a set of supranational corporations—is both timely and in need of further development. Here, the elements of sovereignty are distributed in a complex assemblage with multiple sites, not concentrated in the single will of a people, a king, or a dictator. Familiar debates in International Relations theory between imperialistic and anarchistic readings of a world order either place too much control over events in a dominant power or reduce the world to a quasi-autonomous system exerting restraints on sovereign states. The contemporary world assemblage is marked by two tendencies: (a) neither state authorities, corporate elites, market mechanisms nor international agencies possess sufficient foresight to govern the world intentionally as a system; (b) every state, corporation, labor movement, and supranational movement is nonetheless enabled, contained, and restrained by the larger world assemblage in which it is set. Ambiguities and uncertainties already discernible within sovereignty become magnified as its sites are extended to encompass the world.

Hardt and Negri see how the migration of sovereignty to new sites encourages some states to try to restore a semblance of autonomy that they project into a mythic past by intensifying drives to integrate the population into a nation. But, even as they support the "multitude" against corporate and state priorities, these authors refuse to support this violent course. They refuse the drive to reinstate the nation as the state's bulwark against the new formation of sovereignty.

But things soon take less compelling turns. In a way that recalls Agamben's quest to break the logic of sovereignty, Hardt and Negri also seek a revolutionary transformation of Empire. They seek a dramatic break rather than forging strategies within and against the current order of things to render it more democratic and less bound to the blind compulsions of capital. This desire for transformation, in turn, severs their politics from the insightful institutional analyses they have just launched. The new possibility becomes a vague gesture, reminiscent of the way in which one brand of Marxism proceeded over the last century. Hardt and Negri demand overthrow and refuse to identify what terms or direction it might take:

> Furthermore, we have not yet been able to give any coherent indication of what type of political subjectivities might contest and overthrow the forces of Empire. (p. 205)
>
> Even when we manage to touch on the productive, ontological dimension and the resistances that arise there, we will still not be in a position—not even at the end of this book—to point to any already existing and concrete elaboration of a political alternative to Empire … . It will only arise in practice. (p. 206)
>
> We need a force capable of not only organizing the destructive capacities of the multitude, but also constituting through the desires of the multitude an alternative. (p. 214)

> This is the point when the modern republic ceases to exist and the postmodern posse arises. This is the founding moment of an earthly city that is strong and distinct from any divine city ... Only the multitude through its practical experimentation will offer the models and determine when and how the possible becomes real. (p. 411)

For them, the multitude is not equivalent to the people. The people is forged upon a populace on a politically organized territory, fitting it into the narrow imperatives of a "nationstate." The multitude is those forces in politics, work, and ethos that exceed both the people and the established forces of economic organization.[13] Good enough. But Hardt and Negri then set the multitude against Empire, rather than locating it ambiguously within and outside Empire and showing how various factions of it do and can act to press this global assemblage in new directions. Must the diversion of investment within capitalism toward ecologically sound companies either be reduced to co-optation of the multitude by capital or an act of resistance against the Empire of capitalism? Perhaps these investments act modestly upon capital to stretch its priorities. What about the cross-state citizen divestment movement that helped to end apartheid in South Africa? Does the formation of new forms of property/territory by indigenous peoples participate in the new global assemblage while modifying some of its terms? Or must it be treated as a co-opted movement within Empire? What about movements that stretch the organization of investment and work life within capitalist firms by creating institutional space for gays and women, or by addressing the issue of poverty? Finally, what about a variety of religious movements surging through and across territorial states? Are they inside or outside Empire? The either/or character of such questions presupposes an architecture of Empire tighter than that presented in the authors' best descriptions of the assemblage.

The authors may be at odds with themselves on these questions. The dominant theme is, first, to show how each new effort of change becomes absorbed and contained by the flexible world assemblage and, second, to point to an abstract multitude outside the most highly organized industrial states as agents of vague, fundamental transformation. A subordinate theme, seldom expressed in the summary statements, is to suggest how this supple assemblage with no single authority rising above it could be shoved and pushed in more promising directions without eliminating it as a capitalist assemblage. Again, the dominant tendency is to graft the idea of the multitude onto overthrow of the Empire of Capital.

But in the absence of an imagined alternative linked to a concrete agent, it is counterproductive to join critique to vague, transformational gestures.

Many, otherwise sympathetic, who hear it will fear that the existing formations of production, welfare, safety, accountability, and responsibility might be destroyed with nothing else emerging to replace them at the needed architectural scale. Fear does not decline as a motive to resignation and obedience in the age of Empire. Rather, the new fear lifts Hobbesian fear to a new level of being. It is now that the jerry-rigged, fragile world assemblage upon which production, jobs, finance, and commerce depend will decompose under the pressure of stress without anything expansive or supple enough to replace it. To point vaguely to the promise of overthrow is to spawn such a fear. The most unpromising side of Marxism is thus recapitulated under even less favorable conditions. The result is to paralyze creative action. Thus, under such circumstances, it is better to identify energies and possible sites of action on a variety of fronts to make the assemblage function more robustly in the interests of ordinary people.

It is surprising that religion, which has become both a national and a transnational force with which to contend, plays no significant role in this analysis of Empire. It is pretty much ignored until near the end when a new immanent faith of immanent materialism is projected onto the multitude. But surely Christianity, Judaism, Hinduism, and Buddhism did not subsist as dependent variables until immanent materialism emerged. And, just as surely, that variety of existential faiths is not going to dissolve into this new faith either. It is better to come to terms with the persistence of religious diversity on the globe during a time when the acceleration of speed and the mobilization of capital draw contending faiths into closer and more persistent contact. Today, the goal should be not to dissolve diverse experiences of the sacred into a new common faith, but to fold greater appreciation of the profound contestability of every faith into our self-portrayals and presentations to others. The best place to start this process is with one's own. So I begin by announcing clearly: immanent materialism, while it inspires me existentially and ethically, is apt to seem strange to those uninhabited by it. It is both worthy of my embrace and a profoundly contestable faith. It is surely not rendered unavoidable in the age of Empire, nor are the other contestable faiths with which it seeks to enter into relations of agonistic respect.

Hardt and Negri are caught in a struggle between the immanent radicalism of Gilles Deleuze and the eschatological tendencies of Karl Marx. While their most creative institutional analyses express this cross-fertilization admirably, the eschatological drive of the book prevails. Capital and religion are the major vehicles of that eschatology: in the drives to overcome capital and to transform diverse metaphysical and religious faiths into immanent naturalism. As I see it, again, the diversity of religion is not apt to fade into a new materialist ontology of the multitude, although the intra- and extraterritorialization of multiple faiths contains promising possibilities. And capital, while it may well emerge in a world crisis, is also unlikely to give way to a world economic assemblage that eschews private investment, earnings on interest, wage-labor, and the commodity form. The new world assemblage, just because it is flexible and complex in its architecture, is not amenable to replacement. But for the same reason it may be susceptible to significant stretching and reshaping by a variety of movements situated at multiple sites. The task is to infuse it with more flexibility, inclusivity, and plurality, and to act upon localities, states, supranational capital, religious organizations, and international institutions to redistribute the world assemblage.

Capitalism, Property, and Sovereignty

Consider a process under way that could modify state-capitalist forms of property and governance in the new world assemblage without overturning that assemblage itself. It grows out of the contemporary politics between "settler" states and indigenous populations previously conquered and displaced by them.

Before the advent of modern capitalism, the practice of acquiring mining or oil rights over land occupied by others did not exist. Today, oil and mining companies acquire mining rights to land owned in other respects by others. A new property form is emerging out of capitalism. Indeed, in capitalist states new forces are constantly reshaping the property form. Thus, to take a second example, the privately incorporated, nonprofit university provides a legal forum of governance that stretches the typical practices of individual or corporate ownership. So does the apartment collective.

People do protest vocally about inalienable property rights when the question of distinctive forms of governance over lands previously wrested from indigenous peoples comes up. But they can be offered these examples of previous creativity in the property form within capitalism to loosen them up a little. And be reminded that, in the past, the most creative embellishments have been reserved for those who already control major economic resources. Recall, for instance, that Tocqueville worried about the future effects of the "new manufacturing aristocracy" on the agricultural form of property that he considered to be indispensable to American democracy. But he did not follow that concern with a call to dismantle the aristocracy of capital; he reserved *that* conclusion for those Amerindians who lacked Christianity and, at least he thought, agriculture.

To chart plural practices of property and governance within capitalism is to encourage support for the worldwide movement of indigenous peoples to govern large stretches of territory previously wrested from them. Such practices are being pursued today in large areas of Canada and Australia. New strategies are being proposed for indigenous peoples to participate in world capitalism in ways that stretch and pluralize the paradigmatic practices of capitalist property, ownership, territory, and sovereignty. Indigenous casino capitalism might become a way to generate capital for other productive activities.

Such changes neither overturn global capital nor remain within its most familiar forms. Such modes of governance enable indigenous peoples both to reject the coercive demand that they be stationary peoples with unchangeable customs and to fold traditional elements of spirituality into new practices of territory, property, capital, and governance.

Such achievements, however, cannot be secured by indigenous people alone, one country at a time. They must be promoted through cross-state assemblages of indigenous peoples, backed by corresponding networks of religious leaders and critical public philosophers within and across settler states, processed through active negotiations with finance capital and state officials. Such multisite negotiations might help to alter the ethos of sovereignty and capital alike, without transforming world capitalism into a new world order.

Indeed, old ideas of "place," "land," and "earth" provide new sites for possible metamorphosis today. For instance, a growing number of people in several areas of the world identify the earth as simultaneously a vibrant source of life, a site of diverse energies exceeding possible human mastery, and a fragile planet to be nurtured as a source of sustenance and creative evolution. The earth may be emerging as an immanent field upon which to relocate visceral experiences of identification traditionally reserved for the territorial nation. The earth becomes a rallying cry through which to refashion and tame capital while exceeding the closed prerogatives of the sovereign, territorial nation. The territorial state retains prominence as one site of action, but the drive to the territorial *nation* is challenged from within and without the state.

Consider the irony. In 1968, Apollo 8 sent back pictures of a vivid blue planet suspended in the middle of the solar system, a stunning, bright sphere unlike any other planet observable from the earth itself. This reflected image of the earth, the paradigmatic product of a highly organized capitalist state, underlines for many how unique the earth is by comparison to other planets so far encountered. The others cannot even hold water, while the fine balance that the earth maintains between evaporation and precipitation is sustained to a considerable degree by the behavior of *life* on the planet.[14] That is, without the lush vegetation of the earth, the fragile balance between evaporation and precipitation that human life depends upon would not continue.

Today, states and capital collide and collude to jeopardize balances that are favorable to life. But the image of the planet returned to earth by Apollo 8 also helps to foment a new ethos within that assemblage: a vast microassemblage in which farmers, professors, scientists, religious leaders, and indigenous peoples from several places on earth coalesce to protect the earth/planet from the ravages of global capital. These are not transformative forces. They may also be turned back as they seek to reshape elements in the global assemblage of capital, states, and religions. But, amidst that risk, they do incorporate new energies and possibilities into old practices of sovereignty, territory, property, capital, mastery, nationhood, and faith.

Notes

1. For two essays that are particularly pertinent on this point, see Bonnie Honig, "Declarations of Independence: Arendt and Derrida on the Problem of Founding a Republic," *American Political Science Review* (Winter, 1991), 97–113, and Alan Keenan, "Promises, Promises: The Work of Arendt," *Political Theory* (May, 1994), 297–322.
2. Rousseau, *On the Social Contract: With Geneva Manuscript and Political Economy*, trans. by Judith Masters (New York: St Martin's, 1978), Bk I, p. 46. I discuss this paradox with respect to the relation between territory, global politics, and democracy in Chapter 5 of *The Ethos of Pluralization* (Minneapolis: University of Minnesota Press, 1995). A thoughtful and detailed engagement with its effect on Rousseau's theory is developed by Steven Johnston in *Encountering Tragedy: Rousseau and the Project of Democratic Order* (Ithaca: Cornell University Press, 1999).
3. Rousseau, *On the Social Contract*, pp. 69–70.
4. Giorgio Agamben, *Homo Sacer: Sovereign Power and Bare Life*, trans. by Daniel Heller-Roazen (Stanford: Stanford University Press, 1995), p. 82.
5. Agamben, *Homo Sacer*, p. 83.
6. Agamben, *Homo Sacer*, pp. 44, 59.
7. I explore an ethos of multidimensional pluralism as an alternative to the ethos of the nation in Chapter 3 of *Why I Am Not A Secularist* (Minneapolis: University of Minnesota Press, 1999).
8. Alexis de Tocqueville, *Democracy in America*, 2 vols., trans. by George Lawrence (New York: Harper and Row, 1969), p. 58.
9. Tocqueville, *Democracy in America*, p. 336. I explore Tocqueville's rendering of the relation between the Christian civilization of America and Amerindians who were excluded by it in *The Ethos of Pluralization* (Minneapolis: University of Minnesota Press, 1995), Chapter 6.
10. Tocqueville, *Democracy in America*, p. 294.
11. Gilles Deleuze and Felix Guattari, *A Thousand Plateaus*, trans. by Brian Massumi (Minneapolis: University of Minnesota Press, 1987), p. 214.
12. *Empire* (Cambridge: Harvard University Press, 2000). Pages for the quotes to follow are given in the text of the essay.
13. For a thoughtful review of Empire that explores the meaning and role of the multitude, see Kam Shapiro, "From Dream to Desire: At the Threshold of Old and New Utopias," *Theory & Event*, http://muse.jhu.edu/journals/theory_and_event/v004/4.4r_kam.html
14. Even when the planet was crystallizing into the earth, a "decisive reason why it was able to hold on to these volatile layers of melted comets was the emergence of living organisms that regulated crucial climatic conditions and kept them constant." Tor Norretranders, *The User Illusion*, trans. by Jonathan Syndenham (Viking Press), 1998, p. 340.

CHAPTER 3

Correlating Sovereign and Biopower

MICHAEL DILLON

The production of bare life is the originary activity of sovereignty.
Giorgio Agamben[1]

Power, Idiom, Relation

Power is commonly associated with regimes of government and governance that regularly claim universal, metaphysical status for the rights and competences that comprise them; regimes whose very *raison d'être*, in the form of state sovereignty and *raison d'état*, for example, seek to limit and confine if not altogether rid us of politics. Sovereign power, a form of rule gone global, has also come to develop and deploy modes of destruction whose dissemination and use it finds increasingly impossible to control because these have become integral to its propagation and survival; modes of destruction that put in question the very issue of planetary survival for the human as well as many other species. Despite the fashion of speaking about the demise of sovereignty, political thought and practice have to still struggle with terrains of power throughout which the legitimating narratives, iconography and capabilities of sovereign power remain amongst the most persistent, and powerful and threatening globally. As it has come to dominate our understanding of rule, so sovereign power has come to limit our imagination in relation to the possibility and to the promise of politics.

But power is not a universal or a metaphysical principle that applies to all things at all times across space and time invariant to moment and place. Power, including sovereign power, is idiomatic. Power idioms are formed by the time and the place in which power takes place.[2] The taking place of power also circumscribes the space of the possible for political understanding and political being as well as for a regime of rule. Such a space of the possible is what we might call a political imaginary. Distinguishing political being from modes of rule does not, however, imply that a mode of political being is an escape from power or rule. Instead, it is a different engagement with, and a certain struggle continuously to responsibilize, power and rule. Neither does a political imaginary specify its detail. It circumscribes a terrain of invention and intervention, a political *spielraum* if you will, in which a mode of political understanding and of political being finds expression and enactment. The substantive detail comes in the singularity of those expressions and enactments. Re-engaging the idea of sovereignty, here through reviewing its idiomacy, is essential to revivifying the promise of politics in a world increasingly subject to the rule and injustice associated with technologizing suppression of political imagination in which sovereignty remains so deeply implicated.

Like anything that is idiomatic, power is also a plural thing. It has different modes, moods and moments. There were few analysts of power as alert to its plural idioms and manifestations as Michel Foucault, few as aware as he was of the dense relays of logic and practice that implicated one idiom of power in another even as he insisted on their differences. Few were as insistent as Foucault, too, that the sovereign idiom of power often concealed more than it revealed about the operation of power at the extremities and through capillaries and mechanisms of power that had more to do with truth and knowledge, with war and domination, than with sovereignty and right. Famed for his accounts of disciplinary power/knowledge and of biopower, in which the disciplining of bodies and power over life rather than power over death predominated, Foucault has also been celebrated for his allied claim that we have still not cut off the head of the king.

Once predominant, sovereignty nonetheless remains one of the most important idioms of modern power and perhaps there is still something more general to be observed about its idiomatic enactment of power, even within that heightened sensibility to the plurality of power relations that we owe Foucault, and also in relation to what he called the strategic as opposed to the juridical model of power. In order to explore this possibility further, we are best guided by Foucault's own careful and probing approach to questions of power and its idioms. Rather than any one of his contingent conclusions about the character of modern power, it is Foucault's way of questioning power and power relations that inspires this essay. In particular, he always asked about the how of power. Hence the insistence here on the idiomatic character of power and the determination also to submit the sovereign conception of power to other 'how' questions, questions inspired this time by the additional thought of idiom.

Like every idiom of power, sovereign power provides a grid of intelligibility for why power is ordered as it is, how it is to be enacted and passed on as well as why it should be obeyed. But, again like every idiom of power, expressions of sovereign power are themselves also subject to changing grids of intelligibility in the context of which, and in response to which, their mode and tone of operation change as well. Two concern this chapter: the first is that of the advent of modernity itself, the second is the rise of biopower. Sovereignty co-evolves with both. How else could it be? Foucault taught us that power is above all a relational phenomenon. Sovereignty, too, ironically given its disavowal of relationality in all but the mechanistic transaction of inter-subjective exchanges with other supposed sovereign bodies. For sovereignty is merely a trick, we know, to bring such bodies into political and juridical existence. It is a grid of intelligibility imbricated with other grids of intelligibility and cannot therefore escape the uncanny transitive and transformative logic of being-in-relation. Even when grids of intelligibility encounter each other in their incoherence for one another, an effect courses throughout those grids of intelligibility if only in terms of the way the shock of the strange calls forth some explanation or explication of what simply should not otherwise have been possible or allowable.

Relation—correlation in the title merely to emphasize the point—is one of the most, if not most, elemental issue or matter of concern for thinking. For the philosophizing or theorizing of power, it is thought's most minimal thing. The bare minimum of power is this, relationality. Anterior to its metaphysical doctrines of foundation, relation, not *arche* or anarchy, anterior to any relation—"in relation, not only does the subject tend toward the other with all the indicated implications for the subject, but also the *relatum* of the relation lets the subject come in relation to it."[3]—The very *relatum* of relationality's advent is power's 'limit condition'. Understood as the minimal thing, relationality not only holds towards the nonrelational but also implies a being-towards something that is no longer in the mode of what philosophy and politics have always thought of as the relational; specifically, for example, the relation of concepts, statements and subjects. The very concept of relationality carries with it a reference to the nonrelational: "There is no relation…without a prior opening of the possibility of being-toward-another by which the subject is allowed to arrive 'in' the place of the other."[4] Without this gift of an opening for an subject to turn up in, this turning towards the other, no relation would or could occur. In the very relationality of power, therefore, arises the reference to the other of power. Not, not power. Simply the 'simple complex' of the other of power. This is the occurrence through which the relation eventuates. Such an event is not of the order of relationality and therefore also not of the order of power. It is of the order of the given and of the giving that opens being. At this point arises the question of another justice and the promise as well as the possibility of politics. There is no time or space to travel down this track again. But the track has to be signaled as part of the depiction of sovereignty in terms, for example also, of what its very constitution denies in the process of effecting its idiom of power. It has to be signalled because sovereignty too is relational. Sovereignty's own idiom changes in relation to the changing character of the modern, in relation to its changing location, and also in relation to other idioms of power such as biopower . It also multiplies, since being-in-relation always is a multiplying power in relation to substance not least in terms of the shapes, moods and tones of being-toward something—loving, hating, despairing, fawning, reverencing, measuring, coaxing, exciting, enraging, intimidating, opening, closing, etc. This returns us of course to idiom, to coming into relation and the many different ways of being-in-relation. All of these shapes, moods and tones of being-in-relation also involve power even, albeit differently, in power's relation to the other of power. They also involve the contingency of time and place because to come into relation is very much a matter of chance, as it were, of happenstance.

Foucault himself acknowledged something of all this directly in relation to sovereignty when he recounted how the one massive fact that emerges from his consideration of sovereign power is that the juridico-political theory of sovereignty is related to the reactivation of Roman Law in the middle ages and that it revolved around the problematics of kingship. He also went on to note that it mutated as the very grid of intelligibility that was medieval life underwent at the cataclysm of its dissolution. While it was used as an instrument to constitute and justify the great monarchical administrations, for example, from the sixteenth and seventeenth centuries onward, at the time of the wars of religion, sovereignty became a weapon that circulated on both sides of the religious divide. Employed by Catholic monarchists and Protestant anti-monarchists, it was also used by Protestant monarchies and by Catholics urging dynastic change and regicide, as well as by aristocrats and *parlementaires*, and by the representatives of royal power as well as the last feudalists. It was, he says, "the great instrument of the political and theoretical struggles that took place around systems of power in the sixteenth and seventeenth centuries."[5] Later, it was invoked by parliamentary democracies to construct an alternative to absolute or authoritarian monarchical administrations. In sum, for Foucault, sovereignty has always been about royal power, but in two deeply related senses:

> Either it had to be demonstrated that royal power was invested in a juridical armature, that the monarch was indeed the living body of sovereignty and that his power, even when absolute, was perfectly in keeping with a basic right; or it had to be demonstrated that the power of the sovereign had to be limited, that it had to submit to cer-

tain rules and that, if that power were to retain its legitimacy, it had to be exercised within certain limits. From the Middle Ages onward, the essential role of the theory of right has been to establish the legitimacy of power; the major or central problem around which the theory of right is organized is the problem of sovereignty.[6]

Sovereignty then is about right, and right ultimately becomes a matter of the organization of subjects in their reciprocal relations. Hence, the relational contest now also, at the turn of the twentieth/beginning of the twenty first century, is between the sovereignty of individual rights globally and the sovereignty of states. The same mechanism of power is in play but the grid of intelligibility governing the play of sovereign power has nonetheless mutated once more.

The advent of disciplinary power/knowledge also illustrates this point. "That is why we now find ourselves in a situation where the only existing and apparently solid recourse we have against the usurpations of disciplinary mechanisms and against the rise of a power that is bound up with scientific knowledge is precisely a recourse or a return to a right that is organized around sovereignty, or is articulated on that old principle…..We obviously invoke a right." But, Foucault adds, "having recourse to sovereignty against discipline will not enable us to limit the effects of disciplinary power."[7] And so it has come to pass that, new relational complexes of sovereign juridical, disciplinary power/knowledge and biopower have formed and continue to develop. In the symbiotic relations and relational transfers and exchanges of power relations, sovereignty takes on a different tenor, as it then becomes exposed to other accounts of the life whose deployment and death it ultimately seeks to command. Sovereignty has always been inextricably entwined in the power relations of other modalities of power relations and their respective idioms.

However, we are so drilled into thinking of sovereignty in metaphysical or institutional terms, as the ultimate locus or centre of power and as the institutional setting where that metaphysical foundation is seated, in short as something to be possessed, that we think very little about the idiomatic character of sovereignty and its enactment as an idiom of power, beyond its juridical and legal character, in its relation with the multiple grids of intelligibility that comprise the terrain of modern life forms. Similarly, we are so drilled into thinking of the grid of intelligibility that sovereign power sets for the rest of life that we can easily forget how changing grids of intelligibility across other aspects of life provide a changing backdrop against which the mutation of sovereignty and its modes may also be detected. Backdrop, in fact, is not enough. It may be suggested that sovereignty actively coevolves with the very terrain of existence whose responsibility it assumes but is ultimately unable to master. Sovereignty is then markedly inflected, now, by the many ways in which it is invested in as well as influenced by the changing grid of intelligibility furnished by the complexities and vicissitudes of what is called the modern and what is called biopower.

Sovereignty, Modernity, Idiomacy

Sovereignty remains central, of course, to the political imaginary of the modern. In many ways sovereignty was responsible for bringing about the modern, and modern state sovereignty remains one of the principal means by which modernization is sought, even within already modernized states, as the continuous 'modernization' of Britain throughout the second half of the twentieth century, for example, attests. How can there be politics, the modern asserts, if there is no sovereign? If you aspire to be political, the modern insists, you need the defining strength of the sovereign around you. How then is one to attain and retain sovereignty? Who or what is to be sovereign? What responsibilities are entailed by sovereignty and how is sovereignty to be held accountable for its sovereign actions? What conventions, protocols and laws will best regulate the relation of sovereigns in an international arena of competing sovereignties, also including the rights, rules and logics of sovereign war? Thus did much of the political landscape of political modernity emerge. In many ways this tells us little, however, about the lived character of sovereign power as a way of existing collectively, the tropes, manners, moods and expectations that circumscribe the very possibility of political being and of what politics itself is allowed to be under a regime of sovereignty. It tells us little about the ways in which the experience of sovereignty changes as its locale moves from the medieval to the modern, and how as a lived experience the experience of sovereign subjectivity moves from location to location—Europe to North and South America, Africa and Asia.

It is one thing, therefore, to speak the language of sovereignty and enact the idiom of sovereign power in a world still dominated by the cosmology of the Christian world and its promise of divine salvation, yet another to do so when the grounds of that world have shifted via the privatization of conscience, the de-confessionalization of politics and the retreat of God into an obscurity so enigmatic that His law no longer underwrites the play of sovereign power in idealizations and normalizations of the idiom of sovereignties. Recall, for the purpose of developing this point further, that Foucault speaks eloquently and insistently of the ways in which the individual agent or subject is very much an effect of power: "the individual is one of power's first effects."[8] The same must also be true of sovereign power and of the sovereign. What happens therefore to the experience of sovereign subjectivity when it is played out on a stage quite different from that of the Christian world? The experience of sovereign subjectivity changes.

Modern sovereignty is then an idiom of power so inflected by the violent birth pangs of the modern, so reflective of the ontological and epistemological as well as the aesthetic and political shifts characteristic of modernity, that it seems unlikely to have remained unaffected by modernity's changing grids of intelligibility in the midst of which its own grid of intelligibility for the exercise and legitimation of power relations has had to operate. Modern sovereignty therefore constitutes a distinctive idiom of its own. But what kind of idiom would that be and how would we begin to distinguish it? In what ways has that idiom changed? And in what ways has its changing idiom circumscribed and inflected the space of the possible for political understanding and political being, such that our very experience of politics and our very modern fantasy of self-making and self-grounding as political agents are exhausted by the figure of the sovereign, even when the sovereign is as much villain as savior? There are more questions than can be addressed here. But is it somehow possible to delineate certain idiomatic aspects of modern sovereignty as a changing historical experience and enactment of power rather than a universal principle of political formation? And if we manage to attempt this, how might the findings contribute towards further clarifying the relations between sovereignty as an idiom of power and all those other idioms of modern power to which Foucault directed us in his continuous but unending analytics of power relations, most especially his strategic model of power and of biopower. Finally, if there is to be space for political understanding and political being that is not to be so exhaustively circumscribed by the *spielraum* of sovereignty, and if there is to be an experience of the political that is not monopolized by the experience of sovereignty, we have to make a start at judging sovereignty's idioms as well as its mechanisms of power.

What kind of power play is, instituted by the *spielraum* of modern sovereignty? Well, in the first instance, if we concider Foucault's insistence that the individual is the first effect of power, we can push the observation and insist that so also is the sovereign. That is to say, the first exercise of sovereign power is to create the sovereign. We can go further and also insist that sovereignty, too, has its infinitesimal mechanisms and that these infinitesimal workings work first to effect the sovereign. We can then ask how did the shift from the medieval to the modern affect the infinitesimal workings of sovereignty as an idiom of power, and by that I mean its tonalities as well as its modalities, its moods as well as its mechanisms.

If we follow this line of questioning, there is something in the play of modern sovereignty to suggest, at first, that its idiom of power is essentially tragic. For example, sovereignty seeks to combine subjective being and objective appearance, unified in the figure of the sovereign so that the tragic conflict or antagonizm between being and appearing is played out there classically, for example, in Hobbes' *Leviathan*. Like the sovereign individual, sovereign power furthermore comprises a central contradiction. Its first necessity is to uphold the law. Its second necessity is to be outside the law so that it is able to impart the law, since anything already bound by law cannot initiate law. This profound contradiction is subjected to sustained analysis in Walter Benjamin's "Critique of Violence" and further explored in Derrida's deconstructive reading of Benjamin in "Force of Law." If sovereignty were therefore Greek, that is to say played out on the stage of the Greek world, governed by these twinned necessities, its play would be a tragedy and the sovereign individual tragic.[9]

But modern scholars have often repeated the argument that a properly tragic conflict is not possible in the sphere of the Christian universe, much less that of the modern. As Giorgio Agamben noted, "after the fall, human language cannot be tragic, before the fall it cannot be comic."[10] In other words, the Christian worldview put paid to the tragic. It did so largely through repositioning guilt and promising divine salvation.[11] Divine providence precludes the tragedy of existence, prey to fate and its irresolvable conflict of necessities: to act but to have no guarantee of the probity and effectiveness of one's actions; to know but to know that one can never know with certainty; and to be creative and also created—subject to necessity yet capable of invention in a universe of contesting and contestable demiurgic powers. Jesus unties the knot of the tragic, as much as He does the law of the Jewish people, and reweaves the skeins of existence into a quite different providential fabric ordained by a benign and omnipotent deity. The Messiah, the Trinity and the message of the cross displace the aporias of tragedy's conflicting necessities. Our God Reigns, as the hymn proclaims. His writ inscribes the universe with meaning and His promise of everlasting peace becomes a deliverable guaranteed by the divine absolutism that he enjoys over His creation. History thus passes from the tragic and the heroic to the holy. And so, here at least, the sovereign, as one of sovereign power's first effects, is himself holy and ordained. The idiomatic sovereignty of medieval kingship was thus deeply inflected by the grid of intelligibility furnished by medieval Christianity in ways brilliantly explored by Kantorowicz's study of medieval political theology.[12] But, as Kantorowicz himself documented in painstaking detail, things changed and they did so in their infinitesimal detail as the medieval gave way to the modern world via the great revolutions of the sixteenth and seventeenth centuries.

Mourning Play

In the process of this monumental shift of sensibilities and intelligibilities, Walter Benjamin describes, or rather, since he too is telling a story, *recounts* the demise of a certain Christian "*Heilsgeschichte*" and its partial replacement through a theater of death and destruction, the allegorical *Trauerspiel* or "mourning play" of the early modern baroque world of the sovereign. The "mourning play" is allegorical insofar as the eschatological narrative and institutions in force prior to the Reformation no longer provide an unchallenged principle of cosmic intelligibility and social cohesion. But in contrast to its medieval predecessor, Baroque allegory is less a "conventional expression" than an "expression of convention," and in particular, of its problematic if unavoidable status. With respect to its authority, Benjamin remarks, recalling the analytic of "Critique of Violence," it "is secret as to the dignity of its origin" but "public as to the range of its validity."³ In short, deprived of divine succession, sovereignty must authorize itself and its law in the constituent violence that it employs to found rather than merely uphold an order of law. In doing so, it finds legitimation in having itself continuously inscribed publicly rather than religiously sanctioned divinely...

> "*Le portrait de Cesar, c'est Cesar.*" (*Port Royal* saying)
> "...a detail insignificant in appearance, but what is insignificant in politics? The innumerable edifices that I shall construct must be marked with my name, they must contain attributes, bas reliefs, groups which recall a theme of my history. My arms, my monograms, must be woven-in everywhere. In one place there will be angels who support my crown, in another statues of justice and wisdom which bear my initials ... . For the same reason I want my statue, my bust, my portraits to be in every public establishment especially in the auditorium of the courts; I would be represented in royal costume or on horseback ... . These points are of utmost importance. I consider them essentials.
> It is by these signs, by these emblems, that the person of the sovereign is always present; one lives with him, with his memory, with his thought. The feelings of his absolute sovereignty enters into the most rebellious spirits as the drop of water which falls unceasingly from the rock hollows-out even granite."¹⁴

While contemporary tyrants still follow the imperative of this public iconography, liberal state sovereignty, in alliance with biopower in the form of governance both local and global, also seeks to still inscribe itself on and through bodies individually and publicly; but differently and more intensively, beyond the corporeal and into the somatic.

A corollary of this absence of an original, originating authority, in the political realm, is that the "sovereign," who no longer has power or legitimacy to rule guaranteed by a transparent and unchallengeable cosmic order, is increasingly overshadowed by the "plotter" (in German: *der Intrigant*), whose manipulations and conspiracies attempt to fill the gap opened in the political realm by the decline of the Christian eschatological narrative. Here, Iago comes to mind, as does Hamlet, who, unable to assume the role of sovereign, schemes, plots and stages in a vain attempt to reestablish an inaccessible legitimacy. Benjamin's account of the "origin" of this allegorical theater is tied to a center and a court however "figural" these may be:

"Allegory brings with it its own court; the profusion of emblems is grouped around the figural center, which is never absent from genuine allegories…"[15] Since here what Benjamin calls a "figural center" (*figurales Zentrum*) is a function of that which surrounds it, rather than one that precedes and grounds the structure, and since that which surrounds the center is in constant flux, the result is a certain profound and increasingly prevailing confusion (in this context, Benjamin refers to the title of a play by Lope de Vega, "The Confused Court"). The court is confused insofar as the elements that comprise it are brought together only to be dispersed once again: 'Dispersion' and 'Collection' (*Zerstreuung und Sammlung*) are the laws of this court." Benjamin's discussion thus suggests that, insofar as it is allegorical, a certain spatial-temporal transformability is built into the very structure of the network of modern sovereignty. Implicit in his other analyses, for instance, those related to the relation of sovereignty to the state of exception, is the suggestion that this transformability can be stabilized only through some sort of violent cut/decision/scission or intervention. The burden of this decision in the prevailing confusion of this de-christianizing world of allegory, the continuous plotting simultaneously to secure the legitimacy and efficacy of sovereignty, comes to characterize and even define the late modern idiom of sovereign power as the Schmittean state of emergency becomes the norm. Here, the confusion unmastered by the court and plotter magnifies and ramifies. Entry on stage of this confusion later propels the play of sovereign power towards the assimilation, appropriation and propagation of increasingly arcane knowledge, knowledge that once taught laws and now experiments widely with digital and molecular morphogenesis. Here, Byzantine policy, analytic structures and techniques, spiralling investment in modes of surveillance, harnessings of knowledge and funding of techno-science are even more mannered than the plotting and intrigue of the baroque, no less intense or calculative if differently driven and engineered.

What distinguishes the sovereign of the baroque at the beginning of the modern are features that then continue to characterize with perhaps increasing intensity and ferocity our contemporary knowledge-obsessed sovereignty. The first of these was a shift from a preoccupation with absolute supremacy to the dire responsibility for deciding the state of emergency amidst a court characterized by machination and intrigue. If one of the first effects of sovereign power is the figure of the sovereign individual, here that individual is figured either in terms of martyrdom or tyranny. This central contradiction of sovereignty persists into the modern. The possibilities of instantiating modern power, of instantiating modernization itself, *lie with* the sovereign yet are *not within* the sovereign's power. With the decline of faith and the waning of the Christian enframing, however, the sovereign becomes deprived of the transcendental maneuvers that promised resolution of this central aporia of sovereign power, and begins to encounter only this contradiction instead: "We rise as smoke that disappears in the air,/We rise after the fall, and he who finds lofty heights,/Finds what can topple him."[16]

Here, then, especially in the sovereign as martyr, Christianity no longer provides the believer with their desired and promised salvation, but with a downfall that the crucifix does not transfigure but rather "contrapuntally intensifies."[17] Sovereign freedom no longer finds itself framed by an incalculable but benign outside that it cannot master, yet can trust. The modern sovereign instead faces the necessity of its own movement, which actually requires the continuous transgression of its own principles and laws, most notably its rule of law that knows no authority ultimately other than its own violent instantiation of itself. In fact if it is to repeat and to realize itself as freedom metaphysically conceived but without benefit of faith, it is on its way to becoming, in short, nihilism. Second, freedom, value and necessity combined in the figure of the modern sovereign, deprived of Christianity's portal to the transcendental, act out this contemporary aporia of sovereign power through increasing reliance on the technicity of calculation and machination that finds its apogee in the strategic model of power relations that Foucault initially contrasted so strongly with sovereignty's juridico-political mechanisms. A further intensification of this development, a further dissemination and elaboration of courtly intrigue, via a full-blown realistic account of the strategic manipulation and deployment of power relations with its massive supporting cast of state ministers, chancellors and policy analysts transforms the setting and the plotting of *trauerspiele*, transforming the mourning play of the baroque into the nihilistic knowledge play of the late modern sovereign.

Strategic Knowledge Play: The Correlation of Sovereign and Biopower

Christian sovereignty is unable to be tragic because the grid of intelligibility that enables it is soteriological rather than fated. Modern sovereignty is unable to be Christian since the grid of intelligibility that enables it has almost lost the soteriological plot altogether, ironically in an ever more hysterical insistence on securing security via commanding every conceivable aspect of the life force itself, figured first as bare and now increasingly as emergent life. Moving from the *trauerspiele* via the willing of the will, contemporary

sovereignty enters into a knowledge play with biopolitical biopower relations, the central motif of which is the new correlation of power in the delivery of life to knowledge as experimentation in pursuit of a command of
morphogenesis that turns strategy into life science governed by design
brought to it, architectural strategy, rather than design found in it.
Therefore, what,happens to the experience of sovereign subjectivity when it
operates in a terrain of power relations no longer monopolized, if it ever
was, by its own juridico-political mechanisms? What is there in sovereignty
that nonetheless also allows it to persist and adapt here, and to enter into
symbiotic and contractual relation with other relational idioms of power,
notably biopower? Is there something shared in the very difference? Is there
something nonetheless common in their separate mechanisms? I think so.

Because it is no longer possible to write tragedies, because it is no longer *à
la mode* to write *trauerspiele* either, the mood of late-modern sovereignty
being nihilistic, if pugilistically optimistic, not mourning, it was the realist
who first began to write the script of the knowledge play of contemporary
sovereignty. However, the modern realist was a mutation of *trauerspiele's*
plotter, substituting the hubris of universal 'reason' for the pathos of the universal church in dissolution. Deploying a stock of dramaturgical *realia*, including necessary invocations of classical and early modern figures, Sun Tzu
to Machiavelli, Thuycidides to Clausewitz and stock concepts deprived from
a political anthropology of interest-driven subjectivity, the central problem
for realism was that its anthropological naiveté and a core ideological contradiction increasingly amounted to a bum script for wired 'Princes' gone digital and molecular. The contradiction was not even subtle: a universalist claim
made on behalf of sovereign self-making whose very historicism defined its
sovereign political subject as modern. A system of generalized sentiments,
widely disseminated via cliché and textbooks for the edification of a sovereign
body politic comprising of thoroughly subjected onlookers, also proved an
inadequate text for power relations gone global, gone networked, gone plural, gone 'soft' and above all gone strategic in ways that required a radical re-
vision of the *realia* of the reason that realism proclaimed. In short, it was
assailed by developments that began to offer entirely different narratives and
plots for sovereign power, and opportunities for new power mongers.

Plotting, strategizing and knowing were distinguishing features of modern sovereignty from its earliest inception in the advent of the modern, and
not just in the form of the intriguer. The modern state sovereign has long
been knowledgeable.[18] Comprised in its very structure of a requirement to
know its realm,[19] the sovereign state's appetite for knowledge goes back for
example to statistics, whose very name derives from its earliest association
with the state. Foucault noted this too, of course, which is not to say that
knowing, particularly with respect to the human and then of life, is not

possessed of its own logics, or indeed of its own imperatives to seek a patron in the sovereign and a market there for its wares. Statistics again provide an early illustration.[20] The relation is simply more pervasive and involved now, and its imperatives more compelling and unrestrained.

For Foucault, it was absurd to think of subjects as if they preexisted the relations of power and meaning that actually brought them into play. Creatures of a historically constituted present, human beings are the enactment of material practices systematically organized through discursive economies into which they are thrown. They are always on the way to a future contingently determined by the outcome of the struggles that take place through, for and by those discursively mediated enactments. The taking place of existence in and through worlds opens on also to the 'mystery' of the taking place of existence as such: something to which Foucault addressed himself directly in what turned out to be his last publication "Life, Experience and Science," published in the January–March issue of *Revue de Métaphysique et de Morale* in 1985. Signaled earlier in relation to relation, this is the 'outside' to both freedom and power relations upon which Foucault also insisted.[21]

Second, power is less a commodity that is possessed, for Foucault, than a force that circulates. As a force that circulates it only comes to presence in the context of the freedom of human being acting in effect as a conductive material for power's very circulation and strategic organizing. If we were not free, by which Foucault means radically undetermined creatures governed by no general telos, natural law or historical determination, we would not conduct or enact power relations. We would instead be composed of raw life or raw material whose properties and behavior could be read off from the telos, with natural law or historical determination said to govern our existence. For Foucault, there are no power relations in human affairs without freedom. There is dominance, but that is another thing. Similarly, there is no freedom in human affairs without the existence of power relations.

Herein also lies the explanation for Foucault's account of resistance. All conductive material exhibits resistance to the force that circulates through it. Suffused by this force, conductive material ought not to be conflated with it. Struggle is thus an involuntary manifestation of the temporal freedom of human being for Foucault: "there are no relations of power without resistances; the latter are all the more real and effective because they are formed right at the point where relations of power are exercised; resistance to power does not have to come from elsewhere to be real… it exists all the more by being in the same place as power; hence like power resistance is multiple and can be integrated in global strategies." [22]

While the mediation of power relations via the operation of detailed discursive practices gives form to human existence, through the very enactments that humans themselves play out, Foucault does not equate human being with its specific and historically contingent manifestation through the operation of modes of power relations. There is an excess of (human) being over its (powerful) appearance. Free, in the ways just specified, human conductive material exceeds the force with which it participates while that force circulates strategically through it to fashion human beings into an historical shape and form. This excess is figured in Foucault, and elsewhere in the intellectual resources upon which he draws extensively, as 'possibility', potentiality or virtuality. Ethically, Foucault throws himself on the side of this excess of possibility in which, for him and others, human existence consists. The point is well made by Giorgio Agamben in his short but subtle discussion of Foucault's last essay: "It is clear that what is at issue in Foucault is not simply an epistemological adjustment," Agamben says, "but, rather, another dislocation of the theory of knowledge, one that opens onto entirely unexplored terrains. And it is precisely this terrain which coincides with the field of biopolitics…"[23]

Precisely because it is a force that circulates in human relations, for Foucault there is no escape from power relations. In particular, there is no escape from power relations through knowledge. While he is insistent on not conflating the two, for Foucault there is a mutually disclosive belonging together of power and knowledge.[24] Where there is knowledge, there is also power. Where there is power, there is necessarily also knowledge:

> "power and knowledge directly imply one another; there is no power relation without the correlative constitution of a field of knowledge, nor any knowledge that does not presuppose and constitute at the same time power relations. These… are to be analysed, therefore, not on the basis of a subject of knowledge who is or is not free in relation to the power system, but, on the contrary, the subject who knows, the objects to be known and the modalities of knowledge, must be regarded as many effect of these fundamental implications of power/knowledge and their historical transformations."[25]

The idealization of knowledge as something separate from power relations and emancipatory with respect to power is less an illusion for Foucault, then, than it is a kind of category mistake. Ontologically undecideable and undetermined, human freedom exceeds and resists any final delineation or classification by power relations, while nonetheless only manifesting itself as this form of life, rather than that form of life in virtue of the strategic organization of the relations of power that its very relational existence calls into being. Freedom in the sense that Foucault understands freedom is not something that seeks emancipation through an escape from power relations or, alternatively, through the unalloyed good of the advance of knowledge. As a free existence defined in terms of possibility/potentiality rather than determination, human beings pursue emancipation in an adventure of re-making that is in search of empowered and empowering, but different, practices of self-hood, individual and collective. Power relations do not necessarily and automatically defeat such efforts. Knowledge does not necessarily or automatically guarantee their realization. Freedom is not a powerless condition, and it is underwritten by no guarantees.

> Power relations are thus a positive and not merely a negative thing for Foucault: We must cease once and for all to describe the effects of power in negative terms: it 'excludes', it 'represses', it 'censors', it 'abstracts', it 'masks', it 'conceals'. In fact, power produces; it produces reality; it produces domains of objects and rituals of truth. The individual and the knowledge that may be gained from him belong to this production.[26]

But they do remain strategic. Indeed, power/knowledge in biopower is concerned with cultivating life, making it more developed, productive, secure and so on rather than with threatening death. To do this, the very nature of life processes itself has to become known in its details and dynamics as an object of systematic investigation.

This is the explanation for the term biopower. Power's manifestation as the strategic organization of networks of relations according to different generative principles of formation, regularities and norms of behavior, disclosed by the sciences of power/knowledge, is a creative force. Thus power/knowledge is also inventive. It brings new things to presence. Hence, the modern subject is both one who knows and the one who has to be known, and with biopower and biopolitics known in its changing life forms and processes both individually and in the form of populations. In the process, of course, power/knowledge also and necessarily subjugates, suppresses, outshines and outmatches and therefore also works by erasing from presence, effacing and reducing some things, while elevating and empowering others. These are differentiating and dividing practices that not only constitute inclusions and exclusions but they also modulate intelligibilities, eligibilities, liabilities and legibilities for populations and individuals alike. However, since Foucault has taken so heavily to demote the operation of sovereign power in favor of biopower, diverting attention from the ways in which they also complement each other, Giorgio Agamben's recent work on sovereign power somewhat remedies the imbalance.[27]

All power as strategy presupposes a life that bears the ordering work of power itself. In fact, it is only inasmuch as it does presuppose such a life that power as a strategy institutes itself as a specific and manifests productive ordering of that life. Endorsing Foucault's strategical account of power that presupposes a radically relational freedom as the very medium required for its operation, we can turn that understanding back on the very sovereign power in contra-distinction to which Foucault first differentiated it. Doing so, discloses how the exercise of sovereign power, like biopower, also consists in a strategic maneuver. Here, the metaphysical fiction that sovereign power emanates from a single and unified intentional consciousness is replaced by an analytics of its formal structure that discloses as to how it, too, operates as a strategy of power.

What sovereign power does is institute emergency as the strategic ordering principal of power. The state of emergency/nature is "not a real epoch chronologically prior to the foundation of the city but a principle internal to the city, which appears at the moment the city is considered *tanquam dissoluta*."[28] The foundation of sovereign power in this maneuver "is not an event achieved once and for all but is continually operative in the civil state in the form of the sovereign decision."[29] This ensures the "survival of the state of nature at the very heart of the state."[30] In this sense, the state of nature is something like a state of exception and sovereign power is the power by which "it is permitted to kill without committing homicide and without celebrating sacrifice."[31] "At its very centre," Agamben notes, "the localization-ordering link," of sovereign power, "thus always already contains its own virtual rupture in the form of a suspension of every law."[32] By virtue of its very formal structure, then, the topologizing of sovereign power tends towards the indistinguishability of the spheres of inside/outside, *physis/nomos*, established by it. The state of nature and the state of the exception are simply two sides of a single topological process in which what was "presupposed as external (the state of nature) now reappears, as in a Mobius strip or a Leyden jar, in the inside (as state of exception)." In its topologizing, sovereign power becomes this "very impossibility of distinguishing between inside and outside, nature and exception, *physis* and *nomos*."[33]

The topology of sovereign power is not in fact a space at all. It is a dividing practice. As such it does work. That work is not simply or even primarily, however, to command the domain of the inside of law and of order. Rather, it is to effect a passage between inside and outside, law and violence, *physis* and *nomos*, the command of which itself inaugurates this very form of power. The state of exception and of nature comprises a complex topologizing figure in which not only the exception and the rule but also the states of nature and law, outside and inside, are allowed to pass in and out of phase with one another according to a strategic operation of power, which is know as sovereign. This is why Agamben characterizes it as "the point of indistinction between violence and law, the threshold on which violence passes over into law and law passes over into violence."[34] He concludes: "the sovereign *nomos* is the principle that, joining law and violence, threatens them with indistinction."[35] Similarly that is also why and how all constitutions in establishing a constituted power simultaneously presuppose themselves as constituting power.[36] Sovereign power, whether of the state, the nation, the people or the individual, is simultaneously posed then both "on the violence that posits law and the violence that preserves it."[37]

In short, the work of sovereign power has been the production of bare life, life amenable to the sway of sovereign power. From the standpoint of the operation of sovereign power, bare life is "the originary political element."[38] Without it, there would be no sovereign power. If the first effect of power is to produce the individual, sovereign power produces both the individual sovereign and the bare life that the sovereign requires for its own self-production as transcendent to its subjects (objects). The geopolitics enabled by sovereign practices necessarily, however, also called for, and reproduced, biopolitical effects. As Foucault noted: "more than the problems of a sovereign's legitimate dominion over a territory, what will appear important is the knowledge and development of a state's forces: in a space (Euclidean and global at once) of competition between states, very different from that in which dynastic rivals confronted each other, the major problem is that of a dynamic of the forces and the rational techniques which enable one to intervene in those forces."[39]

Conclusion

Recall the progressive oligarchizing of state power throughout the last century, and the merging of public and private sectors of power, most prominent in the defense sector but by no means confined to that area, characterized by the ways in which sovereign power came to be extensively shared with large private interests. Also consider the many ways in which these power developments not only intensified but also ramified towards the end of the century with a whole variety of new initiatives experimenting in the fusion of public and private powers including, for example, 'privatization,' 'public private finance initiatives,' 'public private partnerships,' 'governance,' 'global governance' and so on. Bear in mind also the great labor of knowledge, of knowledge processing, of data acquisition and statistical accumulation as well as the intensive and extensive modes of surveillance entailed by the vast and expanding scientific study of 'man' resourcing these power developments.

Such a mutation and pluralization of power has not been confined to one form of power, or one region of the world. National and international institutions, developed and developing states, sovereign as well as biopower have all been associated with its growth. Increasingly productive of knowledge as well as reliant upon it, sovereign states came to promote the very idea of knowledge-based or knowledge-intensive societies, and of networked societies globally. In the process, sovereignty's traditional power over death became deeply involved in the production of biopower over life as sovereign authorities became concerned with the more efficient, more knowledgeable, more adaptive, more calculable and more fungible delivery of citizens for sovereignty, for labor, for consumption and for experiment. Here, in the oligarchizing of states, the production of proactive business-friendly states and the experimentation with many modalities of power bearing little or no resemblance to the public/private distinction so functional to liberal modes of political accountability was a promiscuous miscegenating mix of sovereign and biopower, and of complex juridical and biopolitical ways of ordering life.

Clearly driven by capitalistic demands, its allied promotion of carefully calibrated self-regulating freedoms was by no means, however, confined solely to satisfying the interests of global capital. It was addressed to the organization and promotion of a whole variety of other political, cultural, developmental, social and human rights projects nationally and internationally, and these often conflicted with the interests of capital. Compared with classical metaphysical definitions of it, sovereign power also appeared to have become critically weakened to the point where it became popular to talk of the demise of sovereignty. And yet, sovereign power simultaneously also became much more extensive and much more intrusive as well. Newly allied with proliferating forms of biopower, networks of disciplinary power knowledge and surveillance as well as with more cybernetically organized public/private control systems, sovereign power seemed rather to have become re-engineered as one powerful modality of power in an emergent and complex network of powers that has increasingly come to characterize power at the beginning of the Twenty-first century, at one and the same time both global in its reach yet also penetrating deep into the very structure of cellular life.

Thus, the molecularization of biology throughout the fist part of the twentieth century, deeply dependent upon state subsidies and the imperatives of national security, national science and national economy in pursuit of sovereign state ascendancy geopolitically,[40] leading to the discovery of the genetic code and the advent of genetic engineering, has eventuated, for example, in the production of genetically modified seeds and crops whose introduction, in the developing world especially, also becomes integrally associated with correlated changes in the very structure of governments as well as of economies there, with insistence on sovereign liberal constitutions as well as the practices of global liberal governance. Here, championing people's right to be free from famine and starvation has become inextricably involved not simply in the availability of food, or indeed in the changing inter-national economy of food production but also in the very ways in which populations are to be governed constitutionally and through governmental self-regulating freedoms. Hence, also, the same processes now look forward to the bioengineering of biological weapon systems likely to become available to state and nonstate actors alike as the century wears on and state sovereignty plays out its competitive power games biopolitically as well as constitutionally in ways that now systematically incorporate international, nongovernmental and corporate players in biopolitical and sovereign practices.

The complexity of power does not play a zero-sum game in which the advent or strengthening of one form of power necessarily diminishes the other. In truth it was never like this in relations between sovereign and biopower in any way, or between public and private organizations of power. Competition does not mean zero-sum, nor does it mean linear development of different forms of power. Here is a complex self-exciting system of many different ways of organizing populations and resources, and of organizing population as a resource. Thus any power over death, such as that which classically characterized sovereign power, must nonetheless also be deeply implicated simultaneously in the specification of the life whose death it is that it ultimately desires to command. Bio and sovereign power have never been dissociated. They have always been correlated. However mutually implicated in one another these different modalities of power may be, they are nonetheless different. In order to explore this difference, one has to change one's approach, as indeed Foucault did, to the very notion of power itself.

Sovereign and biopolitical idioms of power are therefore closely correlated in the sense that they are technologies of power, complex strategic practices concerned with the ordering of life. However, we begin to understand how they work as power technologies concerned with the strategic orchestration of relationality only when we change our understanding of technology as such. Technology is no mere instrument. Technology, therefore also power, is a way of revealing things, making them available, calculable and fungible so that they can be ordered up, and secured into presence. Power as technology, sovereign power is thus a changing way of being in the world as well. It is one in which the world comes to presence and we encounter ourselves and other things that inhabit it first as intractable difficulty, then as malleable stuff, and now as substance capable of emergent self-design with the ability to have the preferred design principles built into it.

Notes

1. Giorgio Agamben, *Homo Sacer. Sovereign Power and Bare Life* (Stanford: Stanford University Press, 1998), p. 83.
2. For a classic analysis of this in relation to sovereignty, including a devastating critique also of the Westphalian idealization and normalization of sovereignty and its mal-application to and for Africa, see Siba Grovogui, "Regimes of Sovereignty: International Morality and the African Condition," *European Journal of International Relations,* 8(3), 2002: 215–238.

3. Rodolphe Gasché, *Of Minimal Things. Studies on the Notion of Relation* (Stanford: Stanford University Press, 1999), p. 9.
4. Gasché, *Of Minimal Things*, p. 9.
5. Michel Foucault, *Society Must be Defended. Lectures at the Collège de France, 1975–1976* (New York: Picador, 2003), p. 35.
6. Foucault, *Society Must be Defended*, p. 26.
7. Foucault, *Society Must be Defended*, p. 39.
8. Foucault, *Society Must be Defended*, p. 30.
9. Peter Szondi, An Essay on the Tragic (Stanford: Stanford University Press, 2002).
10. Giorgio, Agamben, *The End of the Poem. Studies in Poetics* (Stanford: Stanford University Press, 1999), p. 10.
11. Szondi, *An Essay on the Tragic*.
12. (Kantorowicz, 1957).
13. Walter Benjamin, *Ursprung des deutschen Trauerspiels* (GS 1, Suhrkamp: Frankfurt am Main, 1980),p. 351.
14. Maurice Jolly, *Dialogue in Hell Between Machiavelli and Montesquieu*, quoted in Dillon, G.M. and Everard, J., "Stat(e)ing Australia: Squid Jigging and the Masque of State," *Alternatives*, 17, 1992: 281–312, 281.
15. Walter Benjamin, *Origin of the German Mourning Play* (London: Verso Books, 1988), p. 188.
16. *Leo Armenius*, quoted in Szondi, *An Essay on the Tragic*, p. 77.
17. Szondi, *An Essay on the Tragic*, p. 74.
18. Maurice Pearton, *The Knowledgeable State. Diplomacy War and Technology Since 1890* (London: Burnett Books, 1982).
19. R. Koselleck, *Critique and Crisis. Enlightenment and the Pathogenesis of Modern Society* (Oxford: Berg, 1988).
20. Ian Hacking, *The Taming of Chance* (Cambridge: Cambridge University Press, 1990).
21. This has of course been a central concern of continental thought as a whole. Derrida, for example, puts the point this way: "This unnamable is not an ineffable being which no name could approach: God for example. This unnamable is the play which makes possible nominal effects, the relative unitary and atomic structures that are called names." (Jacques Derrida, *Margins of Philosophy*, trans. by Alan Bass (Chicago: University of Chicago Press, 1982), pp. 26–27). What is unnamable, Giorgio Agamben glosses, is *"that there are names."* (Agamben, *The End of the Poem*, p. 211).
22. Michel Foucault, *Power/Knowledge: Selected Interviews and Other Writings 1972–1977*. (Brighton; Harvester Press, 1980), p. 142.
23. Agamben, *The End of the Poem*, p. 221.
24. (Dean, 2000; and Rose, 2000)
25. Michel Foucault, *Discipline and Punish: The Birth of the Prison* (London: Allen Lane, 1977), pp. 27–28.
26. Foucault, *Discipline and Punish*, p. 194.
27. Agamben, *Homo Sacer*.
28. Agamben, *Homo Sacer*, p. 105.
29. Agamben, *Homo Sacer*, p. 109.
30. Agamben, *Homo Sacer*, p. 106.
31. Agamben, *Homo Sacer*, p. 83.
32. Agamben, *Homo Sacer*, p. 40.
33. Agamben, *Homo Sacer*, p. 37.
34. Agamben, *Homo Sacer*, p. 32.
35. Agamben, *Homo Sacer*, p. 31.
36. Agamben, *Homo Sacer*, p. 40; Jacques Derrida, "Declarations of Independence," *New Political Science*, 15, 1986; Bonnie Honig, "Declarations of Independence: Arendt and Derrida on the Problem of Founding a Republic," *American Political Science Review*, 85(1), 1991; Dillon and Everard. "Stat(e)ing Australia."
37. Agamben, *Homo Sacer*, p. 40.
38. Agamben, *Homo Sacer*, p. 90.
39. Foucault, "Security, Territory, and Population," p. 69.
40. Lily E. Kay, *The Molecular Vision of Life* (Oxford: Oxford University Press, 1993); *Who Wrote the Book of Life. A History of the Genetic Code* (Stanford: Stanford University Press, 2000).

CHAPTER **4**

Time for Politics

ERIN MANNING

Politics Make Time

If politics today seems to be going through a protracted eclipse and appears in a subaltern position with respect to religion, economics, and even the law, that is so because, to the extent to which it has been losing sight of its own onto-logical status, it has failed to confront the transformations that gradually have emptied out its categories and concepts.

Giorgio Agamben[1]

In the aftermath of the September 11 attacks and the ensuing wars in the Middle East, the face of sovereignty in Québec has changed once more. The liberals have had a victory in Québec (April 2003), eclipsing, for the moment, the separatist Parti Québécois, and talk of sovereignty has faded somewhat into the background. A lack of time for any politics that exceeds those of the federalist nation-state can be felt. Indeed, even sovereign ghosts within the Québécois separatist movement are increasingly echoing a sovereignty politics that sounds like federal politics to me.

This reaching toward federalist sovereignty (whether in the name of Canadian or Québécois nationalism) points to a deficiency within politics itself. Rather than turning to the timeliness of the political, rather than questioning how we live together, and rather than taking the risk of transgressing national politics in view of possible worlds of dissension and incommensurability, national politics are upheld as the promise of the sovereign state's dominion over issues such as security, identity and territory, that is, politics without possibility, and Politics indifferent. For, when politics overlaps with sovereignty, we become complicit in a writing of the political that remains enmeshed with the very violence that we may be trying to eclipse.

This dilemma of the political is certainly not confined to Québec. Indeed, as Agamben writes, the political has lost its meaning everywhere in its confrontation with the timelessness of the naturalized state system. Politics takes time, time that is not readily given in this age of quick responses and short-term solutions. To make time for politics, to experience the possibility of a thought that is not a means to an end, a different kind of dialogue must ensue. This, as Rancière points out, is the dialogue of "disagreement." Disagreement involves making time for politics. It includes taking the time to recognize the instances when disagreement is automatically expelled in the name of "politics." It involves taking seriously the moment(s) when politics begins to count.

In the process of making time for politics–when we make the time for disagreement–what becomes more obvious is the false count, that is, the miscount of parts silenced by sovereign politics' lack of time. Politics that takes time makes time to count those who are excluded, to disagree with those who otherwise have "no part." Politics that make time remain divided by a fundamental dispute that foregrounds the fact that a miscount is at the heart of any encounter between independent thinkers. This miscount–a politics that makes time–calls forth an attentiveness to the passing of time, an attentiveness to the manner in which I count in and through time. As Rancière writes: "There is politics–and not just domination–because there is a wrong count of the parts of a whole."[2]

According to Rancière, "politics exists when the natural order of domination is interrupted by the institution of a part of those who have no part."[3] Politics must make time for the disagreement that initiates its enunciation. There is no politics without this discourse, only the order of domination or revolt. Politics is the contentious discursive space, the sum that never equals a whole, the means without an end. Politics is the lack of foundation of any social order. It is a contingent discourse that takes place, and that makes place through time. "Politics only occurs [with] the presupposition of the equality of anyone and everyone, or the paradoxical effectiveness of the sheer contingency of any order."[4] The political moment is an incommensurable break in time.[5] It is the introduction of contingency at the heart of the distribution of speaking bodies. It is the will to speak and to disagree. What is ordinarily seen as politics–the procedures whereby the aggregation and consent of collectivities is achieved–is not politics at all, but rather a form of governance, "the police," in Rancière's terms.

Although not directly identified with the state apparatus, Rancière suggests that "the distribution of places and roles that defines a police regime stems as much from the assumed spontaneity of social relations as from the rigidity of state functions."[6]

The police can be understood as an order of bodies that organizes the allocation of time within a certain territory. Within this allocation of time(lessness), a duration is placed on the necessities of communication, action and exchange. What is promoted is the visibility of the exchange within a time-span that can be measured according to the parameters of the nation's imaginary and the state's spatio-temporality. "Policing is not so much the 'disciplining' of bodies as a rule governing their appearing, a configuration of *occupations* and the properties of the spaces where these occupations are distributed."[7]

To initiate political activity is not sufficient in making time for politics. It is necessary to shift, to make space to make visible what was beyond vision, visible what was hidden, often in the very name of politics. The timeliness of politics is experienced when a discourse that was only heard as noise becomes a platform for dissent, disagreement and change. Political activity does not take place when we hasten to assign blame, when we place the other within a category that will facilitate the organization of that person within the grids of intelligibility, which makes discourse possible within the regime of state sovereignty. A timely politics takes place when we make space and time for two heterogeneous processes to meet, and when there is the possibility of equality between two speaking beings.

Relationships between citizens and states are organized around the imaginary of the nation. This imaginary is enunciated according to a chronology of time. As politics must continually make time for new disagreements, it cannot recognize relationships between citizens and states. It can only recognize "the mechanisms and singular manifestations by which a certain citizenship occurs but never belongs to individuals as such."[8] Hence, politics has no objects or issues of its own. Politics is not a stance, but a discursive engagement with the other, a meeting that is never set up in advance.

> Nothing is political in itself for the political only happens by means of a principle that does not belong to it: equality. . . . Equality is not a given that politics then presses into service, an essence embodied in the law or a goal politics sets itself the task of attaining. It is a mere assumption that needs to be discerned within the practices implementing it.[9]

Politics takes place in the meeting between the police and egalitarian logic and when what is at stake is a subject, or modes of subjectification and when we make time to recognize the multiple that extends beyond community, a multiple that cannot be counted with the arithmetic of police logic. With subjectification (the making of time for the other) comes disidentification (the making of time for politics), which can be considered as the removal of the subject from the naturalization of place. This fissure in the organization of place introduces the possibility for all to be counted because the fissure is the symbol of a subject-space, that is, a space where those of no account are counted, where, as Rancière writes, "a connection is made between having a part and having no part."[10]

The disagreement cannot be settled, but it can be processed. It is this process–a process that takes time, that makes time–that I think of as the political. This process, this time-making, challenges the relationship between the ways of living and saying that define the perceptible organization of time and space. Within the timeliness of politics, what is brought to the fore is language, that is, the implication of the *logos*, the contingency of the moment in which we make a decision to speak one way or another. This is history written differently, not national history replete with its organization of heroes and victims, but a genealogical discourse of timed and spaced events, a momentum in time and a writing in space. This timeliness of politics encourages relationships between different possible worlds to take form.

Relationships between worlds can become political relationships. In the current Québec sovereignty debate, no relationship seeks to be established between worlds, be they ethnic, political or social worlds. Homogeneity of experience is the manner in which the political is written. The cause for this lies as much at the heart of federalism as it does at the heart of separatism, two spaces where the police reigns. Consequently, there is little time for the complex disagreement of politics that would encourage a relationship between worlds. This is the sad irony of Québec politics, where language remains at the epicentre as the central beacon of (in)difference (difference with respect to a "Canadian" Anglo-majority, and sameness with respect to Québec's emphasis on the French language as a tool for identity). As amply demonstrated by the frustrated attempts at re-articulating the political in Québec, in order to create possible worlds, it is not sufficient to posit language as a pillar of difference. It is necessary to communicate that difference, to disagree, to encourage dissent. Unfortunately, these debates never actually achieve a dialogue on the issue of language itself, because, if they did, language could no longer be posited as a homogeneous voice of assent or dissent. "Any interlocutionary situation," writes Rancière, "is split at the outset by the contentious issue–unresolved and conflictual–of knowing what can be deduced from the understanding of a language."[11]

As soon as a common language[12] is posited as the basis for politics, disagreement becomes impossible. Rather, it is the heterogeneity of language (as writing) that is constitutive of politics. This heterogeneity promotes disagreement, which in turn stimulates argument as the opening up of worlds that are not communities but incommensurable spaces of encounter, as disagreement is anathema to organizations of consensual power. Disagreement is the continual negotiation between worlds, a negotiation that is as much poesies as it is politics. It is a listening to the other, a speaking with the other, using all the languages at our disposal. As worlds open themselves onto this heterogeneous playing field, consensus becomes suspect as the glue that holds the "community" together. As Rancière writes, "politics occurs wherever a community with the capacity to argue and to make metaphors is likely, at any time and through anyone's intervention, to crop up."[13]

Politics Take Time

In early December 2000, a series of events occurred that caused reverberations in Québec's political circles. These events are known in Québec as "l'affaire Michaud" (the Michaud affair). I explore the political time in which "l'affaire Michaud" takes shape to set the stage for a further discussion of time and politics. Although the Michaud affair is located in a specificity of time and space, it alerts us to the tendency within so-called politics to ignore the relationship between time and politics.

I first turn to the Michaud affair to expose the manner in which the discourse of sovereignty politics provides a certain vocabulary for politics as a whole in Québec. Then, I turn to Lepage's *Possible Worlds* (Canada 2002) not to draw a conclusion concerning (cultural) politics in Québec, but to expose the manner in which politics can be eradicated through a sense of timelessness on the one hand, or brought to life through a minute attention to the contingencies of time on the other. The Michaud affair and *Possible Worlds* can be seen as synchronous events: in their juxtaposition, they signal that there are always tendencies toward both the erasure and the wilful generation of politics in Québec as elsewhere. I suggest that to adopt a political stance, it is necessary to become aware of which moments are political and which are at pains to eradicate anything but an imposition of a consensuality that deadens the very possibility of politics.

The question that I pose at the outset is the following: is there time for politics today? In the case of the Michaud affair, the answer would seem to be that there is no such time. However, in the case of Lepage's film, I would say that we are always in a potential state where we can make time and take time for politics. The challenge is to begin to be able to distinguish between moments that deny the possibility of politics and those creative moments when dissension is possible, where argument and disagreement are encouraged and where, ultimately, possible worlds can be imagined and constructed. To do so necessitates a sense of what politics can mean, of how time can be made and space altered. In the first case, the Michaud affair, what is palpable is the discouragement vis-à-vis politics, which remains a state affair. In the second case, Lepage's *Possible Worlds*, what we envisage is the tangibility of time as it relates to the construction of juxtaposed worlds.

In the fall of 2000, Yves Michaud, a member of the Parti Québécois and a candidate for the district of Mercier, published a book entitled *Paroles d'un homme libre* (*Words of a Free Man*). On December 5 2000, he was interviewed on a radio talk show by Paul Arcand. On December 13 2000, Michaud was once again invited to speak publicly, this time with the General Commission on the State of the French Language (commission des états généraux sur la langue française). Each of these events focused on questions raised by Michaud in his book, questions having to do with the primacy of race relations in Québec in the aftermath of the 1995 referendum on Québec sovereignty.

During these public forums, Michaud focused on certain key subjects. He repeatedly expressed frustration at the centrality of the Jewish experience in historical and political thought. Michaud accused the Jews of foregrounding Jewish suffering, thereby downplaying the oppression of the Québécois at the hands of Canadian federalists. In an interview with Paul Arcand, Michaud summarized his stance vis-à-vis the Jews by referring to a conversation held earlier that month between himself and a liberal senator. The conversation between the liberal senator and Michaud went something like this: "Are you still a separatist, Yves?" asked the senator. "Yes, I said, yes, I am a separatist like you are a Jew." "It's not the same," said the senator. To which Michaud responded: "It's always your suffering that is foregrounded. You are not the only people in the world who have suffered."[14]

Michaud does not consider his comments to be racist. In the interview with Paul Arcand, he defended his stance with respect to the Jews with the assertion that "we, the Québécois, we have never been racist in our lives. The Jews went to the University of Montreal and elsewhere." In fact, Michaud sees racism being directed *at* him, rather than the other way around. He suggests that the Jews, or, at the least, the recent immigrant populations of Québec, are the racists in this equation. Michaud explains his stance to Paul Arcand by raising a familiar issue, one that received much press after the 1995 referendum: the ethnic vote.

In his book, Michaud examines the voting statistics at length. As he explains to Paul Arcand, his findings reveal that there was not one single "yes" vote in the 12 electoral offices, based on a total of 2275 voters. As a result, claims Michaud,

> we can draw the conclusion that there was an ethnic vote against sovereignty. We lost the referendum because of money and ethnic votes. There is a zero intolerance by the immigrants face to face with us.[15]

"They understand nothing of what we tell them," Michaud continues.

> Most of them are immigrants, neoquébécois who are newly arrived
> on Québec soil. . . . When you arrive in a society, in a new country,
> you take inventory and you try to accompany the people. . . . When
> you think that the angloquébécois population is but 8% of the wider
> Québec population, and that they assimilate 50% of all immigrants,
> it does not make sense. . . . If we do not manage to integrate our im-
> migrants and to assimilate them, well, we will enter a period of
> louisianization, a folklorization of our society.[16]

As can well be surmised, Michaud's comments caused a stir in Québec
political life. From journalists to politicians to academics, responses ranged
from incredulity to support, evoking in many a desire to take an inventory
of sovereignty politics today. In an article published in *La Presse* on the
December 19, 2000 entitled "Les récifs de l'amertume et du ressentiment"
(Tales of Bitterness and Resentment), Mario Roy writes:

> Perhaps what we will finally remember about the Michaud affair is
> its depressing aspect, its retrograde and useless aspect. . . . Michaud's
> tirades come up against what constitutes the essence of Québec. A
> nation that we like to recognize as open and tolerant and which, in
> fact, has been that way, in an honest sense, as far back as we can re-
> member. A nation which, historically, only very marginally partook
> of anti-Semitism.[17]

On the same page, in a letter to the editor, Lorraine Boudreault writes:

> I have been a sovereignist for twenty-seven years. I have always voted
> for the PQ in order to fulfill one of my biggest dreams, to see Québec
> become a nation. . . . I have to wonder what kind of a society houses
> us if we can no longer repeat important facts concerning ethnic pop-
> ulations in Québec without immediately being cast as racist! In
> Québec we live a reverse racism. How can we hope to construct a na-
> tion with people who do not have the courage to affirm themselves
> because they are on their knees before ethnic groups?[18]

I place these two responses side by side to demonstrate what Lucien
Bouchard, the leader of the Parti Québécois at the time, faced in the wake of
the Michaud affair. Lucien Bouchard responded to the Michaud affair by
taking it to the National Assembly, which, in turn, issued an official repri-
mand to Yves Michaud without a forum of response. Michaud was politically silenced, if not cast out of politics completely. A debate on rights of
expression ensued. In an article entitled "Is the National Assembly Abusing

of its Authority," five immigrants to Québec (Ercilia Palacio, Johan Nachmanson, Guadalupe Calderon, Jean Cermakian and Salomon Cohen) responded to the National Assembly's verdict. They wrote:

> Mr. Michaud is a citizen who benefits from the same rights as are accorded to us, the recently arrived. We do not understand how the National Assembly could denounce without nuance, without identifying them, certain of Michaud's comments, thereby pronouncing on the future of a simple citizen who had done nothing but exercise freely his rights of expression in a public forum open to all. . . . We have the impression that, we, newly arrived or members of diverse minorities, are sometimes used like offensive or defensive arms with respect to partisan politics between political parties.[19]

This article highlights the lack of homogeneity under the heading of "the ethnic vote," underlining the fact that the Parti Québécois, in the name of Lucien Bouchard, does not necessarily represent the desires of the ethnic population in Québec by silencing Michaud. The ethnic population cannot be organized so neatly within national politics. Herein lies the irony of the ethnic vote: within the nation, the ethnic presence is cast as the other despite its potential debt to nationalist politics. In other words, there is no time for ethnicity within the discourse of the nation, yet the nation depends on ethnicity to construct its borders between "us" and "them." In this case, ethnicity refuses to give time to Canadian and Québec partisan politics by underplaying its dual role as insiders *and* outsiders of state politics.

Despite the political fervour unleashed by his comments, Michaud refused to retract them. This stubborn resistance in turn prevented Bouchard from publicly regaining face, for the spectre of ethnicity had returned to haunt the discourse of sovereignty in Québec. Bouchard did everything he could to dissociate ethnicity from the sovereign project as he conceives it. In public forums, Bouchard repeated:

> The Québécois are all equal. They have the right to vote for whom they please, and it is not to lose any kind of quality, any kind of merit, any kind of status, to be for or against sovereignty, for or against the Partii Québécois. Prejudice does not have a place within the PQ.[20]

But, despite Bouchard's efforts, the "ethnic vote" had returned as the backbone of sovereign politics. On Thursday, January 11 2001, Lucien Bouchard resigned as head of the Parti Québécois, taking full responsibility for the stagnation of the discourse of sovereignty within public opinion, stating, the interests of his young children as a reason for his resignation.

The majority of his final address was dedicated, however, to the Michaud affair. On the morning after Bouchard's resignation, Lysianne Gagnon, a regular commentator for the Montreal newspaper La Presse, reacted with indignation. "Didn't the sovereignists realize," she writes, "that by condemning Bouchard's decision to turn to the National Assembly, they were shooting themselves in the foot?"[21] Gagnon claimed that Bouchard, was the only politician capable of bringing to fruition the project of sovereignty. Drawing a familiar, although dangerous distinction between civic and ethnic nationalists, Gagnon deplored the absence of civic support for Bouchard's actions. She wrote:

> It was obvious yesterday [during Bouchard's resignation speech], that the Michaud affair was the last drop, the very imposing last drop, that caused the vase to overflow. . . . Bouchard made it clear in December that he would not represent a party that would tolerate banterings such as Michaud's.[22]

Bouchard framed his final speech with a challenge to the candidate who would succeed him as leader of the Parti Québécois. In the words of Bouchard:

> I hope the next political candidate will know better than I how to reaffirm the militancy, how to intensify the sense of identity of the Québec people and how to advance the cause of sovereignty.[23]

There is a certain irony to these comments, as Jean-François Lisée, Bouchard's former political counsellor, notes: "If he, the best amongst us, did not manage to create a sovereign state . . . imagine the difficulty of realizing it."[24]

However, this opinion is not shared by all. The militant wing of the movement for independence did not mourn Bouchard's passing. "Yes, I think it's a good thing that he left," declared Guy Boutiller, president of the Saint-Jean-Baptiste Society of Montreal.[25] "Within Bouchard's party," added Bruno Viens, another candidate to the district of Mercier, "the right to dissidence was difficult to express."[26] Such strong reservations about Bouchard were not heard from the other side of the border. Federalists received Bouchard's resignation with a mixture of respect and relief, respect because of Bouchard's track record as a politician and relief because Bouchard was seen as the politician most likely to generate a legal breach in the Canadian state.

In Québec, a few of the less militant envisaged Bouchard's resignation as "the end of a chapter, not of history itself," suggesting quietly that it may be time for sovereignty politics to be cast aside. "If the mass of the franco-québécois wanted sovereignty, they would have it already, despite 'money' and 'ethnic votes,'" writes André Pratte, journalist for La Presse,

> but the obstinate sovereignists hear nothing. Rather than question-
> ing themselves ... they incriminate others.... The results [of the two
> referendums] do not render sovereignty illegitimate. ... . But they
> should be cause to reflect on the pertinence of the project in light of
> the contemporary Québécois.[27]

Who are the contemporary Québécois and what do they want? This question remains at the periphery of the Michaud affair, begging to be addressed. However, to address this question would necessitate a re-articulation of the politics of sovereignty in Québec, a task too daunting for the majority of politicians in Québec as well as in the rest of Canada. To re-articulate the politics of sovereignty would necessitate a rethinking of what is gained by the segregation of the ethnic vote as the pillar for the failures of politics. Indeed, in Québec, the ethnic vote embodies the paradox of the timeliness of current political structures: the ethnic vote is cast simultaneously as a vital instance of a liberal multicultural politics of assimilation[28] *and* as that which fails to make space for a sovereign Québec nationalism. A re-articulation of the politics of sovereignty would require a critical assessment of sovereignty's nationalist vocabularies of inclusion and exclusion, inciting us to examine the ironic lack of division between separatist and federalist politics in Canada. A re-articulation of sovereignty politics would implore us to ask the question we avoid at all costs: is there time for the political within the vocabulary of the nation, be it in the name of federalism or in the name of separatism?

"There is politics as soon as there is time," writes Geoffrey Bennington.[29] Time signals the potential for a patient re-articulation. Yet, time is also the marker for the devious undertakings of the writing of history, which have a tendency to privilege certain forms of coherence over others. A timeless coherence takes place in the name of the nation, for it is essential to the discourse of the nation that time be measured as the marker for the homogenization of an imaginary. As I imagine it, political time differs from national time. It is time set aside, time outside, time in excess of national time. It departs from the troubling hyphenation of space and time within the vocabulary of the nation. It contests the nation-state's 'within-timeness,' time that recasts politic's capacity to disrupt the stagnant time-line of the nation's imaginary, time that supplements spatial imaginaries with temporalities that challenge the time of the nation-state.[30] Political time, as I am recasting it here, refers to the possibility of rewriting history as genealogy. As histories are rewritten, the times and spaces of their writing can be re-imagined. In so doing, space and time themselves become aspects of a re-articulation of what it means to write, that is, to disagree. This re-writing becomes a political gesture that takes place within a notion of time that exceeds narratives of absolute containment such as those of the nation-state.

The politics that preside over the Michaud affair are national politics. They are politics of the within-timeness of the nation. They are politics indebted to a metaphysical vocabulary of inclusion and exclusion where time is considered to be a stable enunciation of the nation-state's spatial strategies of containment. As long as politics continues to be imagined and understood as the overarching signifier of a national spatio-temporality, politics will remain a championing voice of an exclusionary metaphysics. Such are the politics of sovereignty, politics for which there is no time other than the stultifying timelessness of the nation. Timeless because sovereignty must, according to its biopolitics, preside at the epicentre of the national vocabulary of governmentality as the voice of the law. In other words, sovereignty politics are exclusive politics that make demands on the bodies of those who inhabit the nation-state in an attempt to contain the untimely enunciations of a population that always already exceeds the rule of the sovereign. For, bodies are never acually contained within the body-politic. Bodies exceed sovereignty, always in excess of strict territorialities and identities. Discourses of security uphold not the bodies within the imaginary nation-state, but those always potentially in excess of it.

Sovereignty politics are exclusionary not because they are separatist politics, as in the case of Québec, but because they are indebted to the vocabulary of the nation, wherein politics connotes policy-making practices that codify untimely events. Racism is inscribed within the vocabulary of sovereignty: sovereignty privileges the erection of exclusionary boundaries between us and them, between the inside and outside. Hence, Michaud's comments do not reflect, a priori, the nature of the Parti Québécois as a political party. They speak, first and foremost, about a troubling infatuation with national time at the heart of sovereignty politics. Michaud is thus, paradoxically, neither an emissary for nor a deviant from the Québec separatist arena. Instead, he is an attentive pawn of (federalist) politics, if we understand federalist politics in this case as a politics that cannot think outside the bounds of the nation-state's dominion over territory and identity. On the other side of the political spectrum, we locate Bouchard who, similarly inspired by nationalist rhetoric, found himself dreaming of a politics that could flourish within the measured time of the nation's vocabularies. It was the Michaud affair that tipped the scale, alerting Bouchard to the untimeliness of his political aspirations.

If Québec sovereignty, as it claims, is the re-invention of modes of governance that deviate from federalist practices, it follows that sovereignty should enable a re-articulation that would exceed, or at least be critical of, the politics of the nation. This is not possible. As the Michaud affair highlights, the discourse of sovereignty in Québec is heavily indebted to the very nationalist (federalist) politics from which it attempts to separate itself. The result is an impasse in the political communities on both sides of the Québec border, for how can a dialogue ensue from a monologue? It is in light of this impasse that I view Bouchard's resignation: first and foremost, Bouchard resigned not from the Parti Québécois. He resigned in the face of what he perceived as the impossibility, within the discourse of sovereignty, of giving time to politics. Without time (if we continue to perceive political time as time that has the potential of exceeding national time), there is nothing to discuss. Timelessness is the practice of policy-making that silences the making of politics.

Is Bouchard's resignation really a withdrawal not simply from the governance of Québec sovereignty politics, but from the impasse that accompanies the untimeliness of national political time? Perhaps. Of course, the timelessness of national political time is not a current subject within political circles in Canada, where politics continues to be envisioned and practiced as the policy-enhancing binary of the nation-state's codified spatio-temporality. Time for politics would only exist as a thought if Canada's political vocabulary exceeded policy, that is, if the vocabulary of the nation challenged the separatist/federalist binary.[31] This is not the case either within Québec or the rest of Canada. Québec sovereignty remains a policy-making machine that dreams of the political, but has no recourse to a vocabulary of time that would depart from the sanctions of the nation's 'within-timeness.'

Consequently, the quest for sovereignty in Québec remains at a standstill. Despite its failure at establishing a majority, sovereignty continues to be spoken in the name of national politics. This dream of re-articulation does not bear fruit, for the political demands difference and difference takes time. Within the discourse of sovereignty, there is no time to focus on the heterology of the political. Sovereignty is out of time. If sovereignists did take the time to encounter the political, they would come face to face with the impossibility of the community as a homogeneous political entity, thus taking time to recognize that it is the political that demands re-articulation, and not the nation.

In light of sovereignty's debt to the time of the nation, Bouchard's resignation is as explicable as Michaud's unwillingness to retract his comments. Although one event is not necessarily worthy of the other, both are symptoms of a malaise within political time. Both are stuttering responses to the impasse within politics today. Michaud's comments are expressions of rage that decry the hopeless political situation in which he finds himself. Bouchard's comments betray a resignation in the face of a politics to which he feels he can no longer adequately respond. There is no time for politics in Québec. There is no time to realize Bouchard's dreams. There is no patience for that which is to come, that which cannot once and for all be framed and that which has not yet been thought. Time is withheld, organized and compartmentalized by national policy makers, and itemized in the ongoing eclipse of politics by the policies of national time.

When politics is construed as policy, it betrays itself as a metaphysical construct that secures vocabularies for its re-instatement. In other words, political timelessness upholds structures such as the conflation of identity and territory as a metaphysical ploy that gives the impression of solid foundations. This is created via national histories written around a silencing of the difference that time can make if time is experienced as a moment in passing that remains in excess of normalized territorialities (be they bodies, states, texts, etc). National politics are orchestrated around this silence. Within national policies, there is no time for the political. In the name of governmental organizations, national institutions and official cultural texts, politics as policy silences undecidability in favour of the dream of a concrete vision of governmentality. Politics thus becomes a moral discourse oriented toward its own end. Rather than celebrating the possibility of a re-articulation of its vocabularies, national politics institutes a mute narrative.

"Politics happens in time, against time," writes Bennington. In the swiftness of time, a re-articulation of the political is the injunction to make decisions that are not based on pre-programmed scenarios. To "decide" to re-articulate the political raises the stakes of politics. It is a potentially violent act, violent because it will always risk re-instating the very violence it seeks to exceed. Still, writes Derrida,

> we cannot give up this metaphysical complicity without simultaneously giving up the critical work we are directing against it, without running the risk of erasing difference.[33]

I am faced, then, with the dilemma of "giving meaning" to signs such as "politics" even as I attempt to divest them of that which identifies them within a metaphysical tradition. This is a compromise I must perhaps make in order make time to create possible worlds.

Synchronicity: Possible Worlds

If politics is about time–making time and taking time–, then politics must also be about the contingency of the present. This is the subject of Robert Lepage's recent film, *Possible Worlds*.[34] The main character, in this film Georges Barber, travels between various possible worlds, each of them equally significant and binding. What makes *Possible Worlds* particularly interesting in the context of identifying moments in which time is made and taken for politics is that the film refrains from adopting a moralistic approach to time and synchronicity, allowing itself and its characters to instead remain in the realm of responsibility and choice, will and desire. In this sense, the film is a good example of where the poetic becomes political, where ideas awaken the potential for disagreement and where the moment becomes timely.

> Rancière writes:
> In politics, subjects do not have consistent bodies; they are fluctuating performers who have their moments, places, occurrences, and the peculiar role of inventing *arguments* and demonstrations . . . to bring the nonrelationship into relationship and give place to the nonplace.[35]

In *Possible Worlds*, Georges Barber struggles between the parallel bodies of his consciousness and experience, each of which is as present as the next. There is no moral imperative and no predetermination that would elevate one experience above another. There is no consistency, there is only possibility and choice. In the moment when consciousness shifts, Georges explains to Joyce, properties melt and nothing holds. *Possible Worlds* is about this adjustment to nonplace. This nonplace is not a pre-given entity but a chronotope always in the act of being invented, being spoken and being thought. In *Possible Worlds*, there is no singularity in the sense of a moment set alone in time and space. Instead, there is a synchronicity of experience, and of desire and chance.

This synchronicity can be conceptualized as an enactment of politics. It is an act that admits the complexity of time within its environment. Time is made for the unknown, for the nonrelationship and for the contingent. Within this awakening to the multiplicity of time, the moment is acknowledged as an infinite web of possibilities for which we must assume responsibility. There can be no consensus within this synchronicity. Each decision is an individual locus of potential disagreement. Where consensus is sought, synchronicity is denied as synchronicity implies the impossibility of a reduction to a singular unified centre. Timely juxtaposition complicates the relationship between the police and politics, drawing them apart, forcing politics to disidentify itself with the image of a consensus democracy.

Democracy is usually understood as a political regime and a system of institutions that enable popular sovereignty. Ideally, democracy should not be a parliamentary system or a legitimate state. As Rancière underlines, democracy should be "politic's mode of subjectification."[36] If politics is conceptualized as the disruption of the police, and politics seeks to be democratic, democracy must be understood as the appearance of time within the inoperative community, where appearance is conceptualized as an introduction of visibility, which is a modification of this very visibility. Such a democracy must not be confused with either parties of the state or with society itself. A political democracy of this kind would be nothing more (or less) than a chronotope where the people appear and a dispute is conducted.

Robert Lepage's *Possible Worlds* can be seen as such a space of dissension if we keep in mind Rancière's suggestion that there need not be unbreachable disparity between the political and the poetic. As a poetic enunciation of a democratic encounter with/in time and space, Lepage's film can be encountered as an attempt to initiate a disagreement, and thereby imagine a democratic politics.

As there are many simultaneous moments in *Possible Worlds*, there are various story lines. Rather than recounting the "story" as such (which would be to render linear, to create a consensus within the chronotope of the film), I shall turn instead to a few of the moments of transformation and dissension in the film, moments in which what is at stake is the very incommensurability of the self face to face with the other. The first such moment occurs at the beginning of the film in a conversation between Georges and Joyce. In this scene, Georges enters a cafeteria, the camera framing him standing amongst a succession of partitions, leading the viewer to assume that it is chance that leads him down this particular path. Georges sits down at a table (similar to all the other tables, each of them occupied by doctors/researchers with identical white lab coats) facing Joyce. After introducing himself, they begin to speak.

This scene, like most in the film, is framed by pouring rain. Water figures everywhere in *Possible Worlds* as a symbol, perhaps, of the mutability of life, of the flow between its moments and the simultaneity of its experiences. Georges asks Joyce if she would change anything in her life. Joyce responds that she finds it strange that when asked this question, people usually choose the most simple and trivial things. "How could anything be different from what it is?" she asks. "But surely you've wished you could do things over?" George queries. "Why waste time dreaming about things that could never have happened?" asks Joyce. This exchange sets the tone of the film, suggesting that the present carries within it the possibility of choosing a variety of worlds, where time is a contingency rather than destiny. Time is choice, and living is taking responsibility for that choice. Living in time is to make a political choice to be involved in the construction of a world. To desire another world, a world different from the one in which we have chosen to live, in is to rescind on our will toward the time of our present. It is to un-will the present, or, in Nietzschean terms, to live in *ressentiment*. Nothing is anathema to a politics that makes time more than *ressentiment*.

The dispute that is politics is not a discussion between preconceived partners; it is "an interlocution that undermines the very situation of the interlocution."[31] A pre-determined space cannot house the political. If democracy is conceived as that which makes space for a timely politics, democracy cannot be considered as a specific locus where the people appear. There is democracy only in the contingency of time and place, in the appearance of an other who is not an agent of the state apparatus. A timely politics is not an exchange that occurs between pre-determined subjectivities; A timely politics is a moment between subjectivities-in-process, whose identities waver between possible worlds.

Every attempt at initiating a world is an investment in disagreement. In *Possible Worlds*, disagreement is conceptualized as the complex attempt to make contact with another. This relation to the other involves challenging the relationship with oneself, as can be seen through the exchanges between Georges and Joyce, both of whom seem to be surprised by the nature of the world that they are creating. Choosing a world is especially challenging for Georges, who has the knowledge of the myriad possibilities of his interactions with the others in his life. Even more so than Joyce, he is aware that he is making a choice between worlds. In the world that Georges finally chooses, his love Joyce survives. She does not swim out to sea to communicate with an other she believes is sending her a Morse code SOS signal. Yet, with the end of the film also comes the sense that worlds are not to be contained (hence the water). Invested communication with another—the politics of time—is a constant process of a will-to-desire, a will toward a world. In this instance, politics becomes the choice to challenge the responsibility of the future in a present, as well as the present in the future in a form of Nietzschean eternal recurrence.

In the last scene of the film, Joyce and Georges are at the beach together. Startled by a light in the distance, they run to the edge of the water. Joyce is very disturbed by this event and prepares herself to respond. Yet the light stops, as a result of which she stays with Georges, who is visibly relieved not to have to relive the experience of his wife's drowning. The water remains at the centre of the shot, unstilled and alive, a reminder of the turbulence and fluidity of possible worlds. Shortly before this event, Georges and Joyce are lying on a blanket on the sand. "When I was a girl," Joyce tells Georges, "I thought it was a different world I saw underwater—I can't put it into words." Georges urges her to be more specific. She cannot. Words are not available for this experience of a possible world. The closest Joyce comes to elucidating this possible world is with the word *not*, the pregnant negation she understands as "a bunch of ghostly possibilities." *Not* is the possible world where Joyce refrains from drowning, *not* is the possible world where Georges chooses to love life, and *not* is the expression of the contingency of time, of difference and possibility.

Not is reminiscent of Heidegger's description of the state of encountering *nothing*. In his essay "What is Metaphysics?," Heidegger turns the question "What is there in the world?" into "What is it that is not?"[38] Here, Heidegger aims to show that presence and absence coexist and that presence is incomprehensible without absence. *Possible Worlds* is a dramatization of this eventuality of nothingness. It is a film about the fullness of absence, otherwise understood as possibility. "*Not* is really magical," Joyce explains to Georges, "it is a way of getting around our own ignorance." In *Possible Worlds*, everything revolves around the *not*, around the politics of not knowing, of absence and possibility, around the necessity to get beyond the ontology that invests all its energy in the *is*. Without the "original revelation of the nothing," writes Heidegger, there is "no selfhood and no freedom."[39] Encountering the nothing is the very process of subjectification. "Wish only for what's possible," Joyce tells Georges, which is another way of saying, "wish *not*, will your life."

Rancière writes: "The political community is a community of interruptions, fractures, irregular and local, through which egalitarian logic comes and divides the police community from itself."[40] The intervals of subjectification are fissures constructed between possible worlds, and between times of dissension. When time is made for politics, the in-between of time becomes palpable, as do the uncertainties inherent in the myriad possible turns that the world can take. "Political being-together is a being-between: between identities, between worlds."[41] *Possible Worlds* is about the troubling contingency of life where juxtapositions of time challenge us to take time, to make time for an encounter with worlds that will surprise us, worlds in which we will initiate dissent, where we will disagree, thereby creating, willing, a possible politics.

A possible politics takes time. This time-making is without end, for it exists in the *not*, in the contingency of a moment to come. Sovereign politics are a waste of time. To take time for politics is neither a capturing nor a wasting of time. It is a re-casting of time amongst and between possible worlds. It is a re-articulating of various ways of writing the chronotopes in which we choose to live. To take time for politics is to recognize difference not as ethnicity but as excess to identity and territory. To take time for politics is to exceed the body-politic that seeks to contain the act of decision-making within the bounds of nationally timed narratives. If we take time for politics, we make time that resists narratives of sovereign hierarchy. If we take time for politics, we engage in a poeisis that remains synchronous with the myriad possibilities we have not yet had time to articulate, possibilities in the making.

Notes

1. Giorgio Agamben, *Means Without an End: Notes on Politics*, trans. by Vincenzo Binetti and Cesare Casarino (Minneapolis: Minnesota UP, 2000), p. 1.
2. Jacques Rancière, *Disagreements: Politics and Philosophy*, trans. by J. Rose (Minneapolis: Minnesota UP, 1999), p. 10.
3. Rancière, *Disagreements*, p. 11.
4. Rancière, *Disagreements*, p. 17.
5. That Nietzschean instant at the gateway when the dwarf must decide between two paths ...

6. Rancière, *Disagreements*, p. 29.
7. Rancière, *Disagreements*.
8. Rancière, *Disagreements*, p. 31.
9. Rancière, *Disagreements*, p. 33.
10. Rancière, *Disagreements*, p. 36.
11. Rancière, *Disagreements*, p. 49.
12. The notion of a common language in Québec exists on more than one level. In the most bla-tant case, the common language is French. Political debates have been fought over the question of language in Québec not only to the possible detriment of difference as regards different lan-guages (a large proportion of québécois speak not only English, but also Italian, Hebrew, Portuguese, Vietnamese, etc), but also to the detriment of difference *within* language (i.e., there is only *one* québécois notion of "French" within the discourse of sovereignty politics in Québec). For more on this subject, see Erin Manning, *Ephemeral Territories: Representing Nation, Home and Identity in Canada* (Minneapolis: Minnesota UP, 2003).
13. Ranciere, *Disagreements*, p. 60.
14. Yves Michaud interview with Paul Arcand, *La Presse*, Tuesday, December 19, 2000, A15.
15. Michaud interview with Paul Arcand.
16. Michaud interview with Paul Arcand.
17. Mario Roy, "Les récifs de l'amertume et du ressentiment" (Tales of Bitterness and Resentment), *La Presse*, December 19, 2000, p. A14.
18. Lorraine Boudreault, Letter to the Editor, *La Presse*, December 19, 2000, p. A14.
19. Ercilia Palacio, Johan Nachmanson, Guadalupe Calderon, Jean Cermakian and Salomon Cohen "Is the National Assembly Abusing of its Authority," *Le Devoir*, Wednesday, December 20, 2000, p. A7.
20. Lucien Bouchard *Le Devoir*, Wednesday, December 20, 2000, p. A8.
21. Lysianne Gagnon, *La Presse*, Friday, January 12, 2001, p. A1
22. Lysianne Gagnon, *La Presse*, Friday, January 12, 2001, p. A1.
23. Lucien Bouchard, *La Presse*, Friday, January 12, 2001, p. A2.
24. Jean-François Lisée, *La Presse*, Friday January 12, 2001, p. A3.
25. Guy Boutiller, *La Presse*, Friday, January 12, 2001, p. A3.
26. Bruno Viens, *La Presse*, Friday ,January 12, 2001, p. A3.
27. André Pratte, *La Presse*, Friday, January 12, 2001, p. A12.
28. The multicultural policies in Québec reflect a much more assimilatory stance than those in the rest of Canada. In Québec, for instance, French speaking immigrants are preferred and sought out. These immigrants must send their children to French schools, thus assimilating themselves within French québécois culture and politics.
29. The full text of the quotation is: "Il y a politique dès qu'il y a temps, c'est-à-dire dès que ce n'est plus l'éternité (ou la nature, figure terrestre de l'éternité) c'est-à-dire dès le départ." The piece from which this quote was drawn can be found at http://www.sussex.ac.uk/Users/sffc4/contre.doc
30. Michael Shapiro, "National Times and Other Times: Re-thinking Citizenship," in *Cultural Studies*, No 1, January 2000: p. 9.
31. Policy involves that which is concerned with government and "relies on the distribution of shares and the hierarchy of places and functions" (Rancière 1992: 58).
32. My translation. The original text reads: "La politique se fait dans le temps, contre le temps," See Geoffrey Bennington: http://www.sussex.ac.uk/Users/sffc4/contre.doc
33. Jacques Derrida, "Violence and Metaphysics," in *Writing and Difference*, trans. by A. Bass (Chicago: Chicago UP, 1978), p. 281.
34. Robert Lepage, *Possible Worlds* (Canada, 2000).
35. Ranciere, *Disagreements*, p. 89.
36. Ranciere, *Disagreements*, p. 99.
37. Ranciere, *Disagreements*, p. 100.
38. Martin Heidegger, "What is Metaphysics?" in *Martin Heidegger: Basic Writings* (New York: Harper and Row, 1977), p. 102.
39. Heidegger, "What is Metaphysics?" p. 106.
40. Ranciere, *Disagreements*, p. 137.
41. Ranciere, *Disagreements*.

CHAPTER 5

On the "Triple Frontier" and the "Borderization" of Argentina
A Tale of Zones

GUILLERMINA SERI

This is one of the world's great centers of lawlessness. . . . Every criminal activity that you can possibly think of flourishes here, from drug and arms trafficking to money laundering, counterfeiting, carjacking, contraband and prostitution.

Brazilian Federal Police official[1]

Zoning, the distinction between spaces of safety and spaces of lawlessness and exception, has been the primary activity of sovereign power since its origin. By defining and locating all kinds of contrasts, sovereign power frames and stabilizes its dominion. Whereas the preeminence of the rule of law characterizes "normal" spaces, zones of exception are instead areas in which the juridical order has been suspended. Zones of exception are formless. Within them, different sorts of signs, languages, lives, identities, and forms of production coexist without any recognizable pattern other than crisis and corruption.[2] Anything may take place in these zones, and does take place in them. The threatening, porous, and unstable features of those spots where the exception rules exist in contrast to the legality, morality, and security of the territories that sovereign power takes under its protection. Or, at least, this is what we are led to believe.

Changes in the grammar of sovereignty affect the dynamics of zoning. Traditionally, lawless or juridically "blank" zones of exception were assumed to exist outside the boundaries of the polis—in no man's land or the godless and sinful realm of the barbarian. Yet, as Giorgio Agamben notes, in recent history zones of exception were given specific arrangements *within* the polity—as may be seen in the emergence of concentration camps. Contemporarily, not only do states proceed to define zones of emergency within[3] but also ghettoes and shantytowns in major cities enjoy *de facto* the same status. While the "construction of boundaries between zones of safety and zones of violence"[4] defines the main activity of sovereign power, throughout history such an activity has materialized into different units— from the city-state in ancient times to the nation-state in modernity. In all cases, the differentiation is made between an inside that appears safe and an outside with which danger is associated. Yet, as soon as we approach any specific spot, we discover that the divisions between safe/dangerous, rule of law/state of exception, bios/zoē, reappear on different scales (i.e. world regions, countries, cities, neighborhoods) in such a way that the dynamics of zoning, with its play of insides and outsides, organizes a fractal structure.[5] At all scales, "what enables individuals, homes, schools, and nations to become a zone of safety *or* danger, is an assignation of 'the dangerous' as that which is outside, unknowable, foreign, different, Other."[6]

Zoning thus entails the definition of borders and frontiers, although such a delimitation is never as neat as the image of a linear limit may suggest. The global scenario emerges today as the appropriate scale by which to examine crises, collapses, and processes of *zoning*. They appear more intelligible when approached from the dynamics of a new form of sovereignty that is also global. This form is what Michael Hardt and Antonio Negri call "Empire" and define as "a decentered and deterritorializing apparatus of rule that progressively incorporates the entire global realm within its open, expanding frontiers."[7] Departing from an understanding of space as *open*, imperial power assimilates all existent legal, cultural, and spatial forms in its continuous and unlimited expansion. In the era of global capitalism, power does not attempt to stop but to control and regulate flows of capital, beings, and commodities. Thus, former state borders become *internal regulatory zones*, and entire countries transform themselves into zones that resemble their former borders. Paradoxically, though, in a world in which the identification of actual borders becomes increasingly difficult, the play of sovereignty permanently settles new zonal distinctions, qualifications, and exclusion on all scales. And September 11 constitutes the event that decisively intensified this global dynamic: according to Hardt, "we seem to have entered into a state of emergency post-September 11 with expanded police powers within and outside the United States."[8]

Zoning is a multi-layered process that results from the overlapping and confluence of different kinds of narratives, genres, and practices. The process of zoning turns any narrative able to reinforce a process of othering into a tool of sovereign exclusion. Policing, in addition to tourism, technical assessments of security, and crime rates alongside images of safety and danger crystallized in movies and soap operas, myths and folk tales, and moral judgments, all contribute to making the distinction between spaces of safety and spaces of danger appear natural. By and large, they all converge in manufacturing a space such that whatever it contains appears as exotic, distant, lawless, and alien; in short, as a space that is ontologically other and truly exceptional.

This chapter focuses on the examination of the discursive definition of a zone of exception after September 11—the "triple frontier," on the border between Paraguay, Brazil, and Argentina—as well as on the practical consequences of such a process on Argentina's symbolic and political status following the country's economic and political collapse in December 2001.

The "triple frontier" is the north-east area where Argentina meets Paraguay and Brazil, right next to the Iguazú Falls 1400 km north of Buenos Aires. It is one of the most significant centers of tourism in the region. The area is also characterized as one of the greatest centers of lawlessness in the world and the most significant location of smuggling in South America. Besides smuggling, all kinds of crimes—counterfeiting, prostitution, money laundering, drugs, children and arms trafficking, and terrorist and paramilitary training—are said to take place there.[9] Furthermore, it is suggested that terrorists run businesses related to tourism.

Covering an area of approximately 30 square kilometers, the "triple frontier" includes the cities of Puerto Iguazú in Argentina, Foz do Iguaçu in Brazil, and Ciudad del Este in Paraguay. Two bridges unite the cities: the "Bridge of Friendship," which connects Ciudad del Este with Foz do Iguaçu, and the "Bridge Tancredo Neves," which links Foz do Iguaçu to Puerto Iguazú. With a population of approximately 700,000 people of 62 different nationalities and 22 religions, the "triple frontier" appears as a paradigmatic Babel.[10] Within the area, the city of Ciudad del Este—once characterized by *Forbes* magazine as the "third commercial center in the world" after Hong Kong and Miami[11]—has achieved a reputation for being "the contraband capital of South America." More than 80 clandestine landing-fields in the surrounding jungle endorse such fame.[12]

For decades, the area of the "triple frontier" was invested with meanings of instability and lawlessness, which are usual in border zones and appear more accentuated in this triple border. Yet, its lawlessness appeared to be of the kind that the center is able to tolerate. All this changed dramatically after September 11. Rather than to Babel, the post-September 11 "triple frontier" has been compared to Casablanca during WWII, with a strong presence of local law-enforcement and intelligence agencies, together with their American, Israeli,

German, and Spanish secret service counterparts.[13] Both Brazil and Argentina have intensified controls in the area, with the FBI and the CIA in support.[14] After the economic and political collapse of the country in December 2001, the logic of zoning previously confined to the "triple frontier" reversed and overflowed to the whole territory of Argentina, threatening to stain a larger area within South America. Meanwhile, territories of power shaken after September 11 and the financial crisis in the North began to regain stability.

In what follows, I revisit the conceptual apparatus necessary to examine the production of zones by sovereign power to discuss the process of definition of the "triple frontier" as a zone of exception.

Zoning and Sovereign Power

Sovereign power reproduces and stabilizes itself through zoning. Power is always territorial and always proceeds through territorial partitions. Whereas power can only be exercised in a certain space, it is the presence of power that defines a territory. According to Michel Foucault, "territory is what is controlled by a certain type of power."[15] But, what is sovereignty and how does the activity of *zoning* relate to it? In an attempt to characterize sovereignty by the specific kind of activity that best describes it, Carl Schmitt defines the sovereign as "he who decides on the exception."[16] Every time we face emergencies to define and solve, but for which there are no available norms or principles, the exception, which "is not codified in the existing legal order,"[17] comes to the forefront. The emergency is overcome when the gap between the existing norms and the concrete situation is closed through a decision, and such a decision is ultimate and consequently sovereign. But there is even more to this: the very definition of the situation as exceptional is the product of a similar decision. That is, being sovereign is both being able to define the existence of a situation that exceeds the provisions of the legal order, and to decide how to deal with such a situation. In Schmitt's view, the privileged nature of sovereignty is disclosed in the exception.

With his definition, Schmitt points to the groundless nature of any legal arrangement and its foundation upon a contingent decision. Far from being founded on divine or natural law, Schmitt makes it clear that the juridical order is arbitrarily based upon a decision that is taken in a realm previous to and outside the law—the realm of the exception.[18] That is, the juridical order is ultimately grounded in the realm of the non-juridical.

Giorgio Agamben elaborates Schmitt's definition further in two decisive aspects. First, Agamben shows that the exception is included in the structure of the law: the "normal case" requires the presence of the exception to appear normal itself (i.e. the value of the law becomes apparent only against the background of the state of nature).[19] Thus, the realm of lawlessness belongs to the very structure of the law and makes its existence possible. Second, Agamben argues that the decision that founds the sovereign order is actually a decision about the status of life. Accordingly, Agamben redefines sovereignty as the activity of permanently distinguishing between on the one hand, the life that deserves to be lived and has juridico-political status (*bios*) and on the other, the life that does not and consequently is just a mere biological fact that remains outside the juridical order and whose annihilation does not constitute a crime. Following Aristotle, Agamben calls the latter zoē, or bare life—that is, life deprived of any juridical rights.

As it appears in the foundation of the Western tradition, what makes us human is the recognition of our status as subjects by sovereign power. Thus, for example, Aristotle establishes in his *Politics* that life is *human* only within the polis. In contrast, he considers stateless beings bad or "above humanity"[20]—either barbarians or gods. To the extent that humanity is something we acquire *only* within the political community, those "tribeless, lawless, heartless" outcasts retain the potential for being human, but they are not actually so. Thus, whereas all members of the species homo sapiens share the attribute of biological life—that is, all human beings are primarily zoē—and also share the potential for their life to become *human*, only some among us actually develop this potential, and such a development is the product of political activity. It is the political that turns us into humans and allows our lives to be good lives, but our inclusion in the political realm solely follows a sovereign decision.[21] Thus, Agamben indicates the paradox that "in Western politics, bare life has the peculiar privilege of being that whose exclusion founds the city of men."[22]

Bare life is life in zones of exception. The definitions of the status of life entail a correlated play of localizations and territorial delimitations. Thus, different kinds of lives tend to be either safeguarded in areas of safety and the rule of law or thrown into zones where only the exception rules. The activity of delineating zones discloses a recursive grammar: on the one hand, the sovereign activity defines zones in such a way that forms of life considered worthless are cast out and confined to the outside limits of the polity. On the other hand, from the perspective of sovereign power, forms of life growing beyond the protection of the juridical order appear as worthless. *Zoning* then is the spatial grammar that accompanies the decision about the status of life.

From the very beginning, the spatial delineation of zones also defined moral, legal, and subjective orderings and hierarchies in the narratives that organize the idea of "the West." Starting with them, sovereign power defines through differentiations as to what is excluded as not entirely human, esthetically inferior, morally bad, and ontologically threatening as the opposite and correlated face of the polity.[23] Outcasts, boundaries, and the need for an outside appear in the very foundation of the West in such a way that they reveal the existence of intrinsic links between the *outside* (spaces of exception) and the *inside* (normal spaces) in the structure of sovereign power ultimately grounded on the exception.

So far, sovereign zoning appears as organizing a binary world of norm and exception, inclusion and exclusion, and bios and zoē. However, Agamben argues that with the emergence of concentration camps, a shift occurred in the dynamics of sovereign power during the twentieth century. Agamben defines the camp as "a piece of territory that is placed outside the normal juridical order [yet] it is not simply an external space," because what the camp excludes is "*captured outside* that is included by virtue of its very exclusion."[24] With the organization of concentration camps, spaces of exception acquired a permanent territorial basis for the first time. The concentration camp, where the exception and arbitrary decisions constitute the only rule, expresses the logic of sovereignty in its purity, and therefore appears to Agamben as the main political institution in the contemporary world.

With the emergence of concentration camps, Agamben sees sovereign power beginning to break formerly clear and stable territorial distinctions between legal or "normal" and lawless or exceptional zones. The ordering that results resembles a Möbius strip, in which normality and exception, inside and outside, and the very borders between them become increasingly indistinguishable.[25] Consequently, the emergence of concentration camps heralds "a new nomos of the Earth"[26] that has the camp as its model and "will soon extend itself over the entire planet."[27] Agamben's prediction is based upon the insight that the progressive indistinction between norm and exception implies the spread of the state of exception in such a way that the exception becomes the rule and "the realm of bare life—which is originally situated at the margins of the political order—gradually begins to coincide with the political realm."[28] Yet, one may still wonder as to the kind of shift that the concentration camps represents in the dynamics of sovereign power: do they embody any transformation in the grammar of sovereignty, or do they only make visible the already present structure of the law, always embedded in the exception but hidden behind the illusion of keeping the exception outside?

On the whole, "the world in which The Zone is situated … becomes indistinguishable from The Zone itself."[29] In her discussion of the film *Stalker* by Andrey Tarkovsky, Aida Hozic argues that "the zone" is neither more or less polluted, beautiful, or insecure than "the outside world, to which it is supposed to be contrasted."[30] Thus, if "the zone" must be especially patrolled and isolated, it is just because "it makes sovereign order possible."[31] Consequently, Hozic advances the thesis that in the present world, zoning works fundamentally to maintain the *illusion* of differences between the inside and outside. Therefore, if there are no significant differences between legal and lawless spaces, but the very distinction is still maintained in place only because it constitutes the main substance of sovereign power, hegemonic and symbolic struggles are now a major source for recreating borders and forbidden zones. In the meantime, whole state territories increasingly show features that only their borders used to have, while mobile zones spill over and irregularly stain the global map.

Fundamentally, the dynamics of sovereign power described by Agamben—with its blurring and progressive indistinction of all kinds of clear boundaries—entails a shift towards a global *grammar* of the production of sovereignty and territorial distinctions, and global is the scale in which zoning appears intelligible today. More specifically, Hardt and Negri advance the concept of global sovereignty in their book *Empire*. Empire is the new sovereign that emerges from the magma of capital to satisfy its new global needs of regulation. Modeled upon the republican model of the U.S., imperial sovereignty develops as a "decentered and deterritorializing apparatus of rule that progressively incorporates the entire global realm within its open, expanding frontiers." Far from being hybrid and chaotic, the superposition and indistinction between normality and exception and the generalization of the exception reveal a unique pattern when seen on a global scale, a scale in which there is no outside anymore. Hardt describes it as follows:

> With the decline of national sovereignty there is ever less distinction between inside and outside — and therefore there is the tendency toward the formation of a global space of sovereignty that has no outside (…)[and] there is increasingly little difference between military action (outside the space of sovereign authority) and police action (inside).[32]

Indeed, the definition of crises, collapses, and exceptional situations offers imperial sovereignty opportunities for intervention, expansion, and growth through the securitization of the places where it intervenes.[33] In short, "the juridical power to rule over the exception and the capacity to deploy police force are thus two initial coordinates that define the imperial model of authority,"[34] and Empire expands itself through peaceful forms of intervention, solving the crises it defines.

A Borderless World?

Borders and frontiers are the skin of sovereign power and have always exhibited fascinating and dangerous features. Setting limits to the reach of the law, they strangely partake of the universe of the exception that they are supposed to repel.

Peter Andreas approaches borders as political, symbolic, and fictional *stages*. Andreas emphasizes the symbolic importance of border policing, which he characterizes as a "ceremonial practice, not only a means to an end but an end in itself."[35] In fact, policing is one of the main tools through which sovereign power distinguishes and redefines itself in practical terms between worthy and worthless forms of life, inside and outside, legal areas, and zones of exception. Hence, the treatment of borders and frontiers by sovereign nation-states gives us a sense of what a zone is.

Although borders seem unnecessary in a borderless world, paradoxically the present world appears more and more like a "borderless economy and a barricaded border."[36] The political organization of a world now global requires developing new forms of localization and regulation of flows of peoples, capital, and commodities. In this context, borders do not disappear, but are instead reconfigured and become internal regulatory zones.[37] While border controls become tougher, the grammar of borders reverts over centers and colonizes them. Thus, borderline activities populate most inner cities around the world, as shown by Mike Davis' research on Los Angeles.[38] The politics of zoning that Davis identifies in urban settings—with the use of curfews, strategies of "formal *exclusion* of pariah groups from public space,"[39] and the proliferation of micro bubbles of legality in scenarios of low-intensity war—provides an adequate sense of how zoning works. Similar patterns of zoning are at play in different spatial scales—from the domestic to the international realm—although they are continuously separated and differentiated by sovereign power.[40]

The aforementioned aspects and strategies of zoning can be recognized in the "triple frontier." Although the area already appeared to possess special features, its definition as a zone of exception followed September 11 and had the U.S., Argentinean authorities, and the media as its principal actors.

The "Triple Frontier" a Zone on the Border

> *Deep in the heart of South America, the region where Brazil, Argentina and Paraguay meet has some of the most porous borders—and busiest black markets—in the world.*
>
> *Harris Whitbeck and Ingrid Arneson*[41]

Tourists arrive in the area attracted to both the Iguazú Falls and shopping. The latter is centered in Ciudad del Este.[42] As soon as one leaves any of the bridges that lead to the city, all kinds of indistinguishably authentic or fake imported goods such as Cartier or Rolex watches, Chanel perfumes, Ray-Ban glasses, or Guess jeans offered in hundreds of stores for little money call one's attention. Illegal trade amounts to between $10 and $15 billion every year in Ciudad del Este, and makes the economy of the city probably larger than the economy of Paraguay as a whole.[43]

Such a vibrant economy explains the ethnic and cultural diversity of the area, where migrants from all over the world have come in search of a fortune. Among such a diverse population, the Arabic community—estimated by different sources to range from 7,000 to 23,000 people—is particularly active. Many in the community own stores in Ciudad del Este and live in Foz do Iguaçu, which makes crossing borders part of their daily routine. Estimates are not precise: between 30,000 and 100,000 people are said to cross the border daily.[44] With about 20,000 inhabitants, the small city of Puerto Iguazú on the Argentinean side constitutes the third vertex on the border. Yet, the economic activity in Puerto Iguazú has traditionally been more related to tourism, or at least this is what Argentinean authorities argue while blaming Ciudad del Este and Foz do Iguaçu for everything illegal.

Niches in the world market encompass both legal and illegal activities. Although the state and the smuggler appear as natural enemies, Andreas shows that they are interdependent. Both the opportunities and the nature of smuggling are determined by the state's economic policies: "Laws and consumer demand are the most basic determinants of what smugglers smuggle."[45] Smuggling is business and smugglers are entrepreneurs who simply dare to take advantage of opportunities for profit created by states.

Developed and underdeveloped countries have traditionally subsisted on supplying legal and illegal trade, respectively, to the point that for some countries, "the smuggling-based part of the economy"[46] is the one that appears more integrated to the world market and brings more revenues to the national economy. Frequently, illegal activities favor wealth accumulation and the country's development, in other words illegal activities finance the development of the legal ones, and this applies to both individuals and nations. Britain, a country whose glory was built upon the development of state-sponsored illegal activities such as smuggling and piracy, constitutes the best example of this dynamic. Another classical example is Paraguay, "a major smuggling transshipment hub, a distribution center for the smuggling of America's cigarettes and other products into South America."[47]

Trends in economic policies determine different patterns of smuggling. Thus, during the decades in which import substitution policies prevailed throughout Latin America—from the 1930s to the 1970s—smugglers focused on the provision of glittering imported goods. Yet, once neoliberal market-oriented policies began to be implemented in the region and tariffs and restrictions to imports were lifted, the goods that were being smuggled became widely available at relatively cheap prices, and consequently their supply in the "triple frontier" appeared redundant. An extensive newspaper report in 1997 describes the area as a "ghost triangle": checked by the widespread effects of the Asian crisis, liberal policies towards imports, and economic recession. Local businesses complained as everything they had to offer—perfumes, electronic devices, video-games, watches—was easily found everywhere in Brazil and Argentina. In 1997, about 2,000 stores had closed.[48] The neoliberal shift intensified during the 1990s and redirected smuggling into other (more dangerous) activities such as money laundering, arms, immigrants smuggling, and drug trafficking. According to the U.S. State Department, Paraguay moves between 10 and 40 metric tons of cocaine every year to the United States and Europe, and it grows some of the best-quality marijuana, which is exported mostly to Brazil. Links between Paraguayan criminals and the Revolutionary Armed Forces of Colombia date back to the mid 1990s (FARC).[49] However, what most reports by security analysts, the media, or governmental authorities examine as moral decay and crises calling for U.S. intervention could also be considered as the long-term consequences of neoliberal economic reforms, ultimately fostered by the dynamics of global capital.

Terrorism 1: The Argentinean Israelite Mutual Association (AMIA)

Argentineans know about violence. Yet, the bombing that blew apart the Israeli embassy in Buenos Aires on March 17, 1992, where 28 people died and 250 others were injured, was a new form of violence in the country. At that time, many attributed the bombing to a reaction against Argentina sending troops to the Gulf War in 1991 in support of the U.S. Yet, while conjectures were still discussed, less than two years later, on Monday, July 18, 1994, another bombing reduced the building of the AMIA, the Argentinean Israelite Mutual Association, to rubble. Around 100 people were killed and 120 wounded by this bombing in what constituted the biggest attack against the Diaspora Jewish community after the Holocaust.[50] A few months after the bombing, the Argentinean government announced the introduction of high-tech passports, which led the U.S. Department of State to grant Argentineans the exemption of visas to enter the country in 1996 through the "Visa-Waiver Program."

Only two suspects in the 1994 bombing were sent to prison. After some misleading first evidence and the emergence of hypotheses about a connection to the Iranian government, Argentinean Judge Juan José Galeano's investigation headed to the "triple frontier." At the end of November 2001, Judge Galeano declared Muslim residents in the "triple frontier" responsible for the 1994 bombing. After checking a series of telephone numbers and calls that were made between the "triple frontier" and Buenos Aires before and after the events in AMIA, Judge Galeano proved that residents of the area had provided logistic and financial support for the terrorist attack in Buenos Aires. Evidence also showed that several of the investigated telephone numbers had also been used before the bombing against the Israeli embassy in 1992.

Furthermore, the bomber who drove the car bomb with 300 kg of explosives into the AMIA had been in the zone of the "triple frontier" a few days before, and his two collaborators, now in prison, made calls to the same area.[51]

Terrorism and Tourism

The case of the "triple frontier", Ciudad del Este overall, challenges the distinction between safe and dangerous zones categorized by tourism.[52] Implicit in media and governmental statements that the area is a haven for international terrorism and that Arabic businessmen finance terrorist organizations, what is suggested is that *terrorist organizations themselves run tourist businesses in the region*. The detention of Hezbollah leader Assad Ahmad Barakat by Argentinean and Paraguayan officers illustrates the particular kind of relationship between terrorism and tourism that apparently has developed in the area. Co-owner of one of the biggest shopping malls in Ciudad del Este, Barakat was held responsible for the bombings of the Israeli embassy and the AMIA. Hypotheses linking Arabic terrorists from Hezbolla to businesses led by members of the Arabic community in the "triple frontier" have only become stronger with time. Thus, in his report on Hezbollah, Jeffrey Goldberg notes that the group "took in twelve million dollars in the year 2000" in the area and "washed" them through licit businesses.[53] Another Arabic organization, Hamas, is also suspected of getting funding in the area. In the Iberoamerican Summit held in Lima in November 2001, Brazilian Minister of International Affairs Celso Lafer officially acknowledged the existence of sources financing international terrorism in the "triple frontier."[54] Carlos Altemburger, the Paraguayan chief of investigations on terrorism, also concerns money is sent from the area to the Middle East.[55]

If in recent years "the bodies of tourists have become strategic targets for acts of terrorism"[56]—as for example in Luxor in 1997—the dynamics of the "triple frontier" challenges and reverts this logic. According to the aforementioned narratives, what we would be facing here is an alliance between international terrorism and tourism instead, where terrorist organizations exploit a tourist site to make profits that are then used to finance terrorist attacks elsewhere. Actually, tourism and terrorism may be achieving a virtuous circle in the "triple frontier." The possible connection between businessmen and terrorists constitutes a conjunction that obviously challenges basic categories and splits the grammar of power on which the West relies. The "triple frontier" may then appear as a zone pacified for tourism by terrorists or terrorist supporters, which certainly subverts the dichotomy between security and safety and the correlated process of *zoning*. In this case, the zone would turn into a source of systemic destabilization fed by systemic forces, those of the flows of tourism and capital.

A Border/Zone

If terrorists are really hiding out here, it should be easy for them to go unnoticed.

Larry Rohter[57]

Lisle emphasizes that tourist sites must be both extraordinary and safe: "a geographical imagination full of all the different 'elsewheres' one could visit is further divided into 'zones of safety' (within which the modern tourist gaze operates freely), and 'off limit' areas (where the tourist gaze refuses to enter)."[58] Lisle identifies tourist warnings as one of the tools through which states redirect and channel tourism, recreating the "the safe/danger opposition."[59] Accordingly, after the U.S. and the U.K. jointly attacked Iraq in 1998, the area of the "triple frontier" was immediately considered a "hot zone" by the Argentinean government because of the presence of the Arabic community.[60] And, what about the U.S.? How safe do they consider the area of the "triple frontier"? If borders are porous in general, this one seems to be too fluid for the stability of U.S. security. In the Consular Information Sheet on Argentina, the U.S. government warns Americans about the "presence of members of and support for foreign extremist terrorist groups in the tri-border region of Argentina (Misiones Province)."[61]

"[T]he vanishing tourist gaze is one of the first signs of geopolitical instability,"[62] says Lisle. Accordingly, after September 11 the area of the "triple frontier" was increasingly defined as a "war zone" by the U.S. authorities as tourism was dramatically hindered. In the 15 days immediately after the attack more than 3,000 reservations were cancelled in hotels in Puerto Iguazú.[63] In mid January 2002, a delegation of six U.S. congressmen visited Ciudad del Este for four days "to get a first-hand look at an area considered a 'hot spot' for terrorism in South America."[64] In April 2002, the U.S. State Department warned that Argentina, Paraguay, and Brazil were not able to prevent terrorist attacks originating in Ciudad del Este, while the groups assumed to be there could engage in attacking Israeli and U.S. targets in Latin America if the Israeli-Palestinian conflict were to generalise into a more comprehensive war.

"When war appears on the horizon of the tourist gaze, the discourse of the extraordinary gives way to the discourse of security."[65] Could this take place in the "triple frontier"? In his meeting with the Argentinean President Eduardo Duhalde in March 2002, American President Bush's emissary Mr. Grossman explained that the ongoing war on terrorism in Afghanistan and the Middle East could be prolonged in Colombia and the "triple frontier." Together with Colombia, the "triple frontier" defines the second tier of military targets of the U.S.[66]

Meanwhile, U.S. joint military exercises, training, and subtle forms of intervention escalated in the area after September 11. Latterly, DEA forces have been training Paraguayan soldiers in techniques to combat drug smuggling, which also included counterinsurgency training. Security analyst Sweeney justified the growing U.S. military intervention in the area of the "triple frontier" as an attempt to contain Paraguay, "an increasingly lawless state with a fragile economy, wobbly democratic institutions and deeply ingrained corruption," and prevent it from being swallowed up by international gangs.[67] Preventive forms of intervention like these are characteristic of imperial sovereignty, and are carried out today by appealing to moral reasons. Interventions tend to be unilaterally initiated by the U.S., to identify the enemies as "terrorists," campaign against "mafias" and the drug trade, and ultimately express "the logical form of the exercise of force that follows from a paradigm of legitimation based on a state of permanent exception and police action."[68]

"I shut my eyes — I opened them. Then I saw the Aleph"

In that single gigantic instant I saw millions of acts both delightful and awful; not one of them occupied the same point in space, without overlapping or transparency.

Jorge Luis Borges[69]

In his tale "The Aleph," Jorge Luis Borges describes a tiny magic hole through which all existent things may be seen simultaneously. In the single point of the Aleph, both time and space become senseless dimensions. Everything is in there, and the whole Universe condenses on that point. The first thing that the writer expresses is the impossibility of translating "into words the limitless Aleph." Borges' description of "The Aleph" grasps the ways in which the "triple frontier" has been invested with meaning in recent times, especially after September 11.

"Every criminal activity that you can possibly think of flourishes here..."—a police officer's words illustrate the connotation of excess characteristic of the "triple frontier." The area is permanently given meanings that are different, contradictory and seemingly impossible as coexistents, thus conferring an aura of unreality or magic upon the place. In addition, the image of "the Aleph" also serves to grasp the surprising ways in which all kinds of beings from all over the world suddenly and mysteriously are said to appear in the "triple frontier." As American official Mark Davison declared to Spanish newspaper El País: "that Paraguay was a center of contraband was known... yet during the last years two new problems have appeared: drug trafficking and the smuggling of false visas and passports, which constitute an open door for terrorism." At least 570 illegal immigrants obtain fake I.D.s in Paraguay every year. Tariffs are said to vary according to people's nationality: individuals from Lebanon or other Arab countries pay $900, whereas Korean or Chinese citizens pay $800. According to this narrative, the result is that all sorts of anonymous people have been pouring into Latin America through the portal opened in Paraguay. The airport of Ciudad del Este is indicated as a privileged entry to the zone: there, at least 16 foreigners are said to enter the country illegally on a weekly basis, each one having to pay $5,000 in bribes.

"Every day we have more than 20,000 people crossing that bridge, and you can't stop and inspect them all," a police officer says.[70] After September 11, the *porosity of the border* appeared destabilizing to the U.S. The "triple frontier" was then depicted as a kind of security "hole" through which all forms of dangerous beings were smuggled first into Argentina and then into the U.S. legally with illegally obtained Argentinean I.D.s. If during recent years the "triple frontier" was increasingly invested with meanings of danger by the U.S. government and the American media, the U.S. did not react before the bombings in Buenos Aires in 1992 and 1994, but did so only after September 11. Afterward, the area was defined as a potential zone of war.[71] Accordingly, the media regularly informs us of the U.S. view that the "triple frontier" is one of the "most dangerous" zones in the Americas, and could even destabilize democracies in the region.[72]

Terrorism 2: The September 11 Attacks and the "Triple Frontier"

Crime syndicates from Colombia, Brazil, China, Lebanon, Italy, Russia, Nigeria, Ivory Coast and Ghana are known to be operating in Paraguay.
Jack Sweeney[73]

A month after September 11, the U.S. Office of Counterterrorism accused terrorist organizations Hezbollah and Hamas of raising money and proselytizing in the "triple frontier." Yet, the Paraguayan intelligence service claimed to have warned the U.S. about the presence of Hezbollah activists in Ciudad del Este more than a year before the attacks in New York, whereas Argentinean, Israeli, and American intelligence had worried about the spot since 1994.[74] In mid-November, 2001, CNN transmitted a polemic image: the interior of a house in Kabul identified as a part of Al Qaeda's headquarters, with a poster of the Iguazú Falls. Immediately, rumors started circulating about the links between Al Qaeda and the "triple frontier."[75] Not only Al-Qaeda but also "the Irish Republican Army, ETA (the Basque separatist movement), FARC from Colombia and even neo-Nazi groups from the United States" were said to be present in the area.[76] What could these groups possibly have in common? A strategic alliance of "crossover"—some analysts think—by which all kinds of criminal and terrorist organizations could trade favors and do business in a spot such as the "triple frontier."[77]

Inhabitants of the area do not seem resigned to accept the capricious plays of sovereign zoning, though. Always under surveillance and suspicion, people from the zone of the "triple frontier" sometimes rebel. Immediately before September 11, for three days, more than 3,000 people marched and paralyzed Ciudad del Este, resisting a project to remodel "Puente de la Amistad." Protesters were violently repressed by hundreds of policemen and military personnel.[78] But soon, their voices were not heard anymore: the world after September 11 turned all of them into suspects. The detention of individuals of Lebanese origins in Ciudad del Este after September 11 made members of the Arab community feel like victims of a "witch-hunt"[79] led by the U.S. Also, earlier in November 2001, 65,000 people from the three countries marched under the slogan "Peace without Frontiers" against the process of construction of the zone of the "triple frontier" as a lawless place supporting international terrorism.[80] "It is not possible to accuse without proof," one of the speakers said, while the mayor of Foz de Iguazú claimed that either "proof of the existence of terrorism here is shown, or this international defamation ends." The mayor assessed the damage that the process of zoning was carrying over the "triple frontier": since "tourists are afraid to come due to the media campaign," only two out of the ten million tourists who arrive regularly to the site every year were estimated to have chosen the destination in 2001. Furthermore, by the end of 2001, the international campaign against the "triple frontier" threatened to ruin the business community in the area and efforts such as the creation of a "zona franca" by Argentinean President Duhalde in Puerto Iguazú in March 2002 appeared insufficient to placate the crisis.[81] Despite people's protests and attention now concentrated on Iraq and the Middle East, slowly but steadily the definition of the "triple frontier" as a war zone seems to be in a process of consolidation. Hozic points out that human beings in war zones are construed as "beings in need";[82] accordingly, the treatment of the zone started to include also some humanitarian missions, such as the one consisting of U.S. humanitarian intervention to combat and carry out research on dengue.[83]

The Argentinean Collapse

> *The idea that Argentina does not exist becomes more and more obsessive. Black stains grow in the world atlas. Sometimes, they cover entire countries, or cities that used to be brilliant and participate in the world's life. Now, they are countries without production, without an active population, without an organized economy. (…) Argentina is a country of consumption, but not of production or labor, and its exemplary character is that it rapidly advances towards decadence and decomposition.*
>
> *Alain Touraine*[84]

The existence of radiation from black holes seems to imply that gravitational collapse is not as final and irreversible as we once thought.
Stephen Hawking[85]

After having been applauded internationally as a successful example of orthodox pro-market reforms during the 1990s, the Argentinean economy collapsed in December 2001, together with the political stability of the country, when the Alianza government could not afford to pay its private debtors anymore.[86] Tens of thousands of Argentineans marching on the streets despite a bloody police repression, and the succession of five Presidents in a month give a sense of the gravity of the situation. This may be seen as the outcome of decades of harsh policies of structural adjustment drawn from the lines of international institutions such as the IMF and the World Bank, which ended by dramatically eroding the productive capacity of the country, while unemployment and poverty rates skyrocketed and a $160 billion external debt continued growing in spite of all efforts to control it.[87]

Soon, a massive exodus began. Escaping unemployment, poverty, and insecurity, many Argentineans either took the first flight they could to get out of the country, or applied for passports or visas from their European ancestors' countries, mostly Italy and Spain, or from Israel. Many others decided to take advantage of the U.S. visa-waiver program and entered the country as tourists with the purpose of staying. In 2002, non-official estimates indicated that around 100,000 Argentineans were living in the New York area and that there were about 140,000 others in Miami and South Florida.

Beyond their precise numbers, citizens of a developing country turned into *bare life*, Argentineans, either at home or abroad, began to constitute a mobile, amorphous, and undesirable flow of human bodies that threatened to destabilise spatial orderings wherever they went—Miami, Madrid, New York, Rome. Rapidly, the numbers of the Argentinean diaspora led the U.S. government to exclude Argentina from its "visa-waiver program." Both the lack of security of the Argentinean I.D. and the porosity of the "triple frontier," which according to the U.S. authorities allowed terrorists to launder their identities and enter into the United States with Argentinean passports, were blamed for such a change in policy. As a result, since February 2002, the U.S. Immigration and Naturalization Service once again requires Argentine citizens to carry a visa upon entering the U.S. Not only visas but proof of wealth is required for Argentineans entering the U.S., and U.S. Attorney General John Ashcroft finally acknowledged that the undesirable flow of immigrants was the main reason why the measure was taken. Meanwhile, hunger threatens the once "middle class" society of Latin America.[88]

Although generally correct, Touraine's perception of Argentina in 2002 may be misleading: in his account, decadence and decomposition appear to be the final stage of a process, which they are, only if what we have in mind is modern institutions and patterns. But decadence and decomposition may also be constitutive elements of a permanent state of affairs, when crises and corruption become systemic. Along these lines, Hardt and Negri argue that corruption is simply a symptom of the progressive dissolution of nations, national identities, and territories. The authors observe that far from leading to catastrophes, crises become the force that impels the further expansion of global sovereignty through intervention. Fluidity, corruption, and hybridity seem to be functional to the development of Empires as the movements of simultaneous expansion and "decomposition" of the Roman Empire suggest, in agreement with Hardt and Negri's analysis of the present world.[89] Furthermore, being excluded from protagonism in world history or in the world market is not the same as ceasing to exist. What changes is one's own status: indeed, the collapsed spaces of modernity do not entirely or necessarily disappear but become *zones*, zones of exception that serve as a background to the "normal" world. Accordingly, instead of "hell," President Kirchner could have also said: "We are still in the *zone*," which is the political version of hell.

Concluding Remarks

The goal of the Bush administration is to build an effective surveillance and interdiction fire wall across a major southern route in Paraguay that Colombian and Bolivian drug traffickers use to export cocaine to the United States and Europe. But the U.S. effort comes as Paraguay's political institutions are increasingly at risk of being overwhelmed by powerful international criminal organizations.

Jack Sweeney[90]

Through zoning, walls are constructed—these days against international crime, terrorism, and lawlessness. Through zoning, sovereign power proceeds to delimit spaces of safety and spaces of danger, the latter ruled by the exception, and to stabilize its territorial dominion. Boundaries, which are essential to zoning, tend to be conceived of as neat and linear, however they always define amorphous zones, and not lines, by which it is extremely difficult to tell where limits are. In times of global unrest, though, the ideological claim for neat borders and zones becomes apparent, while the (re)definition of zones helps administer and confine the consequences of crises.

Accordingly, it is my contention that the "borderization" of Argentina after 2001 spread from the discursive definition of the "triple frontier" as a zone of exception, danger, and war, which contributed to the stabilization of the convulsed North. By extending the definition of an exceptional zone from the "triple frontier" to Argentina as a whole and threatening to extend it from Argentina to the rest of South America, the U.S. government attempted to regain the stability and normality that were lost after September 11 and the financial crisis. The latter exploded at three points: Enron, WorldCom, and Argentina, but the bulk of its consequences seems to have been transferred to South America.[91] Meanwhile, normality returned to the New York Stock Market. Sovereign power once again proceeded through *zoning*. After December 2001, a new amorphous zone of exception overflowed from the "triple frontier" to Argentina, and from Argentina endangered the region.[92] Apparently, the framing of the "triple frontier" as a zone of insecurity anticipated the definition of the whole Argentinean country as a similar zone.

Disputes on zoning concern sovereignty and it is possible to see how both the U.S. and the Argentinean governments attempted to resignify the "triple frontier" according to different patterns and with different strategic purposes. Since 2002, seeking to regain stability and credibility, the Argentinean government challenged the direction of the process of *zoning*, in part by disputing the understanding of what occurred in the "triple frontier." Hence, Argentinean officers confined emergency and exception to the area of the "triple frontier" and blamed Ciudad del Este for the crisis: "In case terrorist activity exists, that must be investigated principally in Ciudad del Este and Foz de Iguaçu. Our main task is to avoid filtrations into the country"—said the chief of the Argentinean Gendarmerie.[93] Simultaneously, right after September 11, Puerto Iguazú was presented as "the safest Argentinean city."[94] But the sacrifice of the "triple frontier" and the majority of its inhabitants to the exception was not questioned, though, by any expression of sovereign power and neither by Argentina.

The zone of the "triple frontier" constitutes the heart of South America. Modern Argentina was built upon a deadly attack to this heart, with its participation in the Triple Alliance War that reduced both the process of industrialization of Paraguay in the mid nineteenth century and its male population to dust.[95] Modern Argentina understood itself as being destined to be anything but European, whatever such a thing might mean. After December 2001, though, the heart of the land seemed to be taking revenge and Argentina appeared to be referred to as a zone threatening security in the Americas. Simultaneously, Argentinean nationals looked to many the kind of individuals who inhabit zones—lawless pariahs from a lawless territory. In this case, the logic of construction of borders became the logic of production of the whole territory, which was given the same symbolic attributes that only the "triple frontier" used to exhibit. This in turn reveals the zonal character of borders and the need for both boundaries and zones, those chunks of political hell, in Empire.

Notes

1. Qtd. in Larry Rohter, "Terrorists Are Sought in Latin Smugglers' Haven," The New York Times, September 27, 2001.
2. "Corruption" is understood here, following Michael Hardt and Antonio Negri, as a "general process of decomposition or mutation. . . . We might think of corruption, then, as de-genera-tion—a reverse process of generation and composition, a moment of metamorphosis that po-tentially frees spaces for change." Michael Hardt and Antonio Negri, Empire (Cambridge: Harvard University Press, 1998), p. 201.
3. As for example, the Colombian government did in September 2002 with the creation of two se-curity zones to fight guerrilla groups. Within those "Rehabilitation and Consolidation Zones," the military are allowed to "impose curfews, restrict civilian movement, arrest suspects without a warrant and search vehicles and houses without any kind of legal limitation." See "Colombia creates security zones," BBC, September 22, 2002. URL http://news.bbc.co.uk/1/hi/world/amer-icas/2273680.stm. Accessed October 27, 2003.
4. Aida Hozic, "Zoning, or How to Govern (Cultural) Violence?" Cultural Values, Volume 6 (1), 2002; 183–195.
5. Shapes containing substructures that reproduce the same shape, which in turn are made of sub-structures that reproduce the same shape, and go on "indefinitely like that, never bottoming out in ordinary curves, are called fractals." Douglas Hofstadter, Metamagical Themas: Questing for the Essence of Mind and Pattern (New York: Basic Books, HarperCollins Publishers, 1985), p. 423.
6. Patricia Molloy, "Moral Spaces and Moral Panics. High Schools, War Zones and Other Dangerous Places." URL http://culturemachine.tees.ac.uk/Cmach/Backissues/j004/Articles/molloy.htm. Accessed October 27, 2003.
7. Hardt and Negri, Empire, p. xii.
8. Michael Hardt, "Sovereignty". Theory & Event, 5 (4), 2001.
9. "A half a dozen temporary terrorist training camps are scattered up and down the border from the two cities" argues Tom Huheey. See "Al-Qaeda's Latin American Base," FrontPageMagazine.com, December 9, 2002. URL: http://www.frontpagemag.com/Articles/ReadArticle.asp?ID=4980; also see Francesc Relea, "'Comandos' Terroristas Se Refugian En La Triple Frontera". El País, Andalucía, November 9, 2001.
10. Hugo Ruiz, "Manifestación en la Triple Frontera por "una paz sin fronteras"", La República – Uruguay—12/11/2001. URL http://www.mre.gov.br/acs/interclip2/Diario-WL/Novembro-01/Materias/republica12b.htm. Accessed October 27, 2003.
11. "El Triángulo de los Fantasmas," La Nación, Buenos Aires, October 19, 1997.
12. Henry Raymont, "Crecientes Indicios: la Triple Frontera entre Paraguay, Brasil y Argentina, Refugio de Fundamentalistas Islámicos," InfoLatina S.A. de C.V., August 30, 1998; also, in an ex-tensive article on the "triple frontier," the existence of 500 private landing-fields in Ciudad del Este in 1996 is mentioned. With the construction of Guaraní International Airport, those land-ing-fields were declared illegal ("El Triángulo de los Fantasmas," La Nación, Buenos Aires, October 19, 1997).
13. Martin Edwin Andersen, "Terrorism in Latin America," Reuters, November 26, 2001.
14. Martín Rodríguez Yebra, "La Gendarmería Aumenta los Controles. Fuerzas de Elite en la Triple Frontera," La Nación, Buenos Aires, September 26, 2001.
15. "Not only can the exercise of power only be performed in a certain space, but it is the presence of power that defines a territory—territory is what is controlled by a certain type of power" Michel Foucault, "Preguntas a Michel Foucault sobre la geografía," Microfísica del Poder, La Piqueta, España, p. 116 (my translation).
16. Carl Schmitt, Political Theology (Cambridge, MA: MIT Press, 1985).
17. Schmitt, Political Theology, p. 6. "There exists no norm that is applicable to chaos. For a legal order to make sense, a normal situation must exist, and he is sovereign who definitely decides whether this normal situation actually exists" (Ibid., 13).

18. Schmitt, *Political Theology*, p. 10.
19. Giorgio Agamben, *Homo Sacer: Sovereign Power and Bare Life* (Stanford: Stanford University Press, 1998), p. 22.
20. Agamben, *Homo Sacer*, p. 22
21. Agamben, *Homo Sacer*, p. 7.
22. Agamben, *Homo Sacer*, p. 7.
23. Peter Stallybrass and Allon White, *The Politics and Poetics of Transgression* (Ithaca, NY: Cornell UP, 1986) constitutes a seminal work for the analysis of the links between spatial, aesthetic, moral, and social hierarchies.
24. Giorgio Agamben, *Means Without End* (Minneapolis: University of Minnesota Press, 2000), p. 40.
25. Agamben, *Homo Sacer*, p. 9.
26. The concept of the "nomos of the Earth" is Carl Schmitt's and it refers to different territorial strategies of taking, organizing, distributing, and exploiting the Earth by humans.
27. Agamben, *Homo Sacer*, p. 38.
28 Agamben, *Homo Sacer*, p. 38.
29. Aida Hozic, "Forbidden Places, Tempting Spaces, and Politics of Desire: On Stalker and Beyond." In [edited by Jutta Weldes] *To Seek Out the New Worlds: Science Fiction and International Relations*, (London and New York: Palgrave Macmillan, 2003), p. 3.
30. Hozic, "Forbidden Places," p. 4.
31. Hozic, "Forbidden Places," p. 4.
32. Hardt, "Sovereignty."
33. "While disciplinary power isolates and closes off territories, measures of security lead to an opening and globalisation; while the law wants to prevent and prescribe, security wants to intervene in ongoing processes to direct them. In a word, discipline wants to produce order, while security wants to guide disorder. Since measures of security can only function within a context of freedom of traffic, trade, and individual initiative, Foucault can show that the development of security coincides with the development of liberal ideology. Giorgio Agamben "Security and Terror," *Theory & Event* 5.4 2002.
34. Hardt and Negri, *Empire*, p. 17.
35. Hardt and Negri, *Empire*, p. 11.
36. Peter Andreas, *Border Games* (Ithaca: Cornell University Press),p. x.
37. Andreas, *Border Games*, p. 152.
38. Mike Davis, *City of Quartz : Excavating the Future in Los Angeles* (London: Verso, 1990).
39. Mike Davis, *Ecology of Fear: Los Angeles and the Imagination of Disaster* (New York: Metropolitan Books, 1998), p. 385.
40 Molloy, "Moral Spaces and Moral Panics," p. 3.
41. Harris Whitbeck and Ingrid Arneson, "Terrorists find haven in South America," *CNN*, November 7, 2001, URL: http://www.cnn.com/2001/WORLD/americas/11/07/inv.terror.south/index.html. Accessed October 27, 2003.
42. Larry Rohter, "Terrorists Are Sought in Latin Smugglers' Haven."
43. Henry Raymont, *InfoLatina* S.A. de C.V. August 30, 1998. Also, see Rohter, "Terrorists Are Sought in Latin Smugglers' Haven."
44. Oscar Laski, "Ciudad del Este: Entre las 'Células Dromidas' y un Pueblo Despierto," *Agence France Press*, September 14, 2001.
45. Andreas, *Border Games*, p. 17.
46. Andreas, *Border Games*, p. 17.
47. Andreas, *Border Games*, p. 19.
48. "El Triángulo de los Fantasmas," *La Nación*, Buenos Aires, October 19, 1997.
49. Jack Sweeney, "DEA Boosts its Role in Paraguay." *Stratfor* (Strategic Forecasting, Inc.), URL http://www.mapinc.org
50. Jason F. Isaacson, "Preface" In *Seeking the Truth: the AMIA Bombing Goes to Trial*, edited by Sergio Kiernan (New York: American Jewish Committee, 2001).
51. Sergio Kiernan, *Atrocity in Buenos Aires: the AMIA Bombing, One Year Later* (New York: American Jewish Committee, 1995).
52. Debbie Lisle , "Consuming Danger: Re-Imagining the War-Tourism Divide'", *Alternatives*, 25, 2000: 91–116.
53. Jeffrey Goldberg, "Party of God," *New Yorker*, October 28, 2002.

54. "Cumbre Latinoamericana. Lafer admite que la triple frontera puede financiar terrorismo," *Efe News Services* (U.S.) Inc. Spanish Newswire Services November 24, 2001.
55. Andrea Marchain, "Frontier in Terror Spotlight," *BBC*, September 10, 2002. URL http://news.bbc.co.uk/1/hi/world/americas/2248487.stm. Accessed October 27, 2003.
56. Lisle, "Consuming Danger…," p. 27.
57. Rohter, "Terrorists Are Sought in Latin Smugglers' Haven."
58. Lisle, "Consuming Danger…," p. 8.
59. Lisle, "Consuming Danger…," p. 31.
60. 1998 Efe News Services (U.S.) Inc. Spanish Newswire Services, December 18, 1998, "IRAK-ATAQUE/ARGENTINA. REFUERZAN MEDIDAS DE SEGURIDAD EN PREVENCION DE ATENTADOS."
61. U.S. Department of State, Bureau of Consular Affairs, *Consular Information Sheet September 7, 2001* . URL http://travel.state.gov/argentina.html.
62. Lisle, "Consuming Danger…," p. 13.
63. Yebra, "La Gendarmería aumenta los controles."
64. "Paraguay-US Lawmakers Visit Triple-Border Area in South America," Global News Wire, *EFE News Services* January 14, 2002.
65. Lisle, "Consuming Danger…," p. 7.
66. Juan Castro Olivera, "Malestar de la Comunidad Arabe en la Triple Frontera," *La Nación*, May 22, 1998.
67. Sweeney, "DEA Boosts its Role in Paraguay."
68. Hardt and Negri, *Empire*, pp. 37–38.
69. Jorge Luis Borges, *The Aleph and Other Stories, 1933–1969,* trans. by Norman Thomas di Giovanni (New York: Dutton, 1970).
70. Rohter, "Terrorists Are Sought in Latin Smugglers' Haven."
71. Sweeney, "DEA Boosts its Role in Paraguay."
72. Juan Castro Olivera, "Malestar de la Comunidad Arabe en la triple frontera," *La Nación*, Buenos Aires, May 22, 1998.
73. Sweeney, "DEA Boosts its Role in Paraguay."
74. "U.S., Argentina join forces to battle terrorism" May 23, 1998. *CNN*: http://www.cnn.com/WORLD/americas/9805/23/argentina/index.html. Accessed October 27, 2003. Also see *Agence France Press*, "EEUU Advierte Sobre 'Terroristas Islámicos' en Triple Frontera Argentina, Brasil, Paraguay," Washington, April 30, 2001.
75. Andersen, "Terrorism in Latin America."
76. Huheey, "Al-Qaeda's Latin American Base."
77. Huheey, "Al-Qaeda's Latin American Base."
78. Laski, "Ciudad del Este."
79. Relea, "'Comandos' Terroristas."
80. Ruiz, "'no al terrorismo' en la Triple Frontera."Also see Marchain, "Frontier in Terror Spotlight."
81. "Duhalde Inauguró la Zona Franca de Puerto Iguazú," *La Nación*, March 2, 2002.
82. Hozic, "Zoning, or How to Govern (Cultural) Violence."
83. Rina Bertacini, "Ejercicios militares combinados de Estados Unidos y Argentina en la provincia de Misiones," September 8, 2002. URL http://www.rebelion.org/imperio/rena080902.htm.
84. "Alain Touraine, 'La Argentina es un país que no existe," *Clarín.com*, April 4, 2002. URL http://old.clarin.com/ultimo_momento/notas/2002/04/04/m-368093.htm. Accessed October 27, 2003 *(my translation).*
85. Stephen Hawking, *A Brief History of Time* (New York: Bantam, 1988).
86. "Argentina defaulted on $141bn of international debt at the start of this year," "Investors Count WorldCom costs," *BBC*, June 27, 2002. URL http://news.bbc.co.uk/1/hi/business/2069514.stm. Accessed October 27, 2003.
87. One of the paradoxes in this respect is that, whereas Argentina owes $165 billion, it has already paid $214 billion which shows the structural impossibility of paying the debt.
88. Becky Branford, "Hunger Follows Crisis in Argentina," *BBC*, October 16, 2002. URL http://news.bbc.co.uk/1/hi/business/2307491.stm. Accessed October 27, 2003.
89. C.R.Whittaker, *Frontiers of the Roman Empire: A Social and Economic Study* (London: John Hopkins, 1994).

90. Sweeney, "DEA Boosts its Role in Paraguay."
91. "Enron and Argentina hit JP Morgan," *BBC*, January 17, 2002 URL http://news.bbc.co.uk/1/hi/business/1765321.stm. Accessed October 27, 2003; also see "Investors Count WorldCom costs."
92. Going even further, Alain Touraine suggested that the Argentinean crisis threatened all Latin America, "with the exception of Brazil, Chile, and a part of México," and that the crisis would also reach Europe. Touraine, "La Argentina es un país que no existe."
93. Martín Rodríguez Yebra, "La Gendarmería Aumenta los Controles." (my translation)
94. "El Mundo en Alerta: Reunión del Consejo de Seguridad Interior. Acuerdan Controles contra el Terrorismo," *DyN*, September 28, 2001.
95. Allied to Brazil and Uruguay, Argentina carried out the genocidal Paraguayan war between 1865 and 1870, with the support of Britain. Tulio Halperín Donghi, *Historia Contemporánea de América Latina*, (Buenos Aires: Alianza Editorial, 1992), pp. 253–256.

CHAPTER 6

"The Nation-State and Violence"*
Wim Wenders contra Imperial Sovereignty
MICHAEL J. SHAPIRO

The World Trade Center Towers Come Down; Bin Laden is Wanted "Dead or Alive"

September 11, 2001: after *Al-Qaida* operatives hijacked U.S. passenger planes and crashed them into the towers of the World Trade Center in lower Manhattan, the horrific results of the attack on civilian targets were witnessed by millions around the world. Included in the continually repeated televised sequence was a body falling through the air from over 90 stories up, a doomed worker, hopelessly waving a white flag from a window near the top of one of the towers, and, most stunningly, the two towers imploding with thousands still trapped inside. Because viewers saw these events repeated endlessly in video footage on a television screen, it played like a disaster movie (in video release) without a touch of redemption. But, however it may have seemed, it was (to borrow a phrase from Don DeLillo) "an aberration in the heartland of the real."[1] A nation with the world's most powerful defensive and destructive capabilities had thousands of its citizens victimized by a small group of men with low-tech weapons.

U.S. President George W. Bush's initial reaction was to evoke a wild west scenario. He wanted the alleged mastermind of the attack, Osama Bin Laden,

*This chapter is a version of chapter 6 in my *Methods and Nations: Cultural Governance and the Indigenous Subject* (New York: Routledge, 2004).

"brought to justice" in the manner the world has come to know through western movies. Bin Laden, said Bush, was "wanted, dead or alive." President Bush's resort to the codes of the West (as Hollywood has made them) is not a singular gesture. Richard Slotkin points out that the U.S. is a "gunfighter nation" in one of the dominant collective imaginaries. Pointing to Western films as the genre within which the territorial extension of Euro American national culture (the westward-moving frontier of violence) has been mythologized and celebrated throughout the twentieth century, Slotkin dismisses the more pacific, contractual models of the evolution of American nationhood and locates the machinations of the U.S. as a nation-state in its acts of violent possession.[2] Certainly, the Hollywood version of the "gun fighter nation" looms large in popular as well as official culture. In an episode of the HBO production, *The Sopranos*, Tony Soprano's Uncle Junior says to his head hit man, who is thirsting for violent revenge against some of Tony's overly exuberant minions, "Take it easy, we're not making a Western here."

Doubtless, aspects of America's western experience can provide compelling historical analogies for the events after 9/11, but with varying political inflections, some of which escape the historical frame that the Bush administration sought to impose. One can, for example, revisit the revenge-happy antics that emerged throughout the U.S. in America's Centennial Year, right after General Custer and his cavalry regiment were wiped out by Crazy Horse and his Sioux warriors. Evan Connell's remarks, in his account of the events following the Battle of Little Big Horn, resonate with some of the official and popular reactions to 9/11:

> Reaction throughout the country was no different in 1876 than it is today upon receipt of similar news: shock, followed by disbelief, fury, and a slavering appetite for revenge.[3]

In the 1876 episode, "volunteers popped up like daisies in April" (in "of all places," Sioux City and in Salt Lake City, Springfield, Illinois, and throughout several states, including Arkansas, Nevada, Tennessee, and Texas), egged on by a revenge-lusting media. Among the more incendiary statements in the press was an editorial in the *Chicago Tribune*: "In every case where an inoffensive citizen is slain, let 100 of these red brutes feel the power of a rope properly adjusted under their chins." And in a statement reminiscent of President Bush's, "a group of schoolboys [in Custer's birthplace of New Rumsley, Ohio] took an oath - 'each with his right hand upraised over a McGuffey First Reader' - to kill Sitting Bull on sight."[4]

Connell's gloss on one of America's earlier violent episodes points to a danger that President Bush doubtless neglected in his precipitous evocation of the cinematic "Wild West." Eager to respond to the event with an analogy that legitimates a revenge scenario, he turned to a genre that threatens the legitimation he sought. Robert Burgoyne's observations about westerns and America's self-actualizing narratives disclose this threat. Drawing on a remark by the Cherokee artist and writer Jimmie Durham, who writes, "America's narrative about itself centers upon, has its operational center in a hidden text concerning its relationship with American Indians...the part involving conquest and genocide, [which] remains sacred and consequently obscured," Burgoyne adds that "one of the most durable and effective masks for the disguised operational center of the nation-state has been the western, a genre that has furnished the basic repertoire of national mythology."[5] At a minimum, the classic western films treat, an extended episode of Euro America's expanding (imperial) sovereignty in politically ambiguous ways. But to evoke their messages is not necessarily to legitimate a contemporary version, as an inspection of both a classic and a post western will show. However, before turning to the western to examine how two of them, John Ford's *The Searchers* and Wim Wenders' *Paris Texas*, negotiate and renegotiate the Euro American imperial expansion, I offer an interpretive frame for the historical trajectory of "imperial sovereignty."[6]

Establishing Imperial Sovereignty

In 1876, the biopolitics providing the context for the post Little Big Horn revenge scenario was already in place, having emerged from the Euro American nation-building project. A white American ethnogenesis had already disqualified the political eligibility of Native American nations to a great extent. Whether lamented as a "vanishing race" or abjured as impediments to a commercial model of land use, the "savage" bodies were either dangers to be eliminated or problems for the Euro American "Indian policy." In contrast, the main contemporary biopolitical conceits are post nation-building ones. The bodies to be protected and those to be surveilled and attacked or excluded reflect a genealogy of security practices. To achieve a critical political purchase on the post 9/11 attack on Afghanistan, primarily by U.S. and British forces, aimed at punishing the regime that harbored Osama Bin Laden, and the subsequent security initiatives that involved domestic as well as global forms of criminalization and intelligence gathering (while planning for the preemptive use of force), one must appreciate the historical changes in state sovereignty practices.

As the twentieth century drew to a close, many surmised that war in the post-cold war era would be increasingly framed and influenced by a post sovereignty, globalized set of political and economic forces. While it is certainly the case that capital expansion is not entirely controlled by national decision makers and that many of the "deadly quarrels"[7] recognized as wars in the post cold war era have resulted in the summoning of multinational forces, for example, UN peace keepers and NATO forces, sovereignty commitments have remained central to peace keeping/ war making. To the extent that contemporary warfare has achieved the prefix post, it is post industrial rather than post sovereign. Rather than preparing for a clash of heavily armed tanks and massed armies, those nation-states most involved in managing global conflict are reconceiving the character and tasks of alliance structures. They are also developing global surveillance technologies to perceive threats (hence Paul Virilio's characterization of modern war as "the logistics of perception")[8] and weapons technologies that allow for (allegedly) accurate strikes from a great distance and, when "manned," involve a limited contingent of forces on the ground. Doubtless, we can learn as much about the biopolitics of contemporary sovereignty moves by heeding the minutiae of ballistics and delivery systems, as we can from the pronouncements of "defense intellectuals" about what lives are at stake, where danger lies, and who are the enemies. Weapons design is, among other things, an implementation of sovereignty's approach to sustaining and eliminating forms of life. For example, when James Puckel invented a many-chambered machine gun in the early eighteenth century (a time before the development of the biopolitics of populations), he dedicated his invention to "Defending KING GEORGE your COUNTRY and LAWES."[9]

In addition to distinguishing forms of life, the interpretive elaboration of danger, reflected in battle plans as much as in implements, has a cartographic component. In the contemporary construction of global conflict, to know dangerous bodies is also to know how the landscape of terrorism is being interpreted. Inasmuch as terror can strike anywhere, the terrain of battle must extend to the terrains of everyday life (e.g., to urban environments).[10] To put the issue in general terms, there is a correlation between changing conceptions of the landscape of danger and engagement and alterations in approaches to the recognition and location of bodies: those that are dangerous, those that are vulnerable, those that are regarded as politically eligible (those whose voices are heeded as civically relevant and whose bodies require protection), and those who are either primordially or contingently politically unqualified.

At a minimum, sovereign violence began intensifying after 9/11. Lacking unambiguous venues and easily discernible antagonists, the representation of threat entered a frantic and expansive mode. Paradox abounded as violent choices were made in order to defend (politically qualified) humanity from violence, and the juridical concepts of law and justice were invoked in the process. Jean Baudrillard's remark is apropos:

> What kind of State is that which is able to nip terrorism in the bud and eliminate it? . . . Does it not have to equip itself with its own terrorism and in doing so simply generalize terror at all levels? What is the real price for such security and are we all seriously dreaming about this?[11]

Certainly, however, the process of criminalizing geopolitical antagonists and intensifying intelligence networks predates 9/11. Especially in the U.S. case, ever since the cold war, there has been an increasing ambiguity between conducting warfare and fighting crime. While fighting both the Taliban fighters and *Al-Qaida* operatives in Afghanistan in 2001, the Bush administration refused to grant their adversaries unqualified military status. The assault hovered ambiguously between a search for specific culprits and a military campaign aimed at ending a regime's (the Taliban's) control over the country. At the outset of the war, Secretary of Defense Donald Rumsfeld admitted perplexity about where and what to strike, noting that Afghanistan lacks "high value targets." Moreover, after killing hundreds fighters and at least as many civilians, scores of captives were imprisoned on Guantanamo Bay Cuban, kept in a legal limbo, a zone of juridical indistinction between prisoner of war and criminal status.

The ambiguous status of the captives reflects what two analysts have noted as a post-cold war trend:

> [a] growing gap between traditional security concepts and paradigms and the contemporary practice of security policy . . . the coercive apparatus of the state has been reconfigured and redeployed . . . . [producing a] growing fusion between law enforcement and national security missions, institutions , strategies, and technologies.[12]

Whereas the cold war "security paradigm" distinguished sharply between the external military security of states and its "internal policing functions," the practical and conceptual internal/external separation, which arose historically after states had monopolized force capabilities and largely disarmed their populations, in varying degrees is now being reconceived.[13]

One of the more 'well-known versions of the history of states' monopolization of violence is supplied in Anthony Giddens's sociological gloss on the modern state. His widely accepted treatment of the modern state's history of violence is one of a successful process of the "pacification" of state populations and a subsequent "withdrawal of the military from direct participation in the internal affairs of the state."[14] However appropriate to the history of European states Giddens's linear narrative may be—certainly episodes of militarization in a wide variety of global venues suggest that "military withdrawal from domestic affairs" has not been continuous— trends in post-cold war sovereignty and security practices present a new challenge to the narrative. In addition to a growing use of military technologies for crime fighting, domestically and abroad (for example in U.S. anti narcotic assaults in Colombia), the post 9/11 developments in "homeland security" and the elaboration of a domestic intelligence network, which reconfigures CIA and FBI investigatory functions and insinuates military tribunals into the domestic juridical network in the U.S., dissolve many of the former distinctions between domestic crime fighting and global warfare.[15]

Along with the territorial ambiguities that the new warfare-as-crime-fighting entails, a new biopolitics is emerging. The criminalization of military adversaries has been accompanied by a biometric approach to intelligence and surveillance. The significance of this change becomes evident if one contrasts Giddens' treatment of the surveillance technologies that paralleled the modern state's monopolization of violence with the current ones. Throughout his discussion, Giddens refers primarily to the use of paper trails. He begins with a treatment of the state's use of writing, proceeds to their "coding of information" (47), and concludes with some observations about cultural governance, the sponsoring of printed materials, not only for surveillance but also to enlarge the scope of the public sphere (179). Certainly, the paper trail and/or its electronic realization in the form of computer files remains significant, but the new modes of warfare-as-crime fighting involve the development of a biological rather than merely a paper trail, as new genetic tracing discoveries are being recruited into the intelligence gathering.

Is the biometric, designer weapon far behind? Anticipating the role of biometric coding in futuristic forms of warfare, science fiction writer William Gibson began his novel *Count Zero*, with the following passage:

> They set a SLAMHOUND on Turner's trail in New Delhi, slotted it to his pheromones and the color of his hair. It caught up with him on a street called Chandni Chauk and came scrambling for his rented BMW through a forest of bare brown legs and pedicab tires. Its core was a kilogram or recrystallized hexogene and flaked TNT.[16]

Thanks to advanced cloning technology in Gibson's futuristic war world, "Turner" is reassembled from some of his own parts and some others (eyes and genitals bought on the open market). He lives on as the novel's main character, a commando, operating in a war over R & D products. Whether or not the military logistics of biometric warfare is now under way, the surveillance dimension is being rapidly developed. Also, the use of pheromones in the Gibson account is technologically anachronistic. The technology of DNA tracing, now well developed, is complementing the photograph and paper trial to surveill and intercept dangerous bodies. Shortly after the destruction of the Taliban regime in Afghanistan, U.S. Attorney General John Ashcroft sought changes in federal law "to allow the Federal Bureau of Investigation to maintain a DNA databank of profiles taken from *al Qaida* and Taliban fighters detained in Afghanistan and Cuba."[17] Subsequently, "forensic experts" were dispatched to Afghanistan to test the human tissue found in one of the battlefields to find out whether any of the dead included Bin Laden or his top associates.[18]

Of course, policy makers face legitimation issues when introducing new modes of surveillance and criminalization. When those operating the "reasons of state" are involved in implementing a historically unorthodox "governmentality"—in this case an extraordinary mode of surveillance and management of the global order and the domestic population—they have to produce warrants for the new policy initiatives. Accordingly, after the 9/11 episode, the Bush administration began operating on two fronts to solicit acquiescence to their simultaneous intensification of domestic surveillance and preparation for global military incursions (a strategy of "preemptive defense").[19] On the one hand, there was a feverish search for legal precedents, hence the designation of an American citizen as an "enemy combatant" to apply a law of war that was earlier applied only to foreign nationals. On the other hand, the administration approached film and television producers seeking to encourage them to create patriotic feature films and TV dramas, designed to elicit public support for the new policies.

This latter part of the administration strategy, its cultural governance initiatives aimed at managing popular culture, particularly films and television, occupies much of this chapter's analysis. But to appreciate what the media was being summoned to provide a warrant for, it is necessary first to heed additional dimensions of the historical context, especially the historical changes in the practices of state sovereignty that have ultimately led to the policies for which the administration was seeking compliance. First and foremost, what must be understood is the paradoxical nature of the Bush/Blair attack on Afghanistan's Taliban regime, and the subsequent structures of surveillance (a biopolitics associated with the new imperial sovereignty) that have been put in place both in the U.S. and globally.

In their treatment of "imperial sovereignty," their designation for the post-cold war proliferation of "micro conflicts,"[20] Michael Hardt and Antonio Negri emphasize the new biopolitics: "The realization of modern sovereignty," they assert, "is the birth of biopower."[21] The concept of biopower comes initially from Foucault, who associates it with modernity's reigning governmentality, the increasing concern with managing populations. But it involves a militant, expansionist dimension as well, inasmuch as the modern security state, seeking to protect its population, has increasingly seen the need to preempt threats abroad. For imperial sovereignty, the entire world is both "within its domain and at the frontiers."[22] As the Hardt–Negri quotations imply, sovereignty is both a spatial and a biopolitical phenomenon. While the spatial or territorial aspect is a familiar feature of political theorizing, belonging as it does to a history of nation state formation, the biopolitical aspect has been under-theorized.

Simply put, understanding the biopolitical aspect of state security practices, ranging from the administrative to the violent, requires an approach to sovereignty that treats its nonjuridical dimensions, its constructions of worthy versus unworthy human life. In a brief, but suggestive, section of his investigation of the history of sexuality, Michel Foucault addresses the biopolitics of war in the modern era, asserting that whereas wars were once "waged in the name of the sovereign who must be defended," now, "they are waged in behalf of the existence of everyone . . . the decision that initiates them and the one that terminates them are in fact increasingly informed by the naked question of survival;" killing takes place "in the name of life necessity."[23]

However, Foucault's treatment of the biopolitics of the sovereignty–war connection is underdeveloped and merely suggestive. Giorgio Agamben provides an elaboration of Foucault's introduction of the biopolitical dimension of governing by elaborating Foucault's insight about the change in the legitimation of war from protecting the inviolability of the sovereign to implicating a broader model of life. This broadening of the issue permits analysis of a wide range of state actions aimed at "administering life."[24] In particular, Agamben argues that modern sovereignty has been reinflected by the "politicization of life."[25] He notes that sovereignty, at the level of executive decision making, operates in a process of making exceptions in order to use extra-legal force (in violation of territorial sovereignty) on behalf of some aspect of human existence. Rather than functioning entirely within a legal framework, it exists in a zone of "indistinction" between violence and the law.[26] This topology of sovereignty, a paradoxical conjunction of force and judiciousness, achieved clear expression in a Bush-quoting banner headline in USA Today on October 10, 2001: "Bombs 'Tighten the net of Justice.'"

To appreciate what appears to be paradoxical—the sovereignty-affirming significance of a violation of territorial sovereignties—one must recognize with Agamben that sovereignty-as-enactment exists at "the intersection between the juridico-legal and biopolitical models of power."[27] Moreover, Agamben's approach effaces the inside boundary, as in his model, expendable lives are included exclusions. Sovereignty's biopolitical imperatives, realized in the making of exceptions (contemporary historical examples include U.S. missile strikes in the Sudan, and NATO's "humanitarian intervention" in Kosovo, as well as a joint "allied" strike on Afghanistan) are derived from the power to administer life. To invoke Agamben's terms, sovereign power is deployed to distinguish "bare life" (that part of humanity that is excluded from political protection) from politically qualified life and thus, as Agamben puts it, to kill without committing homicide.[28]

Yet, Agamben's approach to sovereignty, like Foucault's, is under-specified with respect to current changes in political orders, especially as they affect legitimations for war. As William Connolly has put it, Agamben's attention to "the modern intensification of biopolitics . . . pays little heed to the changed global context."[29] In a global context, the most significant post-cold war change in the model of life upon which sovereignty's approach to peace keeping/war making is predicated is from a biopolitics of "population" (the collective identity to which Foucault was referring when he spoke of war on behalf of "the existence of everyone") to a biopolitics of "humanity." In the latter conception of life, those who must be defended (as well as those who are criminalized) constitute a new class of bodies to be protected and a new set of threatening ones to be confronted. Thus, for example, British Prime Minister Tony Blair, a leading proponent of contemporary "peace keeping," introduces the concept of "positive engagement" (as opposed to the cold war concepts of defense and deterrence) to refer to intervention on behalf of an endangered humanity rather than simply the population of the UK or even of the populations of the states within the NATO alliance.[30] Moreover, some months after 9/11, President Bush claimed that the defense of the U.S. will require military responses to "evil" regimes that harbor or support "terrorism."

Bush and Blair's approach to war and peace exemplifies the new approach to the system of state sovereignty within the Western Alliance. Rather than abandoning a system of sovereignty, it is an expansive, cooperative venture in which cooperation is no longer constituted as merely an alliance against a common threat. It involves, instead, preparation for engagement with what are regarded as disruptive modes of violence (threats to "peace") within sovereign territories. The new venture requires, in the words of one analyst, whose observation fits the current attack on Afghanistan, "a coalition of war and humanitarianism," where politics is deployed in the form of humanitarian war.[31] This expansive, imperial sovereignty has echoes from the pasts of both countries. It harks back to the territorial and biopolitical aspects of the imperial expansion involved in the United States' European heritage, or, more specifically, the imperial transfer that was precipitated after American independence.

The Imperial Transfer

On the one hand, the colonization of North America was part of the British imperial project. Even though the war of independence created a historical rift in the "imperial transfer,"[32] the mythography emanating initially from both English and American historiography, and subsequently from novels and films, has created an articulation of an Anglo-American ideological project, which is especially evident in cinematic versions of Elizabeth's reign. As Curtis Breight summarizes it, "Elizabethan England was deployed in cinema as both a model and a warning: a model of heroic resistance to some potent external threat." Also, the films "provide a myth of innocent origins well suited to the rise of imperial America."[33]

But imposing a smooth historical continuity on the English-American forms of nation building and expansion has had to face a disruptive historical event. As Breight points out, the American Revolution constituted a daunting problem for the imperial transfer. The fact of the revolt of the American colony creates a rift in the transfer narrative. Breight argues that "the mythmakers [who sought narratively to heal the rift] turned to Elizabethan England as the true origin of both Britain and the United States,"[34] and he sees this mythography deeply embedded in a series of feature films about Queen Elizabeth's England, in which English and American actors together challenge the Spanish tyranny and, seemingly, hint that it constitutes an earlier version of the tyranny that Hitler sought to impose on twentieth-century Europe.

A variety of genres in the early twentieth century reflect and articulate the imperial transfer, primarily in their representations of the Euro-American imperial expansion westward. Among the notable texts are the illustrations of Frederick Remington, who, like his friends, Theodore Roosevelt and Owen Wister, contributed to the imperial transfer by constructing a primarily Europeanized West, featuring heroic and aristocratic white cowboys, and images of horsemanship and guns, featured as the moral center of the new West.[35] In addition to his vast corpus of paintings and drawings (numbering 2,750)[36], as well as sculptures and writings, Remington served as a journalist in two episodes of U.S. imperial expansion. On the continental front, he served as an "artist war correspondent" with General Miles in his campaign against the Apaches in 1886.[37] Subsequently, he helped to sell the U.S.'s takeover of Spanish colonial possessions, helping to build anti-Spanish sentiment before and during what he called "the Cowboy's War" by providing illustrations for Hearst's *New York Journal*, for example, his drawing of a strip search of an American woman by "the evil Spaniards" and his famous painting of the war, *The Charge of the Rough Riders at San Juan Hill*, arguably another version of his "'last Cavalier' myth," which constructed the cowboy as a modern version of the European knight.[38]

Cinema: The New History-Making Genre

While Remington participated in legitimating Euro-America's imperial consolidation, primarily with drawing and painting technologies at the turn of the century, the film genre was to take over this role throughout the twentieth century. Perhaps the most significant linkage is between Remington's role and that of John Ford, a connection that is most manifest in the way the two rendered the social history of the West. Remington rendered the process of Euro-American settlement and the Native American resistance by exploring types. In his celebration of imperial expansion, he represented not only the cowboy and the Indian warrior but also the old mountain man, the French Canadian trapper, and the Mexican vaquero, among others.[39] This version of the biopolitics of the expansion westward was to be taken up by John Ford in his first epic western film, *Stagecoach*.

In *Stagecoach*, Ford constructs the American West as an evolving social order, which is represented both within the stagecoach itself (a microcosm of that evolving order) and by the types that Ford treats as those to be superseded (caricatures of Mexicans and Indians).[40] *Stagecoach* is therefore primarily a celebration of Euro-American expansion. Despite the few satiric moments in which the film anticipates the complications Ford was to insinuate into the West's racial-spatial order in his later films, for the most part, *Stagecoach* evinces no ambivalence about the displacement of Native American nationhood. However, subsequently, in arguably one of the most significant twentieth-century films, *The Searchers*, Ford's West becomes more complicated. Most notably, John Wayne, who is unambiguously heroic in *Stagecoach* as The Ringo Kid (saving the stage's passengers from an attack by menacing Indians), becomes, as Ethan Edwards, both hero and anti-hero in *The Searchers*. He is, at once, an Indian hating racist and an exemplar of heroic masculinity, wise in the ways of his adversaries and protective of those with whom he is associated.

The details of the family drama in the film—it is implied that Ethan has had a romantic attachment to his brother's wife—are less important than the historical context and social setting. Ford's film maps the expanding world of post-civil war America and reenacts the encounters among white settlers, Spanish aristocrats, and Indian nations, shortly after Texas had become independent. The film's historical moment is right after Texas had violently extricated itself from Mexican control and was in a period of ongoing war with the Comanches (who were not defeated until the "Red River War of 1874-75). In the film, a Comanche war party led by Scarface, kills Ethan's brother and wife, rapes, mutilates and kills their eldest daughter Lucy, and carries off Debbie, the younger daughter. The episode precipitates a captivity narrative (one of the oldest modes of American literature). The main searchers are Ethan and young Martin Pawley, a part Cherokee, whose Indianness is constantly disparaged by Ethan during their quest to find Debbie and exact revenge for the massacre. The search proceeds for five years, allowing Ford to present the articulation of generational and historical times. Ethan's paternal relationship with Martin (which he resists until making his will near the end of the film) sets a background for Ethan Edwards' antimiscegenation fixation and sets in motion the same biopolitical forces at work in the novels of James Fenimore Cooper, espe-cially *The Pioneers*, which seek to contain the contradictions in America's Indian policy by establishing interrelationships between Anglo and Native American heritages. Although Ethan ultimately resists the impulse, he has sworn to kill Debbie when he finds her because she has become an intimate of a Comanche and, in his words, is "no longer white." Although Ford's film is somewhat more ambivalent about the ethnogenesis of the Euro-American state than Cooper, he offers a similar resolution, put into the mouth of Mrs. Joergenson, the mother of Martin Pawley's "intended," Lucy. At one point, she remarks that the West will have a white future, but perhaps not until "all their bones are in the ground."

Nevertheless, Ford's film is not simply a narrative of white civilization displacing savage Indianness in the West. As is the case with Ford's films in general, a strictly narrative account misses the play of opposing forces and world views that clash in the film. Indeed, Ford's film anticipates the "dys-narrative" aspect of later, so-called "experimental cinema,"[41] *The Searchers* contains a resolution-inhibiting encounter between two different orders of coherence: the narrative and the structural. While in the narrative register, a resolution occurs because Ethan decides to bring Debbie home rather than killing her, structurally much of the imagery—stark juxtapositions be-tween dark domestic interiors and a wide, seemingly untamable land-scape—suggests that the space is too large to afford easy incorporation into the cultural habitus of any group. Moreover, there is no clear dividing line between Euro and Native Americans. Certainly, Indian trading practices are juxtaposed to Native American trading practices, most notably the differ-ence between the Double Eagle coins that Ethan throws around and the trade that Martin effects for a blanket, (while he is unaware that he is also acquiring a wife). But Ethan and his adversary, Scarface, operate with similar revenge motives, and Ethan, despite his articulated contempt for Indians, displays many instances of Indianness, for example, speaking Comanche, desecrating a corpse to compromise its spiritual future, and scalping the dead Scarface. Moreover, the different groups are also similar in their violence. The scene of Ethan's family's burned farmhouse and dead bodies is parallel to a scene of a burned Indian village with dead bodies, courtesy of the Seventh Cavalry.

Most significantly, the antagonisms and boundary protection exhibited by Ethan Edwards are juxtaposed to that of a searcher who is seemingly pe-ripheral to the main search, old Mose Harper, the man who actually finds the missing Debbie without even trying (and whose various appearances constitute a dysnarrative). Although the humorous antics of Mose tend to be treated by viewers as mere comic relief (for example, while he and the other Texas Rangers are under fire during a ferocious Indian attack, he exclaims, "thank thee Lord for what we are about to receive), Mose can be seen instead as one who operates outside of the racial-spatial order and its attendant antagonisms. While controlling territory, seeking revenge, and, in general, having one's ethnos dominate the landscape is what drives Ethan and Scarface, Mose is unimpressed with boundaries and enemies. In one scene, when chasing Indians is on the agenda, he begins an Indian dance instead of grabbing a weapon. Also, when he appears at each key juncture in the story, first at the farmhouse when the Rangers form a posse in search of stolen cattle, then as he returns to see the farmhouse burned, and toward the end when he is asked to report on Debbie's whereabouts, a rocking chair is central to the scene. In the first, he sits in a rocker inside the house and, on taking his leave, thanks his hostess for the chair (while the others mention only the coffee). In the second scene, he finds the rocker outside the burned out farmhouse, and while the others are dealing with their anger and grief, he sits down to rock. Finally, in the third scene, he promises the information to Ethan about how to find Debbie in exchange for a promise of his very own rocking chair. Rather than merely portraying a demented and lazy loafer, through the character Mose, Ford's film offers a different kind of life world, one in which the drive is to abide without ethnic enmity and territorial displacement. For this reason, among others, the film cannot be easily enlisted along with those texts that warrant or celebrate the nineteenth-century version of Euro-American imperial expansion.

Subsequently, the more critical "post westerns," which emerged in the last two decades of the twentieth century, have also addressed themselves to the consequences of the Euro-American imperial expansion in the west, often with cinematic references to Ford's westerns. Among these, German director, Wim Wenders's *Paris Texas* is especially noteworthy here because it begins with a cinematic reflection on *The Searchers*. Certainly, in *The Searchers*, as in Ford's other westerns, the Indians are primarily props. Within the narrative register of the films (at times undercut with visual moments), white stories are foregrounded and Indians have primarily "iconic" roles.[42] In one of his later films, *Cheyenne Autumn* (1964), the Cheyenne, oppressed while attempting to return to their homelands in the North, become somewhat more central to the story than the Indians in other Ford westerns. Also, in an observation that helps to frame Wenders's cinematic disruption of the mythic west in *Paris Texas*, Ford makes the point in *Cheyenne Autumn* that white language constitutes a cognitive imperialism; it is undoubtedly the most effective weapon used to displace and conquer Indianness in the west. Although the signs of an Indian presence in Wenders's West are minimal, the hints of their former presence incorporates Ford's observation regarding the role of language and, moreover, aligns his film with Burgoyne's above-noted treatment of the western as "one of the most durable and effective masks for the disguised operational center of the nation-state"... [its] ... "hidden text concerning its relationship with American Indians."

Paris Texas

Reminiscent of the opening scene in *The Searchers* (after a song about what makes a man wander accompanies the opening credits, the first scene in *The Searchers* shows John Wayne riding in from a vast panorama in Monument Valley), Wenders's film begins with a man, Travis, wandering over a large western landscape, close to the Mexican border, before he collapses in a small isolated gas station store, where he has sought something to drink. Seemingly affirming Ford's insight into the role of language, when Travis' brother, Walt, comes from California to fetch him, Travis is speechless for much of their journey. Although some of the film's narrative can be quarantined within a Freudian family story (particularly one oriented around patriarchal violence), the implied historical narrative (and dysnarrative) it conveys provides a more effective political gloss.[43] Travis and his brother begin their journey to California without dialogue and with significantly different relationships to language. Travis is without speech, and Walt, who summons him back into language, is a not simply a prototypical middle class man mouthing unremarkable platitudes but also someone whose company makes roadside billboards.

Walt's vocation reflects Ford's *Cheyenne Autumn* point about white words taking over the West, but with a decidedly Wenders inflection. Wenders's West is "*the* place [in America] where things fall apart."[44] For Wenders, the West has been abandoned, "civilization simply passed through," so that now, for example, instead of numerous people "in the middle of a desert you come across a road sign reading: 375 Street."[45] As Wenders puts it, the West, holds "names and writing ... a lot of signboards, cinema facades, billboards half worn away by the elements, already falling apart."[46] Given this version of the West, *Paris Texas*' Walt represents Euro-America's contemporary habitus. Instead of the settlers' homes, around which the action in Ford's films takes place, there are signs and billboards. As Wenders notes, "a man will paint a big sign first of all, and then the sign counts for more than the building."[47] Los Angeles, Walt's place of residence, represents the ultimate in an ersatz relationship with place (where representations trump built structures): "I was walking around in downtown Los Angeles, and all of a sudden down this dead end I saw a painted wall with its make believe windows and a dainty awning."[48]

Wenders exhibits America's contemporary name-dominated habitus in his filming of *Paris Texas*. The dominating imagistic aspect of the film's focus on signs is reflected in the "location scouting" stills, taken before the filming began; they include motel signs, road signs, abandoned café buildings with names in large lettering, and, most tellingly, a small, almost effaced sign in the midst of an empty desert tract, which reads "Western World Development Tract 6271."[49] Rather than seeing America's "world of names" as merely a commentary on a contemporary rift between person and place, *Paris Texas* offers hints of a history of violent displacement that the naming-dominated white American habitus overcodes. Here, Wenders is likely influenced by the Austrian novelist, Peter Handke, as the expressions "world of names" and "places of names" appear often in Handke's short novel, *Slow Home Coming*, which features a contrast between the Native American mode of dwelling in Alaska and the Euro-American mode of dwelling in cities such as Berkeley (where apartment buildings have "colonized woods"), Denver, and New York. In the latter mode, for example, the Northern Lights, which has cosmological significance, for Native Americans is reduced to the name of a street "Northern Lights Boulevard" in a California city.[50]

To discern this aspect of the film, one must recognize the relays it creates between individual and collective stories. At the individual level, Travis, once he is summoned back into language, recovers the memory of his violence toward his wife, Jane. At the end of his personal search, which is consummated when he restores the relationship between Jane and their son, Hunter, he is able to verbalize his past violent acts and take responsibility for them. At another level, the film ponders Euro-America's collective violence, primarily through images rather than its major narrative thread. When Travis returns to his son Hunter, after a long encounter with his wife, the film cuts to an alley where the words "RACE, BLOOD, LAND" are written on a wall. At roughly the same time, the camera shows a large head of a Native American woman, as part of a mural on the wall and an African-American version of the Statue of Liberty. Yet another aspect of the history of imperialism is thematized. When Travis finally converses with his brother, Walt, we learn that they are Hispanic on their mother's side. Subsequently, Travis sings a melancholy Spanish song while in Walt's home, and later, he renews his familiarity with his Hispanic side in a conversation with his brother and sister-in-law's Mexican maid, Carmelita, who asks him identity questions to help him select a mode of dress and a body language.

One ready-to-hand interpretation of the mixture of cultural and national codes—including the disjunctive Paris-Texas, a German Doctor who treats Travis after he collapses, Walt's wife, who is French, and the Spanish maid, Carmelita—is to evoke the idea of cultural conflict.[51] While cultural conflict is one of Wenders' cinematic signatures (it is also central to his *An American Friend*, and is very much a part of this film), the concept of *critical translation* should also be applied. After Walter Benjamin's insight that the translator is coming to terms with her/his own national-cultural-linguistic self-understanding while making sense of a foreign text, one can read Wenders's approach to Euro-America's violent past as not only a recovery of American history but also as a reflection on Germany's Nazi past. Wenders's disjunctive assemblage of signs from both a German and an American past makes present, albeit ambiguously, the process through which memory becomes "history."

Again, Handke's *Slow Homecoming* provides a prototext. His main character, the Austrian geologist, Valentin Sorger, discovers the violence of names on the American continent while, at the same time, seeking to come to terms with the violence of the Nazi period in Germany and Austria. Attempting, to evince a "science of peace" in the present, through his simultaneous reading of America and Europe, Handke's Sorger discovers that he must first free himself from being an unreflective part of his national patrimony, from being "the faithful replica of death-cult masters."[52] Like Handke (and also like the novelist, Thomas Pynchon, who offers a similar translation, linking the Nazi death machine and American violence within a satyric assault on America's domestic repression and violent imperialism of the 1960s, in his *Gravity's Rainbow*),[53] Wenders effects a simultaneous treatment of Nazi German and Euro-America's racial violence. He does this most dramatically through the above-noted slogans and figures on the wall, but he also evokes the violence of Germany's past through the Doctor, who treats Travis, who, after his collapse, "falls literally into the world of language."[54] The Doctor turns out to be "corrupt and greedy"; his demand of a large payment from Walt as a ransom for Travis is another aspect of Wenders's critical look backward at the biopolitics of Germany during the Nazi period.

Ultimately, Wenders's *Paris Texas* contains a strong narrative similarity to Ford's *The Searchers* inasmuch as both searchers, Ethan and Travis, remain loners at the end of the stories. But in *The Searchers,* Ford, as in his other westerns, displays an ambivalent position on myth, seeing it as both destructive and necessary ("print the legend" as he says through a newspaper editor in *The Man Who Shot Liberty Valance*). His films have continued to produce a West that by 1893, as Slotkin notes, had been historically "closed," as "a geographical place and a set of facts requiring historical explanation." Instead, it is ready-to-hand for people (for example, President Bush) to use as an unproblematic mythic West, "a set of symbols that *constituted* an explanation of history."[55] By contrast, Wenders is unambivalently hostile to national myth, both Germany's and America's, and unlike Ford, he is unambivalently hostile to violence, which for Wenders has no heroes. As a result, in *Paris Texas*, he restores the West as a place whose history must be reopened, as a set of symbols requiring critical explanation.

Hollywood at War

Wenders returns to the issue of American violence in his *The End of Violence*. However, before examining that film, which is prescient with respect to the domestic aspect of America's contemporary "war on terrorism," I return to Ford, to the historic cinema-war relationship more generally, and then to Hollywood's role in what CNN has called "America's New War." Ford's *The Searchers* and some of his subsequent westerns both technically and narratively produce a West that cannot be unambiguously articulated with a heroic or democratic account of the U.S.'s developing continental nationhood in the nineteenth century. In particular, the films make it evident that America's Indian wars, along with the less violent aspects of the Euro-Native American encounter constitute a troubled past that haunts attempts at either celebrating or exonerating subsequent war policies. The recent World War II film, *Code Breakers* (2002), which honors the role of Navajo code talkers, enlisted to stymie Japanese intelligence, is doubtless aimed at creating a more hospitable Euro-American–Native American relationship by emphasizing a collaboration in a (relatively) morally unambiguous war, at a time when the U.S.'s increasingly aggressive war policy faces severe domestic and global criticism.

For much of the twentieth century, regimes involved in warring violence looked to film as a genre well-positioned to encourage national allegiance. Ford himself was enlisted in the making of documentaries supportive of the allied cause in World War II (as were other major film directors such as Howard Hawks and Frank Capra). Joseph Goebbels, the Nazi propaganda minister, enthralled by the reality effects and their subtle persuasiveness in Hollywood films, created a substantial cinema propaganda campaign, which has been subjected to critical commentary ever since. For example, well aware of the film–war policy relationship in general and the case of Nazi Germany in particular, critical theorist and film director Alexander Kluge locates those film and television dramas that seem to provide a "universalistic representation of reality" as especially insidious. They belong, he argues, to a "pseudo public sphere," which aids and abets the "imperialism of consciousness" that is mandated in state projects of cultural governance.[56]

As is well known, such mandates are intensified in wartime. In the British case, for example, there was an unchallenged celebration of the war effort in feature films during World War II. In particular, such films as *For Freedom, Convoy Ships With Wings, In Which We Serve, We Dive at Dawn, and San Demetrio, London*, combined patriotic drama and realism "to find a formula for the war narrative that would prove acceptable to audiences and critics."[57] Hollywood's U.S. role during World War II is similar. For example, the "B movie crime fighter," Ronald Reagan, who, as Michael Rogin famously shows, subsequently took his "Hollywood identity to Washington," made patriotic films during the war (before turning to his role as an unambiguous hero in westerns).[58]

The Washington–Hollywood romance had cooled considerably by the 1960s, especially as a result of the critical Vietnam War feature films, which made it difficult to incorporate that war into a patriotic scenario.[59] However, by the 1990s, after the Gulf War helped cure what promilitary people called "the Vietnam syndrome" (a popular resistance toward military adventurism), the U.S. "defense" establishment sought to enlist Hollywood in its training as well as its public relations projects. In August of 1999, in what the designer of the relationship called "a marriage made in heaven," "an unprecedented collaboration between the Pentagon and Hollywood" was effected. The U.S. Army announced the formation of an "Institute for Creative Technologies" at the University of Southern California (chosen because of its close ties to Hollywood). As a *Los Angeles Times* business reporter put it "the entertainment industry is expected to use [cutting edge technologies] to improve its motion special effects, make video games more realistic . . . [and] to help the creators of military simulations develop better story lines that are believable and engaging."[60]

The new and friendly military–Hollywood relationship was in the news again after the September 11 attack and subsequent U.S.–British assault on the Taliban regime in Afghanistan. The Bush administration approached Hollywood film directors to enlist their talents in the "war on terrorism." In early November, 2002, the media carried a story about a meeting between White House advisor, Karl Rowe, and several dozen top television and film executives. Aware of the film industry's role in World War II, the Bush administration wanted "patriotic war movies" that characterized the early years of that war.[61] After the meeting, "nearly a dozen" patriotic war movies were under production (for example, the above-mentioned *Windtalkers*), and television dramas followed suit. Among the most notable of the TV genre was an episode of *JAG* (a CBS drama about military lawyers). The April 30, 2002 episode, produced with the Pentagon's help, featured a trial of a defiant *Al Qaida* terrorist (doubtless modeled after Zacarias Moussaoui, the alleged twentieth hijacker) by a military tribunal at which he receives a "fair trial" (a promise by Defense Secretary Rumsfeld to the media after the tribunal plan was floated). As one commentary notes:

> The strategy behind the "Tribunal" episode is more transparent than ever: the show creates the wish-fulfillment fantasy of capturing a

terrorist responsible for the attacks, depicts an idealized military, yet ends with an ominous threat of more terror in the works, affirming the government's real-life message that America must remain vigilant.[62]

Extending the media campaign to trials is not surprising given the extraordinary legal quandary the government is in. Alleged plotters are to be tried by military tribunals that operate without the presumption of innocence of the accused and on the basis of some evidence that their attorneys cannot see. In some cases, U.S. citizens are being held without trial, as the Bush administration places intelligence gathering above the rights of the accused, arguing that a state of war justifies the abrogation of rights. As intelligence gathering by FBI agents is creating a pervasive climate of intimidation, even extended to surveillance of people's library borrowing profiles, and as the White House encourages the population at large to take on a surveillant attitude (passing information on what they see as suspicious activities to government agencies), the entertainment industry is being suborned. For example, Hollywood stars are shown answering phones for September 11 charities in three-minute trailers released in theaters throughout the country. Also, in general, the relationship between the Bush administration and studio executives is positive. As one White House official Hollywood notes, is "way out in front of us in getting patriotic messages out just like the Hollywood community was in World War II."[63] Perhaps, Wim Wenders can be summoned again, this time to reflect on the current episode of imperial violence and as an antidote to the U.S. entertainment industry's complicity in it.

Wim Wenders' *The End of Violence*

After having treated, allegorically, much of Euro America's initial enactment of imperial sovereignty in *Paris Texas*, Wenders undertook a powerful meditation in an attempt to eliminate all violent crime in *The End of Violence* (1997). His approach in the film articulates cinematically with what Baudrillard has suggested about ending terror, when (as noted above) he remarks that to "nip terror in the bud," a state would have "to equip itself with its own terrorism and in doing so simply generalize terror at all levels." *The End of Violence* is set in a Los Angeles that has been equipped to surveill and totally eliminate all violent crime. But at the same time, through one of the characters, a Salvadorean woman hired to spy on a surveillance technician, the film treats the issue of U.S. imperial sovereignty, especially as it aids and abets both domestic and foreign aspects of state violence.

The End of Violence addresses itself to a parallel system of power and violence, articulated by the Hollywood film industry and a panoptic surveillant, and ultimately a terrorist government. Two management-of-violence persona and their venues are featured at the outset. First, there is Hollywood producer Mike Max, whose specialty is violent crime thrillers. He manages his film production empire from a distance, connecting with his staff with his laptop computer, while seated on his Malibu patio, overlooking the Pacific Ocean. At the same time, Ray Bering manages an anti-crime project in which satellites monitor Los Angeles streets with hidden cameras whose visual data are processed in his planetarium-like building on a Los Angeles hilltop (the Griffith Observatory).

The two become linked when Max receives an email from Bering, which details the satellite monitoring of the city. Because Max's vocation is suspect and Ray himself is under surveillance, Max is subsequently abducted by henchmen sent to kill him. They fail to carry it out when, after Max delays them with promises of wealth, they are mysteriously shot, after which Max goes underground, becoming part of the work crew of Mexican gardeners who manage the grounds of his estate. Once Ray is ultimately murdered (because his scrutiny of the stills from the killing of the henchmen is reported by the suborned Salvadorean woman, posing as a cleaning woman, hired to spy on him), it becomes clear that the process of seeking to end violence is a cure more violent than its objects of attention.

At the same time that the narrative carries the film forward, making clear that the brave new world of a crime-free Los Angeles is far more horrific than the prior version, Wenders' film provides two levels of intimacy in a world increasingly reliant on distance. Cinematically, the painterly dimension of the film (for example, a diner scene that evokes Edward Hopper's *Nighthawks* [1942]) evokes an esthetics of the city that is unavailable on the digitalized versions that make their way onto Max's and Bering's screens. At another level, Max and Bering are shown in their respective moments of intimate attachment. For Bering, his devoted and caring relationship with his father (who is shown in a room full of books and working with an older technology, a typewriter) contrasts with his distant relationship with the rest of the city. Also, when the extension of his intimacy to the Salvadoreian cleaning woman, with whom he has an affair, ends in his death (when she reports his suspicious activity), it is implied that ending violence also radically compromises the possibility of intimate attachments.

In Max's undercover sojourn, living with his Mexican gardeners, the film offers another episode of intimacy. In contrast with his earlier laptop-mediated distance from Los Angeles' infrastructure, Max enjoys an episode of comradely and familial belonging, which contrasts dramatically with the cold distance in his broken marriage. The making of violent representations had kept the life world of Mike Max at a distance. In particular, he had not been in touch with a laboring infrastructure, which results from transnational relationships and, among other things, made possible his leisurely pool-side working style. Although no global structural supplements are offered to tell us how the gardeners are recruited into their profession, the transnational relationships that attend "the end of violence" in Los Angeles are supplied through the implied biography of Bering's maid/lover Mathilda.

Mathilda, whose family was wiped out by death squads (supported, as history has shown, by U.S. policy) has scars that, until they become intimate, Ray Bering admits he had never noticed. At the end of the film, the anticrime FBI unit that was responsible for killing Bering also threatens to kill Matlilda. Following the logic of a totalizing approach to ending all violence, the antiviolence organization turns out to be threatened by its own employees, at least one of whom, ironically, is recruited because of the complicity of an antiviolence organization in global violence. Through "the domestic" Mathilda, then, the boundary between domestic and global violence is effaced. The antiviolence project has eventuated in a vast, secret, and largely unseen organization of state terror.

Conclusion: Cultural Governance and Political Critique

> Listen . . . listen: this is war's evensong, the War's canonical hour, and the night is real.
>
> Thomas Pynchon, Gravity's Rainbow

After 9/11, life began imitating Wenders's feature film The End of Violence, as the Bush administration's "war on terror" turned to the creation of a domestic surveillance network, a suspension of due process for both citizen and noncitizen suspects, and a set of plans for military assaults on countries that support "terrorists" in direct or indirect ways (activated with an assault on Iraq on March 19, 2003). Among other things, the CIA–FBI nexus, which is part of the new "Homeland Security" project, is at least as intimidating as the end-of-violence organization that Wenders depicts in his film. Wenders's film is not moralistic. Instead of harping on a specific message, it begins with a query to Director Mike Max from an off-screen voice:"Define violence. You're making a movie about it. Shouldn't you know what it is?" Max resists a definitive answer. Similarly, rather than defining violence, Wenders's film contemplates it, treating especially the relays between shooting (in a filmic sense) and shooting to kill.

Another dimension of cinematic shooting, however, is shooting to influence. Much of The End of Violence's focus is on artistic media. For example, the film's meditation on the violence–artistic media relationship includes an episode of artistic readings at a Los Angeles performance venue, where Ade, an

African-American poet, mimes a white teenager being molested by her father. Also, at another point, a character ponders the question of whether observing nuclear particles can affect their behavior. Such moments speak to the question of the power of the arts to affect how people act. While this issue will always escape definitive conclusion, certainly one can place more confidence in the effect of the arts on how people think. It is doubtless this assumption that drives the Bush administration's attempt to enlist the entertainment industry to produce patriotic, policy-friendly features and dramas.

Yet, as I noted with respect to Bush's turn to the classic western, artistic productions are open to continuing interpretation. Thus, for example, although the Jerry Bruckheimer/Ridley Scott treatment of the U.S. intervention in Somalia, *Black Hawk Down*, drew optimistic administration support (the Washington premier was attended by Secretary of Defense Rumsfeld and Vice President Cheney),[64] the film did not necessarily provide the romantic *soldatesque* that the administration expected. Although the film portrays an unsuccessful attempt to eliminate a political leader involved in violence unfavorable to American interests (now part of the administration's war agenda), it does not clearly valorize the policy or the attempt. Certainly, its version of good guys (American soldiers engaged in resolute duty and often heroic mutual support) and the bad guys (murderous Somali mercenaries) plays into the administration's hands, but at the same time, no clear point of view on the policy or its failed implementation strikes the viewer. Ultimately, at a historical moment when a government is seeking support from the arts to extend its sphere of imperial violence while, at the same time, closing what has been one of history's most open societies, the arts can be mobilized to resist. Its archives remain open to a process in which memory can never be constructed as definitive history. Those who would use films in particular or the arts in general to achieve quiescence can never rest assured.

Notes

1. DeLillo was commenting on an earlier history making/shaking event, the assassination of President John F. Kennedy. See Don DeLillo, *Libra* (New York: Viking, 1988), p. 15.
2. See Richard Slotkin, *Gunfighter Nation* (New York: Atheneum, 1992).
3. Evan Connell, *Son of the Morning Star: Custer and the Little Bighorn* (New York: Harper Collins, 1984), p. 330.
4. Evan Connell, *Son of the Morning Star*, pp. 331–332.
5. Robert Burgoyne, *Film Nation: Hollywood Looks at U.S. History* (Minneapolis: University of Minnesota Press, 1997), p. 48.
6. Michael Hardt and Antonio Negri use the concept of "imperial sovereignty to identify the post cold war conflicts which, they argue are not organized around one central conflict but rather though a flexible network of microconflicts." *Empire* (Cambridge, Massachusetts: Harvard University Press, 2000), p. 201. I am expanding the concept to identify all episodes of state violence undertaken in the name of shaping and sustaining its territorial and biopolitical coherence.

7. The quoted expression comes from Lewis Frye Richardson, *Statistics of Deadly Quarrels* (Pittsburgh: Boxwood Press, 1960).
8. Paul Virilio, *War and Cinema: The Logistics of Perception*, trans. by Patrick Camiller (New York: Verso, 1989).
9. John Ellis, *The Social History of the Machine Gun* (Baltimore: Johns Hopkins University Press, 1975), p. 13.
10. Among those articulating this war imaginary is Ralph Peters, "Our Soldiers, Their Cities," *Parameters* 26(1), Spring 1996: 43–50.
11. Jean Baudrillard, "The Seismic Order," (1991). Found on the web at http://www.uta.edu/english/apt/collab/texts/sedismic.html
12. Peter Andreas and Richard Price, "From War Fighting to Crime Fighting: Transforming the American national security State," *International Studies Review* 3(3), Fall 2001: 31.
13. Quotations in *Ibid*, p. 33.
14. Anthony Giddens, *The Nation-State and Violence* (Berkeley: University of California Press, 1985), p. 192.
15. For example, on June 11, 2002, The New York Times reported the arrest of an American citizen, whom the Attorney General alleged to be an Al Qaida operative. Commenting on his legal status, Ashcroft said, he is an "enemy combatant . . . We have acted with legal authority both under the laws of war and clear Supreme Court precedent, which establishes that the military may detain a United States citizen who has joined the enemy and has entered our country to carry out hostile acts." And Deputy Defense Secretary Paul F. Wolfowitz said that the suspect, Mr. Al-Mujahir was being held "under the laws of war." David Stout, "U.S. Arrests Man Accused of 'Dirty Bomb' Attack," *New York Times* on the web: (http://www.nytimes.com/2002/06/10/national/10CND-TERROR.html).
16. William Gibson, *Count Zero* (New York: Ace Books, 1987), p. 1.
17. David Johnson, "Law Change Sought to Set UP DNA Databank for Captured Qaida Fighters," *The New York Times on the Web*, March 2, 2002 (http:www.nytimes.com/2002/03/06/national/06DNA.html.).
18. Dexter Filkins, "U.S. Is Studying DNA of Dead Al Qaida and Taliban Combatants," *The New York Times on the Web*, March 15, 2002 (http://www.nytimes.com/2002/03/15/international/asia/15AFGH.html.).
19. *The New York Times* 6/17/2002, p. 1.
20. Michael Hardt and Antonio Negri, *Empire*, p. 201.
21. Hardt and Negri, *Empire*, p. 89.
22. Hardt and Negri, *Empire*, p. 171.
23. Michel Foucault, *History of Sexuality*, trans. by Robert Hurley (New York: Vintage, 1998), p. 137.
24. Foucault, *History of Sexuality*.
25. Giorgio Agamben, *Homo Sacer: Sovereign Power and Bare Life*, trans. by Daniel Heller-Roazen (Stanford CA: Stanford University Press, 1998), pp. 119–125.
26. Agamben, *Homo Sacer*, p. 19.
27. Agamben, *Homo Sacer*, p. 6.
28. Agamben, *Homo Sacer*, p. 83.
29. William E. Connolly, "The Complexity of Sovereignty," this volume, pp. 23–40.
30. Exemplary is Tony Blair's speech, "Enlightened Patriotism," (at the Lord Mayor's banquet, London, Monday 13 November 2000) at http://www.fco.gov.uk/news/speechtext.asp?4374.
31. Robert Redeker, "In Place of Politics: Humanitarianism and War." In *Masters of the Universe? NATO's Balkan Crusade*, edited by Tariq Ali (New York: Verso, 2000), p. 172.
32. The expression "imperial transfer" belongs to Christopher Hitchens; see his *Blood, Class, and Nostalgia: Anglo-American Ironies* (New York: Farrar, Straus & Giroux,1990). The expression is used by Curtis C. Breight, *Surveillance, Militarism and Drama in the Elizabethan Era* (New York: St, Martins, 1996), pp. 15–17, to treat the genre history - especially feature films - of Elizabethan militarization.
33. Breight, *Surveillance, Militarism and Drama*, p. 17. The films include *Elizabeth the Queen*, or *The Private Lives of Elizabeth and Essex* (1939), *Young Bess* (1953), and *The Virgin Queen* (1955).
34. Breight, *Surveillance, Militarism and Drama*, p. 14.
35. Theodore Roosevelt's most exemplary contribution in this regard is his epic, *The Winning of the West* (New York: G.Putnam, 1889), while Owen Wister's is his "The Evolution of the Cow-Puncher." In *Owen Wister's West* , edited by Robert Murray Davis (Albuquerque: University of New Mexico Press, 1987), pp. 33–53.

36. Noted in William H. Goetzmann and William N. Goetzmann, *The West of the Imagination* (New York: W. W. Norton, 1986), p. 238.
37. Goetzmann and Goetzmann, *The West of the Imagination*, p. 241.
38. Goetzmann and Goetzmann, *The West of the Imagination*, p. 251.
39. Goetzmann and Goetzmann, *The West of the Imagination*, p. 242.
40. In his analysis of the Cooper-Wister contrast and its influence on Westerns, John Cawelti, employs the expression "evolving social order" and argues that Cooper's West neglected it, simply juxtaposing a civilized East with natural West: *The Six-Gun Mystique Sequel* (Bowling Green, Ohio: Bowling Green University Popular Press, 1999), p. 66.
41. On the anti-diegetic aspects of experimental cinema, see Andre Gardies, *Le Cinema de Robbe-Grillet: Essai semiocritique* (Paris: Albatross, 1983).
42. This point is made by Tag Gallagher, "Angels Gambol Where They Will: *John Ford's Indians*. In *The Western Reader*, edited by Jim Kitses and Greg Rickman (New York: Limelight, 1998), p. 273.
43. Certainly Sam Shepard who wrote the screenplay is known for his psychological Freudian-oriented plots. For a treatment that offers a psychoanalytic reading of the film, see Donald L. Carveth, "The Borderland Dilemma in *Paris Texas*: Psychoanalytic Approaches to Sam Shepard," *Psyart: A Hyperlink Journal for Psychological Study of Arts* at: http:www.clas.ufl.edu/ipsa/journal/articles/psyart1997/carvet01.htm.
44. Conversation with Alain Bergala in Wim Wenders, *Written in the West* (Munich: Shirmer, 1987), p. 11.
45. Wenders, *Written in the West*.
46. Wenders, *Written in the West*, p. 9.
47. Wenders, *Written in the West*, p. 13.
48. Wenders, *Written in the West*, p. 16.
49. The "location scouting" stills can be seen in Chris Sievernich, editor. *Wim Wenders-Sam Shepard: Paris Texas* (Nordlinger, Germany: Greno, 1984), pp. 98–99.
50. Peter Handke, "The Long Way Around," in *Slow Homecoming* (New York: Farrar/Straus/Giroux, 1985), p. 76. Both authors of the screenplay of *Paris Texas*, Wenders and Sam Shepard are familiar with Handke's novels. Wenders worked with Handke on a screen play for one of Handke's earlier novels (*The Anxiety of the Goaltender During the Penalty Kick*), and Shepard reviewed *Slow Homecoming* in the *New York Times Book Review*.
51. This is the interpretive resort of Phillip Kolker and Peter Beicken, in their excellent reading of the film "Paris, Texas: Between the Winds," in Kolker and Beicken, *The Films of Wim Wenders: Cinema as Vision and Desire* (New York: Cambridge University Press, 1993), p. 125.
52. Handke, *Slow Homecoming*, p. 114.
53. Thomas Pynchon, *Gravity's Rainbow* (New York: Viking, 1973).
54. This apt expression is in Kolker and Beicken, "Paris Texas: Between the Winds," p. 120.
55. Quotations from Slotkin, *Gunfighter Nation*, p. 212.
56. Alexander Kluge "On Film and the Public Sphere," trans. by Thomas Y. Levin and Miriam B Hansen *New German Critique*, 24–25, Fall/Winter, 1981–1982: p. 21.
57. James Chapman, *The British at War: Cinema State and Propaganda* (1939–1945), p. 181.
58. Michael Rogin, *Ronald Reagan, the Movie and Other Episodes in Political Demonology* (Berkeley: University of California Press, 1987), p. 37.
59. See for example, Karen Rasmussen and Sharon D. Downey, "Dialectical Disorientation in Vietnam War Films: Subversion of the Mythology of War," *Quarterly Journal of Speech*, 77(2), May 1991: 176–195, and for a more general treatment, which locates the Vietnam War film in a historical trajectory of war-film relationships, see Tom Englehardt, *The End of Victory Culture* (New York: Basic Books, 1995).
60. Karen Kaplan, "Anita Jones' Proposal Links up Army and USC, *Los Angeles Times*, August 18, 1999.
61. Rick Lyman, "White House Sets Meeting With Film Executives to Discuss War on Terrorism," *New York Times*, November 8, 2001, p. 8.
62. Caryn James, "TV's Take on Government in a Terror-Filled World," *New York Times*, April 30, 2002 (on the web at http://www.nytimes.com/2002/04/30/arts/30JAME.html).
63. "Act II: Hollywood waves the flag and is redeemed": The cover story in *Christian Science Monitor* 12/21/2001, p. 1.
64. See Geoffrey Gray, "'Black Hawk' Damned," *The Village Voice* 47(6), February 12, 2002: 26.

CHAPTER 7

Killing Canadians
The International Politics of Capital Punishment

PATRICIA MOLLOY

I came in on a Canadian passport, which I had kept current all these years, for travelling as a Canadian is perhaps the easiest way to find safe passage. In a crisis, everyone wants to be one of us. We're known globally for our innocuousness, our apparent harmlessness. No wonder our passports are the most forged in the world.

Catherine Bush, *The Rules of Engagement*[1]

Nguyen Thi Hiep's Body

Within Vietnamese culture, it is customary to bury the bodily remains of a deceased member close to where that person had lived their life, in other words, close to home. According to Vietnamese law, however, human remains cannot be exhumed and moved within three years of burial, thus presenting an international conundrum with regard to the rightful resting place for the body of Nguyen Thi Hiep, a Canadian citizen executed in April 2000 for drug trafficking in Vietnam, her country of native origin. For four months, Hiep's body lay buried in a shallow grave within the walls of a Hanoi prison courtyard, in a low field subject to washout in the torrential spring rains, while her family, Canadian officials, and lawyers argued for its release and transport for reburial in Canada. Hiep's two sons insisted that Canada is where their mother belongs. After reneging on its promise to release the body in May (Hiep's sons having traveled from Canada to Vietnam for that very purpose), the Vietnam government eventually, on "humanitarian grounds," agreed in August to release Hiep's remains to her family for reburial at a site of their choice—as long as it was in Vietnam.

Complicating the struggle both to preserve Hiep's life and to return her "home" following her death is the ever contentious issue of citizenship and its ambiguous relation to home and nationhood, identity and difference. Indeed, difference can neither be thought of nor lived outside the space of identity even when one's identity is pluralized[2] (or, in Hiep's case, hyphenated); just as identity cannot be thought of outside the power relations of statist notions of citizenship. Modern political life authorizes a "citizen/nation/state ensemble" that governs the subject, placing spacial limits on the possibilities of action and meaning. The privilege accorded this triad, as Nevzat Soguk argues, is such that identities that fall outside the boundaries of the territorial nation-state, the figure of the refugee, for example, come to represent a lack. The refugee lacks the security of the citizen-subject's home, sociocultural affiliation, and ties to community. Given this lack of community, refugees lack proper ties with the state and thus lack the state's protection and representation within and by its democratic institutions. The refugee, says Soguk, represents a disruption "in the conditions of normality in life imagined in terms of the hierarchy of the citizen/nation/state ensemble."[3]

Democracy itself is an activity allowed by the hierarchy of this ensemble and thus has become territorialized, reserved for the citizen-subject within the protective (and bounded) space of the sovereign state. The territorial state is accorded its significance precisely "because it becomes the sole provider and protector of that space, which presumably is the only place enabling both citizenship and democracy."[4] The territorial sovereign state is thus the sole dispenser and guarantor of what we call "rights" insofar as, with the advent of modernity, rights are only available to the citizen.[5] This is not to say, however, that *all* citizens equally enjoy the citizen-subject status and the rights offered by the territorial state and its democratic institutions. In addition to that of the refugee, migrant bodies and incarcerated bodies also disrupt the certainties of the citizen/nation/state hierarchy, and lack the privilege it otherwise affords. As I shall argue, the incarcerated citizen, the death-row inmate in particular, lacks many of the ties to community and democratic rights of full citizen-subjects. The death-row inmate lives in what Giorgio Agamben terms a state of exception and under the suspension of law: the point where the violence of law and the law of violence enter a *zone of indistinction,*[6] and when incarcerated in a state outside of one's own country of citizenship, it becomes all the more complicated given the limits of sovereign power, its jurisdiction, over life and death.

At the limits of the jurisdiction of two sovereign powers lies Nguyen Thi Hiep's body—the corpse itself a site of territorial contest, literally refusing to stay put.[7] Whilst Hiep had been a Canadian citizen since 1982, Vietnam does not recognize dual citizenship. Thus, for Vietnamese officials, Hiep's Vietnamese-ness rendered her Canadian-ness inconsequential.[8] It could be said, then, that whereas the refugee might lack the citizenship and the security that it ostensibly provides, a dual citizen such as Hiep suffers from an *excess* of citizenship, doubly inscribed as both "inside" and "outside" not one but two sovereign states. Hiep's ties to Vietnam and Canada effectively cancel each other out, placing her in one of several zones of indistinction which I will elaborate in this chapter. First, however, it is necessary to look more closely at Hiep's case.

Quiet Diplomacy and Good Governance

I began by chronicling the fate of Hiep's (already) dead body rather than the events leading up to her death for several reasons; the first being that while claims to "identity" may indeed be an indispensible feature of human life,[9] they do not cease with death. The second, and related, reason is the (not so) simple fact that the plight of Hiep's burial and body received far more coverage in the Canadian news media than her arrest, trial, and conviction four years before, and subsequent diplomatic efforts to have her case reinvestigated in light of (overwhelming) evidence that she was an unwitting pawn in an international drug ring.

One of the most popular narrative accounts provided to Canadians writes Hiep's death as the inevitable result of the barbarism of a non-democratic state that refused to act in good faith with the benevolent, more "civilized" democracy that we call Canada. The irony here is that, as one of Hiep's lawyers even admitted, her death may have equally resulted from the failure of a Canadian-style "quiet diplomacy." Secretary of State for the Asia-Pacific Region Raymond Chan, who met with Vietnamese officials in 1996 and 1998 with reference to the case (while on trade missions), stated that the Canadian government had not considered adopting a more forceful approach as "people don't want to be bullied.... We don't try to lecture them. We try to explain to them that it's important for us to have bilateral relationships."[10]

This decidedly was not the stance taken by Rubin "Hurricane" Carter of Toronto's Association in Defence of the Wrongfully Convicted (ADWC), and subject of Norman Jewison's 1999 film *The Hurricane*. Indeed, Carter, who following a White House screening of the film enlisted the help of U.S. President Bill Clinton in successfully postponing Hiep's execution in December 1999, had argued all along for a louder and more public protest of Hiep's conviction and death sentence. Nonetheless, lawyer James Lockyer, appointed by the ADWC to represent Hiep and her mother (imprisoned in Hanoi under the same charges), felt that too much publicity might offend Hanoi leaders and therefore seal her fate and, against the advice of Carter, instead led a "quiet campaign" to secure Hiep's release—a move he subsequently redefined as a "fatal mistake."[11] Without any warning to the Canadian government or her family, after three years on death row shackled in a rat-infested cell, in a stunning display of sovereignty, Hiep was executed by a firing squad just weeks before an international delegation consisting of Carter, the Reverend Jesse Jackson, representatives of Amnesty International, federal prosecutors, and RCMP investigators were scheduled to arrive in Hanoi to meet with Vietnamese prosecutors and present new evidence in the case. Also, this occurred a few months short of the Vietnamese government's provision of amnesty to 12,000 prisoners in conjunction with its celebrations marking the 25th anniversary of the end of the Vietnam War.[12]

Once notified, the Canadian government was (now) quick to publicly condemn the execution, and as a Canadian spokesperson for Amnesty International has pointed out, this in itself was somewhat of a diplomatic departure. "It may not sound like the strongest language, but 'regret,' 'disappoint,' and 'concerned' is the usual wording (in diplomatic circles). Using the word 'condemn' is strong."[13] Canada's ambassador to Vietnam, Cecile Latour, who was in Canada at the time of Hiep's execution, was recalled for consultation, and Foreign Affairs Minister Lloyd Axworthy announced within days of the execution that the Canadian government was canceling a program intended to assist Vietnam in joining the World Trade Organization, and would boycott the official celebrations of the end of the war. A week later, in an even louder diplomatic voice, Canada suspended all ministerial contact with the Vietnam government and announced the cancelation of pending aid programs, including a $5 million proposal on legal reform and a $3 million initiative "to promote good governance."[14] As Axworthy put it, "For a government that is celebrating 25 years, this shows that there are some lessons that haven't been learned. And if you're going to be part of the international community of countries, there are certain rules one has to live with."[15] Indeed, Axworthy promised a complete review of all of Canada's international relations with Vietnam. Moreover, while the Canadian government was busy revoking its bilateral relations with Vietnam, lawyer James Lockyer was calling for an internationalization of the case "so that countries that execute people can appreciate that there is a downside to killing their own citizens and foreign citizens."[16] But while the Canadian government may indeed have withdrawn its support of "good governance" in Vietnam, efforts to internationalize capital punishment as a global problem must be careful not to overlook the specific workings of sovereign politics and its distinction from humanitarianism. Before we wrestle with this, however, it bears noting that whilst Hiep's execution may have re-sulted in Canada's re-evaluation of its neighborly relations with Vietnam, the execution of Canadian citizen Stanley Faulder in the United States less than a year before did not result in a similar diplomatic chill.

The Nine Lives of Stanley Faulder

Canada's condemnation of Nguyen Thi Hiep's killing, and severing diplo-matic relations with Vietnam could, in some respects, be considered safe, or at least easier than suspending relations with its more powerful neighbor to the south. In other words, following the execution of Stanley Faulder in Texas in June 1999, Canada did not withdraw its ambassador to the United States. Nor were trade or any other sanctions imposed,[17] even with the ac-knowledgement by the Texas government that Faulder's rights under the Vienna Convention on Consular Relations had been violated some twenty years before.[18] Axworthy and Ambassador Raymond Chretien (nephew of Prime Minister Jean Chretien) did, however, repeatedly appeal for clemency for the former Alberta mechanic, the first Canadian to be executed in the United States since 1952.

Faulder's ninth appeal for clemency reads like a gripping television drama, and indeed was a well-aired news item at the time. A five-member international delegation, including South African Archbishop Desmond Tutu, Rubin Carter, and Joyce Milgaard (mother of David Milgaard who had spent twenty-three years in prison in Canada for a murder he did not commit), traveled to Texas to put pressure on a U.S. District Court of Appeals to uphold a stay of execution granted to Faulder on December 9, 1998 by a Texas district court and subsequently overturned by a federal appeals court. Adding fuel to the fire, that very week, U.S. Secretary of State Madeline Albright had appealed to (then) Texas Governor George W. Bush to grant at least a thirty-day reprieve to examine Faulder's case in light of the violation of the Vienna Treaty. And just fifteen minutes before he was scheduled to die by lethal injection, Faulder was granted an indefinite stay of execution by the U.S. Supreme Court on December 10, 1998—International Human Rights Day and the 50th anniversary of the Universal Declaration of Human Rights. It was the ninth reprieve for Faulder since his initial conviction in 1977 for the murder of Inez Phillips (head of a wealthy Texas oil family), the ninth time he was marked as a "dead man" and allowed to live, and the last time he would be spared at the last minute.[19] Despite the intervention of the Inter-American Commission on Human Rights (the human rights enforcement agency of the Organization of American States) and a law suit filed by lawyer Sandra Babcock under the (rarely cited) Alien Tort Claims Act, by which foreign citizens may sue the United States government for "harm or damages resulting from breaches of the laws of nations," in June 1999, Stan Faulder did indeed become the first Canadian citizen to be executed within American borders in almost fifty years.[20]

In many respects, however, Faulder, like Hiep and any other death-row inmate, was already dead or at best suspended in what Giorgio Agamben terms a "limit zone" between life and death, both inside and outside, included as a politically unqualified life ("bare life") and yet excluded from political community altogether. "Like the fence of the [concentration] camp, the interval between death sentence and execution delimits an extratemporal and extraterritorial threshold in which the human body is separated from its normal political status and abandoned, in a state of exception, to the most extreme misfortunes."[21] With the pardon and remission of a death sentence being one of the most extreme manifestations of sovereign power over life and death (biopolitics), in a state of exception, any such "subjection to experimentation" will result in either returning the body to life, "or definitively consign it to the death to which it already belongs."[22] In this zone of indistinction, in being included *as* excluded, the person condemned to die by sovereign authority becomes the equivalent of *homo sacer*, the figure of "sacred man" who can be killed yet not sacrificed, murdered without the commission of homicide. Indeed, the bare life, the expendable life, of *homo sacer* is life exposed to death, life *available* to be killed.[23]

For Agamben, the figure of *homo sacer* is crucial to the advent of modernity and the juridical order of the West. It is in the zones of indistinction that bare life is both subject to and object of state political order. More specifically, it is upon the body of *homo sacer* and in the realm of bare life that state power is exercised and organized. Sovereign violence is "founded not upon a pact but on the exclusive inclusion of bare life in the state."[24] Indeed, it is the subject's capacity to be killed that forms the new political body of the West.[25] But it is also in the realm of bare life that *homo sacer* is emancipated, with the birth of democracy and the demand for human rights.[26] It is in the form of rights that politically unqualified bare life now fully enters into the structure of the state becoming the very foundation of its legitimacy. For Agamben, "the declarations of rights is the originary figure of the inscription of bare life in the juridico-political order of the nation-state."[27] In other words, the rise of human rights discourse and democracy *paralleled* that of the modern sovereign state itself.[28] I will return to the implications that these zones of indistinction bring to bear in terms of how we regard the internationalization of capital punishment as a human rights issue later. Next, I want to examine another, albeit fictitious, "case study" that I think impacted upon the Canadian psyche in making such a demand.

Law, Order, and the "True North"

On December 9, 1998, in the same week of Stan Faulder's ninth appeal for clemency, NBC aired an episode of the popular American television drama *Law and Order* entitled "True North," whose theme elicited considerable controversy in Canada (where the program is also broadcast on the Canadian Television Network, or CTV). In so titling the episode, the show's writers and producers acknowledge, through irony, an icon of Canadian identity. The words "the true North [strong and free]" are contained within the lyrics of the Canadian national anthem and the phrase itself is often used in self-reference (in much the same way as "home of the brave" stands in for "America" in the lexicon of popular discourse). It is also the name of an Ontario micro-brewery beer. Here, however, for the savvy viewer the trueness of the true North is cast in doubt before the first scene even begins, and then proceeds to a state of transparency.

In keeping with the traditional format of the show, the episode begins with a police investigation of the murders of John Harker, a wealthy New York software executive, and his young daughter who had been at home in their fashionable Manhattan apartment, while an errant Mrs. Harker is unaccounted for. While tracking down the prime suspect, Mrs. Harker's friend Doris Nichols, that same night, the detectives find Stephanie Harker, having just fatally shot Doris outside a restaurant in what seemed to be a case of self-defense at that time . The shocked and bewildered Mrs. Harker relayed that Doris "went crazy," had shot her husband (with whom Mrs. Harker said she had been having an affair) and step-daughter and had attacked Mrs. Harker herself, scratching her badly, before Harker grabbed the gun in fear for her own life. In investigating the case further, however, detectives Briscoe and Curtis discover that things are not quite as they appear, or rather, that Stephanie Harker is really not who she says she is. It seems that the same Manhattan socialite, who attends regular meetings of her book club in posh restaurants, is the daughter of a souvenir shop owner in Niagara Falls, Ontario, has a flair for the wild life, a penchant for booze and drugs and illicit extra-marital sex, and whose husband was threatening to divorce her. Once the investigation reveals evidence that Mrs. Harker had contracted Doris Nichols to kill her husband, and subsequently shot Nichols not in self-defense but cold blood, Harker flees back to her native Ontario where she is arrested.

The second half of the show then details the legal (and to a lesser degree moral) conundrum of the State of New York in securing an extradition agreement from the Canadian government, which is reluctant to do so unless assurances are made that the death penalty not be imposed for Mrs. Harker's crimes. The New York District Attorney's Office begrudgingly agrees to take the death penalty off the table in exchange for Mrs. Harker herself. The tale, and the law, takes a bit of a twist, however, when the police subsequently come to suspect that Stephanie Harker had earlier killed her husband's first wife in Buffalo, New York, and withdraws its promise not to prosecute Harker's case as a capital offence. With the terms of the extradition agreement now violated, the Canadian authorities refuse to hand over Mrs. Harker. Not to be outdone, the Assistant D.A. threatens to suspend the operations of the Manhattan branch of the (fictitious) Commonwealth Bank of Canada, as Harker's local branch in Canada is withholding key evidence concerning her payment to Nichols for the contracted murder. Now outdone, the Canadian authorities extradite Mrs. Harker to the United States where she is tried, convicted, and sentenced to death.

That this has never happened "in reality" could be one of the reasons why True North was not a big hit with its Canadian viewers. In addition, there is an underlying tone that Stephanie Harker "got what she deserved," made easier by her portrayal as a completely unsympathetic character, unremorseful and lying from the very start. And, moreover, with an axe to grind against Americans. Her one loyal (and Canadian) friend blurted out on the witness stand that Stephanie had been hard done by by an American boy when she was younger, leaving her bitter. But it was Stephanie herself who cooked her own (Canada) goose. During her testimony, the poised young Mrs. Harker begins to explain what it was like growing up on the Canada/U.S. border, constantly being looked down upon by Americans who thought they were better than her, and later snubbed by those in her (husband's) social circle upon her marriage to Harker. She loses her cool and when completely unhinged, angrily screams how nobody, no American that is ("they're all snobs"), will ever look down on or walk all over her ever again.

Parallel to this uncovering of Mrs. Harker's "true" identity, wherein the "harmless Canadian" is revealed as a lying, gold-digging, vengeful, sexual predator, and serial killer—a life not worthy of being lived—is a stripping bare of "Canada" itself. Whilst the focus of the sovereign disciplinary gaze in "True North" is upon the bare life of Stephanie Harker, the Canadian juridical order (and cultural identity) is also subject to scrutiny. Canada's non-compliance with capital punishment, formally abolished by parliament in 1976, is put to the test throughout the show.[29] For example, when Assistant D.A. Abbey Carmichael pays a visit to the Canadian Consulate to request Harker's extradition she is, to begin with, greeted by an official who looks more like a clown complete with a polka-dotted bow tie. Also, when Carmichael challenges him that while under Canadian law the state may choose not to extradite a person facing the death sentence, it does not necessarily *have* to, his reply that it is a moral issue elicits a sneer from the A.D.A.

With claims of moral righteousness being made by both sides, Stephanie Harker's biological (politically unqualified) life becomes the political playing field for two mutually opposing and irreconcilable demands for, and visions of, justice. Even more so than with Nguyen Thi Hiep and Stanley Faulder, the bare life of "Stephanie Harker" is a life inscribed by and subject to the strategic ordering, the violence, of not just one sovereign state, but two. Ultimately, as Carmichael would have it, Mrs. Harker was, literally, sold out by her "own" country. For it was only with the threat of shutting down the bank in Manhattan that the Canadian government agreed to relinquish its own claim on Stephanie Harker's life, or as Carmichael remarks, "money talks." But complicating the political and economic playing field of Stephanie Harker's expendable life is a particularly gendered biopolitical (b)ordering of human life and sovereign existence. Stephanie is alternatively described as either young and attractive or deadly and lethal, a sexual deviant who, in preying on American men, is a threat to the nation as a whole. Thus, here, the seemingly separate terrains of the sexual and the juridical form their own zone of indistinction.

Enter at Your Own Risk: The Biopolitics of Borders

As previously mentioned, the airing of "True North" generated controversy, thanks to *Law and Order*'s (sizeable) Canadian audience. As to whether the timing of the episode added fuel to the demands for clemency for Stan Faulder, I can only speculate. However, following Faulder's December 1998 stay of execution, Texas Governor George W. Bush issued somewhat of a warning to those who dwell north of the 49th parallel. Bush declared that, "If you're a Canadian and come to our state, don't murder anybody."[30] Or, as *Law and Order*'s fictive New York District Attorney, Adam Schiff, sardonically remarked following the sentencing of Stephanie Harker, "enter at your own risk." For Canada's Foreign Affairs Minister, Lloyd Axworthy, Faulder's ninth stay brought home the urgency of the message. "What was at stake was the importance of protecting the rights of Canadians who travel abroad. And broader than that, the rights of all people in this global age to receive basic minimum standards of protection."[31] Indeed, the very same year, Canada had become a signatory to a universal moratorium on the death penalty presented to the International Commission on Human Rights.

Given its international commitment to abolishing capital punishment in the interests of human rights, it might therefore seem odd that Canada recently came under fire both at home and afar for seeking to extradite two of its own citizens to face murder charges, and the death sentence, in Washington State. Here, the innocuousness of the Canadian way, as described by the heroine in Catherine Bush's novel, is itself a fiction. The "real life" counterparts to Stephanie Harker, British Columbians Atif Rafay and Glen Sebastian Burns, were, when I wrote the initial draft of this paper in February of 2001, awaiting the Supreme Court of Canada's ruling on whether the federal government should be forced to seek guarantees that the death penalty will not be imposed on any Canadian citizens extradited to a foreign country to face murder charges. In fact, the Burns/Rafay case represents the first time that the Canadian government did *not* ask for a such a guarantee and on that basis in 1997 the B.C. Court of Appeal over-turned (then) Justice Minister Allan Rock's 1996 decision to extradite.[32] Lawyers for Burns and Rafay appeared before the Supreme Court on May 23, 2000 to argue that their execution in the United States would violate their rights under the Canadian Charter of Rights and Freedoms, a move that, much to the chagrin of the federal government, was endorsed by the Italian Senate in an unprecedented granting by the Supreme Court of "in-tervenor status" to a foreign country without a "tangible interest" in the case.[33] For the federal government, the Supreme Court of Canada is not the proper forum for a foreign government's "political mission."[34] However, the Italian Senate, which is heading a campaign for a global abolishment of cap-ital punishment, sees itself in "an advantageous geographical position" to advise Canadian judges of legal developments in European countries that prohibit extradition to countries imposing the death sentence. Moreover, for Italy, Canada's behavior in relation to Rafay and Burns was nothing short of "barbaric" for a country that had already signed an international human rights agreement. Or as an anti-death penalty activist put it, the sit-uation of Canadians facing execution in foreign countries is "a human rights issue, not a law and order issue."[35]

But *is* it? To be more precise, *why* are human rights issues not considered as belonging in the realm of law and order, or politics? For example, why, was releasing Nguyen Thi Hiep's body considered a "humanitarian" and not a "political" gesture? Whether extraditing Burns and Rafay is a political or a human rights issue is not only well worth asking, but crucial, as the degree to which these are even separable, as Agamben argues, constitutes the "extreme phase of the separation of the rights of man from the rights of the citizen."[36] As previously noted, for Agamben rights are available only to the citizen, ac-complished in the passage from a divinely assigned royal sovereignty of the *ancien regime* to the form of national sovereignty that we associate with the modern state. In the process of the new state order, the subject is transformed into a citizen, thereby severing the distinction between "the principle of na-tivity" (simple birth, or bare life as such) and "the principle of sovereignty" (the politicization of bare life through biopolitics) which had been separated in the *ancien regime*. The principles of nativity and sovereignty are now united in the body of the "sovereign subject," which becomes the foundation of the new nation-state. "Birth", says Agamben, immediately becomes "nation" such that there is no longer a distinction between the two terms.

In Agamben's analysis, the most extreme (and logical) consequence of this "hidden difference" between birth and nation in the twentieth century appeared in the form of Nazism and fascism, "that is, two properly biopolitical movements that made of natural life the exemplary place of the sovereign decision."[37] To be sure, Nazism's racism and eugenics, he argues, are comprehensible only in the context of the birth-nation link, which had lost considerable force by the time of the First World War, and has led to the demand for human rights. He writes:

> On the one hand, the nation-states become greatly concerned with natural life, discriminating within it between a so-to-speak authentic life and a life lacking every political value. ... On the other hand, the very rights of man that once made sense as the presupposition of the rights of the citizen are now progressively separated from and used outside the context of citizenship, for the sake of the supposed representation and protection of a bare life that is more and more driven to the margins of nation-states, ultimately to be recodified into a new national identity.[38]

Thus given the contradictory character of this process, the various international organizations and committees (such as the League of Nations and the later United Nations), which claim not a "political" but a solely "humanitarian" mission, can, according to Agamben, only fail. Ultimately, humanitarian organizations "can only grasp human life in the form of bare or sacred life, and therefore, despite themselves, maintain a secret solidarity with the very powers they ought to fight."[39]

Jenny Edkins argues that the broader implication of this is that a liberal humanitarianism that purports to challenge sovereign authority for the sake of a common humanity instead turns out to be the very manner in which sovereign order, and sovereign violence, is achieved. The "new humanitarianism" such as that witnessed through NATO's intervention in Kosovo, for example, is but a new form of sovereign politics.[40] Here, refugee bodies were interned in "camps" often surrounded by high metal fences and barbed wire. Forced to leave their vehicles, money, and documents at the border, they were left in possession only of their (bare) lives. Moreover, Edkins argues that even once returned to their homes, Kosovar refugees did not cease to be *homines sacri*. Indeed, "in their victimhood, they were constituted as without any political voice." The refugee or victim is included by liberal humanitarians only "through a surrender of *political* status"[41] (my emphasis).

What is at stake, therefore, in the separation of human rights from politics, is the very future of politics. For Agamben, what is especially crucial for that future is precisely the recognition that the entrance of *zoe* (simple natural life) into the *polis*, which had been separated in classical western politics, is the decisive event of modernity. To be sure, the politicization of bare life (the inclusion of that which is excluded) signals a radical transformation in the categories of classical thought *and* political possibility. He writes that "if politics today seems to be passing through a lasting eclipse, this is because politics has failed to reckon with this foundational event of modernity."[42] With the classical distinctions between public/private, inside/outside, and right/left already dissolving into zones of indistinction, it is *only* an interrogation of the link between bare life and politics that will bring the political out of its own concealment "and at the same time, return thought to its practical calling."[43] Any attempt to rethink the political space of the West must in fact proceed from the awareness that there is no longer a distinction between *zoe* and *bios*, between private life and political existence.[44]

My argument here, then, is that it is less a question of whether capital punishment is a human rights or a political issue, but of what gets left out when it is designated *as* a solely humanitarian concern. At the same time, it is not a case of simply consigning capital punishment to the juridico-political realm, but recognizing the consequences of the biopolitical ordering brought about by the modern state in its juridical guise. As Agamben says, once we have had the concentration camp, there is no going back to the classical distinctions of the *polis*. The possibility of distinguishing between our biological body and our political body is forever lost.[45] Thus, what he calls the "enigmas" of the last century (such as Nazism) will be solved only on the biopolitical terrain on which they were founded.[46]

Atif Rafay and Sebastian Burns, living for six years in a state of exception and under the suspension of law, had no rights to their so-called life under either of the sovereign powers governing them. In the limit zone between life and death, the terms "life" and "death" themselves become political rather than biological concepts, acquiring their political meaning only at the moment of a decision. For Agamben, the moving border between life and death is thus a *biopolitical* border,[47] the threshold of the exercise of sovereign power. As is, I would suggest, the seemingly topographical border that separates (and unites) the sovereign powers presiding over the life, and death, of Atif Rafay and Sebastian Burns, and any others who may (and will) come to occupy a similar limit zone.

Conclusions

The good news, however, is that on February 15, 2001, the Supreme Court of Canada ruled 9-0 that Burns and Rafay may be extradited to the United States only if it guarantees that they would not face execution. For Burns and Rafay, the decision eventually handed down by the court means that they get to "live," or at least to continue their biological existence, once they cross the border. For those working on abolishing capital punishment worldwide, the Canadian decision sets an important precedent in stopping the international traffic of human life and death. According to an Amnesty International lawyer observing the proceedings, the Burns and Rafay decision means that non-Canadians are also covered by the court decision. Had this been the case a decade ago, American citizens Joseph Kindler and Charles Ng (wanted for murder in the United States and captured in Canada) would not have been extradited to the U.S. when they attempted, and failed, a similar bid in 1991.[48]

Moreover, the Canadian decision has serious ramifications for future extraditions of suspects wanted in connection with the September 11, 2001, terrorist attacks on the World Trade Center and U.S. Pentagon. Not only are Canadian authorities unlikely to relinquish any possible suspects, Spain has already refused to hand over eight arrested Al Qaeda members for U.S. indictment unless assurances are granted that they will not face the death penalty or trial in a military tribunal recently established by former Texas Governor George W. Bush, now at the presidential helm. With other members of the European Union likely to follow the lead taken by Spain,[49] and more and more countries joining the international ban on capital punishment, what will happen in the months, and years to come, is anybody's guess.

The tribunal, set up by the Pentagon precisely in order to ignore rights normally accorded U.S. non-citizens and other foreign defendants, has the authority to deny defendants' rights to choose their own counsel and also has the power to impose the death penalty without the unanimous agreement of jurors required in a regular court of law. Hence, the "us" and "them" binarism of sovereign distinction is now even further welded to the American polity. According to Vice President Dick Cheney, non-U.S.-citizen terrorist suspects are *not* entitled to the same rights as the American citizens they are accused of targetting. As he put it, "They don't deserve the same guarantees and safeguards that we use for an American citizen." Likewise, for Attorney General John Ashcroft, "Foreign terrorists who commit war crimes against the United States in my judgement are not entitled to and do not deserve the protections of the American Constitution."[50] The National Institute of Military Justice in Washington defines the rights, and jurisdiction, of citizenship somewhat differently. "As a *citizen of the world*, one could assume they ought to be entitled to the same human civil rights under various international treaties the United States has co-signed on."[51] (emphasis added).

Nonetheless, Canada was at odds with the United States once again over the treatment of Canadian citizen Shakir Ali Baloch, whose detention in the

U.S. since September 20, 2001 (without any charges being laid) only came to light in November of the same year (when family members contacted the Department of Foreign Affairs for help in locating him) and would seem, once again, to violate the Vienna Convention on Consular Relations. As with Stanley Faulder almost twenty-five years ago, Baloch was not notified of his right to contact Canadian representatives. Baloch was one of more than 1000 people detained in the United States since September 11, 460 of whom had been jailed for three months on alleged immigration violations.[52] Also, although the U.S. State Department had, at that point, not disclosed whether he was being held under immigration rules or new anti-terrorist legislation, in the wake of September 11, there appears to be little distinction between "immigrants" and "terrorists," the latter label being the discretion of the President, the sovereign, himself.[53] One thing we can be sure of, then, is that without serious adjustment, the sovereign practices of law and order across biopolitical borders will continue to determine the bodies and lives of *homines sacri* anywhere and everywhere. What must be adjusted, however, is not just sovereign practices in and of themselves, but how we conceive of the relationship among sovereignty, politics, and law. Most importantly, it is perhaps in recognizing capital punishment as the drawing of biopolitical borders (rather than our "internationalizing" capital punishment) that we can "return thought to its practical calling," as Agamben asks us to do.

Notes

This paper was initially presented at the panel "Racism, Rage and Human Rights: Still Seeking the Ethical in the International," at the International Studies Association annual conference in February 2001. For her kind and insightful discussant comments, I'd like to thank Jenny Edkins. I also thank Jenny, Mike Shapiro, and Veronique Pin-Fat for post-conference suggestions and editorial encouragement as the Burns and Rafay plot continued to unfold and as the world kept changing as this volume came together. For their comments and help in writing the initial draft, I owe a huge debt to Hilary Davis and Mario DiPaolantonio. Special thanks are also due to Dave Parkinson of the Canadian Coalition Against the Death Penalty, my initial encounter with whom constitutes probably the best "it's a small world" story of all time.

1. Catherine Bush, *The Rules of Engagement* (Toronto: HarperFlamingoCanada, 2000), p. 154.
2. William E. Connolly, *Identity\Difference: Democratic Negotiations of Political Paradox* (Ithaca and London: Cornell University Press, 1991), p. 158.
3. Nevzat Soguk, *States and Strangers: Refugees and Displacements of Statecraft* (Minneapolis and London: University of Minnesota Press, 1999), pp. 18–19.
4. Soguk, *States and Strangers*, pp. 211–212.

5. See Giorgio Agamben, *Homo Sacer: Sovereign Power and Bare Life* (Stanford, California: Standford University Press, 1998), pp. 126–135.

6. Agamben, *Homo Sacer*, pp. 31–32.

7. Due to heavy rains and the shallowness of the grave, Hiep's body had to be weighted down to keep it "in place." Thanks to Mario DiPaolantonio for this information.

8. However, *as* a dual citizen, Hiep's identity as wholly "Canadian" was incomplete. As political scientist Kim Nossal has argued, Hiep's "ethnicity" may have worked against her. Had she been a Canadian of Caucasian origin, Hiep might not have been dealt with as severely by Vietnamese authorities. See Sharon Oosthoek, "Canadians are not invulnerable," *The Hamilton Spectator* on http://www.hamiltonspectator.com/context/220755.html.

9. Connolly, p. 158.

10. Quoted in "Vietnam defends execution of Canadian…", *The Globe and Mail* (Saturday, April 29, 2000).

11. Ibid. See also *Vietnam News Analysis,* May 20, 2000. http://www.vietquoc.com/may20-00.htm

12. In September 2000 another 8,000 prisoners were released in a promised second wave of amnesty. Among those were Tran Thi Cam, Nguyen Thi Hiep's mother, released on "humanitarian" grounds.

13. Alex Neve, quoted by Sharon Oosthoek, "Canadians are not invulnerable," *The Hamilton Spectator.*

14. Allan Thompson, "Chretien condemns Canadian's execution, Rift with Vietnam widens as Ottawa steps up pressure," *The Toronto Star,* May 2, 2000.

15. Quoted by Allan Thompson, "Ottawa protests woman's execution, Canada withdraws ambassador to Vietnam," *The Toronto Star,* April 28, 2000.

16. See "Activists denounce execution of Canadian woman in Vietnam," *Vietnam Executes Innocent Canadian: IN THE NEWS.* http://ccadp.org/canadavietnam.htm.

17. Canada didn't suspend trade with Vietnam either as the volume of trade was considered by Axworthy to be too negligible to make a difference. See "Vietnam defends execution of Canadian," note p. 8.

18. While Texas authorities did admit that the international treaty, which guarantees the right of those arrested or detained in foreign countries to contact their native governments for assistance, was broken in Faulder's case, officials laid blame on a 20 year-old clerical error. Faulder had served 15 years on death row before his family or the Canadian government were notified of his arrest. See Kathleen Kenna, "Court turns down Faulder bid," *The Toronto Star,* Jan. 26, 1999; and Kathleen Kenna, "Tutu seeks mercy for Albertan," *The Toronto Star* n.d., both available on http://ccadp.org/faulder.htm.

19. Faulder's conviction was overturned in 1979 by the Texas Court of Appeals on the grounds that his confession was obtained by coercive means. His second trial was prosecuted not by a district attorney but a private lawyer hired by the Philips family under a special provision of Texas law. See *Dallas Morning News* Editorial, Dec. 4, 1998, on http://ccadp.org/faulder.htm.

20. See "New Law Suit Seeks Halt to Faulder Execution," http://ccadp.org/faulder.htm.

21. Agamben, *Homo Sacer*, p. 159.

22. Agamben, *Homo Sacer*, p. 159.

23. Michael Dillon and Julian Reid, "Global Governance, Liberal Peace, and Complex Emergency," *Alternatives,* 25, Jan. 2000: 131.

24. Agamben, *Homo Sacer*, p. 107.

25. Agamben, *Homo Sacer*, p. 125.

26. Jenny Edkins, "Sovereign Power, Zones of Indistinction, and the Camp," *Alternatives,* 25, Jan. 2000: p. 7.

27. Agamben, *Homo Sacer*, p. 127.

28. Edkins, "Sovereign Power, Zones of Indistinction, and the Camp," p. 18.

29. The last execution in Canada occured in Toronto in 1962. In 1967, Lester B. Pearson's Liberal government abolished capital punishment for all but the killing of police officers and prison guards and in 1976 the Trudeau government formally abolished it for all offences. In 1987 when the Brian Mulroney Conservative government held a free vote in the House of Commons on a motion to reinstate, it was defeated by 148-127. And on Dec. 10, 1998, the date of Stanley Faulder's ninth stay of execution, Canada passed legislation removing all references to capital punishment from the National Defence Act.

30. Quoted in Kathleen Kenna, "Faulder gets last minute reprieve," *The Toronto Star*, Thursday Dec. 10, 1998, A12.
31. Quoted by Kathleen Kenna, "Last-minute reprieve for Canadian," *The Toronto Star* Friday, Dec. 11, 1998, A1.
32. See Valerie Lawton, "B.C. pair take extradition fight to Supreme Court," *The Toronto Star* Wednesday May 24, 2000, A2.
33. Ibid. See also, Janice Tibbetts, "Supreme Court gives intervenor status to Italy," *The National Post*, April 17, 2000.
34. Justice Department lawyer, Rob Frater, quoted in Tibbetts.
35. Tracy Lamourie quoted in Brian Shields, "Baby killer looks to Canada for mercy," *The Beacon News*, Saturday, October 7, 2000. See http://ccadp.org/news2000.htm.
36. Agamben, *Homo Sacer*, p. 133.
37. Agamben, *Homo Sacer*, pp. 128–129.
38. Agamben, *Homo Sacer*, pp. 132–133.
39. Agamben, *Homo Sacer*, p. 133.
40. Edkins, "Sovereign Power, Zones of Indistinction, and the Camp," p. 18.
41. Edkins, "Sovereign Power, Zones of Indistinction, and the Camp," p. 19.
42. Agamben, *Homo Sacer*, p. 4.
43. Agamben, *Homo Sacer*, pp. 4–5.
44. Agamben, *Homo Sacer*, p. 187.
45. Agamben, *Homo Sacer*, p. 188.
46. Agamben, *Homo Sacer*, p. 4.
47. Agamben, *Homo Sacer*, p. 164. Here Agamben is referring particularly to the "neomort" (bodies kept alive for transplant), the overcomatose patient (eg. Karen Quinlan) who wavers between life and death, and the *"faux vivant"* (the body kept alive soley by artificial life-support); all of whom are capable of being killed by medical decision, in other words, without the commission of homicide.
48. See Kirk Makin, "Top court speaks out against execution," *Globe and Mail*, Friday, February 16, 2001, A1, A9.
49. See William Safire "Kangaroo Courts," *The New York Times*, November 26, 2001.
50. Quoted in Bryan Robinson, "Due Process or Star Chamber? Critics Worry Military Tribunals Will Violate Terror Suspects' Rights," http://abcnews.go.com/sections/us/DailyNews/military tribunals011115.html. See "Military Tribunals in Bush Country: News articles about the new American police state," on http://ccadp.org/policestate.htm.
51. Ibid.
52. See Sheldon Alberts, "Ottawa files a rare note of protest after citizen is denied access to consular officials," *The National Post*, Wednesday, January 2, 2002, A1, A10; and Colin Freeze, "U.S. jailing of Canadian man may breach consular treaty," *The Globe and Mail*, Thursday, January 3, 2002, A10.
53. Under the order which established the military tribunals, the president determines who is considered a terrorist suspect to be detained by the Department of Defense. See Bryan Robinson "Due Process or Star Chamber?" For a Girardian take on the post-Sept. 11 scapegoating of Arab and Muslim Americans, see Larry George, "9–11: Pharmacotic War," *Theory and Event*, 5(4) (http://www.muse.jhu.edu/journals/theory_and_event/v005.4).

CHAPTER 8

Fictional Development Sovereignties

CHRISTINE SYLVESTER

"Development" is a realm of what has been described as a vast Empire of post-imperialist international relations.[1] It is the domain of information and economy that produces and ultimately sustains a global order of uneven progress. The development enterprise scatters widely across a decentered and deterritorializing Empire. It stretches from the northern to southern portions of the globe, where the poor people supposedly cluster, and from western to eastern European countries accessioning after the Cold War. "Over there" and "over here" in the more privileged quadrants, an intellectual cum organizational apparatus partially generates and administers knowledge/power machineries that "create the very world [they] inhabit" as "permanent, eternal, and necessary."[2] Necessary to what? To a global hierarchy of production and consumption.

The chief administrators of development within Empire are the once-were colonial powers as well as key contemporary financial giants—IMF, World Bank, and WTO—national overseas aid departments, nongovernmental organizations, corporations and banks, local governments and bureaucracies, plus scores of consultants and development experts. These comprise a development police force that both spreads and monitors the rule of uneven progress with words about the good market, good governance, sustainability, poverty reduction, adjustment, liberalization, and so on. Inducing development conflicts as it goes along, Empire also mutes conflict, to some degree, through aid and weapons. Further, it keeps its development wing going by creating subjectivities, "needs, social relations, bodies and minds"[3] aspiring to or celebrating a certain kind of progress. The logic seems to predict "smooth space" in a world where, in fact, African societies both experience and elude imperial policing, while winning East Asians wrap imperium around local practices that resist and embrace the international flow of ideas, products, and people.[4]

Despite the incongruities, the empire of development within Empire has its ways with people. Its multi-pitched voice is sovereign. Marxists and neoliberals alike pledge allegiance to development progress, while post-colonial analysts answer back to histories of the colonial phase of imperium written from western perspectives.[5] Those taking one of many postmodern turns are fascinated by such icons of imperial development fiction as the "peasantry,"[6] the "grass-roots,"[7] the "expert,"[8] and the idea of "helping" the other.[9] With humanitarian intervention *au courant* in these quarters of Empire, as "alternative development" used to be,[10] the development circle closes around itself. Explains Jenny Edkins, "just as the role of the revolution in the transition to modern state rule can be seen as an ironic strengthening of central authority, so the role of humanitarian intervention can be seen as a tightening of a global structure of authority and control."[11]

The sovereignty of development leaps off library shelves and surrounds its students. Great works and great development theories written from rationalist, scientific, machine mindsets reign. Other literatures about development—novels, poetry, memoirs, drama—are tagged as "art," the stuff of dreams and memories, colors and prosaics, entertainment, and extracurricularity. These are unsovereign vehicles and voices. Rationalists, maintains Dipesh Chakrabarty, think their way "gives us some kind of X-ray vision into the social, that it gives us access to a level of reality somehow deeper than the everyday."[12] This reality may not be more vivid than one depicted in a memoir, novel, or poem, but it is deemed more accurate, and it is organized in development spheres of Empire around and by language used in control-validating ways. Indeed, Hardt and Negri argue that language and communications control "the sense of direction of the imaginary that runs throughout communicative communities."[13] Louiza Odysseos adds that rationalist progress "dismisses mythic and comic narratives as valid perspectives on social life…"[14] as though narrative did not underlie all enterprises that use language to communicate stories about truth, and as though words were not "meeting points and places of rest. We meet there, in and across cultures and languages, to unload the burden of mental images. This constant unloading ties words to a complex web of myths."[15] With narrowed development vocabularies, which control the range and ordering of words that qualify as useful, spaces are smoothed around populations whose stories and lives are fitted to and for them.

It is the seemingly unsovereign fiction of sovereign development within Empire—the myths promulgated and the ways readers/writers/texts create, change, and defy them—that occupies our attention here. I have two literary events of the realm to explore: Sekai Nzenza Shand's *Songs to an African Sunset: A Zimbabwean Story* and Mira Stout's *One Thousand Chestnut Trees*.[16] Both are autobiographical memoirs revolving around travel from developed lands to poorer homelands of childhood (Zimbabwe) or to an imagined geospace (Korea) not heretofore experienced directly. The travelers are not entirely of the places they inhabit or visit. They live within internations of globalization, somewhere between the center and the periphery, between west and somewhere else, in shadows cast by police lights, and in the words that form on soft paper instead of authoritative newsprint. Nonetheless, they are always already in the Empire, even when trying to escape it by going "home" to a less imperial local. The crux of the issue here is not only how Empire is revealed, but whether these travelers realize that their books are addressing, writing, rewriting, or resisting development sovereignties within Empire .

Sovereignty and Home

Nzenza-Shand and Stout set out to go home—to a place that is sovereign in our minds. "Home" to the former is Matabeleland, Zimbabwe, the rural place of childhood and immediate family. It is an outpost of Empire and of development logic within Empire, that is to say, it is one of those places globalization forgot.[17] Nzenza-Shand is a citizen of Australia, who has a PhD from the University of Melbourne, worked for a while as a nurse in Britain, and has married a white man. She is of Australia and of Zimbabwe. Stout hails from the East Coast of the United States, where she was born to a Korean mother and an American father. She lives in a city where sovereign progress struts the streets and desires simultaneously to stay put and to go imperial "over there" and put everything straight. Traveling to Korea is a trip to a past she has not directly known but senses she cannot fully develop without.

Zimbabwe, the former colony of Britain in Southern Africa, is the kind of place that swarms with development helpers, adjusters, and defiers and yet edges downward over time rather than up. South Korea is an OECD country in East Asia with a split soul: its other half glares at it, or pines for it, across a demilitarized zone. A fast developer in the 1980s, this former colony of Japan, and military center for the United States, exemplifies for the core what can be accomplished when modernization is embraced aggressively, single-mindedly, and also with a felicitous mix of Asian and Western values. Zimbabwe, by contrast, is a lament.

Off go two women to validate or refute constructed memories, myths, and localities about their homely "other halves." We see them setting out on a "...private hoo, hoo of passion/amplified across countries/and continents, the breath taken..."[18] Daughters on the "History Train," with its "upholstery coming unpicked," have a chance to "Imagine marrying your cousin, the one/displaced up or sideways..."[19] From afar, Stout imagines everyone in Korea in the mold of the odd uncle who comes to the USA periodically like some displaced skeleton. For much of her tale, he is someone she implicitly would not wish to marry:

> At last our breakfast arrived. Still feeling unwell after his long journey, my uncle faced a modest fried egg and toast. He hesitated a moment, but with a final scowl of concentration seized the sides of the egg white with his fingers, and crammed the whole object in his mouth in one piece. Head bowed and cheeks bulging, he chewed the egg penitently, as if ridding his plate of an obstacle...Never having seen an egg dispatched in this way, I began to laugh, but my mother's eyes stopped me like a pair of bullets.[20]

Nzenza-Shand views her husband, Adam, as the one the village back home probably regrets seeing a favorite daughter marry:

> Uncle Chakwanda, who had arrived from the main village, appointed himself mechanic to our stricken automobile. He had never fixed anything more complex than a windlass or a paraffin lamp but led Adam away in search of "parts" to fix the oil sump. Adam followed him, his shoulders drooping, all his power as a civilized Westerner visibly ebbing away. An hour later the two of them returned with a half-tube of two-party epoxy cement, with which Uncle Chakwanda intended to restore the damage to the pride of German engineering—the BMW.
>
> "It will never work. This old man must be bloody crazy," said Adam, laughing without an ounce of mirth. "Has anybody else got a car around here? Maybe there's a farmhouse somewhere that has a phone."
>
> Everyone laughed at the sight of the white man covered in oil and dust, looking wildly around for some sign of hope—an electric light in the distance, an aeroplane flying overhead, some ingenious technology to help him out of his predicament.[21]

The predicaments of travelers sizing up their displaced "cousins": cultural gaucheness from outpost development empire comes to the core and core rationalities become gauche in an imperial outpost. Nzenza-Shand and Stout are more or less aware of the ironies surrounding their representations of the other. But Sampson asks a broader question: "...Could you greet each other?/Or does that fundamental/correlation impel you/past the words' handshake/clicking the childsafe/locks on the door?..."[22] Is travel through spaces of development empire an exercise in being at home wherever Empire is (smooth), going home to authentic narratives Empire has managed to separate well (escape); or, a case of writing oneself out of the problematic of Empire and it development through "...letters that don't arrive..."[23]

A Korea Odyssey

> After my uncle's return to Seoul, life in Manhattan resumed its former shape as if he had not been there are all...When I tried to picture Hong-do's life in Seoul, I could not...Besides, it was too draining to imagine a world beyond New York.[24]

The imperial seal operates to close off a self-satisfied, but unfulfilled core from places beyond the horizon where ships drop into hot, demon-infested hells, planes do not fly, and letters do not arrive—indeed, "...I sat down to think of things to tell my uncle –in the letter I never wrote to him..."[25] On his last visit to the USA, odd uncle had transmogrified into a person Stout yearned to remember, because "Korea had grown nearly real to me...[and] I suspected that when he left, the floating embryo of coded dynasties, diagrams, religious precepts and war-dates might perish. Korea would exist only in the unfinished, idealized monument my mother's memory had carved...."[26] Would this uncle remember her and that big American city he once inhabited or would he be swallowed up by the mysteries of distance? "I wanted to be there in the background, and to appear across the table from him, years later. But I couldn't break into his memories. Too much flesh, and glass, and time sealed them."[27] The coda are fragile. They can smooth out through forgetting or smooth idealized rememberings. In either case, Stout fears that she will not be able to control her memory and thus could become a pawn in someone else's hoo hoo of passion, someone else's story.

Our heroine's initial attempts to remember her uncle and his ways and her efforts to keep in distant "touch" across Empire reduce to a gesture of multiculturalism: she visits a local Korean restaurant. Her gastronomical romp with the far off does not quite work because it is disembodied— "without him the experience felt somewhat hollow."[28] Without him, the food of his land is deficient, for "it" cannot compensate for her lack of knowledge of him, for her tendency, as Uma Narayan puts it in another context, to eat more than she understands.[29] He is a necessary ingredient of her story, her place in Empire, her understanding of the world, and her tastebuds. With him, she might just unload a burden of mental images, travel

well, cross the Empire. Without him, the "flimsy template of Korean awareness dissolved quickly…"[30]

"…Displaced Up or Sideways…"[31]

"Progress" of an imperial-twisting kind intervenes. Moving flats within New
York, Stout finds herself with a garbage strike in the new neighborhood,
which sends up "an almighty stench of food, cooked and rotting," a "frighten-
ing-looking gas stove," and a bathroom in which "toilet-flushing involved two
trips to the kitchen tap with a bucket."[32] Food from elsewhere wafts unlovely:
"I awoke in the morning lightly coated in a dew of congealed felafel exhala-
tion…"[33] Although the Manhattan side of Empire has myths of hierarchy and
separation to uphold, Stout's whiffs and chores of common urbanity have her
and her uncle "moored in the same harbour on separate submarines…I invited him aboard my vessel, he never stayed long; he seemed to know about
the leaks. I should have done better; made the necessary repairs to accommodate him."[34] The challenges and words could have met up.

His spot in Empire nudges the center outwards and "home" in a homely
way, through her mother. It is not that something definitive happens that
fuels the journey to Seoul. The demands of life in New York undo Stout, and
from a mother's unplumbed history rises a ghost of an alternative. A ghost it
is only, for mother has never sent up romantic images of herself and Korea.
She turns her head away from her daughter's polite kisses. She uses the word
"respect" in ways that have diminishing resonance in student-revolutionary
America—"to me, it meant politeness; to her, it meant *filial piety*—children
revering their parents. How did one revere?"[35] Mother is reserved and still
about her past, with reference points so elsewhere that she thinks learning
modern American literature is "a colossal waste of time."[36] One might say
that she is a guardian of alien cultural riches, a silent emissary for words that
she assumes her western rationalist daughter should but cannot appreciate.[37]

Still, with New York merging into Seoul surreptitiously, and with "[m]y
heart…an empty frame, waiting,"[38] Stout strikes out for Korea, carrying
with her that naïve aspiration so characteristic of imperial relations: "I
might begin to build a sort of makeshift bridge from West to East, between
my mother and myself."[39] Stout can pinpoint this smoothing desire as an
"over-optimistic, even a grandiose idea,"[40] one that enables her, perhaps, to
unload a burden and greet the other. Unlike the tourist passing through exotic places, mucking them up, and coming home to the myriad imagined
safe spots of the imperial core, she glimpses the anti-imperial imperative: "I
might have to change."[41] At the same time, she does not yet realize that her
mother's archaic tone, her uncle's oddities, are not of some time prior to the
cool contempt of New York or belonging to some place of quaintness. They

are the "now" Stout seeks both to integrate and to escape. Chakrabarty says more broadly that "the archaic comes into the modern, not as a remnant of another time but as something constitutive of the present."[42] And those things archaic and now—those things static yet covariant in fragmentary ways—stand as challenges to any sovereignty that would sweep away the past, prescribe the best future, and dominate the present.

Stout's history train takes her into the mother's past, to the girl who is six in 1936 and learning the Japanese tea ceremony, to the girl on the verge of womanhood at fourteen, who loves Seoul but learns to hail an empire of "'*Hai*' Yes, to everything in Japanese but to feel '*Anio*', No, in Korean, in our hearts."[43] She becomes a woman of twenty in 1950, who witnesses pandemonium in Seoul and hears her father ask an old man near him: "'What is happening?...' 'They say the Communists will be here by sunset. Everyone is heading south. Look at them panic!'"[44] She is at the US airbase at Kimpo during the ensuing war, working as a secretary, and eating Spam with mashed potatoes, when the Chinese "volunteers" march on Seoul. Then, '[t]he Americans on the base [became]...dispirited and sour. I wondered at their outward indifference to the refugees, and regretted some of the men's complacency toward the decimation of the people and country they had come to protect. I overheard some of them expressing hatred for Korea."[45] She is in Pusan then, recalling with the hindsight of the present that "Korea was being subjected to the heaviest and most continuous bombing ever recorded in history."[46] She is there on the airstrip in Pusan, violin-case by her side in July 1951, suddenly about to depart for Columbia University on a full music scholarship. "The scale of my voyage only then sank in to me, and I felt a sudden pang of fear, mixed with chagrin, guilt and bursting hope."[47]

Fear. Fear is everywhere in the Empire. But who narrates here? Where is she placed? Who is moving, traveling on "the Disneyland-blue Korean Air jumbo?..." "Already the world's parameters were shifting in a weird direction."[48] "*Prease fasten your seatbewts fo randing. Komapsumnida!*"[49] Randing rhere? Stout sees the high-rise apartment buildings of Seoul, each a twin to the one next to it. "You knew where you were because there was an enormous number, at least forty feet high, painted on the side of every building, as if designed so that airline pilots could orient themselves at fifteen thousand feet."[50] Inside one of these now, "the sound of Schumann [was] being played vigorously on a piano in the next room."[51] Breakfast for most of the family consisted of rice, fish, and hot kimchi. "The room was lined with many books in a variety of languages."[52] "...I could have been in Los Angeles, Bonn, or Buenos Aires."[53] The Empire is here in its ubiquitous designs for urban living.

Development is seemingly everywhere too: in western fashions, in the upcoming Seoul Olympics, in pro-democracy reforms cautiously undertaken by one of the last military leaders of the country. Even her uncle, Hong-do, tells a development tale that could be a set piece from the World Bank:

> "The press is already much freer than it was. Legislation has been passed to improve conditions and wages for workers… . The age limit for travel has been lowered to thirty from forty-five."
> "There was a ban on travel?"
> "Yes, foreign travel. You could only go away on business before. To strengthen the economy. Ploughing tourist money back into the domestic sector. I hear it's still hard to get a passport unless you're rich, with connections, but that will soon be relaxed. All the protectionist markets are being opened up now that redevelopment is nearly complete," said Hong-do, smoking a Marlboro with the window cracked open."[54]

Little doubt that his Korea is a proud and rising star of the Empire, complete with fading memories and cigarettes dangling from its modern mouth.

Stout, though, is "slightly miffed imagining that tourists must mistake Seoul for a newly-minted city, aping the commercial development of the rest of the world."[55] She wants to protect Korea from corruption. But, it is too late. The Empire is a flowing and corrupting phenomenon. Asking to see the house where her grandparents hid when the North invaded Seoul in the early 1950s, she is told that "[t]he whole character of the place has changed. The low houses and courtyards are replaced with chain-link fence and ugly warehouses."[56] Development has been through this imperial space. New York arrived long before Stout did.

Stout does not see this. She waxes romantic about Korea and its effects on people. Uncle Hong-do is no longer the outpost bumpkin stumbling around New York, but "utterly friendly, direct, and uncomplicated."[57] In Seoul, he seems "grown up"[58] and so does she. See how easy it is: people from different parts of Empire successfully influence each other's development. It makes for a dreamy, smooth narrative. Yet, even she has to admit that the dynamic must be more complicated than this; she cannot really "work out the reason for the change between us…"[59] She has packed well and is growing up, but she misses some tools necessary to cross the Empire, be herself within it, while casting a critical eye on its mythologies.[60] In other words, Stout is traveling spaces that pose a difficult art of appropriate engagement; yet, she is not world-traveling in ways that could call the sovereignty of imperial myths into question.

"Seoul, Cradled in the Lap of the Blue Zig-zagging Mountains, Looked Transformed"[61]

Stout sits listening to AFKN (American Forces Korean Network) news in the background while her hosts explain their relationship with the development empire: "Our ideal is the Choson dynasty: our age of enlightenment...when the arts and sciences flourished under King Sejong the Great. So much of our culture has been wiped out by war and invasion that we have become tenacious about our heritage."[62] Never mind that the late Choson era is known for unprecedented moral laxity, overindulgence by elites, and a decadence with few bounds—conditions that helped pave the road to Japanese colonization. Stout's elite hosts view American forces as another temporary element in a history ("until our stability is more concrete"[63]) leading inexorably back to native forms of enlightenment. After the American license plates vanish, like the Japanese emperor did earlier, the mythologies of the hermit Choson kingdom can replant the soil; for "we do not want the American way of life; the cult of the individual, the broken families, high crime and drug abuse, the uneducated masses."[64] Yet, the project of validating local culture "confirms the 'powers of the West' even as it tries to challenge it."[65] Her hosts would retain "the sit-coms, and the American pizza chains, and pop music, and fashions, which are not *all* bad."[66] The zero-sum scenario casting imperial culture against local ways is not threatened, apparently, by the mall-crazy consumerism one sees in Korea. The product space can be smooth while the cultural spaces are idealized into places well apart: "We believe in the old ways of respect and selflessness."[67]

Stout is not fully persuaded. "But what about the role of women? You work outside the home, Mrs. Park, isn't that contradictory to the Confucian way, where women stay home and must obey men?" Mrs. Park cocked her head to one side. "Yes, but we pick what we like best about Western culture, and leave out that which does not suit us."[68] A moment later, she relates a similar contradiction enacted by Korea's university students: "they have demonstrations in support of traditional Korean farming methods, but spend their money on American fast food and T-shirts with English slogans printed on them, and some poor girls have double-eyelid operations to look more Western..."[69] Myths develop on all sides—myths of glocalizing choices, of resistance, of selected cooperation. The webs of informational economy spin.

Although Stout has her moments of critique, she has little to say about the class she is running with in Korea. Awaiting a colleague at the Regency Hotel, she remarks that her surroundings "happened to be owned by Hong-do's mother-in-law, along with a petroleum processing plant, shipbuilding company, construction business, fibre-optic manufacturing base, tennis racquet factory, sport-shoe factory, and bicycle business."[70] In other words, Hong-do's mother-in-law is a *chaebol* owner! She is highly placed with one of the major corporate conglomerates on the Korean development scene, one of the megabusinesses accused of nepotism and corruption, but without which, the Korean tiger could not have emerged with such development elan. This means that Hong-do, the erstwhile odd uncle from some corner of the known world is, in fact, a higher flier than his Big Apple niece in the core. Stout will know something of his life—"[c]leaning staff dressed like organ-grinder monkeys in ubiquitous white gloves and bellhop hats"[71] —from New York, where stretch limos purr down the avenues to watering holes in establishments cousin to the Regency.

Stout wants only the cultural pluses of Korea, not the nuances that provide any culture with"justifications for practices or institutions that were unjust and exclusionary and worked to disempower and marginalize a great many of the inhabitants…"[72] She is the American discovering good-hearted Koreans and the cream of their political economy. She thus stands in indignation at a memorial to a Korean queen who died at the hands of Japanese imperialists. "Why," she wants to know, " is there not more information?"[73] on this atrocity? To Narayan, "the religious or metaphysical views of an elite social group at a particular historical moment may be taken as the defining components of the 'world views' of all…"[74] And thus Miss Cho, Stout's personal guide, tells Stout that "[e]very Korean schoolchild knows the significance of this place"…"Maybe we don't care enough what outsiders think."[75] That "we." Whoever "we" is, Stout aches to be part of "it," an insider to what seems the great, united, and subordinated story creating "an emerging, and alien, feeling of fraternity."[76]

Perhaps Stout cannot move beyond a romanticizing solipsism while she is in a world city that parallels New York. The food in Seoul elicits some sense of home. A concert at the National Theatre is a *déjà vu*—even though she has not seen that type of performance before—"for some reason, it did not *feel* as foreign as it looked and sounded."[77] An evening of entertainment ends with the popular folk tune *Arirang* and Stout, again with romantic aplomb, tells us "I knew I had never heard the song before, but the melody penetrated the pit of my stomach, and inexplicable tears ran down my face as the entirely Korean audience stood together and sang it."[78] Entirely Korean? Is anyone "entirely"? Stout steadies her imperial rebel cum "bridge-building" lenses.

She is tempted for a short while to stay on in the Korean homebase she has invented. Yet, Stout believes uncritically that to do so would be disastrous. It "would involve a renunciation of everything and everyone I knew. Telephone wire and written correspondence could not conquer the distances involved…[I]n choosing to stay, one's commitment to exile would need to be total; a form of taking the veil."[79] To stay in Korea, even the Korea of elites, requires her to lose sovereign development! And under the veil is another fear: The local will stare back or, worse, ignore her: What if "[e]yes brushed over you as if you did not quite count, you were an aberration, a blip that would be smoothed over by the next manifestly white or coloured face that came into view."[80] It is all too much. Even smoother myths of the old homestead win out.

Stout takes a last trip with her uncle to the mountains. It is her final opportunity to become "displaced up or sideways."[81] Stout tells us that still "I longed for something impossible: for a gentle unfolding of secrets; for a geological deceleration of time; for scars to be reversed; for my family to undie."[82] As she "unloads the burden of mental images…" that tie "words to a complex web of myths,"[83] she finds myth all the way down. Korea is a myth. In fact, it is "fiery and cold, insular and gregarious, ancient and modern, urban and rural, frenetic and serene, ugly and beautiful, refined and earthy, spicy and bland, drunken and monastic, sentimental and harsh…"[84] Her desire "to graft onto Korea"[85] is also a myth: "…I might always be looking through a pane of glass, at a slight remove from whatever joys and tests lay in store. Or perhaps that was an excuse:"[86]

> Sitting next to my uncle, I felt suddenly far away from him. He was sewn tightly into this landscape with many invisible threads, too closely stitched in to see it the way I did, upside-down and sideways like an astronaut in zero gravity. Nothing could cut him loose from it the way I was now, floating and twisting in the slipstream of this aborted mission. Cool, minute particles of detachment started gathering around me as I sat in the car. I felt empty, as if a part of me had already left, and had boarded the aeroplane back West… although I'd experienced tantalizing moments of familiarity, it was also the most alien place I had ever known.[87]

In the end, Stout produces Korea as sufficiently alien from her "true" world, from the production of imperial development with which she is familiar. She takes her hoo and goes "home." The Empire narrows her words, restakes its ground, cuts off the letters, and hugs her with the detachment of an anthropological perspective, which has seen the other and has bowed to its separateness in respect.[88]

A Zimbabwean Story

> It was one of those spectacular postcard images: the Zimbabwean sun was slowly turning into a huge red ball on the horizon. Everything around us glowed as we jumped over puddles of water, following the narrow path through tall green grass.[89]

Nzenza-Shand can readily imagine the world beyond Melbourne, Australia, where she lives. Unlike Stout *en voyage* to Korea, "[m]emories of my childhood flooded my thoughts, just as the sunset bathed the granite boulders on the nearby hillside."[90] Nzenza-Shand is home in Zimbabawe partly on a journey of commiseration for relatives who had passed away recently due to AIDS, the health scourge of this imperial outpost. (AIDS—illness in general—is something that Stout does not mention with reference to her trip "home" to Korea.) Nzenza-Shand is also going on a journey of self-hood through a "roots experience" that confronts hybrid identity in an Empire of spaces policed to be separate.

During her years in Melbourne, Nzenza-Shand was bombarded with questions about her culture and background, the types of questions that Narayan sees heaped onto those westerners see as authentic insiders.[91] "What is Africa like? Do you go back to your village?... . What is African food like? ...How far is Zimbabwe from Rwanda?"[92] She is meant to be an expert on a whole continent, one about which there is relatively little information circulating through Empire, except news of wars and development deficiencies. Not being in the dark about Empire and its effects, the privileged, developed, and controlling local of Australia becomes Nzenza-Shand's space of darkness:

> In Melbourne, I had once joined a women's co-operative where I was identified as an NESB, which stood for Non-English Speaking Background. But I did not want labels. What my Australian women friends did not know was that I started learning to speak English on my father's lap, long before teachers at the mission school taught me how to behave like a 'civilised' English person. I did not view myself as an NESB and I really did not like being called ethnic, black or disadvantaged.[93]

Defiantly a woman beyond Empire, unfooled by the smooth spaces created by moving goods and people, money, and ideas, Nzenza-Shand knows she is a label, a non, and ultimately a myth: "Oh, I wish I could come with you to see the lions and the elephants...May I come and stay with you if I ever decide not to go to Bali?"[94] Imperial words unburden themselves and stick in her side.

Yet Nzenza-Shand, Ms Right-On resister, also desires Empire for awhile, "wanting desperately to be Australian."[95] The imperial center seeks out peripheral culture and the outpost wants a center spot. "But I also worried that somehow these people felt privileged to have me around because, in their eyes, I was different and exotic."[96] She, a celebrity from fashionably poor parts of Empire, uses imperial informationalizing channels to move along the economic hierarchy as the sister from afar with "rich yuppie friends."[97] There is an echo in the chamber: Miss Cho tells Stout that "If the West doesn't know who we are, so what? We know."[98]

"We." A person of Nzenza-Shand's appearance, gender, and culture finds herself in an imperial museum, where visitors gawk at and intrude upon the not-we. "Being black, African and a woman was enough for people to feel that they could ask about my personal life in public. Going back to Zimbabwe meant that I would be anonymous."⁹⁹ The escape: the inter-territorializing masking device. Meanwhile, Stout seeks less anonymity by going to Korea. The two do not meet up, but the myths they stalk will intersect.

Going Back to Commerce

Nzenza-Shand's return to Zimbabwe commences in rural mountains, a kindred place to Stout's ending spot. Mother lives here. The sagas of daily life unfold familiarly here. Development lessons of rural Africa are also rife, or not, as the case may be. Until 1980, white settler Rhodesians were the developers, backed up from the imperialist center by the British government. Zimbabweans take up the wand next, with the well-wishes of the world, and emerge from sanctions into a heavily globalising Empire. In other words, as Korea experiences a tremendous push toward industrialization, Zimbabwe becomes a state subject to the development practices of a post-imperialist, and somewhat post-state Empire.

Nzenza-Shand knows the postcolonial development logic for outback Empire from first-hand experiences: in July 1996, she worked in the northern district of Omay in Zimbabwe, "as one of the 'Western' aid workers committed to sustainable development in the region."¹⁰⁰ Omay is what she refers to as a forgotten region composed of a forgotten group of Tonga people in predominantly Shona- and Ndebele-speaking Zimbabwe. Post-independence, a place like this is a feeding ground for practitioners of development, each carrying a different version of sovereign progress in their words:

> "We will teach the Tonga how to farm," declared a zealous young aid worker in an air-conditioned office in Melbourne. "We will build schools for them," said his counterpart in Oslo. "They do not have cattle because of the tsetse flies, so let's give them tractors to plough the land," said a New Yorker. A group of English workers from the Save the Children Fund flew to Omay and began to teach the locals how to grow vegetables. UNICEF introduced feeding programmes for all children under five. And a women's church group in Denmark sent the Tonga truckloads of secondhand clothes."¹⁰¹

Nzenza-Shand is distressed by what she sees but is also part of the privileged wing of development: "There I was, dressed up like a Westerner—sunhat, sunglasses, brown safari skirt and blouse, and comfortable walking boots."¹⁰² She records the problems that people in Omay report to her, "[f]eeling guilty and helpless"¹⁰³ one minute and then enjoying "a double gin and tonic on a comfortable chair overlooking the vast expanse of water out in front of me. Every so often, a speedboat full of tourists on their way out for sundowner drinks or their evening game-viewing would disturb the glassy surface of Lake Kariba."[104] She is a rationalist. She is a helper. She is a myth. She resists myths.

Now, Nzenza-Shand is with her mother, far from the din of development music, far from the aid workers and the tractors and the sundowners. Abiding by none of the development creeds that have ensnared her daughter, Mother is up early to conduct some business in her own way. She will exchange an old steer for a heifer, "or, failing that [find]…someone who would simply sell a heifer without entering into an exchange."[105] There is much languid conversation on the walk down the hill: remembrances chug along on the history train. The world of myth is openly omnipresent, although a bit tarnished by a healthy local scepticism that is often denied imperial outpost societies by sovereignties of rationalism (West/the rest):

> "Do water spirits still take people away to train them as traditional healers?"
> I asked Amai.
> "Did they ever do that?"
> "Well, when we were growing up there were always these stories in which we were advised to stay away from deep waterholes if we did not want water spirits to capture us. Because if they did, no-one saw or heard about you for many years, but your people would know that the water spirits were keeping you safe and training you to be a traditional healer…"
> "I think that may have happened long ago—before our great-grandparents were born," said Amai. Trying to speak to her about myths and folktales never yielded much: she was always sceptical.[106]

She and her neighbors are not sceptical about the economic options provided by imperial international relations. Emilia will sell a heifer to Nzenza-Shand's mother and use the money to "go to South Africa and buy a sewing machine. Then I will be able to make school uniforms and sell them at the local schools."[107] Nzenza-Shand remarks that Emilia is just "one of the many hard-working women whose economic survival depended on buying goods in South Africa or Botswana and reselling them in Zimbabwe,"[108] often for three times the price they paid. Of course, there are opportunity costs: a wait in queue for a visa, twelve hours on the bus, a night of fitful sleep on the floor of the bus station, a round of the outlets in Johannesburg in the morning, and back again on the bus to Zimbabwe. The informationalizing Empire makes the trip possible. The lower status of this imperial region makes the work necessary. An uneven distribution of technology and income makes the drudgery of this informal economic activity inescapable ("permanent, eternal"). But it is not smooth.

Outpost Parties
Nzenza-Shand does not spend her entire time, or even most of it, in the rural area of her birth. She lives with her husband in Harare. It is the mid-1990s, a time when supermarket shelves are stocked with imported and local goods brought in through the liberalized market. The buses are running. Architectures of the new Harare reach into the sky. From today's vantage point, it is remarkable to recall that in the early 1990s, the government of Robert Mugabe insisted that its economic development adjustments were "home grown." He boasted that he had not capitulated to the World Bank and the IMF. He was not facing externally imposed conditionalities. The "enlightened Marxist" was simply adjusting the economy on his own, at home, free of development pressures from Empire.

Today, of course, the productive economy of Zimbabwe has indisputably failed on nearly all dimensions. It has not moved in circular or lateral or webbing ways, as can happen across Empire, but has gone backward, downhill to the point of near overall collapse and certain collapse of the food-producing sector. The informational and market Empire may have been instrumental in tempting Mugabe into its web, but Empire is decentralized and Zimbabwe is its own place now, where "enlightened Marxism" turns cruel and despotic, and no one "out there" does much of anything about that: "[I]mperial power can no longer resolve the conflict of social forces through mediatory schemata that displace the terms of conflict [as, arguably, the Lancaster House Constitution establishing Zimbabwe did by wrapping conflictual issues of white properties and internal opposition within the black independence struggle in legal niceties]. The social conflicts that constitute the political confront one another directly without mediations of any sort. This is the essential novelty of the imperial situation"[109]

But it is still the mid-1990s and Nzenza-Shand parties in Harare. At one gathering, she learns that some women of new Zimbabwe are raunchy, sassy, and sexually confident: "A heavily pregnant woman in her early thirties…approaches the guests. Apart from a pair of lacy knickers and a bra, she is wearing nothing. Her abdomen and face have been painted with coloured designs. Some of the drawings on her stomach are almost pornographic."[110] It is a baby shower, Harare style. About fifty women are dancing together, some taking on male movements while others perform as women. One of Nzenza-Shand's dance partners, who is acting "male," announces her imminent departure:

"So soon?" I say. "It is only 7 p.m."

"I am not going home yet. You see, I promised my boyfriend that I would meet him for a drink at seven. I told my husband that I would be back by nine. I have two hours to be with my lover. So let me disappear."

"What if your husband comes by looking for you?" asks Rita, who has overheard her.

Tell him I have gone to the funeral of a colleague's relative."[111]

Like some women of Seoul, some Harare women try to pick and choose their identity components in ways that go unnoticed in Hardt's and Negri's account of Empire. Empire bears down on women as workers and shows the indistinguishability of economics and culture; yet, Empire can also offer women points of resistance. Those sad, ubiquitous funerals become excuses for escape, or the baby shower, which fulfills the old role of village aunts—helping a woman prepare for birth—becomes segmented into spaces where middle-class women also flaunt new economic and cultural power:

> They are mostly urban, middle-class women who, like me, have studied abroad and benefited from Zimbabwean independence; among them are lawyers, doctors, nurses, teachers and self-employed businesswomen. Many of them have a rural background like mine...these women only go back there occasionally—for a funeral, for instance.[112]

Here is the twist: "In comparison to their Western counterparts, these women's lives are quite comfortable. Most have a full-time housekeeper, nanny or gardener...the majority of women at this party have houses set on one or two acres, complete with swimming pool and tennis court."[113] And their baby shower is informational within Empire, which is to say it communicates words to and about what it means to be a confident, contemporary urban "woman."

Shift to the Australian High Commissioner's residence and a cocktail party for Australian and Zimbabwean rugby players. The company here is diplomatic, expatriot, government. The atmosphere is "very formal, restrained,"[114] and, "[t]here are only three black women here—myself, the wife of one of the Zimbabwean government officials and an elderly waitress."[115] Development scripts thrust knowledge/power brokers into arcadias of Empire. Meanwhile, the absent women may be at "home" taking lovers: "What do you think, Sekai? Are black men better at it? This is not the first time I have been asked that question."[116] Nor is it the first time she has been disenchanted by imperial company.

Of course, most Zimbabwean women are not at city parties. Their events are of a different nature and Nzenza-Shand knows this well. The relative struck down by AIDS has a second burial and with it a party of sorts: "In Shona culture, it is believed that when an adult dies his spirit wanders all over the place waiting to be united with the ancestors at a second burial ceremony; the ceremony is also a kind of homecoming for the spirit, who is reunited with his family. It was thus a time for celebration…"[117] In such ceremonies, it falls to the women to brew beer and to the widow to make a decision about her future. Will she "remain single or be inherited by a male member of the family?"[118] Traditions of yesteryear mingle with the information of today: "You will have to jump over Charles's possessions first before you choose a husband," said Vongai, who had flown in from Melbourne the evening before. Under her traditional wraparound cloth, she wore a pair of skin-tight bicycle shorts; she planned to sneak off for her daily jog later on."[119] Rudo, the widow in question, is in from New York and a United Nations position. "Why should I feel guilty?, "asked Rudo. "I have not been unfaithful to my late husband. I do not see why I cannot jump—or even fly!—over his possessions."[120] And she does so. But she will not take one of the local men for her new husband. "Who does she think she is?" I heard Uncle Chakwanda mutter. "A woman of her age cannot live without a man."[121] The myths carry on. The Empire does too and adds words to the other's songs, creating a medley of sovereignless sounds:

> At the end of this weekend, my sisters and I would all climb back into our four-wheel drives and return to Harare; some of us would then travel on to cold, rainy cities in Europe, Australia or the States, where we would not hear Shona spoken for months on end. I could not help wondering how much longer our homestead would exist; gradually, the village and all its people, myself included, were being swallowed up by modernity….I comforted myself with the reassuring thought that however far my journey took me, I would always be connected to this place.[122]

Fictions

> If the First World and the Third World, center and periphery, North and South were ever really separated along national lines, today they clearly infuse one another, distributing inequalities and barriers along multiple and fractured lines… . Empire is characterized by the close proximity of extremely unequal populations, which creates a situation of permanent social danger and requires the powerful apparatuses of the society of control to ensure separation and guarantee the new management of social space.[123]

Of course, we know about the interparticulations of contemporary life, the proximities, the dangers, the power, and the urge to separate and manage spaces if we cannot world-travel them in ways that hybridize our experiences and identities. Hardt and Negri want us to remember "the powerful apparatuses of the society of control to ensure separation."[124] They want us to see sovereignty simultaneously evaporating and holding on. They have us putting our ears to the ground to hear the Empire's politics of communication, which is a politics of fear and danger that segments us and governs us. One does not have to take on board the entire Hardt and Negri study to appreciate many of the chords it strikes.[125]

Stout and Nzenza-Shand go on journeys home that both reaffirm the sovereign and proclaim the hybrid—in themselves and in others around them. Of the two, Nzenza-Shand is the more savvy. She cannot hail from an imperial outpost that the centers most fear without recognizing that at the base of all the questions posed by her white friends in Melbourne and at the core of the welcome that she is given in some Australian circles is fear. From this fear emerges what Hardt and Negri refer to as "the problem of imperial administration," which is "to manage this process of integration and therefore to pacify, mobilize, and control the separated and segmented social forces... not by imposing a coherent social apparatus but by controlling differences."[126] Nzenza-Shand's differences are controlled in Australia and tolerated in a Zimbabwe that has fictionalized many of its own traditional sovereignties. In the telling of the stories to new audiences, the content shifts, the baby showers go naked, the widow remains on her own, and Mother is sceptical. Meanwhile, the information-brokering development types, from somewhere else in Empire, are excluded from good local parties. They do not see Charles' widow jump over his possessions or the running pants under wraparound skirts. Rather, they replay fusty parties of times past and try to control the goings on that have escaped their control.

Fittingly, Nzenza-Shand is in a quandry at the end of her journey:

Few people ventured up here; most of the villagers were content to look up occasionally from their toil in the fields to contemplate the talismanic mountain where the ancestors reposed. Once, like them, I had unthinkingly accepted the power of Dengedza [the mountain near her home village.] Now, full of Western learning and scepticism, I had to climb the mountain to feel impressed by it, crashing up through the undergrowth, putting families of quail to flight. And I didn't even know what to say to the ancestors when I got to the top.[127]

Words fail her. Her location is unsettled. The spaces are not smooth, authentic, or policed entirely by Empire. There is little development. There is development everywhere. Nzenza-Shand is of the Empire and at some distance from its cries for sovereignty. She is back and forth to and fro. She will leave Zimbabwe shortly, but she will not seek to escape letters to both places.

Stout is differently placed with her words and her worlds. Her background is more of a mystery to her, and, by implication, to the reader. We travel with her as she discovers Korea and embraces Korea and then escapes "home" to a center, where she thinks she will not have to occupy the same fearful contradictions that she finds in a Hermit Kingdom within Empire. She packs up her X-ray vision and takes the hoo of her imaginary to another place:

> "We're nearly home, " he said. His spirits had bounced back with typical Korean tenacity. I didn't know what had cheered him up. I still couldn't tell what he was thinking about. Remembering the night he'd left New York, with the cold threat of an indefinite parting and reproachful failure hanging in the air between us, it suddenly seemed a miracle that I should be here at all, and that we had even attempted what we had done, despite it having been a small fiasco.[128]

Stout's world has come full circle to itself. She has been in a fiasco "over there" and must get back to "over here," the place where things make sense. She must govern herself with the local effectiveness of Empire. In the end, it all comes down to the far-fetched, fictional prospect of her having to renounce everything and everyone if she stays in this ultimately unfathomable, unreadable land. It is better to catch the sovereignty of imperial administration. New York, here we come.

It is something of a pity that Stout and Nzenza-Shand perform their roles in this development drama so predictably. They are myths to themselves and to the readers who approach them. The African woman wryly sees through the smokescreens of the West, able to world-travel effectively—as her village neighbors are able to ship off to South Africa in order to get some business done—because she must do so to survive.[129] The Western woman with Asian eyes and a hybrid background is not able "to meet there, in and across cultures and languages, to unload the burden of mental images."[130] Her words simply do not fit the Korea she invents: "My uncle and I turned right at the next junction and joined a winking, swarming body of taillights and headlights that flowed into Seoul in an unintelligible language of motion."[131] Nzenza-Shand has one of many trips home. Stout has an unintelligible, winking escape.

Ah, but "in Empire, no subjectivity is outside, and all places have been subsumed in a general 'non-place.'"[132] Both Stout and Nzenza-Shand are part of the larger flows of populations and people that make all of us minorities in our places, whether we can see that or not.[133] Perhaps Hardt and Negri overstate the claim that "the exodus from localism, the transgression of customs and boundaries, and the desertion from sovereignty were the operative forces in the liberation of the Third World."[134] For it is hardly the case that Zimbabwe is liberated today, and hardly the case that the frantic pace in Seoul is all dynamism and excitement rather than some sacrifice of esthetics. Yet, it is a Korean Uncle who remains optimistic and in good spirits at the end. The Zimbabwean widow also does her duty to the village and remains autonomous from its controls. Women who travel traditions of baby showers recast them. These people have fictionalized the old sovereignties—be these the controls of tradition or of imperial development administration. Their texts are powerful, subversive in unplaces that evoke place, that resonate with myth, and that intersect elsewhere.

It is the non-place, then, that breeds new myths, new localisms, and new challenges to Empire. Letters from such places arrive via traveling interspatial relatives, who relate alternative development truths using seemingly other-than-rationalist sources. These tales and the practices behind them might be thought of as some of the immeasurables that Hardt and Negri spot across Empire.[135] Full of words that have no smooth spaces, the stories within stories, if not all those passing on the tales, resist narrowings of words and deeds. Gleefully at times, stubbornly most often, these stories mark out and glide onto non-places the rationalists fear: "Come on. We'll never make it at this rate. I hope there's a shelter somewhere if we get stuck," said Hong-do walking on ahead."[136]

Notes

1. Michael Hardt and Antonio Negri, *Empire* (Cambridge, Massachusetts: Harvard University Press, 2000).
2. Hardt and Negri, *Empire*, p. 11.
3. Hardt and Negri, *Empire*, p. 32.
4. See the critique, e.g., of Tarak Barkawi and Mark Laffey, "Retrieving theImperial: *Empire* and International Relations," *Millennium: Journal of International Studies*, 31(1), 2002:109–27.
5. Dipesh Chakrabarty, *Provincializing Europe: Postcolonial Thought and Historical Difference* (Princeton: Princeton University Press, 2000).
6. Arturo Escobar, *Encountering Development* (Princeton: Princeton University Press, 1994).
7. Christine Sylvester, "Development Poetics," *Alternatives*, 25(13), 2000:335–351.
8. Jane Parpart, "Deconstructing the Development 'Expert': Gender, Development and the 'Vulnerable Groups.' In *Feminism/Postmodernism/Development*, edited by Marianne Marchand and Jane Parpart (London: Routledge, 1995), pp. 221–243.
9. Marianne Gronemeyer, "Helping." In *The Development Dictionary: A Guide to Knowledge as Power*, edited by Wolfgang Sachs (London: Zed Books, 1992), pp. 53–69.
10. Jan Nederveen Pieterse, "My Paradigm or Yours: Alternative Development, Post-Development, Reflexive Development," *Development and Change*, 29, 1998:343–373.
11. Jenny Edkins, "Sovereign Power, Zones of Indistinction, and the Camp," *Alternatives* 25(1), 2000: 20.
12. Chakrabarty, *Provincializing Europe*, p. 239.
13. Hardt and Negri, *Empire*, p. 32.
14. Louiza Odysseos, "Laughing Matters: Peace, Democracy and the Challenge of the Comic Narrative," *Millennium: Journal of International Studies*, 30(3), 2001:710.
15. Costas Constantinou, "Hippopolis/Cynopolis," *Millennium: Journal of International Studies*, 30(3), 2001:788.

16. Sekai Nzenza-Shand, *Songs to an African Sunset: A Zimbabwean Story* (Melbourne: Lonely Planet Publications, 1997) and Mira Stout, *One Thousand Chestnut Trees* (London: Flamingo, 1997).
17. Neil Smith, "The Satanic Geographies of Globalization: Uneven Development in the 1990s," *Public Culture*, 10(1), 1997:169–189.
18. Fiona Sampson, "History Train," *Alternatives*, 25(3), 2000:285.
19. Sampson, "History Train."
20. Stout, *One Thousand*, p. 6.
21. Nzenza-Shand, *Songs*, pp. 28–29.
22. Sampson, 'History Train," p. 285. For another framing of these questions, see Sara Ahmed, *Strange Encounters: Embodying Others in Post-Coloniality* (London: Routledge, 2000), chapter 4.
23. Sampson, "History Train."
24. Stout, *One Thousand*, p. 18.
25. Stout, *One Thousand*.
26. Stout, *One Thousand*, p. 16.
27. Stout, *One Thousand*, p. 17.
28. Stout, *One Thousand*, p. 18.
29. Uma Narayan, *Dislocating Culture: Identities, Traditions, and Third World Feminism* (New York: Routledge, 1997), p. 183.
30. Stout, *One Thousand*, p. 18.
31. Sampson, "History Train," p. 285.
32. Stout, *One Thousand*, p. 20.
33. Stout, *One Thousand*, p. 21.
34. Stout, *One Thousand*, p. 28.
35. Stout, *One Thousand*, p. 52 [emphasis in original].
36. Stout, *One Thousand*, p. 52.
37. See Narayan, *Dislocating Cultures*, pp. 130–132.
38. Stout, *One Thousand*, p. 55.
39. Stout, *One Thousand*, p. 55.
40. Stout, *One Thousand*, p. 55.
41. Stout, *One Thousand*, p. 55.
42. Chakrabarty, *Provincializing Europe*, p. 251.
43. Stout, *One Thousand*, p. 121.
44. Stout, *One Thousand*, pp. 175–176.
45. Stout, *One Thousand*, pp. 215–216.
46. Stout, *One Thousand*, p. 219.
47. Stout, *One Thousand*, p. 225.
48. Stout, *One Thousand*, p. 229.
49. Stout, *One Thousand*, p. 230.
50. Stout, *One Thousand*, p. 232.
51. Stout, *One Thousand*, p. 233.
52. Stout, *One Thousand*.
53. Stout, *One Thousand*, p. 234.
54. Stout, *One Thousand*, pp. 236–237.
55. Stout, *One Thousand*, p. 237.
56. Stout, *One Thousand*, p. 244.
57. Stout, *One Thousand*, p. 243.
58. Stout, *One Thousand*.
59. Stout, *One Thousand*.
60. Christine Sylvester, *Feminist International Relations: An Unfinished Journey* (Cambridge: Cambridge University Press, 2002), chapter 14.
61. Stout, *One Thousand*, p. 242.
62. Stout, *One Thousand*, p. 247.
63. Stout, *One Thousand*.
64. Stout, *One Thousand*.
65. Narayan, *Dislocating Cultures*, p. 130.
66. Stout, *One Thousand*, p. 247 [emphasis in original].
67. Stout, *One Thousand*.
68. Stout, *One Thousand*, pp. 247–248.

69. Stout, *One Thousand*, p. 249.
70. Stout, *One Thousand*, p. 251.
71. Stout, *One Thousand*, p. 252.
72. Narayan, *Dislocating Cultures*, p. 129.
73. Stout, *One Thousand*, p. 254.
74. Narayan, *Dislocating Cultures*, p. 129.
75. Stout, *One Thousand*, p. 254.
76. Stout, *One Thousand*, p. 256.
77. Stout, *One Thousand*, p. 259.
78. Stout, *One Thousand*, p. 260.
79. Stout, *One Thousand*, p. 295.
80. Stout, *One Thousand*, p. 262.
81. Sampson, " History Train," p. 285.
82. Stout, *One Thousand*, pp. 311–312.
83. Constantinou, " Hippoppopolis," p. 788.
84. Stout, *One Thousand*, p. 323.
85. Stout, *One Thousand*.
86. Stout, *One Thousand*.
87. Stout, *One Thousand*, pp. 232–233.
88. Narayan, *Dislocating Cultures*, pp. 124–127.
89. Nzenza-Shand, *Songs*, p. 9.
90. Nzenza-Shand, *Songs*.
91. Narayan, *Dislocating Cultures*, p. 142.
92. Nzenza-Shand, *Songs*, p. 23.
93. Nzenza-Shand, *Songs*, p. 22.
94. Nzenza-Shand, *Songs*, p. 23.
95. Nzenza-Shand, *Songs*, p. 22.
96. Nzenza-Shand, *Songs*, p. 23.
97. Nzenza-Shand, *Songs*.
98. Stout, *One Thousand*, p. 266 [emphasis in original].
99. Nzenza-Shand, *Songs*, p. 24.
100. Nzenza-Shand, *Songs*, p. 203.
101. Nzenza-Shand, *Songs*, p. 202.
102. Nzenza-Shand, *Songs*, p. 203.
103. Nzenza-Shand, *Songs*, p. 219.
104. Nzenza-Shand, *Songs*, p. 219.
105. Nzenza-Shand, *Songs*, p. 178.
106. Nzenza-Shand, *Songs*, p. 181.
107. Nzenza-Shand, *Songs*, pp. 194–195.
108. Nzenza-Shand, *Songs*, p. 195.
109. Hardt and Negri, *Empire*, p. 393.
110. Nzenza-Shand, *Songs*, p. 154.
111. Nzenza-Shand, *Songs*, p. 163.
112. Nzenza-Shand, *Songs*, p. 157.
113. Nzenza-Shand, *Songs*.
114. Nzenza-Shand, *Songs*, p. 167.
115. Nzenza-Shand, *Songs*, p. 168.
116. Nzenza-Shand, *Songs*, pp. 174–175.
117. Nzenza-Shand, *Songs*, p. 221.
118. Nzenza-Shand, *Songs*, p. 222.
119. Nzenza-Shand, *Songs*, p. 224.
120. Nzenza-Shand, *Songs*, pp. 224–225.
121. Nzenza-Shand, *Songs*, p. 234.
122. Nzenza-Shand, *Songs*, p. 239.
123. Hardt and Negri, *Empire*, 335, pp. 336–337.
124. Hardt and Negri, *Empire*, p. 337.
125. Manfred Steger, Review of Hardt and Negri's *Empire*. *American Political Science Review*, 96(1), 2002:264–265.

126. Hardt and Negri, *Empire*, pp. 239–240.
127. Nzenza-Shand, *Songs*, pp. 238–239.
128. Stout, *One Thousand*, p. 324.
129. Christine Sylvester, "African and Western Feminisms: World-Traveling the Tendencies and Possibilities," *Signs: Journal of Women in Culture and Society*, 20(4), 1995:941–969.
130. Constantinou, "Hippopolis," p. 788.
131. Stout, *One Thousand*, p. 324.
132. Hardt and Negri, *Empire*, p. 353.
133. Etienne Balibar, " Ambiguous Universality," *Differences: Journal of Feminist Cultural Studies*, 7(1), 1995:48–74.
134. Hardt and Negri, *Empire*, p. 363.
135. Hardt and Negri, *Empire*, p. 357.
136. Stout, *One Thousand*, p. 318.

CHAPTER **9**

Creating/Negotiating Interstices
Indigenous Sovereignties

KARENA SHAW

Discourses and practices of sovereignty provide the most powerful—and perhaps most dangerous—of political terrains for marginalized groups. It is these discourses and practices through which some of the most important movements of the 20th Century were articulated, not least those of nationalism, anti-colonialism, and self-determination. Sovereignty has framed political possibility, enabling and legitimating resistances to hegemony and the emergence of new political agents and subjectivities. However, as many others have suggested, sovereignty remains at best an ambivalent discourse for marginalized peoples, deeply embedded as it is in an ontology that assumes and reproduces their marginalization.[1]

The ambivalent potential of sovereignty is expressed with unusual clarity in the lives and politics of indigenous peoples. It is no accident that this is the case: it was, after all, the "Savages of America" who constituted the "other" or border guard for some of the first, and still most powerful, articulations of the necessity and desirability of sovereignty.[2] And it is indigenous peoples in places such as North America who have perhaps most consistently not only experienced but constituted its violent undersides. The lives, politics, and selves of indigenous peoples thus express intricate terrains of power produced by discourses and practices of sovereignty. However, this is not to say that Aboriginal peoples have only been victims of sovereignty. Although produced as marginal by sovereignty discourse, indigenous people have creatively engaged their situated-ness through complex rearticulations of selves, communities, and power in and through these discourses and practices. Their struggles illustrate, in very concrete ways, both the potential and constraints embedded in them. Insofar as we seem to be living through a period characterized by the rearticulation of political possibility through and in relation to discourses and practices of sovereignty, this renders the struggles of indigenous peoples in, through, and against these discourses a vital site for thinking about the future of politics. In particular, the struggles of indigenous peoples provide a critical lens on sovereignty, revealing and politicizing the violences that have been its conditions of possibility. Their struggles thus pose important challenges to contemporary efforts to constitute new forms and practices of political authority in and through sovereignty, as well as revealing ways forward in relation to this terrain.

My analysis here rests upon an understanding of sovereignty as the discourses and practices through which political authority has been constituted and legitimated, particularly, at least since early modernity, in the form of the sovereign state. The same discourses and practices through which the sovereign state was articulated, though, have also been seized and deployed in relation to other efforts to constitute legitimate authorities, not least those seeking to resist or delegitimize assertions of sovereign authority over them. It is these discourses and practices that have constituted the political terrain of modernity, through which we have come to understand our selves—both individually and collectively—and the terrains of power and resistance that shape our lives. One of the most revealing accounts of how these discourses and practices work, and what their necessities and possibilities are, is that articulated by Thomas Hobbes in the early chapters of *Leviathan*. Although generally, more attention is paid to the structures of politics he sets out after Chapter 13, in the early part of his work, Hobbes articulates the conditions of possibility for political community, enacting the practice of sovereignty. This takes the form of the production of a shared ontology, expressed as human nature, which in turn establishes the necessity of a shared authority through which "natural" differences arising from human nature can be mediated. His practice of sovereignty—of the creation of the shared ontology that creates the conditions of possibility for, necessity and character of shared authority—then provides the sovereign state architecture as the necessary solution to the violent differences amongst individuals. In this way, through the practice of sovereignty, Hobbes establishes a shared ontology as the precondition for legitimate authority, the precise character of that ontology in turn dictating the form it must take: the sovereign state.

The discourses and practices of sovereignty as deployed by indigenous peoples continue to reproduce this architecture as articulated by Hobbes: they continue to rely on the production of shared ontologies, expressed as identities-in-difference, as the condition of possibility for claims to legitimate authority. My analysis here focuses on a specific moment of indigenous politics in Canada in an effort to explore some of the complex political terrains produced by this practice of sovereignty, both for indigenous peoples and for others who seek to think politically, and thus through and in relation to the architecture of sovereignty. Although indigenous politics provides my lens, the analysis is importantly focused on sovereignty and the dangers embedded in it, and on critical challenges this suggests. In other words, the critique is directed toward those of us who benefit from and might too quickly assume and reproduce the necessity of sovereignty, rather than toward those who have politicized it and are seeking to rearticulate it as a terrain of political possibility. The problem for indigenous peoples is less sovereignty *per se*, than the refusal of those who have benefited from it to seriously engage it as a problem, rather than assuming it as a solution.

The moment I focus on emerged in 1992, in relation to a referendum on proposed changes to the Constitution of Canada. The proposed changes included a Constitutional guarantee of the right to self-government for indigenous peoples in Canada. Perhaps surprisingly, the referendum was opposed by many indigenous groups in Canada. An examination of one of the groups who opposed the referendum, the Native Women's Association of Canada (NWAC), reveals how discourses and practices of sovereignty have shaped the political possibility for indigenous peoples, and some of the broader implications of their struggles to reshape this terrain in ways that will enable them to respond to the past violences effected by it. The chapter begins with an explication of NWAC's resistance to the referendum and moves on to an exploration of the terrain of politics it revealed, and the role of discourses and practices of sovereignty in shaping this terrain. It concludes with an argument that indigenous struggles through and against sovereignty pose some of the most important challenges, but also most suggestive resources, for thinking about the future of politics.

The Constitutional Referendum: Precipice or Turning Point?

In 1992, after long and often torturous negotiations, including the most extensive and intense debate over indigenous rights the country had ever seen, a new proposal for Constitutional reform in Canada, the Charlottetown Accord, was announced. To many people's surprise, it included a Constitutional guarantee of Aboriginal[3] peoples' right to self-government.[4] This appeared to be a crucial victory for Aboriginal peoples of Canada, and was touted as such extensively by the negotiators. With great fanfare, the Charlottetown Accord was presented to the public for approval in the form of a non-binding referendum. The guarantee of a right to self-government was only one of many proposed reforms, and Aboriginal leaders were concerned that if the referendum were defeated, this would be taken as a defeat for self-government, when the majority of voters might be rejecting it for other reasons. However, with their reservations expressed, they agreed to the referendum and launched into an intensive campaign to promote the Accord.

The referendum thus appeared set to be a crucial victory for Aboriginal politics. Although the exact meaning and effects of the self-government guarantee were far from clear, it indicated a formal foothold on which future relationships could be based, a potentially very different basis for interaction between the Canadian government and Aboriginal peoples. However, as the referendum campaign progressed, the inclusion of the self-government guarantee began to appear increasingly problematic. Not only was there significant opposition to the Accord for a variety of reasons unrelated to the guarantee, but, more importantly, one after the other, many Aboriginal organizations and groups began to speak out in opposition to the proposal. While this opposition was not unexpected by negotiators, it sent shock waves through many observers of Aboriginal politics. It appeared that just at the moment of unprecedented success, the identity of interests that facilitated the rise of Aboriginal politics to the national agenda was fracturing deeply, throwing into question the future of federal-level Aboriginal politics.

Things took a turn for the worse when the Referendum failed to pass for a variety of reasons. Initially, Ovide Mercredi, chief of the major pan-Indian organization that negotiated the Accord, accused Canadians of once again turning their backs on the plight of and their responsibilities to Aboriginal peoples. He called for a separate tally of the Aboriginal votes. However, when this tally came in he was forced to confront a very different picture:

> Of the Indians who did bother to cast a ballot, 62.1 percent were against the Charlottetown deal—an even higher percentage than among other Canadians. The Northwest Territories was the only place west of the Maritimes where a majority of Indian voters supported it. Saskatchewan Indians rejected their leaders' pleas and voted 55 percent against. Mercredi's home province of Manitoba led all comers with an 81.6 percent rejection. It was a different story amongst the Inuit, in whose isolated villages individual votes could be identified. They voted 75 percent in favour.[5]

The reasons for this opposition varied widely—some did not trust the federal-level negotiators, some were content with the status quo, some disliked particular elements of the Accord, and so on. However, all of these specific complaints had combined into a significant oppositional force.

This apparent fracture was a turning point for Aboriginal politics. By splintering what had come to appear as a solid and widely accepted identity of political interests, it made visible the complexity of and potential conflicts within Aboriginal politics. Some commentators have mourned this as a setback.[6] However, I believe that the complexity it revealed, and the explicit engagement with the nature, potential, and dangers of the dominant forms of sovereignty that have ensued, have considerably enriched contemporary Aboriginal politics. In particular, the resistance of some groups revealed the ways in which the struggle for sovereignty and self-determination was in danger of perpetuating past violences that can be traced to the embeddedness of discourses and practices of sovereignty in colonial relations. This danger was revealed perhaps most effectively in the campaign of NWAC, which brought to the surface a history of Aboriginal–settler interaction and an analysis of the current state of Aboriginal politics that had previously received relatively little attention from either the mainstream press or the large Aboriginal organizations.

NWAC's Challenge

NWAC's opposition to the Charlottetown Accord centered around two related concerns.[7] First, they protested the lack of representation of Aboriginal women's concerns at the negotiating table. Although the federal government had funded four organizations representing Aboriginal peoples to participate in negotiations, they refused to fund an organization specifically focused on representing Aboriginal women.[8] In response to this, NWAC argued that one effect of colonization on Aboriginal communities was the disruption of traditional gender roles through the imposition of patriarchal structures and forms of government.

> The legal and political struggle by Aboriginal women was not only against an insensitive federal government. It was also against the Aboriginal male establishment created under the *Indian Act*. The *Indian Act* has imposed upon us a patriarchal system and patriarchal laws which favour men. Only men could give Indian status and band membership. At one time, only men could vote in band elections. By 1971, this patriarchal system was so ingrained [through]out our communities, that 'patriarchy' was seen as a 'traditional trait'.[9]

Because of this, they argued, Aboriginal women were not, and could not be, adequately represented at the Constitutional negotiating table by male Aboriginal leaders:

> Some of our women say that our governments—White and Aboriginal—don't give a damn about us! We are telling you this situation will not change without our involvement in self-government and in Constitutional discussions. Aboriginal men could take the initiative and give us a place at the table. Have they done that? No they have not. Aboriginal women want to take their rightful place at the Constitutional table. We are a 'distinct and insular' minority belonging to another culture from which we have been separated.[10]

This argument in turn leads to their second concern: they argued that the political disempowerment of Aboriginal women, combined with the other effects of colonialism that continued to plague their communities, meant that institutionalization of self-government at this time and without the participation of Aboriginal women was premature and dangerous:

> Some Aboriginal women have said no to self-government. Some of our women do not want more power, money and control in the hands of men in our communities …. We do not want you to create Aboriginal governments with white powers and white philosophies in our communities. We do not want the western hierarchical power structure which you have given us.[11]

> Why are we so worried as women? We have never discussed self-government in our communities. There is much to be learned. We are living in chaos in our communities. We have a disproportionately high rate of child sexual abuse and incest. We have wife battering, gang rapes, drug and alcohol abuse and every kind of perversion imaginable has been imported into our daily lives. The development of programs, services, and policies for handling domestic violence has been placed in the hands of men. Has it resulted in a reduction in this kind of violence? Is a woman or a child safe in their own home in an Aboriginal community? The statistics show this is not the case. As one woman said, people are killing each other in our communities. Do they want to govern that? Men rarely speak of family violence. Men rarely speak of incest. Men rarely speak of gang rape and what they are doing about it.[12]

Although they strongly supported the argument that self-government is an Aboriginal right and should be recognized,[13] they argued that the definition and implementation of this right must include Aboriginal women in a way that so far had not been the case:

> What we want to get across to Canadians is our right as women to have a voice in deciding upon the definition of Aboriginal government powers. It is not simply a case of recognizing that we have a right to self determination and self-government. Aboriginal

women also have sexual equality rights. We want those rights respected. Governments cannot simply choose to recognize the patriarchal forms of government which now exist in our communities. The band councils and the Chiefs who preside over our lives are not our traditional form of government. The Chiefs have taken it upon themselves to decide that they will be the final rectifiers of the Aboriginal package of rights. We are telling you, we have a right, as women, to be part of that decision. Recognizing the inherent right to self-government does not mean recognizing and blessing the patriarchy created in our communities by a foreign government. Aboriginal women are not asking for chaos in our communities. We want the equality to which we are entitled as women.[14]

Thus, addressing these questions will require broader participation than is currently in effect in the Constitutional negotiations. Indeed, perhaps a different locus for those negotiations:

We want community decision making. We want consent powers. We want the people in the communities to decide upon their form of government. We want those Aboriginal women who are still banished from their communities to have a vote, some land, and a house in their homeland, in the community in which they were born. There are those among the Chiefs who would deny us a voice, who would deny us a place and those who wish we would simply go away until they have settled this political business. We are not going to go away.[15]

At the very least, they argued, the Canadian Charter of Rights and Freedoms should apply to Aboriginal governments in order to ensure that Aboriginal citizens had recourse to a higher legal authority than their local tribal governments, in this way ensuring that they would be able to exercise their political rights. This was a position that was strongly opposed by the representatives of most of the organizations at the negotiating table.[16] These organizations claimed that the Charter's basis of individual rights was in conflict with Aboriginal philosophy and culture, where rights are held by the group rather than the individual. Further, many Aboriginal leaders argued that the application of the Charter to Aboriginal governments would limit Aboriginal sovereignty.[17]

In response to this argument, NWAC's position paper invokes the *Charter of the United Nations* and the *Universal Declaration on Human Rights* to support the position that individual rights are fundamental and cannot be compromised for the benefit of the collective.

The Native Women's Association of Canada supports individual rights. These rights are so fundamental that, once removed, you no longer have a human being. Aboriginal Women are human beings and we have rights which cannot be denied or removed at the whim of any government. That is how fundamental these individual Charter rights are. These views are in conflict with many Aboriginal leaders and legal theoreticians who advocate for recognition by Canada of sovereignty, self-government and collective rights. It is their unwavering view of the male Aboriginal leadership [sic] that the 'collective' comes first, and that it will decide the rights of individuals.

As Aboriginal women, we can look at nations around the world which have placed collective and cultural rights ahead of women's sexual equality rights. Some nations have found sexual equality interferes with tradition, custom and history. Sexual equality rights have been guaranteed to women around the world. But, like Canada's Charter, the United Nations has allowed nations to 'opt out' of these international instruments.[18]

The history of Aboriginal leadership's treatment of Aboriginal women's concerns shows a frightening tendency to repeat the decision to rank women's rights second to collective rights. Thus, they argue, the application of the Charter should not be left to Aboriginal governments:

> The Native Women's Association of Canada recognizes that there is a clash between collective rights of sovereign Aboriginal governments and individual rights of women. Stripped of equality by patriarchal laws which created 'male privilege' as the norm on reserve lands, Aboriginal women have a tremendous struggle to regain their social position. We want the *Canadian Charter of Rights and Freedoms* to apply to Aboriginal governments.[19]

Further, they argue that they want the federal government to take responsibility for other effects of colonization in their communities as well:

> Yes, we want rights—individual and collective rights. But we want our governments to have responsibilities, too. The Federal government does not get off so easy, either. We are not asking the Federal government to dump us out the door. Self-government is not going to solve our social, economic, cultural and political problems. After 400 years of colonization, Aboriginal communities, Aboriginal families, and Aboriginal structures are devastated. Self-government will be meaningless without the land, money and resources to ensure our self-determination.[20]

NWAC's position paper is fascinating. It draws on some of the most powerful concepts in contemporary political thought—human rights, representation, autonomy, community—in order to negotiate a treacherous political terrain. It also seeks to disrupt not only the existing context of Aboriginal politics but also the political space constituted by sovereignty, appealing as it does to international discourses and institutions in an attempt to counter the dual sovereignties of the Canadian state and Aboriginal organizations. It expresses a hairline judgment and considerable bravery. The achievement of a potential constitutional guarantee of the right to self-government in the context of hundreds of years of colonization seemed incredible. To many—not least Aboriginal leaders—for NWAC to stymie this was irresponsible, to say the least. Although they combined their position with a commitment to self-government in the longer term, it was not an easy position to adopt. That they were motivated to do so is in part an expression of their perception of the stakes of the struggle: the stakes of sovereignty. Before exploring this in more depth, I want to turn to trace some of the contexts revealed by NWAC's intervention. These contexts, in turn, reveal the depth of challenge that their intervention posed.

The Context, and the Politics of Context

Perhaps the most important aspect of NWAC's paper is the way it contextualized the problem of self-government within the complex history of colonialism. This history, both distant and recent, that grounds NWAC's argument, provides a crucial background to understanding the effects of their strategy and, importantly, the ways in which the terrain of politics has been deeply shaped and framed by discourses and practices of sovereignty. For indigenous peoples in North America, of course, discourses and practices of modern sovereignty are synonymous with those of colonialism. As has been argued in relation to colonial processes elsewhere in the world,[21] the history of colonization of Aboriginal nations in Canada is characterized by a systematic attack upon and reorganization of gender roles and hierarchies within Aboriginal communities. As M. Annette Jaimes argues, because Aboriginal women often traditionally held significant political and social power in their communities, "[t]he reduction of the status held by women within indigenous nations was a first priority for European colonizers eager to weaken and destabilize target societies."[22] This resulted in the fact that: "the disempowerment of native women corresponded precisely with the extension of colonial domination of each indigenous nation."[23]

There is significant evidence to support this claim in the history of "Indian policy" in Canada.[24] Along with a sustained attack on indigenous self-government, Canadian Indian policy included an extensive attack on women's roles, responsibilities, and political participation. For example, the Indian Act of 1876 assigned fewer fundamental rights to women than to men; most crucially, women were denied the right of full participation in band affairs.[25] Women were not allowed to hold electoral office, to vote for male representatives, or even to speak at public meetings. As the government extended its presence to all aspects of Aboriginal peoples lives through further expansions to the Indian Act, women's property rights, economic activities, and social and legal status were all drastically limited.

Perhaps the most crucial legal move through which this disempowerment of Aboriginal women occurred was through the question of Indian "Status." The 1869 Indian Act not only contained regulations governing all aspects of life on Aboriginal reserves, and replaced traditional forms of Aboriginal government with "democratized" forms,[26] it also specified regulations about who was, and was not, a "Status" Indian. To be Status meant that you were a member of a band, and had access to all of the special services from the government, including housing on the reserve, medical, property, inheritance, educational, and voting rights. One of the regulations stipulated that Status would descend patrilinearly (directly opposed to many Aboriginal bands' traditional social structures). This meant that if an Aboriginal man married a non-Aboriginal woman, she would gain Status, as would their children. However, if an Aboriginal woman married a non-Aboriginal man, she and all her children would permanently lose Status. They would be unable to live on the reserve, even if there was a divorce later, would not receive any health care, would not be able to vote in band elections, and so on. The implications of this are obvious—not only did it force women to marry within bands if they wanted to maintain band membership, it also ensured that Aboriginal men could marry whomever they liked. It meant that every Aboriginal woman was dependent on a man, father or husband, for Status. This particular element of the Indian Act was a crucial site of Aboriginal women's, and often men's, activism throughout the late 1800 and early 1900s.

Thus the colonization of Aboriginal peoples in Canada took place not only through the disruption of traditional political and social structures, but, as part of this, through a fundamental disruption of traditional gender roles and responsibilities. Just as one of the crucial axes of conflict in many bands today is between "traditional" political structures, including hereditary roles and responsibilities for leadership, and "Indian Act" structures of governance, characterized by "democratic" elections that sometimes have less than democratic effects,[27] another crucial axis involves tensions between "traditional" gender roles and those produced by colonial structures. In both cases, these conflicts are in large part a legacy of colonialism. In both cases, also, the distinctions and their political effects often become muddled, as when activists such as NWAC are branded as "a bunch of women libbers who fight for their own, individual rights."[28] An effort to discredit the activists by attributing their ideas to White (colonial) sources (feminism), this kind of political rhetoric also conceals the historical reality of Aboriginal women's positions in their communities. Thus, the political effects of distinctions between "tradition" and "colonialism" make these discursive strategies high stakes games.

The effects of the gendered nature of the colonial history of Aboriginal peoples in Canada emerged with particular clarity when Aboriginal women began to protest their condition in the 1970s. One example of this is described in a collection of oral histories compiled by Janet Silman.[29] In 1977, a group of Maliseet women on the Tobique reserve in New Brunswick began to organize to protest the situation of women on their reserve: property titles to homes were in the names of men, and some men had kicked out their wives and children, who were then left stranded with nowhere to live, unable to get another house. In addition, the band government failed to provide them with other support services. Meanwhile, some of the men remarried non-Aboriginal women, who gained Status and lived in the homes of their new husbands. At the same time, any woman who returned to the reserve but was non-Status because she had married a non-Aboriginal man (often unaware that this would cause her to lose status) would find herself unable to receive any support from the band. A group of women mobilized, eventually occupying the band offices for over four months, insisting that their needs be met. Their actions were met with extreme resistance, violence, ridicule, indifference, and almost everything but action. Not only was the band government unresponsive and in fact aggressive, but other band members were as well. The reserve became completely polarized. Neither federal nor provincial governments, nor national Aboriginal organizations, would intervene, claiming it was an internal matter. The women eventually focused their efforts on the Status question, realizing that until they had legal and political rights on their own reserve, they would be unable to seriously alter the situation they faced.

The question of Status had already been the site of significant activism on the part of indigenous women. The issue had been raised a number of times, most recently in a case where two women, Lavell and Bedard, took their complaints to the Supreme Court of Canada (1973). They argued that the regulation of Status under the Indian Act should be considered as sexual discrimination under the Canadian Bill of Rights. In response, the Supreme Court argued that it could not use the Bill of Rights to overrule the Indian Act, which conferred a special status and separate government on Aboriginal peoples.[30] Perhaps more important than the decision, however, was what the struggles around it revealed to Aboriginal women activists about their leaders. The case proved to be an illustration of the ways in which, as Fiske put it: "The NIB[31] and other male-dominated organizations confronted women's struggles by adopting discourses from dominant society that reflected the extent to which they had internalized the patri-centric privileges offered them by colonial society."[32] The largest pan-Indian organizations went to court to argue against Lavell and Bedard: "engag(ing) the women in a lengthy, bitter confrontation over the nature of 'Indian rights' and 'women's rights,' asserting that women's rights must not be obtained at the expense of self-government powers."[33] When the Supreme Court ruled against Lavell and Bedard, Aboriginal women were left doubly disempowered, with no legal recourse within Canada or through their Aboriginal governments.

The Tobique women picked up this history, and, realizing they had no further recourse to address the Status issue within Canada, they filed a formal complaint against the Canadian government in the United Nations (December 29, 1977) on behalf of Sandra Lovelace, one of the members of the group. Lovelace had married a non-Aboriginal man, whom she later di-vorced, only to return to the band and discover that she and her children were non-Status and therefore could not live on the reserve, let alone access any social services through the reserve. After four years of delays by the Canadian government and heavy lobbying by Aboriginal women across Canada, the United Nations Human Rights Committee found Canada to be in violation of the International Covenant on Civil and Political Rights, owing to the fact that the Indian Act denied Sandra Lovelace the legal right to live in the community of her birth. While this decision was embarrassing for the Canadian government, it could not force the Canadian government to change the Act. The issue dragged on for much longer before the Canadian government finally (in 1985) passed an amendment to the Indian Act, Bill C-31, in an attempt to resolve the Status issue.[34]

The National Indian Brotherhood, the largest pan-Indian organization at the time, protested this attempted resolution as well. Rather than arguing, as they had in the Lavell and Bedard case, that Bill C-31 would be an infringement on their sovereignty, they protested it as having potentially assimilative effects: "Denying systematic sexual discrimination in their own ranks, the male leadership alleged its opposition derived from a real fear that western philosophical traditions of individual human rights would undermine the collective identity of Aboriginal peoples and the sacred traditions that bind individuals into a mutually-obliged collectivity."[35] As might be predicted from this opposition, even upon the passage of Bill C-31, the struggles of Aboriginal women continued as many band govern-ments either refused to implement the changes or dragged their feet, claim-ing either that the changes were unjust or that they simply did not have the resources to effect them.[36] Struggles like these characterize the history of Aboriginal women's attempts to have their concerns addressed at the level of federal Aboriginal political organizations, and provide a context for NWAC's position of opposition to the Charlottetown Accord.[37]

While this history and evidence would suggest a strong legitimacy for NWAC's position, we should be careful before we hasten to accuse Aboriginal leaders of sexism or condemn Aboriginal political structures as inherently patriarchal. Considering the strategic field faced by Aboriginal leaders and the nature of pan-Indian political strategies, the challenges posed by NWAC are serious ones. Although some of the responses to NWAC, as to Lavell and Bedard, have exhibited a certain intolerance for Aboriginal women's concerns inasmuch as they have attempted to discredit rather than seriously engage these women, this is in part an expression of the depth and stakes of the challenges posed by their claims.

Challenges and Implications

The context invoked by NWAC's paper not only provides depth to their claims but it also reveals something of the broader terrain of indigenous politics, and the role of discourses and practices of sovereignty in shaping this terrain. For example, considering the assimilative history of Canadian policy (the ways in which Canadian legislation was aimed directly at the destruction of collective cultural identities and the forced inculcation of a liberal individualist subjectivity) and considering the potential implications of these concepts gaining a legal foothold against Aboriginal governments (i.e., legal claims to individual property rights leading to dissolution of collective resources), some concern on the part of Aboriginal leaders is clearly understandable. In reaction to the history of forced assimilation, the rise of Aboriginal nationalism had been grounded in the promise of not having to constantly resist government attempts at assimilation. Challenges to this promise, especially when it seemed to be so close to fulfillment, would hardly be warmly received.[38]

Even more to the point, these challenges potentially raised the specter of more than a limitation of their sovereignty; they raised the specter of losing the moral and legal groundwork for their claims. As with other nationalist struggles, pan-indigenous nationalism in Canada developed through the constitution of a shared ontology, expressed in an identity of interests. This was no easy matter, given the diversity of indigenous groups in Canada: there are hundreds of tribal communities in Canada, scattered over a huge territory, representing at least ten linguistic groups, they have several different statuses in relation to the government of Canada,[39] they live with a range of different social and economic conditions: some are located on or have claims to rich deposits of natural resources or large tracts of land while others are largely urbanized or dispersed, their histories of contact with settlers and the status of traditional economies vary widely, and so on. These differences often led to very different ideas about what policies were most urgent or what strategies should be pursued. Not surprisingly, given the logics of sovereignty, the strategy used to overcome these differences was the establishment of an identity constituted through opposition to "white" or non-Aboriginal culture. Thus, in the rise of federal Aboriginal politics, we can trace the development of an essentialized "Indian" identity defined in opposition to all things "white." In this respect, their strategy precisely mirrored that of Thomas Hobbes when he produced the ontology of the modern subject that in turn illustrated the necessity of sovereignty, thus authorizing it, and its violences.

Given that this identity-in-difference provided the authorization of their collective claims, their strategic position was deeply threatened by NWAC's arguments. In asserting that Aboriginal women constitute a "distinct and insular" minority, NWAC not only threw into question the representativeness of the Aboriginal organizations, they also threw into question the underlying identity-of-difference that grounded their claims. The story NWAC tells denies the absolute difference between Aboriginal and non-Aboriginal, instead pointing to shared traits, political, and social structures ("patriarchy") that express an underlying continuity. Although these commonalties are expressions or effects of colonialism, their presence nonetheless enables a wedge to be drawn in the strategic alliance, either in the form of arguments that they are not "real Indians" but rather are "just like us" but claiming special rights, or in the form of arguments that they are not adequately democratic, "developed", or "mature" to be considered responsible. Both are clearly expressions of the history of Canadian sovereignty discourse and its embeddedness in the colonial project, but, because of this, each is still potentially a potent line of critique, especially considering the precarious support for Aboriginal sovereignty.

This is especially true given the assumptions about identity and ethnicity that characterized Canadian negotiators' approaches to Aboriginality, assumptions that are clearly recognizable effects of Canadian sovereignty discourse.

> Much of government policy reflects what I call the 'hydraulic Indian' view of ethnicity. This view depicts an Indian or native person as a cylinder which, at some unidentified point in history, was full to the top of 'Indianness,' that is, traditional Indian culture. As time passed, and as Indians adopted non-native ways, the level of 'Indianness' dropped to the point where the cylinder now is nearly empty.[40]

This essentialized concept of ethnicity was fed by the construction of "Indianness" as all things non-White. Because "Indian" identity/ethnicity rested upon the same terms as their earlier colonization, the "authenticity" of their ethnicity was evaluated by these terms. This measure of authenticity could then be used to discredit Aboriginal political claims based on this essential difference between Aboriginals and Whites:

> Racial characteristics and traditional cultural elements such as language, religion, weapons, tools, transport, and clothing were the criteria adopted [by the dominant society to determine who was and was not an Indian]. Aboriginal people and culture were taken to have existed in a pure form before contact, but to have been 'diluted' through interbreeding and acculturation. This erosion of Indian race and culture was used to discredit contemporary Indian claims to aboriginal rights on the grounds that the claimants had ceased to be Indians.[41]

This danger forces Aboriginal leaders to be constantly reasserting and emphasizing the authenticity of the distinction between Aboriginal and non-Aboriginal, treading a fine line of argument that changes and developments, seen as indications of "Whiteness" by this measure of ethnicity, should not interfere with legal and political claims. By this measure, NWAC was clearly posing a serious challenge. By emphasizing the effects that colonialism has had in terms of the inculcation of colonial ideologies, political, and social structures (problems), they potentially opened Aboriginal organizations to the accusation that their "distinct" identity claims are fraudulent. Although it was clearly not their intention to argue against the "authenticity" of Aboriginal identity, their strategy forced the articulation of legal and political claims away from the identity and ethnicity they rested on. This produced a kind of "credibility gap" for Aboriginal leaders, especially in the short term, which is crucial in the context of fast-moving Constitutional negotiations.

However, NWAC's challenge also reveals potential dangers inherent within the strategy being pursued by Aboriginal leaders. The definition of ethnicity they were working both within and against also potentially "freezes" Aboriginal culture in time, unable to institute the kinds of developmental changes that may be necessary to survive in the world as it is. "This is a truncated and static understanding of ethnicity, one that freezes cultural idioms in some historic moment. It fails to comprehend that ethnicity is a process that unfolds over time as groups continually select and reinterpret diverse cultural forms around them (Aboriginal and non-Aboriginal) in defining themselves as distinct from the larger society."[42] Thus, an essentialized notion of Aboriginality also—in the effort to assert its legitimacy—runs the risk of erasing or minimizing the effects of colonialism on their societies. Because they have to prove their authenticity, measured in relation to their "pre-contact" selves (or how they were written in Canadian sovereignty discourse), they have to deny the effects of colonialism (thus minimizing claims for assistance in addressing these effects). In other words, these discourses of authenticity themselves become mechanisms of colonization. In a desperate attempt to oust the government, the extent of its presence within Aboriginal cultures, identities, selves, and politics, is concealed. While this might seem to be a minimal danger from Aboriginal leaders' perspectives—operating on the belief that success in sovereignty claims will mean that they will have the resources to address these problems—NWAC is clearly more concerned that the effects of colonialism be taken seriously as part of the process of moving toward sovereignty. They also want to insist that responsibility for remedying them remain at least in part with the federal government.

These challenges posed by NWAC's strategy reveal why their demands are not easily addressed at the federal level, and thus why at times they have been responded to less than gracefully by Aboriginal leaders. The kind of response by Aboriginal leaders is telling, though. As NWAC's paper points out, the tendency was to discredit NWAC by rendering them not "real" Indians: "When Aboriginal women demand sexual equality, we are accused of being feminists. We are accused of dividing our community along sexist lines."[43] This response by Aboriginal leaders emerges directly from the necessity of maintaining a homogenized/essentialized identity to ground sovereignty claims. It also clearly expresses the potential violences of sovereignty discourse: in order to maintain legitimacy, the sovereign must be able to maintain a coherent self, and thus a clear "inside"/"outside" distinction. In this context, the inscription of inside and outside—the reproduction of the sovereignty of the "self"—requires the exclusion of others (Aboriginal women) from that self through discourses of authenticity. While perhaps strategically crucial in the short run, in the longer run, it produces a festering problem—as it did in NWAC's opposition to the 1992 Referendum.

Most crucially, however, this tension needs to be understood as an effect, in part, of how sovereignty discourse has already produced the strategic field in ways that constrain Aboriginal political expression. As their claims (their very subjectivities) are dependent on sovereignty discourse, they have to produce themselves according to its mold. Always requiring a violent[44] production of "self" and thus "other," this becomes multiply treacherous when the "other" (in this case, indigenous peoples) tries to produce itself as the "self" (sovereign). The multiple differences of situation, history, and ontology amongst Aboriginal peoples must be erased or homogenized in order to claim sovereignty on their colonizers' terms. The situation of NWAC in the Constitutional discussions thus reproduces the role that indigenous peoples played in the constitution of sovereignty in North

America: they mark the edges, constituting the margin. They are the ones who come to mark what is and is not sovereign, precisely in their exclusion, whether self-imposed or forced upon them, from it. This leaves us with crucial questions about the long-term effects of sovereignty discourse. In the past, the claim has always been that the violences brought about by sovereignty discourses and practices were "regrettable necessities," unfortunate but necessary because without sovereignty, political community is not possible.[45] Such a claim reproduces and strengthens sovereignty, insofar as it reinscribes its role as the very condition of possibility for politics, and thus its constitution as something pre-political. But we should have no small suspicion here regarding how this claim is deployed. Indigenous groups no less: it has provided the justification for their past treatment.

Indigenous leaders in the negotiations clearly considered it a worthwhile gamble: the potential achievement of sovereignty was the precondition for resolving and responding to these "secondary" concerns. NWAC was not willing to take this gamble, insisting instead upon the constitution of a different kind of sovereignty, one that might provide a recognition of the complex historical interconnections amongst indigenous and settler communities constituted through colonialism. They argued that a sovereignty that was grounded in this would provide a better starting point for self-government. However, this would also require a renegotiation of sovereignty discourse itself: the constitution of a sovereignty grounded in a non-essentialized identity. In the absence of this, either the federal Aboriginal claims fail, discredited by the inability to exhibit the appropriate signs of sovereignty, or NWAC's concerns are excluded and they become the underside or "other" that enables the emerging recognition of Aboriginal sovereignty. During the Constitutional Referendum, the strategic field faced by Aboriginal politics seemed almost this sharply defined. Thus, insofar as one accepts this either/or expression of political necessity, the defeat of the Referendum, in particular its resounding defeat by Aboriginal peoples, appears disheartening.

In my view, though, the defeat might be considered as a defeat of the particular strategy of sovereignty in play, an unwillingness to live by its terms. It thus might facilitate an opening for a rearticulation of sovereignty discourse through Aboriginality and Aboriginal politics, and vice versa, perhaps opening the possibility of a rewriting of the history of sovereignty's "regrettable necessity." From this perspective, rather than viewing NWAC's position as a strategic disaster—a failure to support Aboriginal sovereignty at the crucial moment—one might read it as a challenge to a particular form of sovereignty politics. Read this way, what is striking about NWAC's position is the vision of politics that they articulate. Clearly sharing a desire for Aboriginal communities to emerge from their colonized past, their vision nonetheless is grounded in a concern for the health and viability of their communities rather than an abstract and formalistic legal guarantee of their status as autonomous units. Thus, rather than legal status granted by colonizers being the precondition for the necessary changes that Aboriginal communities seek, the reverse becomes true. The internal viability of the communities becomes the crucial site of political action. A politics of "inside" dominates, with necessary connections to the "outside" in order to enable these politics.

Of course, even this articulation of politics is grounded in a language of sovereignty, as was clear from NWAC's position paper. Rather than an escape from sovereignty, it provides a potential rearticulation of it that refocuses its meaning and effects in relation to Aboriginal communities. Further, this strategy itself is dependent on the sovereignty strategy already being pursued, inasmuch as it is articulated through and in reference to those discourses. In other words, I am far from recommending that NWAC's political vision supplant the dominant strategies: there is a dangerous element to their discursive strategies as well. As federal Aboriginal leaders know all too well and the history of Aboriginal-Canadian relations exhibits tenfold, the only reason Aboriginal peoples were receiving the attention and concessions they were was because of the strength of the sovereignty claim they could mobilize. While NWAC's desire to focus on social problems is crucial, a strong sovereignty claim is quite possibly the condition of possibility for accessing the resources necessary to realize such a focus.

Thus, there is a dynamic tension expressed by the conflict between NWAC and federal pan-Indian organizations. This tension is produced by how sovereignty discourse shapes politics, especially for those, like Aboriginal peoples, who have been so clearly marked and located within sovereignty discourse. This tension is a dangerous one, but also, crucially, a productive one. It is an expression of serious contradictions and challenges that are deeply embedded in modern political thought and practices. Thus, they need to be opened up and worked on rather than "resolved" at a symbolic or formal level. The crucial thing that must be resisted is closure, which is the assumption that the struggles expressed by these tensions can and should be contained within existing structures and discourses. To assume this is to seriously underestimate the complexity of the political terrain faced by Aboriginal peoples. So far, if my sympathy seems to lean toward NWAC's strategy, it is because they (if only because they are the weaker party) seem to be resisting this kind of closure most strongly, insofar as they are resisting the inscription of a potentially violent version of sovereignty politics. This resistance to sovereignty as a solution and emphasis on a rearticulation of the political express a more promising sense of the politics of "political space," suggesting the dynamism that Aboriginal politics must force upon the articulation of political space.

The development of the discourse on Aboriginal women's concerns in the intervening years seems to be an illustration of the positive effects of NWAC's strategy, even though much of this discourse emerged through critiques of their strategy. For example, compare the following analysis, developed recently by Turpel-Lafond, to NWAC's. Turpel-Lafond clearly expresses a negotiation of these tensions that keeps alive a complex political space, one where the possibilities for addressing both sovereignty and colonization, both gender and tradition simultaneously appear to open up.

> It is essential that you separate two concepts that are in the foreground here so as not to be confused. On the one hand, it is important to understand the position that First Nations women occupy both historically and in the real contemporary sense, in some of our communities, particularly those which are matriarchal, and to appreciate how this position was attacked by the Canadian state. On the other hand, it is essential not to confuse First Nations women's suppressed status as a result of state-imposed legal definitions and institutional structures in the *Indian Act,* with a reaction translatable into a desire to have what non-native women or men have in this society. The former is patriarchy, the latter is paternalism. Both were imposed upon us as communities and as individuals. We do not want continued patriarchy nor do we want paternalistic prescriptions for our future paths. We want to extricate ourselves from both of these debilitating forces. At the same time, it is wholly distracting and irresponsible to place the blame for First Nations women's experiences at the feet of First Nations men. Yet, neither can we exonerate them today when they are shown the context yet decide to ignore it and embrace learned patriarchy.[46]

This description of the political terrain suggests a more subtle and flexible vision of the possibilities for sovereignty while holding firm on the necessity of some form of self-determination. Insofar as political strategies can be crafted through a recognition of this kind of complexity, and sovereignties formed that recognize and negotiate the complex effects of colonialism, we will see forms of sovereignty emerge that resist some of the now familiar violences of modern sovereignty. This would be a considerable achievement. Given the live struggle with this complexity in indigenous politics at diverse sites, such a reformulation is likely to emerge from their political activities.[47]

The 1992 Referendum did indeed mark the end of a particular form of Aboriginal politics, and there is cause for some regret on that front. However, the assumption that this means that "we're back where we started" is not appropriate either. For one thing, it remains clear that a renegotiation of Canadian sovereignty cannot take place in the absence of a consideration of and reconciliation with its colonial past. The magnitude of this project has also become clearer. More importantly, however, it has galvanized Aboriginal politics in important ways toward more promising rearticulations of sovereignty. In these rearticulations, we will find some of the most promising resources for thinking about the future of politics.

Notes

1. I develop an argument for why this is the case in Karena Shaw, *Leviathan's Angels: Indigenous Politics and the Limits of the Political* (PhD Dissertation, The Johns Hopkins University, 1999), pp. 15–38. Partha Chatterjee provides an astute analysis of the ambivalent potential of sovereignty discourse in nationalist struggles in *Nationalist Thought and the Colonial World: A Derivative Discourse?* (London: Zed Books, 1986) and "Colonialism, Nationalism and Colonialized Women: The Contest in India" *American Ethnologist*, 16(4), 1989: pp. 622–633.
2. Indigenous peoples play this role perhaps most famously in both Thomas Hobbes' *Leviathan* and John Locke's *Second Treatise on Government*.
3. Indigenous peoples in Canada are variously referred to—and refer to themselves—as indigenous, Aboriginal, and Native Canadians; Inuit, Indians, First Nations, and Métis refer to more specific groups. In this paper my usage shifts amongst these depending on the usage in the situation or material under discussion. Although I could standardize it, there is, of course, a politics to this.
4. For a summary of the proposed reform, see Menno Boldt, *Surviving as Indians: The Challenge of Self-Government* (Toronto: University of Toronto Press, 1993), pp. 94–108. For rich explorations of the relationship between indigenous peoples and Canadian political and legal structures, see John Borrows, *Recovering Canada: The Resurgence of Indigenous Law* (Toronto: University of Toronto Press, 2002); Patrick Macklem, *Indigenous Difference and the Constitution of Canada* (Toronto: University of Toronto Press, 2001); Alan C. Cairns, *Citizens Plus, Aboriginal Peoples and the Canadian State* (Vancouver: UBC Press, 2000).
5. Dan Smith, *The Seventh Fire: The Struggle for Aboriginal Government* (Toronto: Key Porter Books, Ltd, 1993), p. 231. Smith's analysis of Aboriginal participation in Constitutional reform, consistent with his analysis of the many other elements of Aboriginal politics, provides a much richer sense of the intricacies of the negotiations, the development of Aboriginal political organizations, and the personalities involved than I attempt here.
6. Smith, *The Seventh Fire*, p. 221.
7. While NWAC was the largest and most well-organized Aboriginal women's organization at the time, it was by no means the only one, nor do I have any basis for evaluating how broadly representative it was of Aboriginal women's concerns. There was certainly a lot of debate about whether or not it was a legitimate expression of the majority of Aboriginal women's views; however, it is clear that they did represent a significant number of Aboriginal women.
8. The four groups that were funded were the Assembly of First Nations (representing Status Indians), the Native Council Canada (representing non-Status), the Métis National Council, and the Inuit Tapirisat of Canada.
9. Gail Stacey Moore, "Statement on the Canada Package," Position Paper: Native Women's Association of Canada (February 2, 1992), p. 4.
10. Moore, "Statement on the Canada Package," pp. 6–7.
11. Moore, "Statement on the Canada Package," p. 9.
12. Moore, "Statement on the Canada Package," p. 16.
13. Moore, "Statement on the Canada Package," p. 8.
14. Moore, "Statement on the Canada Package," pp. 8–9.
15. Moore, "Statement on the Canada Package," pp. 9–10.

16. However, it was ultimately accepted in a compromise move: the Charter would apply, but governments could opt out on matters concerning cultural identity through a "notwithstanding" clause.

17. Moore, "Statement on the Canada Package, pp. 9–10.

18. Moore, "Statement on the Canada Package, pp. 11–12. This passage, it seems to me, poignantly illustrates the political implications of Judith Butler's argument about the meaning and practice of the universal. See Judith Butler, Ernesto Laclau and Slavoj Zizek, *Contingency, Hegemony, Universality* (London: Verso, 2000), pp. 11–43, 137–182.

19. Moore, "Statement on the Canada Package," p. 13.

20. Moore, "Statement on the Canada Package," p. 17.

21. See, for example, Partha Chatterjee, *Nationalist Thought in the Colonial World*, and "Colonialism, Nationalism and Colonized Women"; Rey Chow, *Women and Chinese Modernity: The Politics of Reading Between West and East* (Minneapolis: University of Minnesota Press, 1990); Andrew Parker, Mary Russo, Doris Sommer and Patricia Yaeger, editors *Nationalisms and Sexualities* (New York: Routledge, 1992); Kumkum Sangari and Sudesh Vaid, editors *Recasting Women: Essays in Indian Colonial History* (New Brunswick: Rutgers University Press, 1990); Ashis Nandy, *The Intimate Enemy: Loss and Recovery of Self under Colonialism* (Delhi: Oxford University Press, 1983) and *The Illegitimacy of Nationalism* (Delhi: Oxford University Press, 1994); Chandra Mohanty, Ann Russo and Lourdes Torres, editors *Third World Women and the Politics of Feminism* (Bloomington: Indiana University Press, 1991); Gayatri Spivak, *In Other Worlds: Essays in Cultural Politics* (New York: Routledge, 1988).

22. M. Annette Jaimes, editor *The State of Native America: Genocide, Colonization and Resistance* (Boston: South End Press, 1992), pp. 318–319.

23. Jaimes, *The State of Native America*, p. 323. A powerful argument that a disruption of gender roles was crucial to the colonization of the Huron and Motengnais communities, as well as a careful analysis of how this disruption was enacted, is made by Karen Anderson, *Chain Her By One Foot: The subjugation of native women in Seventeenth Century New France* (London: Routledge, 1993).

24. For a more sustained analysis of how this history was shaped by and articulated through discourses and practices of sovereignty, see Karena Shaw, *Leviathan's Angels*, Chapter 3.

25. Much of my information about the history of gender in Indian policy is drawn from Jo-Anne Fiske "Child of the State, Mother of the Nation: Aboriginal Women and the Ideology of Motherhood" in *Culture*, 13(1), 1993: 17–35; although see also Joyce Green, "Sexual Equality and Indian Government: An Analysis of Bill C-31 Amendments to the Indian Act" in *Native Studies Review*, 1(2), 1985: 81–95; Kathleen Jamieson, *Indian Women and the Law in Canada: Citizens Minus* (Ottawa: Minister of Supply and Services, 1978) and "Sex Discrimination and the Indian Act," in J. Rick Ponting, editor *The Arduous Journey: Canadian Indians and Decolonization* (Toronto: McLelland and Stewart, 1986); Janet Silman, *Enough is Enough: Aboriginal Women Speak Out* (Toronto: The Women's Press, 1987); Ellen Turpel "Aboriginal Peoples and the Canadian Charter of Rights and Freedom," *Canadian Womens Studies/les cahiers de la femme*, 10(2&3), 1989: 149–157; Mary Ellen Turpel-Lafond, "Patriarchy and Paternalism: The Legacy of the Canadian State for First Nations Women", Wendy Moss, "The Canadian State and Indian Women: The Struggle for Sex Equality Under the Indian Act" and Teressa Anne Nahanee, "Indian Women, Sex Equality and the Charter." In *Women and the Canadian State/Les Femmes et l'Etat Canadien*, edited by Caroline Andrew and Sandra Rodgers (Montreal & Kingston: McGill-Queen's University Press, 1997).

26. "Democratized" on a modern, European model, emphasizing individualized political subjectivities, representation, and property regimes. While there is an extensive debate about the contribution of North American indigenous political systems to this model, what is beyond question is that many of the institutions and practices of governance of these groups contained internal logics and practices of legitimation that have considerable affinities with "democracy." What is also beyond question is that these institutions and practices were not recognized and respected as such.

27. These conflicts are complex, very important, and nearly impossible to generalize about. In some cases, the "traditional" leadership is a very progressive anti-colonial force, and in other cases the elected or "Indian Act" leadership is. In most cases, the distinction is not nearly as clear cut as this. There are several different case studies or analyses of how these issues, essentially the effects of colonialism, play out; see, for example, Gerald Alfred, *Heeding the Voices of our*

Ancestors (Toronto: Oxford University Press, 1995) and *Peace, Power, Righteousness: An Indigenous Manifesto* (Toronto: Oxford University Press, 1999); Menno Boldt, *Surviving as Indians*; Geoffrey York, *People of the Pines: The Warriors and the Legacy of Oka* (Boston/Toronto: Little Brown, 1991) and *The Dispossessed: Life and Death in Native Canada* (Toronto: McArthur & Company, 1999).

28. Fiske, "Child of the State…", p. 21.
29. Janet Silman, *Enough is Enough*.
30. This, then, is the background for the argument about whether the Charter should apply to Aboriginal governments or not. Aboriginal leaders saw this as a victory in that it reinforced the idea that their governmental structures should have a separate status from Canadian ones. Ironically, of course, the Indian Act is an act of Canadian legislation. Nonetheless, this decision was seen as a confirmation of their sovereign status.
31. The National Indian Brotherhood, the predecessor of the Assembly of First Nations, the most prominent pan-Indian federal level organization.
32. Fiske, "Child of the State…", p. 21.
33. Fiske, "Child of the State…"
34. See Joyce Green, "Sexual Equality and Indian Government…" for an analysis of the changes contained within Bill C-31. As may be obvious, deeply embedded in this case are some of the same logics and paradoxes of sovereignty revealed in the larger narrative: the UN couldn't "force" Canada to change its law; this would be a violation of sovereignty. However Canada is in general acutely sensitive to external criticism of its human rights record—it is crucial to its international political practices—and so was more likely to respond to pressure in this regard than other, also "sovereign", countries.
35. Fiske, "Child of the State…", p. 22. Here, we see the roots of NWAC's concern that Aboriginal governments would put "community rights" ahead of women's sexual equality rights.
36. The federal government refused to provide adequate resources for many reserves to accommodate the sudden influx of women and children who regained their Status through Bill C-31. There are many discussions of Bill C-31, and the impact it has had on aboriginal communities, and its success or failure. Some examples include Joyce Green, "Sexual Equality and Indian Government…"; Gerald Alfred, *Heeding the Voice of our Ancestors*; Katherine Beaty Chiste, "Aboriginal Women and Self-Government: Challenging Leviathan," *American Indian Culture and Research Journal*, 18(3), 1994: 19–43; Menno Boldt, *Surviving as Indians*; Wendy Moss, "The Canadian State and Indian Women…"; Teressa Anne Nahanee, "Indian Women, Sex Equality and the Charter".
37. It is important to emphasize that there have been many other forms of Aboriginal women's activism, some more effective. Part of my argument is that these particular kinds of impasses/struggles arise as a result of the discursive political context in which the action takes place. Thus, rather than making an argument about the inherent sexism of male Aboriginal leaders or the patriarchal structures of Aboriginal politics (each of which might be important concerns, although I am in no position to consider them here), I am attempting to show how the strategies themselves—in this case the reliance on sovereignty discourse particularly—produce these kinds of conflicts. I hope this becomes clearer below.
38. This itself is an expression of a particular kind of idealism on the part of Aboriginal leaders, a belief in the sovereignty myth: that sovereignty itself was the precondition for solving all of their woes.
39. There are Status, Non-Status, Métis, and Inuit; some bands have treaties with the government, others do not, and so on. Each of these "identities" has specific formal and informal relations to government. For an analysis of how these differences affect political goals and vision, see Menno Boldt and J. Anthony Long, *The Quest for Justice: Aboriginal Peoples and Aboriginal Rights* (Toronto: University of Toronto Press, 1985), Part 1.
40. Boldt and Long, *The Quest for Justice*, p. 146.
41. M. Annette Jaimes, *The State of Native America*, pp. 322–323.
42. Boldt and Long, *The Quest for Justice*, p. 146.
43. Moore, "Statement on the Caexnada Package," p. 10.
44. "Violent" in the sense of requiring the imposition of dualistic categories on "realities" that are usually more complex, which in turn shapes and frames the possibilities of those thus defined.
45. This is Alexis de Tocqueville's language, used to describe the treatment of indigenous peoples in North America in *Democracy in America: Vol. 1* (New York: Vintage Books, 1990 [1835]). For

him, they were the sacrificial blood that secured sovereignty. I develop an analysis of this in relation to the treatment of indigenous peoples in Canada in *Leviathan's Angels*, Chapter 3.

46. Mary Ellen Turpel-Lafond, "Patriarchy and Paternalism...", p. 71. For another recent engagement with the challenges and possibilities faced by contemporary Aboriginal women, see Kim Anderson, *A Recognition of Being: Reconstructing Native Womanhood* (Toronto: Sumach Press, 2000).

47. Some suggestions for how this is happening can be found in the literatures cited above, but see also: Marie Battiste, editor *Reclaiming Indigenous Voice and Vision* (Vancouver: UBC Press, 2000); Claire Smith and Graeme K. Ward, editors *Indigenous Cultures in an Interconnected World* (Vancouver, UBC Press, 2000).

CHAPTER 10

Ebola Takes to the Road
Mobilizing Viruses in Defense of the Nation-State

JORGE FERNANDES

Medical police, like all police science, is an art of defense.[1]

A dark skin was seen not only as a badge of shame for its wearer. Now we were evil incarnate, the mask of long agony and violent death.[2]

Colette Matshimoseka arrived at Toronto's Pearson International Airport on the cold morning of February 3, 2001. After a seemingly interminable flight that took her from Kinshasa to Addis Ababa, Rome, Newark, and Toronto, she drove to Hamilton, where she stayed with friends. During her first night in Hamilton, Matshimoseka fell ill: "She had a headache, no appetite, she was confused."[3] The next morning, Sunday, February 4, she was taken by ambulance to Henderson General Hospital in Hamilton. The emergency room physicians, suspecting she was suffering from a "low-grade malaria," admitted her. Their differential diagnosis took a sinister, if not predictable, turn, "especially considering where she [Colette Matshimoseka] came from,"[4] when the Hospital's consulting infectious disease specialist, Dr. Douglas MacPherson, expanded the differential to include Ebola and a host of other hemorrhagic fevers such as Lassa, Marburg, and Crimean-Congo. Dr. MacPherson's differential set in motion a network of public health and media machines that would transform Matshimoseka into North America's "first case of Ebola."[5]

The responses to Matshimoseka's hospitalization are instructive, for they betray a level of anxiety that reveals much about Ebola's metaphorical force in the West's geopolitical imaginary. Reactions ranged from Dr. MacPherson's confident assertion that the general population was at minimal risk of contracting Ebola to those of nurses and lab workers who kept their "children home from school and daycare for fear of passing any virus to children."[6] A nurse, scheduled to wed days after Matshimoseka's hospitalization, declared that she "was unsure if she should leave the country for her honeymoon while she waits through the incubation period."[7] Similarly, Mario Posteraro, president of the local ambulance workers' union, remarked that "a number of paramedics . . . are actually questioning their choice of profession." He adds: "We work in unpredictable, unsanitary conditions and put ourselves at great risk because the deadly virus [Ebola] may be hidden behind some other symptomology."[8] Debbie Mattina, a representative of the Hospital's lab workers, summarized the Hospital staff's feeling when she commented: "They're not sure if they should kiss their husbands or hug their children. These are people whose lives have been interrupted."[9]

I cite these responses not to discount the risks of contagion or to decry the Hospital workers' and the community's fears: hemorrhagic viruses have effected great human costs in societies throughout central Africa and Latin America. Nevertheless, of all pathogens that "threaten" the globe, Ebola is, at best, a minor contributor. As Michael Fumento reminded readers of the *National Post*: "We hardly need be reminded of the continent's [Africa] AIDS problem. But additionally each year Sub-Saharan Africa suffers half a million deaths from tuberculosis, and almost 700,000 from malaria. Diarrhea—often a laughing matter in First World countries—kills about 900,000."[10] Although morbidity and mortality statistics cannot adequately account for the suffering caused by Ebola, Lassa, and other hemorrhagic viruses, they do, however, highlight the discordance between the number of lives affected by these viruses, less than 500 deaths since 1995, and the fear they engender.

To understand the fear that these viruses inspire, we must look beyond medical and public health discourses. Popular culture's preoccupation with Ebola, unlike malaria, for example, does not rest in its virulence, although this is a recurring concern, but in the horror associated with the illness.[11] Richard Preston equates the illness's end-stage with "the secret detonation of an atomic bomb,"[12] a "terminal meltdown."[13] After death, a "sort of shock-related meltdown occurs . . . the corpse's connective tissue, skin, and organs . . . begin to liquefy."[14] These descriptions signal the body's loss of physical and metaphorical containment. They mark Ebola's caustic effect on the body as a symbolic frontier between the self and the Other. The acute hemorrhage that comprises Ebola's end-stage resonates not only with medical discourse and social taboos about blood contagion, a discursive threat made acutely resonant by the AIDS pandemic, but also finds its socio-political complement in anxieties related to the body politic's vulnerability to increased cross-border flows of populations. This transforms viruses, Ebola in particular, into the subject of a complex matrix of enactments about the nature of difference and the possibility of disciplining the flows of bodies.

Colette Matshimoseka's story highlights the homology between Ebola's disruption of the body's integrity and the anxiety about the nation-state's decreased viability as a stable cultural and linguistic site. Matshimoseka's lab results were returned less than a week after her hospitalization. The results were greeted by newspaper headlines asking Canadians to "breathe easy" for it was "not quite the plague."[15] However, while Canadians breathed easy, Matshimoseka's problems were far from over. For while she no longer was the unwitting agent of "an international health scare,"[16] articles were beginning to appear in newspapers throughout Canada suggesting that "she is under investigation by immigration officials, who say she may be linked to diamond smuggling."[17] Statements by the Royal Canadian Mounted Police that it had met with immigration officials and had found "no reason to go any further" with the investigation did not put an end to Matshimoseka's plight.[18] She soon found herself at the center of a debate about the burden that immigrants posed on Canada's health system. Newspapers reported that the Hamilton Health Sciences Corporation was likely "stuck with more than $60,000 in medical bills" incurred in caring for her.[19] Matshimoseka became the lightning-rod for appeals to reform the health and immigration system by requiring "the federal government to cover the costs of [caring for] visitors it allows into the country."[20] Matshimoseka is the focal point in these narratives' shifting angles. Whether as a carrier of Ebola, as a courier of illegal diamonds, or as an emblem of the immigrant's burden on Canada's limited resources, she is alien, undesirable, and threatening.

Matshimoseka's story exposes the discursive pathways linking the rising interest in "superbugs" with the meta-machines that transform the migrant into a potential carrier and thus a threat to the health of the body politic. Much has been said about the recent proliferation of contagion narratives. These approach the genre as a by-product of AIDS "blood culture," of an internal anxiety about the disruptive qualities of the epidemic. While this is a productive take, I argue that the "community of discourse" engendered by the fear of viral pandemics is a productive terrain for an analysis of the mechanisms by which nation-states code bodies and arrest their flow, thus safeguarding the nation-state's role as an authoring locus of qualified life.[21] In other words, I approach the signifiers of the 1980s "blood culture," AIDS and Ebola, as social signs that offer a symptomatology of our present disquiet about globalization and the end of the supremacy of nation-states. I demonstrate how present attempts at addressing the proliferation of encounters, brought about most significantly by the end of the colonial empires, offer a glimpse into the conditions governing the phenomenon of globalization and the resistances they engender.

Of Mallon, McCarthy, and Matshimoseka: Constructing the Social Being

In a September 2000 interview on National Public Radio, *Newsday* health and science journalist Laurie Garrett described her fear and excitement at the CIA's invitation to brief its agents on the dangers of emergent viruses. She recounted being overcome by a wave of panic when asked for her social security number as she drove past the security gates of the Central Intelligence Agency in Langley, Virginia. Her journey to the inner sanctum of American security discourse began with her coverage of the 1995 Ebola outbreak in Kikwit, Zaire, for which she was awarded the 1996 Pulitzer prize. Garrett's work has since moved in rapid succession from explanatory, scientific journalism to policy and advocacy, making her a leading spokesperson on the dangers of emergent diseases.

Garrett's ascent to the role of policy advisor traces the renewed concern with public health in national security discourse. Shortly before winning the Pulitzer, Garrett published a volume titled *The Coming Plague: Newly Emergent Diseases in a World Out of Balance*.[22] The volume, with a millenarian sensibility, exhaustively catalogues global outbreaks of new and old illnesses, scripting a frightening picture of a world on the verge of disaster. Frustrated by the failure of governments to prevent disease outbreaks, she set out to explore the shortcomings of "global public health" infrastructures in a sequel titled *Betrayal of Trust: The Collapse of Global Public Health*.[23]

Advances in medicine and regulatory practices after world war II led to a decline in interest and support for public health. The divestiture in public health, Garrett contends, coincides with a world made "completely vulnerable" by the transnationalization of production and the post-Cold War ideological fractures.[24] Garrett's understanding of the world's vulnerability is consonant with the triumphalist neo-liberal "revolution." It maintains that late-modern decentralization of production and the concomitant acceleration of trans-border flows of goods and people increase the risks of cross-border movement of biological agents. Moreover, she suggests that the risks associated with population movements exceed the dangers of contagion. By accelerating cultural and political encounters, the late modern population flows threaten the nation-state's political viability by heightening the likelihood of conflicts.

Garrett's reading echoes the anxieties manifest in Samuel Huntington's diagnosis of present conflicts in "The Clash of Civilizations?" Huntington's essay questions realist international relations' ability to satisfactorily explain contemporary conflicts. While he preserves, if attenuated, the agency of nation-states, he contends that in the "new world" order, "conflict between civilizations will supplant ideological and other forms of conflict as the dominant global form of conflict."[25] Although Huntington displaces a state-centered political imaginary with a civilizational heuristic, he leaves the realist theory's rationalist core unaltered. It is the unit and not the mode of analysis that changes. In his civilizational frame, "kin-country syndrome" replaces "political ideology and traditional balance of power considerations as the basis for cooperation and coalitions."[26] The resulting civilizational construct preserves the world's intelligibility by anchoring conflicts and tensions in immutable, ontological differences. While Garrett's and Huntington's models share a culturalist focus, Garrett is less sanguine about the intelligibility of modern conflict. Inasmuch as she eschews civilizational categories, her world does not succumb to civilization's centripetal force, but fragments in a plurality of cultures and voices that render conflict not only present but unpredictable.

Garrett's fractious political matrix lends itself to a heightened sense of insecurity. For unlike the Cold War nuclear détente, which assumed equilibrium in the destructive powers of states, a gross power asymmetry defines the present political landscape. The proliferation of political agents and enmities, though not eclipsing conventional warfare, gives rise to novel, "asymmetric warfare."[27] Non-state agents vying for power no longer seek competitive advantage by acquiring nuclear weapons, but use more affordable and ready-at-hand technologies. Among these, biotechnology surfaces as the most powerful. The easy conversion of pathogens into potent biological weapons makes them the "poor man's atom bomb."[28]

The resulting scenario effects a profound anxiety about our collective capacity to control deadly pathogens, and increases our fears about the terroristic uses of bioengineering technologies. Garrett accords this biological uncertainty with a need to de-emphasize Cold War conceptions of security, premised upon exclusive notions of state agency. Most significantly, she contends, the ideas about security that have governed policymaking in past decades should be retooled to place biological threats at the center of national security discussions.

This analysis is, however, problematic. In embracing normative notions of risk, Garrett fails to account for the nation-state's use of public health to enact a recuperative discourse. This failure is evident in her analysis of the 1994 outbreak of pneumonic plague in Surat, India. In 1987, 28 years after the last recorded incident of plague, the Indian government abandoned its public health surveillance of *Yersinia pestis*—the vector of bubonic and pneumonic plagues.[29] This would have dire consequences, when, in October

1994, physicians in Surat, Gujarat state, began reporting cases of pneumonic plague. In the weeks prior to the Surat outbreak, peasants returning to Beed District in Maharashtra, a few hundred kilometers East of Surat, fell ill from bubonic plague. Seeking treatment and refuge, many migrated to Surat where the bacterium they carried thrived in the City's densely populated and squalid streets.[30]

Surat's lack of an adequate public health infrastructure proved disastrous. A prosperous industrial city in the West, the City is home to approximately 2.2 million inhabitants, 40 percent of whom are imported laborers working in clothing mills and diamond-polishing and gold industries. While the City is home to some of India's wealthiest merchants, its laborers live in slums. In the slums, where conditions were made worse by the monsoon flooding of the river Tapti, the bubonic plague converted into pneumonic plague, a more virulent and contagious variant. Faced with the disease's "explosive spread," the municipal authorities declared Surat "plague threatened" within days of the first recorded cases.[31] The declaration sent a wave of panic through the population, half a million of which fled the City. In the exodus were "workers and hospital staff, including physicians," further jeopardizing the City's imperiled medical infrastructure.[32]

While the moneyed elite sought the first means of transport out of the City and the poor hunted rats, India's federal bureaucracy was silent. For days, "the government strenuously denied any outbreak of plague."[33] In part, the government's reticence was a reaction to earlier incidents of melioidosis in Pune, Maharashtra state. Not wanting to exacerbate the citizenry's fears by mistaking melioidosis, a bacterial infection, with pneumonic plague, India's National Institute of Communicable Diseases (NICD) was slow in conducting the assays.[34] There were, however, more instrumental reasons for the government's reticence and equivocation. First, keenly aware of its dependence on global financial networks, India feared that acknowledging Surat's outbreak would adversely impact its markets. Narasimha Rao's cabinet "took more than ten days to discuss the Surat outbreak after it occurred, and even then it focused not so much on containing the disease as on reassuring the world business community."[35] The government's fear proved warranted when, weeks into the outbreak, the Bombay stock market fell some 213 points, 5% of its total value. Second, the region's volatile political atmosphere complicated matters further. Coterminous with the outbreaks were popular outcries denouncing countries from the United States to Bangladesh for their purported involvement in the plague. Newspaper editorials and political pundits contended that the outbreaks in Beed and Surat were a result of genetically engineered bacterium released on the unsuspecting population by American and/or former Soviet scientists. Still others maintained that the outbreaks were rumors promulgated by Pakistan and Bangladesh to undermine India's national security.[36] While the government busied itself sifting through these narratives, the plague raged in Surat, killing 56 people and infecting some 453 others.[37]

The international community responded to the outbreak with "unthinking panic." The United States, for example, went into a heightened state of alert. Rudy Giuliani, New York City's mayor, a City with an average of 31 daily flights from India, asked City officials to bar all flights from India. When convinced that the measure was ill advised, the City adopted the Centers for Disease Control and Prevention's (CDC) recommendations and mobilized Immigration and Naturalization Service (INS) agents, physicians, and flight crews into a network of "passive surveillance."[38] They were charged with identifying and quarantining persons suffering from coughs, chills, and fever as potential carriers of plague. The United States' reactions, however, were pale in comparison to those of South Asian and Gulf states. Countries in the Gulf responded by boycotting "such outrageously misnamed plague-carrying items as Indian postage stamps, oranges, Madras bolts of silk, and Bangalore computer chips."[39] Others, like Bangladesh, one of India's closest neighbors, closed their borders to Indian citizens, prompting a commentator to remark, "Indian rats are unlikely to observe such restrictions."[40]

In the wake of the plague, India became a "global pariah," And as Praful Bidwai asserts, "the Indian elite discovers for the first time what untouchability is."[41] These articulations of distance as national forms of individuation are overlooked by Garrett's focus on the international communities' ineffectual responses to the outbreak as evidence of a public health system in crisis. Bangladeshi and American responses to Surat's outbreak are neither mere illustrations of the "inanity" of international reactions nor simple reminders of our collective vulnerability to diseases. They enact a discourse of surveillance that operates within a thick symbolic space. Bangladesh's border closing, for example, exceeds the public health-cum-medical discourse. Its supplementarity unmasks the "absence of presence" in nationalist discourse.[42] It is a gesture of self-creation and of self-articulation in the face of contested regional and global politics. That is, the international community's responses to the outbreak betray a reflex to secure borders in a world of vanishing boundaries.

By overlooking epidemiology's boundary-creating impulse, Garrett renders her analysis silent on the bio-politics of public health. This is evinced in her canonical history of American public health. In her bio-political drama, turn of the 20th century New York City is the principal character. The City's billing is an extension of its history as the primary port of entry for millions of European immigrants. Although New York City stages an intersection between urbanization, migration, and health, Garrett restricts her focus to the association between the rise of public health and the ascent of a sizeable urban middle class. She contends that in the absence of an established middle class "the rich simply lived separate and unequal lives . . . raising their families through private systems of health, education, and cultural training."[43] The geographical and material distance between the rich and the poor lessened the drive for public health infrastructures. The upper class understood the gulf as an insurance against the putative source of epidemics: poverty and its attendant social and moral turpitude. Thus, Garrett maintains, public health discourse, whether as sanitary or germ theory, would not find wide acceptance until the post-World War I rise of an urban middle class, a class that "supported public education, recognized and abhorred corruption, and, as home owners, had an investment in their cities."[44]

While the stark and symbolic distance between the upper and lower classes depended on gross forms of violence and proved relatively easy to sustain, the rise of an urban middle class demanded a more complex mode of class surveillance.[45] Public health's referents, contagion and cleanliness, were active tropes in the new technology of governamentality. In the industrial cities of the late 1800s, teeming with immigrant blue-collar workers, these tropes functioned not simply as scaffolds of a preventive science, but "held the potential of deepening every social divide."[46] In other words, public health discourse naturalized class hierarchies by instilling in the urban proletariat the belief that the discipline to fight dirt and grime was a reflection of moral rectitude and the cornerstone of middle class propriety. As Richard and Claudia Bushman note, "cleanliness had social power because it was a moral ideal and thus a standard of judgment. Cleanliness values bore on all who wished to better their lives or felt the sting of invidious class comparisons."[47] Public health discourse thus simultaneously substantiated America's democratic mythos—the belief that class ascendancy was attainable through the assimilation of prescribed social values—and fueled deep social divides. It transformed Garrett's New York City from an immunologically coherent metonym for the nation into a national mise-en-scène of encounter, accelerating America's elemental political struggles.[48]

The violence of public health's bio-political agency is most powerfully illustrated by Mary Mallon's biography. Mallon, a young Irish immigrant cook, led a socially invisible life, like countless immigrant women living in New York. In 1907, her life, and by extension America's cultural lexicon, would be forever changed by a visit from George Soper. Soper, a sanitary engineer and an adherent of the germ theory, had been hired by the Thompsons, a wealthy New York City family, to investigate an outbreak of typhoid at their summer rental home in Oyster Bay, Long Island.[49] Armed with the theory of healthy carriers of typhoid, he became convinced that Mallon, who had been employed by the Thompsons at Oyster Bay, was the crucial link in the outbreak. However, when he confronted her at her employer's Park Avenue residence, Mallon was far from hospitable to Soper's contention that she was responsible for the outbreaks.

Convinced of her guilt, Soper appealed to Dr. Hermann Biggs at the New York City Health Department. Soper found an attentive audience in Biggs. Intrigued by Soper's evidence, Biggs sent Dr. Josephine Baker, the sanitary superintendent's assistant, to collect samples from Mallon. In her first attempt, Dr. Baker was no more successful than Soper had been. However, emboldened by public health's new juridical authority, she returned and under police escort took Mallon to Willard Parker hospital, where tests found her to carry *Salmonella typhi*. New York City's health department found itself ill-equipped to manage its first healthy typhoid carrier. Thus, while City health officials debated the case's immediate policy challenges, Mallon was remanded to North Brother Island.

Unconvinced of the health department's diagnosis, Mallon sought every legal and scientific avenue to contest her quarantine. In 1910, she won her freedom by signing an affidavit promising not to seek employment as a cook. Her freedom was short-lived. Investigating an outbreak of typhoid at the Sloane Maternity hospital, public health agents traced the source of the bacillus to the hospital's new cook, Mary Mallon. This time, she would be exiled to North Brother Island for the remainder of her life.

Mallon, as a biographical subject, has all but receded from America's historical imaginary. What remains is the ubiquitous metaphor, Typhoid Mary. The metaphor realizes its place in America's social imaginary by activating the fundamental attribute of modern subjectification: its governmental imprimatur. Thus, as a narrative of being, modern "life-writing" traces not the unfolding of a being-in-the-world, but outlines the contours of the governmental. In other words, biography traces the emergence of the subject.[50] Therefore, it is not surprising when nearly a century after she was first exiled to North Brother Island, Garrett encapsulates Mallon's life as follows:

> But after her release Mallon illegally returned to that profession under a pseudonym. When Biggs's staff tracked the belligerent and thoroughly uncooperative woman down, they exiled her to that island again, this time for the rest of her days. She would forever be remembered as Typhoid Mary.[51]

Garrett's adjectival arsenal marks Mallon as "belligerent" and "thoroughly uncooperative," and therefore deserving exile. Her biography of Mallon demonstrates the supremacy of public health as a social genre by reducing Mallon's 69 years of life into a medico-juridical account of non-compliance.

The significance of non-compliance is best understood in the context of a praxis of social control framed, in part, through discourses of social responsibility. At stake in Mallon's legal battle to refrain from giving specimens to the City's health officials and to resist involuntary confinement was not only her freedom against intrusion by the state, but her very Americanness. Mallon's Americanness is weighed in decidedly gendered terms. Her unwillingness to sacrifice herself for the good of "America" raises questions about her fitness as a citizen and, more importantly, as a woman/mother. In other words, in questioning public health's juridico-political mandate, she falters in her womanly duty to birth and nurture a healthy nation. This profoundly resonates with the turn of the 20th century angst about the role of American women in safeguarding the country against "race suicide." Increased industrialization and the promise of greater leisure for American-middle class women induced deep cultural anxieties. The new-woman's "refusal of domesticity and reproduction" was interpreted as a challenge to the social order and by extension a portent of America's cultural and political demise.[52] The disquiet over gender roles, complicated in no small measure by the influx of immigrants, is evident in the gender markers associated with Mallon.[53] She is described as a transgressive, recalcitrant, and "masculine woman."[54] Soper's description is especially telling. He notes: "nothing was so distinctive about her as her walk, unless it was her mind. The two had a peculiarity in common . . . Mary walked more like a man than a woman and . . . her mind has a distinct masculine character ."[55] Thus, insofar as she failed to conform to prescribed models of femininity, she was disqual-ified as a citizen and exiled from the nation.

The public health inscriptions that gave rise to Typhoid Mary as a field of signification were much bolstered by the Cold War. Germ theory, which had ushered in the first major shift in public health discourse, found powerful complements in post-World War II advances in virology and immunology. Their discursive preeminence, however, exceeded scientific advances. Inasmuch as they construe the body as bounded entities requir-ing strict internal surveillance, immunology and virology participate in an intricate commerce of security metaphors with the state. Immunology "as a map of systems of 'difference'" offered the state a naturalizing, scientific language.[56] Through a double-mirroring, the modern state came to under-stand itself engaged in differentiation, laboring, like the immune system, to distinguish the self from the non-self. The healthy carrier is thus a danger to the body politic not because she is a silent carrier of deadly "germs," but because she is a "border figure." Her existence between illness and health, between citizenship and exile defies conventions and authority, disrupting the state's ability to recognize and construct the self.

In Cold War narratives, reactions to the disruptive impact of border figures feature prominently. The suspicion that the stranger's differences might not rise above the threshold of recognition is an overriding, if at times an unconscious, element of America's cultural and political landscape. Prior to the end of the First World War, America relied largely on a visual grammar of difference. The Other was knowable by the color of his skin, the texture of his hair, the shape of his nose, and by the visual syntagma of race. The Bolshevik revolution unsettled this visual syntax by introducing new ideological elements. After 1917, the face, the visual matrix of transparency, becomes, more than ever, the locus of the uncanny. It no longer obeyed a simple binarism of reflection, a visual index of the self and the Other. The Cold War, like a house of horror's distorting mirrors, deformed the face, reflecting back an image that was at once homely and unhomely. The Cold War's every reflection registered the suspicion that behind the familiar hid the stranger, the Communist Other.[57]

The neurosis induced by the fear of a visually indiscernible Other found patent articulation in the 1938 creation of the House Un-American Activities Committee (HUAC). A standing committee of the House of Representatives under the leadership of Martin Dies, Representative of Texas, the HUAC sought to root out disloyalty and subversion. If the Other could not be recognized by his face, he would be made recognizable through his utterances. The speech act involved in renouncing membership in the Communist party—"I am not nor have I ever been a member of the Communist party"—was at once a linguistic performance of citizenship and, more importantly, an act of biological incorporation. The Committee's paranoiac posture, seeing a Communist plot in every dissenting gesture, betrays the conceptual limitations of the nation as a geo-culturally contiguous space. It traces a diagram of relationships that constitutes the nation as a political and immunological community.

To fully understand the relationship between the Red Scare's immunological accent and the production of the nation as an "imagined immunity," we must survey the post-Cold War extension of the discourse's dominant tropes.[58] If the Red Scare inaugurated the nation as an immunity discourse, the discourse found its full expression in the HIV/AIDS epidemic. The HUAC hearings sought not simply to uncover individual ideological attachments, but to disentangle ideological communities. For this reason, an individual's declaration of allegiance, in and of itself, was insufficient. The accused demonstrated his social responsibility by participating in a project of contact tracing. He had to expose those whom he knew or thought to be "contaminated." Similarly, the story of HIV/AIDS is the story of contact tracing as an act of citizenship.

One of the dominant HIV/AIDS narratives accords the epidemic a unique position in the annals of public health.[59] Adherents to the "AIDS exceptionalism" narrative contend that the political and legal upheaval that attends the epidemic have suspended public health's use of time-tested technologies, such as routine testing, reporting, contact tracing, and notification, for identifying and tracking at-risk groups, contributing to the continued rise in rates of infection. The AIDS exceptionalism argument does not, however, speak to the concerns of AIDS activists, namely, the relationship between epidemiology and governmentality. For, as Catherine Waldby argues, HIV testing illustrates, à la "Typhoid Mary," the construction of an epidemiological map.[60] Testing does not merely isolate the virus, but marks dangerous behaviors and delimits at-risk communities. The resulting map is, therefore, not a disinterested construction. As opponents of routine testing have asserted, the identification of HIV/AIDS with the gay community renders testing positive for the virus a *de facto* affirmation of homosexuality.[61] The test is, they maintain, less a screen for the HIV virus than a determination of identity.[62]

The exceptionalism of AIDS suggests that a correlation between a weakened public health infrastructure and the increased incidence of HIV/AIDS is animated not by a concern for the well-being of sufferers, but by the fear that the ecology of behaviors associated with the HIV virus—homosexuality and intravenous drug use—elude state surveillance.[63] The imbrication of the spaces of HIV/AIDS with the extra-legal spaces of homosexuality and drug use converts persons living with AIDS into border figures against which the state enacts a discourse of belonging and citizenship. The use of HIV/AIDS in a theater of citizenship is powerfully affirmed in the battles over entitlement. Much as in Mary Mallon's case nearly a century earlier, the social negotiations over the AIDS epidemic are political and cultural acts that rest on the legal conception of the family, and, by extension, on the necessary qualifications for lawful incorporation into the nation. For too many in the AIDS community, protracted legal battles punctuate the disease's end-stage. Often during this stage or soon after a patient's death, parents and family members return to contest powers of attorney and wills. The state's refusal to acknowledge non-traditional family arrangements leaves partners and support networks powerless against the legal onslaught by the patient's biological, state-sanctioned family. The state harnesses this medico-juridical nexus to reaffirm the definition of the family as a bio-legal entity and as the foundational precursor to the nation-state. In so doing, it not only excludes gays from an important domain of legal protection but it also marks them as marginal to the nation.[64]

These enactments of public health's bio-power, the use of HIV to arrest the fluid discourse of belonging, are absent from analysis such as Garrett's. Garrett's *Betrayal of Trust* deflects the imprint of citizenship manifest in the transformation of the subject into a "social being." As both Mary Mallon's case and the HIV/AIDS epidemic illustrate, public health transforms the carrier's micro-political network into a metaphor of the macro-political. Private behaviors and structures of belonging are made to accord with a national imaginary: citizenship becomes an act of piety. Garrett's narrative invokes a Lockean social contract to justify public health impinging on social freedoms. The curtailing of individual autonomy is deemed a necessary sacrifice that ensures the collective good and preserves the nation's viability. This narrative functions through the simultaneous play of exclusion and inclusion. In a defensive act, the state excludes the carrier from the nation by cordoning him within an epidemiological community. The exclusion is, however, never complete, for the state relies on the internal presence of the carrier to deploy the narrative of citizenship-as-sacrifice as an essential attribute of patriotism. Paradoxically, the state's reliance on the carrier's liminality disrupts the national narrative by destabilizing the sacrosanct role of borders, a complication that public health addresses by resorting to a geo-political narrative of origin: enter Colette Matshimoseka.

The "Wall of Disease"

Randy Shilts' celebrated history of the initial years of the HIV/AIDS epidemic in the United States, *And the Band Played On*,[65] begins with a detailed account of the illness and death of Margrethe Rask, a Danish surgeon working in Abumombazi, northern Zaire. The account, as with so many (ex)colonial missionary biographies, follows a predictable trajectory: it is both a tale of heroism and sacrifice and a morality play. Dr. Rask, an energetic health crusader, forfeits a lucrative career in "the sprawling modern hospitals of Copenhagen" to brave the risks of "primitive medicine" in a region of the world that "sire(s) new diseases with nightmarish regularity."[66] Therefore, it was not a cause for alarm when she began complaining of fatigue and gastric ailments. Deemed consistent with the illnesses endemic to the region, her symptoms were addressed accordingly, and, as a testament to her dedication and tenacity, she immersed herself in the clinic's perennial medical and logistical crises despite growing fatigue and weight loss. By the winter of 1976, however, persistent fatigue, a growing list of symptoms, and an unstable lymphatic system forced her to return to Denmark for treatment, which did not provide any relief. Denmark's leading specialists were unable to explain her low T-cell count and the myriad opportunistic infections that plagued her. After months of tests and treatments, Dr. Rask died on December 12, 1977 of *Pneumocystis carinii*.

Given the experiences of the early years of the HIV/AIDS epidemic in the United States, Margrethe Rask's story is hardly unique. Therefore, it is curious that Shilts begins his account by locating HIV/AIDS not in New York or San Francisco, his geographical subjects, but in Abumombazi, Zaire. However, when placed in the context of Western HIV/AIDS narratives, Shilts' choice of Central Africa as an anchor for his account reveals an instinct that finds Africa too often the starting point of narratives about viral pandemics.[67] This narratival finger pointing betrays efforts at reconciling the presence of the carrier within the West's "immunological community." To understand this reflex that fixes Africa as the locus of origin of viral pandemics, we must return to the intersection of imagined immunity, travel, and geopolitics.

In 1994, *The Atlantic Monthly* ran a cover story by Robert Kaplan titled "The Coming Anarchy: How scarcity, crime, overpopulation, tribalism, and disease are rapidly destroying the social fabric of our planet." The essay begins as follows:

> The Minister's eyes were like egg yolks, an aftereffect of some of the many illnesses, malaria especially, endemic in his country. There was also an irrefutable sadness in his eyes. He spoke in a slow and cracking voice, the voice of hope about to expire.[68]

Kaplan's informant, "my friend the Minister," is anonymous. Kaplan is silent about the minister's identity, for, he tells us, he fears, were he to reveal his source, the official's "life would be threatened."[69] His subsequent remarks, however, index a different intent. In Kaplan's apocalyptic future, Africa has a prophetic, if dystopic, role.[70] West African countries, from Liberia to Nigeria, conjure the Chicagos of the future, the bands of "armed burglars, carjackers, muggers," and "the groups of young men with restless and scanning eyes" that haunt the futurist's dreams.[71]

Kaplan holds the implosion of postcolonial states responsible for the systemic problems that are now *de rigueur* in Africa and elsewhere in the South. He draws a causal connection between the "very unstable social fluid," resulting from the collapse of nation-states—and famines, deforestation, soil erosion, flooding and the explosive rise of epidemics. He maintains that these conditions, taken as a whole have replaced recognizable, operative national boundaries by "walls of disease." He writes:

> Africa may today be more dangerous in this regard than it was in 1862, before antibiotics, when the explorer Sir Richard Francis Burton describes the health situation on the continent as "deadly, a Golgotha, a Jehannum."[72]

Echoing early 19th century travel writers, Kaplan represents the Africa of the future as an impenetrable fortress of malaria and warring natives. The imagined "wall of disease" reactivates the colonial grammar of signification: Africa is again alien; it is the dark, blank, and unexplored continent of Victorian atlases.[73]

Through the evocation of over-coded imagery, Kaplan re-primitivizes Africa, a move that is of singular import in writings about epidemics. The trope of the primitive delimits a boundary between the North and the

South that transforms the latter into a location where pathogens "practice on local populations in preparation for pandemics."[74] Kaplan's primitivist bio-cartography, however, differs from past articulations in its appreciation of late-modernity's deterritorializing flows of bodies and cultures. For in negating the notion that "disorder [does] not travel,"[75] he sets diseases in motion and affirms the possibility that the next outbreak will come from outside Western borders.

The bio-geographical provenance, the attribution of place to disease enabled by the primitive trope, captures the flows of diseases within a rigid discursive frame that incites a border creating terror.[76] In marking emergent diseases as pre-modern presences, the West exteriorizes the historicopolitical and geographical loci of superbugs, which explains Shilts' consignation of HIV/AIDS to Abumombazi, Zaire. More importantly, by locating the origin of superbugs elsewhere, the West creates the condition of possibility for a global capture that arrests globalization's destabilizing flows. Put differently, while in Mary Mallon's case and that of the Red Scare, the threat was connsidered to be internal to the nation-state, the projection of present destabilizing forces onto an exterior presence constitutes a rearticulation of sovereignty and international relations. States employ late-modernity's agent of terror, the superbug, to reclaim the viability of nation-states against the global movements of peoples and cultures. In the emerging discourse, the inwardly focused immunological grammar of earlier public health discourses can no longer sustain biopolitical discourses. The state has recourse to virology for linguistic and epistemic scaffolding. For, contrary to immunology, virology's preoccupation is not with recognition writ large, but with border surveillance. It defines the self not through the internal policing of a figurative community, the disambiguating of the self from the non-self, but through the rigid policing of the body's boundaries.

The state's appropriation of immunology's and virology's grammar is not, however, a mutually exclusive proposition. The function of disease as a metaphor of the body politic is neither exclusively inwardly nor outwardly directed. The virological and immunological grammars are conjunctural. They provide the nation with a means to regulate internal and external threats to its stability. However, the present prominence of viral metaphors is symptomatic of a change in statist concerns. The post-1989 purported neo-liberal triumph has lessened anxieties about ideological disintegration while heightening concerns about the cultural, linguistic, and political implications of globalization's deterritorializing force. Virology is thus of great import for it provides a matrix of signification for contemporary border surveillance.

Viruses, like HIV, expose our collective vulnerability, our species' being-in-common, while they reveal our differential susceptibility, a fact demonstrated by the expression "living with HIV." The phrase, meant to capture our shifting medical and cultural relationship with HIV, obscures a wide and growing gap between the effects of class, gender, race, and geography on persons infected with the virus. It conceals, for example, the prohibitive prices of the drugs responsible for the transformation of HIV/AIDS into a chronic ailment, a disease with which very few can afford to live. It is, however, to the inherent mobility of pathogens, to their potential for smoothing spaces and leveling differences that the "wall of disease" reacts. The quarantining of the cultural and geographic Other within a global epidemiological map negates the possibility of an immunological species-being. Rather, it affirms a new (inter)national relations that fractures the globe into distinct and incompatible bio-cultural regions. The new "inter" of the emergent international relations expands the family's constitutive ontopolitical role. Familial co-sanguinity assumes a civilizational-cum-regional scope, a structure that, in part, sustains Huntington's civilizational map. Huntington's use of the term "kin-country" is not accidental. It sustains a geopolitical construct that reclaims the viability of nation-states by staging cultural and political encounters as bio-ontological confrontations.

Wolfgang Petersen's *Outbreak*, released in 1995, illustrates this matrix at work. Briefly summarized, the film tracks a string of events leading to an outbreak of the fictive Motaba, "a rare killer from the jungles of Zaire," in the town of Cedar Creek, California. *Outbreak* begins, as does Shilts' *And the Band Played On*, with a detour. The film's opening scene is a flashback to 1967. The location, Motaba River Valley, Zaire, is a fallen Eden. Gunfire and explosions interrupt the camera's flyover of the tranquil rainforest canopy. The camera captures the chaos that reigns below in an extreme close-up of howling monkeys running from soldiers in pitched gunfight. Petersen's gaze is not, however, merely ethnographic. He does not restrict himself to reporting on the conflict inside or outside the camera's frame. Rather, the reason for the detour becomes evident when the camera pans onto a mercenary camp, where, in a makeshift hospital, American and Belgian mercenaries have been laid down not by bullets, but by a mysterious disease: the dreaded Motaba. The opening scene's visual syntax, the juxtaposition of the jungle, war, and disease, structures the ideological scaffolding that supports the film's narrative.

To the jungle/Zaire's chaos and disorder, *Outbreak* counterpoises the orderliness of the U.S. Army Medical Research Institute of Infectious Diseases (USAMRIID). Petersen's camera creates a structural homology between the opening scenes' jungle flyover and the camera's movement through the Institute's spatial grid. Through a steady-cam sequence, the film moves through the laboratories' progressively higher bio-safety levels, arriving at level four, the "hot zone." The bio-safety levels denote a scale of danger that runs from familiar pathogens, Pneumococcus and Salmonella, to exotic killers such as Ebola, Lassa, and Hanta viruses. The camera's movement enacts a spatial narrative of danger. The greater the distance from the familiar, from the Institute's bureaucratic center, the more pronounced the danger of contagion.[77] The film, however, disciplines the possibility of contagion in the laboratory. Increased layers of protection accompany the camera's movement toward the "hot zone." Computers, security cameras, armed guards, and radiation scrubbers regulate the traffic between each successive level. In controlling the possibility of infection, the film furthers the distinction between the lab and the jungle. The Army laboratories are heterotopic spaces that not only contain the world's most virulent organism, but, more importantly, create a "space that is other, another space, as perfect, as meticulous, as well arranged as ours is messy, ill constructed, and jumbled."[78]

Petersen reproduces the heterotopy between the jungle and the lab by contrasting the USAMRIID's intensely regulated space to the fluidity and vulnerability of the home. The camera cuts in quick succession from the laboratory's ascetic order to the disarray of Colonel Sam Daniels' (Dustin Hoffman) home. The two filmic spaces overlap in their differential relation to the jungle's encroaching disorder. The laboratory's vigilance against the "killer from the jungles of Zaire" stands in marked relief to the innocent disorder of Sam's kitchen. This juxtaposition renders transparent Petersen's choice of USAMRIID.[79] As Laurie Garrett suggests, it implicitly acknowledges biological threats, as belonging to the military domain.[80] Moreover, through a sustained metonymy between the family and the nation, Outbreak references the innocence signified by the kitchen, the family's symbolic center, to the nation's vulnerability. Colonel Daniels and Major Salt's (Cuba Gooding, Jr.) search for Motaba's carrier, an African monkey set loose in the woods of Cedar Creek, completes this metonymic arch. Seated at the kitchen table a young girl draws pictures of the monkey, which has taken residence outside her kitchen windows, while in the background a television news brief asks for the public's help in locating the dangerous animal. The television, through the news anchor's allocution, places the kitchen squarely within the nation's civic space. It effaces the borders between the kitchen's private space and the nation's public space, transforming the girl's naive drawings into a nationally ominous sign.

The complex family/nation finds full expression in Petersen's folding onto the epidemiological thriller the melodrama of Sam and Robby's (Rene Russo) failed marriage. After years of living and working together, the "virus hunter's" marriage succumbs to the job's pressures. The dangers posed by the virus are, therefore, not restricted to individuals, but extend to the nation's formative social and civic bonds. A contact tracing montage that follows the aerosolized virus, expelled by a cough, as it moves through a crowded movie theater captures Motaba's threat to the body politic. The virus' path through

Fig. 10.1 Reconciled by Motaba, from *Outbreak*, 1995, directed by Wolfgang Petersen.

the theater links the audience into the social and civic entity that is Cedar Creek, a "small town, like a family."[81] Motaba's infective flight, however, disrupts the very social and civic bonds it traces. It transmutes all familial contact, every act of affection, into a potentially deadly gesture. While this milieu proves toxic to most families, it has the obverse effect on Sam and Robby. As Karen Schneider has observed, Motaba's "profoundly unnatural breakdown of the patriarchical family unit can only be averted by the concerted reconstitution of the heterosexual team working together to fend off the monstrous."[82] The outbreak in Cedar Creek stages the reunion of the divorced couple. Sent by the CDC to Cedar Creek to help control the outbreak, Robby pricks herself with a contaminated needle whilst treating a patient. Her infection crystallizes Sam's efforts to find a serum. With a husband's devotion, he violates his superior's every order in his search. He demonstrates his heroic commitment to the family when, in violation of isolation protocols and unsure that the serum he has found will work, he removes his mask to touch Robby's hand to his face. The touch, unmediated by the biohazard suit, restores the couple's bond and gestures to the survival of heteronormal family and, by extension, the nation (see Fig. 10.1).

Conclusion

In the aftermath of the terrorist attacks of September 11, 2001, the U. S. sought to mobilize the country and justify its actions against the Taliban and Al Qaeda by calling on the function of history as a traumatic memory.

Newspaper and television reports reached back to the history of the Second World War and gave new life to Japan's attack on Pearl Harbor. Ignoring the comparison's obvious shortfalls, the attack on Pearl Harbor became an overarching signifier. Others, like President Bush, sought grander historical perspectives. In an address to the reporters on the White House lawn, Bush compared the United States' "war on terrorism" to the Crusades: it is a holy war, a religious confrontation of good versus evil.[83] Whatever the historical scale of the comparisons, they share a Manichean understanding of the world. In the words of Tod Lindberg, editor of *Policy Review*, echoing an earlier remark by President Bush, foreign governments are "either with us and against the terrorists, or against us and with them."

The fear that Al Qaeda's agents, blinded by their putative hate for the U.S., would seek to infect the country with deadly viruses has captured the public's imagination. The state's participation in the construction of a climate of anxiety, exemplified most notably in the Homeland Security's color-coded advisory system and in the heightened alarm about the threat of smallpox, "secretly works towards the production of emergencies."[84] The state of emergency that these anxieties produce is placed in the service of an apparatus of surveillance that recovers territorial sovereignty by equating foreign accents and darker skin color with deadly agents. It seeks to contain the Others' deterritorializing presence through a narrative of "imagined immunities."

Notes

1. Johann Peter Frank, *A System of Complete Medical Police: Selections from Johann Peter Frank* (Baltimore: Johns Hopkins University Press, 1976), p. 12.
2. John Edgar Wideman, *Fever: Twelve Stories* (New York: Penguin, 1990).
3. Mary Vallis, "Woman with Mysterious Illness on Life-Support," *National Post*, February 9, 2001.
4. Anne Marie Owens, "Deadly Virus Not Ruled out, Public Told Not to Panic," *National Post*, February 7, 2001.
5. Kem Kilpatrick, "Canada's Ebola Scare over but Questions Just Beginning," *Canadian Medical Association Journal*, 164(7), 2001: 1031. Although the West is the space where the fear of the virus is most acutely demonstrated, it has not spared the South. In January 2001, Saudi Arabia "banned all Ugandan Muslim pilgrims from attending the annual Hajj pilgrimage." Frank Gardner, "Hajj Pilgrims Barred in Ebola Scare," *BBC News*, January 23, 2001.
6. Adrian Humphreys, "Mystery Illness: Health Canada Rules out Ebola," *National Post*, February 8, 2001.
7. Humphreys, "Mystery Illness: Health Canada Rules out Ebola."
8. Vallis, "Woman with Mysterious Illness on Life-Support."
9. Humphreys, "Mystery Illness: Health Canada Rules out Ebola."
10. Michael Fumento, "Ebola Fever Sweeps the West," *National Post*, January 31, 2001.
11. See Joseph B. McCormick and Susan Fisher-Hoch, *Level 4: Virus Hunters of the C.D.C.* (New York: Barnes & Nobles, 1999).
12. Richard Preston, *The Hot Zone* (New York: Random House, 1994), pp. 68–69.
13. Preston, *The Hot Zone*, p. 272.
14. Preston, *The Hot Zone*, p. 75.
15. "Not Quite the Plague," *National Post*, February 9, 2001.
16. "Hospital on Hook for Ebola Scare Medical Bill," *National Post*, March 13, 2001.

17. Heather Sokoloff, "Congo Woman in Ebola Scare Leaves the Hospital," *National Post*, March 5, 2001.
18. "Police Will Not Probe Congolese Woman," *The Toronto Star*, March 6, 2001.
19. Joanna Fretich, "Ebola Scare Costly for Hospital," *The Toronto Star*, March 13, 2001.
20. Fretich, "Ebola Scare Costly for Hospital."
21. Giorgio Agamben, *Homo Sacer: Sovereignty, Power and Bare Life* (Stanford: Stanford University Press, 1998), p. 15.
22. Laurie Garrett, *The Coming Plague: Newly Emerging Diseases in a World out of Balance* (New York: Penguin Books, 1995).
23. Laurie Garrett, *Betrayal of Trust: The Collapse of Global Public Health* (New York: Hyperion, 2000), p. 2.
24. See Laurie Garrett, "The Return of Infectious Disease," *Foreign Affairs* 74(1), 1996; Laurie Garrett, "The Nightmare of Bioterrorism," *Foreign Affairs* 80 (1), 2000.
25. Samuel P. Huntington, *The Clash of Civilizations?: The Debate* (New York: Foreign Affairs, 1996), p. 24.
26. Huntington, *The Clash of Civilizations?*, pp. 12–13.
27. Steven M. Block, "The Growing Threat of Biological Weapons," *American Scientist*, 89(1), 2001: 28.
28. Block, "The Growing Threat of Biological Weapons," p. 32.
29. Garrett, *Betrayal of Trust: The Collapse of Global Public Health*, pp. 15–49.
30. Praful Bidwai, "Plague Warning," *The Nation*, October 3, 1994. This is by no means a universally accepted causal model for the Surat outbreak. Researchers have suggested that the cause for Surat's outbreak might be found in the human contact with plague-infested dead and dying animals brought to the city by the monsoon floods. See, for example, I. J. Catanach, "The 'Globalization' of Disease? India and the Plague," *Journal of World History* 12(1), 2001: 147.
31. D. T. Dennis, "Plague in India: Lessons for Public Health Everywhere," *British Medical Journal*, 309(6959), 1994.
32. Sanjay Kumar, "Plague in India," *The Lancet*, 344(8927), 1994: 941.
33. Bidwai, "Plague Warning," p. 480.
34. T. Jacobson John, "Final Thoughts on India's 1994 Plague Outbreak," *The Lancet*, 346(8977), 1995: 765.
35. Bidwai, "Plague Warning," p. 481.
36. Some commentators saw the plague as a divine sign of all that was amiss with India. See, for example, Francois Gautier, "The Horror That Is Bharat," *The Indian Express*, September 11, 2000.
37. Kumar, "Plague in India," p. 941.
38. Curtis L. Fritz, D.V.M., Ph.D., David T. Dennis, M.D., M.P.H., Margaret A. Tipple, M.D., Grant L. Campbell, M.D., Ph.D., Charles R. McCance, B.A., and Duane J. Gubler, Sc.D., "Surveillance for Pneumonic Plague in the United States During an International Emergency: A Model for Control of Imported Emerging Diseases," Emerging Infectious Diseases, 2(1), 1996: 30–36.
39. Garrett, *Betrayal of Trust: The Collapse of Global Public Health*, p. 48.
40. Editorial, "Plague in India: Time to Forget the Symptoms and Tackle the Disease," *The Lancet*, 344(8929), 1994.
41. Bidwai, "Plague Warning," p. 481.
42. Christine Howells, *Derrida: Deconstruction from Phenomenology to Ethics* (Cambridge, UK: Polity Press, 1999), p. 41.
43. Garrett, *Betrayal of Trust: The Collapse of Global Public Health*, p. 284.
44. Garrett, *Betrayal of Trust: The Collapse of Global Public Health*, p. 284.
45. For a discussion of how the "economy of social goods" is employed in the maintenance of social hierarchies, see Pierre Bourdieu, *Distinction : A Social Critique of the Judgement of Taste* (Cambridge, Massachusetts: Harvard University Press, 1984).
46. Richard L. Bushman and Claudia L. Bushman, "The Early History of Cleanliness in America," *Journal of American History*, 74, 1988: 1230.
47. Bushman and Bushman, "The Early History of Cleanliness in America," p. 1228.
48. For a revealing study of New York City's role in American political and racial discourse, see Ann Douglas, *Terrible Honesty: Mongrel Manhattan in the 1920s* (New York: The Noonday Press, 1995). See also C.L.R. James, *Mariners, Renegades, Castaways: The Story of Hermann Melville and the World We Live In* (Dartmouth: University Press of New England, 2001).
49. Judith Walzer Leavitt, *Typhoid Mary: Captive to the Public's Health* (Boston: Beacon Press, 1996), p. 14.

50. See Michel Foucault, *The History of Sexuality*, 1st American ed. (New York: Pantheon Books, 1978).
51. Garrett, *Betrayal of Trust: The Collapse of Global Public Health*, p. 300.
52. Priscilla Wald, "Cultures and Carriers: 'Typhoid Mary' and the Science of Social Control," *Social Text*, 15(3 and 4), 1997: 202.
53. For a discussion of the general climate that surrounded immigration at the turn of the century America, see Matthew Frye Jacobson, *Barbarian Virtues: The United States Encounters Foreign People at Home and Abroad, 1876–1917* (New York: Hill and Wang, 2000).
54. Wald, "Cultures and Carriers: 'Typhoid Mary' and the Science of Social Control," p. 196.
55. Soper quoted in Leavitt, *Typhoid Mary: Captive to the Public's Health*, pp. 106–107.
56. Donna Harraway, *Simians, Cyborgs, and Women: The Reinvention of Nature* (New York: Routledge, 1991), p. 217.
57. This anxiety is well documented in the post-WWII popularity of the invasion of the body snatcher sub-genre of science fiction films. See, for example, Don Siegel's 1956 *Invasion of the Body Snatcher* and Philip Kaufman's 1978 film of the same title.
58. For a discussion of "imagined immunities," see Priscilla Wald, "Imagined Immunities." In *Cultural Studies and Political Theory*, edited by Jodi Dean (Ithaca: Cornell University Press, 2000).
59. Chandler Burr, "The Aids Exception: Privacy Vs. Public Health," *The Atlantic Monthly*, June 1997.
60. Catherine Waldby, *AIDS and the Body Politics: Biomedicine and Sexual Difference* (New York: Routledge, 1996), p. 100.
61. For a detailed history of the HIV/AIDS epidemic in the United States, see Randy Shilts, *And the Band Played On: Politics, People and the AIDS Epidemic* (New York: St. Martin's Press, 2000).
62. For an example of the refusal to identify HIV/AIDS with the heterosexual community, see Michael Fumento, *The Myth of Heterosexual AIDS* (Washington, DC: Regnery Publishing, Inc., 1993).
63. For a discussion of homosexuality as an ecology, see Gabriel Rotello, *Sexual Ecology: AIDS and the Destiny of Gay Men* (New York: Dutton, 1997).
64. For an analysis of the construction of space and belonging in the "age of AIDS," see Lauren Berlant, "Live Sex Acts [Parental Advisory: Explicit Material." In *In near Ruins: Cultural Theory at the End of the Century*, edited by Nicholas B. Dirks (Minneapolis: University of Minnesota Press, 1998). See also Katherine Boo, "What Mother Teresa Could Learn in a Leather Bar," *The Washington Monthly*, June 1991.
65. Shilts, *And the Band Played On: Politics, People and the AIDS Epidemic*.
66. Shilts, *And the Band Played On: Politics, People and the AIDS Epidemic*, p. 4.
67. For two narratives that trace the origins of HIV/AIDS to Africa, see Mirko D. Grmek, *History of AIDS: Emergence and Origin of a Modern Pandemic*, trans.by Russel C. Maulitz and Jacalyn Duffin (Princeton: Princeton University Press, 1990); Edward Hooper, *The River: A Journey to the Source of HIV and AIDS* (New York: Little, Brown & Company, 2000).
68. Robert D. Kaplan, "The Coming Anarchy," *The Atlantic Monthly*, February 1994, p. 44.
69. Kaplan, "The Coming Anarchy."
70. Although Kaplan reserves his most acerbic comments to West Africa, his observations are not limited to the African continent. His vision of a dystopic future encompasses the entire South.
71. The Chicago Kaplan cites in his essay is a cardboard shantytown in the outskirts of Abidjan, the Ivory Coast.
72. Kaplan, "The Coming Anarchy," p. 46.
73. Kaplan, "The Coming Anarchy," p. 46.
74. Heather Schell, "Outbursts!: A Chilling True Story About Emerging-Virus Narratives and Pandemic Social Change," *Configurations*, 5(1), 1997: 115.
75. Schell, "Outbursts!"
76. Marie Louise Pratt offers an insightful analysis of the relationship between European scientific discourse, especially in its attempts to construct a universal taxonomic structure, and the fixing of the Other within a historic negative. See Mary Louise Pratt, *Imperial Eyes: Travel Writing and Transculturation* (New York: Routledge, 1992).
77. For a treatment of the link between spatial dislocation and danger, see Mary W. Helms, *Ulysses' Sail: An Ethnographic Odyssey of Power, Knowledge, and Geographic Distance* (Princeton: Princeton University Press, 1988).

78. Michel Foucault, "Of Other Spaces," *Diacritics*, 16(1), 1986: 27.
79. In Robin Cook's *Outbreak,* the agents are researchers at the CDC. Despite their title of epidemiological agents, they are civilian physicians who volunteer to work in CDC's special pathogens labs. This lends the work a clear distance from the more military aspect of Peteresen's Outbreak.
80. The film explores the other side of this equation when Sam learns that the U.S. army, under the leadership of General Donald McClintock (Donald Sutherland), had been exploring the possible uses of Motaba as a biological weapon.
81. Laurence Dworet and Robert Roy Pool, "Outbreak," edited by Wolfgang Petersen, 1995.
82. Karen Schneider, "With Violence If Necessary," *Journal of Popular Film and Television* 27(1), 1999: 8.
83. For responses to George W Bush's September 16, 2001 comments to reporters, see Anne E. Kornblut and Charles Radin, "Bush Image of Crusade Upsets Potential Allies," Boston Globe, September 18, 2001.
84. Giorgio Agamben, "Security and Terror," *Theory and Event*, 5(4), 2002.

CHAPTER 11

"In Search of Agency"

Beyond the "Old/New" Biopolitics of Sovereignty in Bosnia[1]

JASMINA HUSANOVIĆ

. . . Now the city is breached; of a dissolved form,
Sarajevo reminds of a postmodern work of fantastic proportions
There is so much suffering, so many cheap feelings: no one cries.
Death is universal and kitsch is universal . . .

From the poem 'Sarajevo' by Semezdin Mehmedinović[2]

The recent war and post-war times in Bosnia witnessed prime examples of hidden 'fantasmatic' and post-political matrices of sovereignty-as-enactment. To use Giorgio Agamben's terminology, the evidence in support of this statement are, multifarious politicizations of bare life, sovereign attempts to eliminate the biopolitically fractured people/People through ethno-national imaginaries, and other instances of the contemporary emergence of indistinct terrains in familiar topological figures.[3] These indistinct terrains, however, do host modalities of political agency that resist and possibly traverse the sovereign biopolitical predicaments. My aim here is to identify and assess the emergence of agents that might be deemed as acting emancipatorily with respect to the matrices of post-politics and sovereignty-as-enactment in the context of war and post-war Bosnia. This searching stance is specifically directed at some interesting instances of grassroots activism in Bosnia of the last decade.[4] Before this, shedding an Agambenian light on this Bosnian decade is in order.

Casting Agembenian Lights on Bosnia of the 1990s

As Agamben has argued, the dissolution of traditional State organisms in the former Yugoslavia (and Eastern Europe),

> should be viewed not as a re-emergence of the natural state of strug-gle of all against all - which functions as a prelude to new social contracts and new national and State localisations—but rather as the coming to light of the state of exception as the permanent structure of juridico-political de-localisation and dis-location. Political organisation is not regressing toward outdated forms; rather, premonitory events are, like bloody masses, announcing the new *nomos* of the earth, which (if its grounding principle is not called into question) will soon extend itself over the entire planet.[5]

Indeed, in Bosnia of the last decade, it has been an almost facile observation to remark how exceptions have become norms.[6] According to Agamben, this is the situation in which the state of exception overflows its spatio-temporal boundaries and coincides with the normal order. Once 'life' as the fundamental referent of the modern power and state organization becomes inscribed into 'order,' Right seeps into Left, public into private, and ex-communist regimes become the ethno-nationalist, racist ones. Here, the line between the decision on life (biopolitics) and the decision on death (thanatopolitics) becomes indistinct,[7] and it is an easy step to go from 'nor-mality' to 'war,' and vice versa. This is the background for the shift of the old leftist elites of the former Yugoslavia to supporting the ethnic cleansing only seemingly and misleadingly 'overnight'; it is also the background of their 'sudden' reversal into creators and expected implementers of peace accords.

The agents from the 'outside' intervening in the war situation also cannot be exempt from this mise-en-scène of biopolitics/thanatopolitics. The majority of Bosnian citizens have good reasons to consider Western humanitarianism as the greatest cynicism of all that happened to them. Many of them recognize the present-day separation between humanitari-anism and politics as the most debilitating war experience—in other words, as a frightening testament to the separation between man and citizen, *zoe* and *bios*, bare life and politically qualified life.[8] The tragedy of Srebrenica, whose inhabitants considered themselves the inmates of the biggest concentration camp in Europe,[9] attests to the vicissitudes of depoliticized humanitarianism that failed to master the camp.

The Bosnian war revealed the actual nature of the relationship between the biological and the political as a relationship of identity, equivalence, immediacy, and/or coincidence between the two. Therefore, in modern biopolitics, "life and politics—originally divided, and linked together by means of the no-man's-land of the state of exception that is inhabited by bare life—begin to become one."[10] Grassroots practices discussed in this article later show an awareness of this state of affairs. Thus, the title of probably the best film[11] about the Bosnian war, *No Man's Land*, directed by Danis Tanović, metaphorizes Bosnia as a whole. It subtly points out that the no-man's-land of the state of exception (where all life is bare life, as opposed to politically quali-fied life, and all politics is exception[12]) has been extended to the entire modern political space, the nation-state being its foremost enactment. All questions are biopolitical-thanatopolitical as the film's ultimate question encapsulates: is the man on the mine in no man's land to live or to die? Moreover, this no-man's-land of the state of exception is "produced at the point at which the political system of the modern nation-state, which was founded on the functional nexus between a determinate localisation (land) and a determinate order (the State) and mediated by automatic rules for the inscription of life (birth of the nation), enters into a lasting crisis."[13] It is surprise that those operating under the cloak of sovereign or ethno-national politics in the former Yugoslavia and Bosnia have assumed the care of the nation's biological life (or death) as their primary task. The structure of the nation-state defined by the trinity land/ Ortung–order/Ordnung–birth has been ruptured not in its first two but in its third element, which marks "the inscription of bare life (the birth that thus be-comes nation) within the two of them."[14] Because the old mechanisms regu-lating this inscription in the former Yugoslavia, and especially Bosnia, stopped functioning, finding new regulators became an urgent task for the sovereign, ethno-national forces. The siege of the cities and civilians, expulsions, massacres, and camps, were all responses to the impossibility of a smooth inscription of life into order and land. They were the "sign of the system's inability to function without being transformed into a lethal machine."[15]

No more a temporary suspension of the juridico-political order occur-ring elsewhere, the state of exception became a new and stable spatial arrangement for most Bosnians in 1992. It was inhabited by bare life that could no longer be inscribed into the old order. This traumatic event did come as a total surprise, but only because the hidden matrices of politics were misrecognized. What underpinned the trauma was what Agamben sees as the extreme "disassociation of birth (bare life) and the nation-state,"[16] and this very disjunction—manifested either as the camp, or the Sarajevo siege, or Srebrenica's safe haven, and so forth—proved to be the crux of today's politics. Bosnian socio-political landscapes assumed a para-doxical character hosting an order of exception without localization, and a permanent localisation of exception without order. Far from being unique in this regard, Bosnians have thus experienced an oxymoronic state: a dislocating localization that exceeds conventional political space and into which every form of life and every rule can be assimilated.[17] This experience is oxymoronic in another sense too, a sense that relates to human and political praxis: it has had both a debilitating and a promisingly liberating impact on political subjectivization and practice.

This is because a critical reflection following the trauma of war or the political leads one to recognize instances such as siege or refugee fate as an essentially varied metamorphosis of the camp itself. Agamben rightly claims that this peculiar dislocating localization called the camp is the hidden matrix of today's politics and has added itself as the fourth element to the broken triad between the state, the nation (birth), and land.[18] He maintains that this is the central feature of the developments taking place in the former Yugoslav territories. These developments are neither redefining the old system according to new ethnic and territorial arrangements nor reproducing the standard European nation-state project. Rather, they are about "an incurable rupture of the old nomos and a dislocation of populations and human lives along entirely new lines of flight."[19] Considering that it has become increasingly impossible for the principle of the inscription of life in the order of the nation-state to function as it used to, new 'lunatic' regulative measures and definitions are to be expected to occur so as to secure as smooth a functioning of the principle as possible. Ethnic rape camps in Bosnia are a pertinent example of these new measures fighting the increasing disparity between naked life and nation-state.[20] The state of the refugee reveals that the modern project of the nation-state with its three elements of territory, order, and birth has been severely ruptured in Bosnia. The phenomenon of the refugee shows the rupture as being present at the site where birth turns into nation, where bare life in inscribed into Ortung and Ordnung, or where 'people' become 'People.' Occupying or symbolizing/materializing this rupture, the refugee has not only been a testament to the subjection to sovereign or ethno-national logic in Bosnia it has also been the figure around which emancipatory gestures related to the nation-state power have emerged.

Where are these resistances and transformations, engendered by the very experience of 'bare life'/'zone of indistinction,' that traverse the fantasmatic biopolitical post-politics to be found? Are there any (new) clusters between vision, space, and agency inhabiting Bosnians zones of indistinction that proceed in such directions? I located one such vision/space/agency congealment in certain grass-roots practices within the women-dominated or women-oriented civil or non-governmental sector.[21] This is hardly a surprising or radically innovative step since the state of liminality or exception has been actively and continuously lived, poeticized, politicized, and acted upon in Bosnia in the 1990s and even now. How did certain grassroots activities become a phenomenon of freedom[22] by introducing the exercise of this freedom into various petrified institutionalizations of life/speech around them? The agencies and subjectivities at the grassroots level of civil society (dominated by and related to women and refugees, as the two rather overlapping categories in Bosnian contexts) occurred at, and rather palpably acted upon, the sites of exceptional or liminal fractures within biopolitical sovereign regimes operating in Bosnia in the last decade. Their voices and visions might have been weak, inarticulate, suppressed or marginalized, but their practice found some space to enact its promise, if only partially. [23] This promise relates to their acts as the instances of what Yannis Stavrakakis calls post-fantasmatic or post-conventional politics.[24] My approach is specifically directed toward the two organizations, MEDICA Zenica and BOSPO Tuzla, which embodied this promise in the realm of grassroots activism[25] in Bosnia. Before this, some theoretical trajectories informing my account of emancipatory political practice and agency in the state of liminality will be described.[26]

Theorizing Emancipatory Political Practice in the Zones of Indistinction/Liminality: a Žižek–Agamben Dialogue

An Agamben–Žižek dialogue is a productive vector in approaching, thinking, and possibly reinforcing certain grassroots activities in Bosnia as congealments of liminal visions, spaces, and agencies that embody the emancipatory promise. One reason for this is that earlier casting of Agambenian lights on some Bosnian 'realities' of the 1990s is complemented in an important sense by Slavoj Žižek's insights into emancipatory political projects. Hence, a second reason: instigating a productive dialogue between Žižek's and Agamben's reverberates, with this particular search for emancipatory political practice and agency in the context of Bosnian grassroots activism.[27] An examination of their key works[28] reveals not only the existence of the multifarious resonances between Žižekian themes with Agamben's insights into biopolitics but also the need to construe a more in-depth dialogue correlating and engaging the two.[29]

Going through, or coming close to, or merely witnessing this limit-experience is therefore politically vital. Žižek and Agamben agree not only on this point but also on the following ones:

- inclusion/exclusion is the originary categorial pair within the political;
- there is an inner solidarity between totalitarianism and democracy, for they both rely on biopolitics whose secret cipher is Homo Sacer/camp;
- these, as most modern political projects, are wedded to the nation-state's politicization of bare life; and
- political and/or symbolic community itself is founded upon the exception of bare life/Homo Sacer (Agamben) as the excremental/ excluded remainder of the social edifice (Žižek), and so forth.

In addition to this, Žižek is concerned with the political kernel behind the questions posed by Muslim/Homo Sacer/bare life figure, the questions that pertain to thresholds or limit situations that we are all about to cross not only in the camp but also whenever subjected to modern biopolitics: for him, today we are all Homo Sacer.[30] However, Homo Sacer is also the void or the very background for the emergence of symbolic vision and action with an emancipatory political potential.[31] So, the most important overlap between their theorizings is as follows: whilst Agamben views bare life to be both the site where state power is organized and where it is possible to emancipate oneself from it[32], Žižek insists that the subjective identification with the excluded, with the non-part of social/political/symbolic, edifice is the authentic (and, I would add, emancipatory) political act.[33] This is what underpins the new politics for Agamben[34], or the emancipatory project for Žižek[35]: they both aim to traverse sovereign or ideological or other traps within the consumerist society of spectacle and its post-ideological post-political universe. In this sense, Agembenian acts of free praxis or constituting power that traverse sovereignty[36] and Žižekian subversive gestures of political subjectivisation against the instituted symbolic orders[37] go hand in hand. They are the spaces of states that occur through (new categories of) human action and human thought, and reunite life with a political form through a truly emancipatory striving.

It is the limits of human experience that foster such gestures of political subjectivization, action, and thought, and in which to search for the agency of emancipatory politics. The liminal experiences of all the horrors of life's politicization and inscription into the sovereign order are particularly profound in war as a simultaneity between the state of exception, the liminal experiential situation, and the zone of indistinction. This is one of the reasons why in such turbulent spaces/times, radically new political gestures and subjectivities emerge.[38] The first subjectivizing gesture is to act negatively by wiping the slate clean, and the second involves initiating such a political subjectivization that seeks positivity in alternative metaphoric spaces and visions.[39] This, for instance, may be a metaphoric elevation of a universal wrong (for example, a particular (de)politicization of bare life) shared by all subjects/objects of the symbolic and political order. Žižek thinks of this longing for community, even if 'only' metaphoric, as the non-ideological utopian kernel upon which to subvert ideological domination in a radical, democratic way;[40] for Agamben, such a non-statist community is based on whatever singularity is the core of the forthcoming politics.[41]

Political subjectivizations and gestures inspired by the metaphoric Universal (such as this universal ideal of non-statist singular community), by the unconditional demands for *égaliberté*, by the identification with the fate of the excluded, are the very grounds for emancipatory projects. In these projects, one must continually conduct a voluntary exodus from the sovereign order and find a *refugium* away from the logic/fantasy of the nation-state (even if these exits and refuges are 'merely' symbolic and/or metaphoric). This requires further gestures: identifying with the non-part of the instituted ideological order, assuming a form-of-life (political existence) that problematizes the politicization of bare life through sovereign biopolitics, resisting being gentrified by the instituted symbolic or biopolitical orders, and so forth. These traits, frequently displayed by (some) grassroots engagements of (some) Bosnian NGOs, point to the traversal of fantasies implied by the nation-state and underpinning sovereign and symbolic/ideological orders. This traversal being the truly utopian moment that unsettles the contingent ideological order, explores the (im)possible and retains hope and belief in the very exercise of political practice.[42]

A Supplement: Biopolitics and Liminality

In the instance of (Bosnian) war, the sometimes hidden seeping of the populational and the territorial elements into each other within the state/sovereign project has inescapably come to the fore.[43] In a position where every day is about situating, protecting, injuring, losing, preserving, giving up, and relating to the body in myriad ways, life and death become (de/re)politicized to their very 'core' however constituted or posited they are. Wars at the turn of the millennia prompt us to focus on the triad body–life/death–space, and this intensifying aspect of biopower at work in the war situation has profoundly affected and inspired grassroots activism in Bosnia and emancipatory political gestures situated therein.

Turner's social anthropological investigation of *communitas* as a modality of social interrelatedness and as a fact of everyone's experience, which is opposed to the concept of social structure, provides some interesting insights in this regard.[44] Turner's category of *communitas* is referred to as an anti-structure that relies on three aspects of culture: liminality, outsiderhood, and structural inferiority.[45] When the subjects, the liminars, are stripped of their symbolic/structural positions and enter the state of liminality, "*communitas* emerges, if not as a spontaneous expression of sociability, at least in a cultural and normative form—stressing equality and comradeship as norms."[46] Considering that this is also the state of outsiderhood, it means that a member of *communitas* is set outside the structural/symbolic arrangements, either permanently and by ascription, or situationally and temporarily, or voluntarily.[47] The third major cultural aspect that pertains to *communitas* is structural inferiority that can also be either permanent or temporary, voluntary or otherwise.[48] These liminal situations can be embraced voluntarily; they require taking cognizance of oneself where one can/may decide to become, or identify with the outsider, the marginal, the liminar, and the structurally inferior. Moreover, the symbolic operation of liminality and *communitas*, both essentially 'anti-structures' (or opposites of social structures in the social anthropological understanding), heavily relies on metaphors and metaphorizations.[49]

As Turner points out, the dissolution of the social/symbolic/cultural structures due to a crisis does not result only in fragmentation and *anomie* but also "sometimes gives a *communitas* a positive opportunity."[50] Therefore, war simultaneously entails a potentiality of rather strong instances of *communitas* emerging in many diverse and perhaps unexpected sites of the social. *Communitas* hence gets generated as a basic human interlinkage, equated with love and solidarity, non-dependent upon conventions and sanctions and revolving around the non-symbolic non-cultural kernel of one's social existence. This opens the space for freedom and creativity of thought/praxis. On the other hand, a voluntary *communitas* is always-already present as the basis for a genuinely creative action and thought. The existence of such anti-structures bonding together those who are in exile and strangers from the positive and instituted symbolic order attests to the primordial human modality of the relationship that questions the instituted itself. These are the foundations from which symbolic/ material revolutions and political changes originate. Certain Bosnian grassroots activism are an example of such *communitas* engendered by war-induced liminalities that is also hosting Žižekian subjective political gestures.

The similarities between Turner's, Žižek's, and Agamben's insights on emancipatory political practices successfully reveal as to how the experience of war affects the social fabric in a way that produces not only closures but also openings for emancipatory gestures and agencies behind them. The impact of the war on the unsettling of symbolic structures is not only characterized or instigated by intensified practices of biopower but is also always already accompanied by what social anthropology views as the anti-structure and political theory as emancipatory politics: the emergence of liminal *communitas* that engages in promising political practices. These anti-structures have an emancipatory potential that might foster the Žižekian-Agambenian view of emancipatory politics. How, then, do certain practices within grassroots activism in war and post-war Bosnia fit into this view of emancipatory political practice in the state of liminality/exception?

Grassroots Practices of Resistance and Traversal: Living/Acting upon Liminality in (Post-) War Bosnia

> As Foucault once wrote, we are animals in whose politics our very life as living beings is at stake. Living in the state of exception that has now become the rule has meant also this: our private biological body

has become indistinguishable from our body politic, experiences that once used to be called political suddenly were confined to our biological body, and private experiences present themselves all of a sudden outside us as body politic. We have had to grow used to thinking and writing in such a confusion of bodies and places, of outside and inside, or what is speechless and what has words with which to speak, of what is enslaved and what is free, of what is need and what is desire. This has meant—why not admit it?—experiencing absolute impotence, bumping against solitude and speechlessness over and over again precisely there where we were expecting company and words. We have endured such an impotence as best we could while being surrounded on every side by the din of the media, which were defining the new planetary political space in which exception has become the rule. *But it is by starting from this uncertain terrain and from this opaque zone of indistinction that today we must once again find the path of another politics, of another body, of another word. I would not feel up to forgoing this indistinction of public and private, of biological body and body politic, of zoe and bios, for any reason whatsoever. It is here that I must find my space once again—here or nowhere else. Only a politics that starts from such an awareness can interest me.*[51]

The ethos Agamben expressed here seems to be relating precisely to the experiences, feelings, urges, and commitments of many people who decided to protest against the logic behind the Bosnian war by engaging in grassroots activism. The absolute helplessness experienced in the war is never final: speechlessness and solitude produced by sovereign biopolitics (which is, through the war, looking for new reinscriptions of life in its own terms, vocabularies, and companionships) are countered by the alternative searches for words and company, as a way of resisting and traversing this very biopolitical logic/fantasy. Grassroots activism is inextricable from newly emerging (political) subjectivities who seek deeds, company, and words in this direction. This has frequently been the case in the civil society sector related to or led by women and/or refugees (these two categories significantly overlapping) in Bosnia that sprang to life in the war period. The ethico-political commitments fueling their acts and searches emanated from the terrains of quotidian life that were engulfed by the liminal and the exceptional (equals normal), and thus fostered a peculiar sense of *communitas*. Solidarity felt between those sharing the Agambenian ethos from the above quote and partaking in newly emerging forms of *communitas* has operated as the bond of alternative collectivity, and thus also as a specific political bond that turned against and extended beyond the nation-state and conventional politics. The actualizations of such processes and structures, which are antithetical to the state project in one way or the other, could be observed in some of the emerging practices in the network of non-governmental organizations (NGOs) within civil society.[52]

Whence Agency?: The Smell of Quotidian Biopolitical Siege

Political agency, which is potentially or actually emancipatory with re-gard to the sovereign biopolitical discourses and practices, and which springs from biopolitical fractures is a complex matter. How does it emerge? How do new political subjectivities arise from the quotidian sieges under-taken by the biopolitical? Personal experiences and work within Bosnian civil society (or 'non-governmental') scene, as well as extensive dialogues and debates with other grassroots activists over the last decade, prompt me toward an unusual image. This example pertains to a particular bodily experience of body politics: the experience of a specific smell and its mem-ory. Bosnian grassroots activists recount a common memory of a specific smell-centered experience that had a similar and strong impact upon them. This was often the universally uniform smell of numerous 'collective centres for displaced people' (people exiled from other parts of Bosnia) and its impact on those who were in a position to reflect and/or act upon it. Other experiences that were centered around the particular smell include the following sites: aid distribution centers, shelters during the bombardments, and other 'crowded' spaces. 'Crowded' is the key word here—the smell was a symptom of human collectivity (and individuality) stripped naked in front of the totalizing biopolitical gaze. All the places with the smell as the symptom of exclusion from the inscribed/inscribing order can be consid-ered as politically/socially akin to the camp.

However, in contrast to the depoliticization they were subject to, those col-lective centers or shelters were also the sites where many seeds of radicalized grassroots actions sprouted, grew, intensified, and spread. These sites—each of which was situated at, or embodied, the biopolitical fracture between people and People made particularly violent by the war—amplified or produced rad-ically new (and yet symbolically and culturally embedded) ethico-political commitments, hence, the increased momentum toward persistent practice 'against' and 'beyond' the reified social and political realities and fantasies.[53] The war appeared to the 'new' activists to be an 'ordinary' though hyphenated bodily experience (just of a higher grade on the biopolitical spectrum). In the situation of war, the omnipresent biopolitical fracture itself could be sensed and comprehended more easily.[54] The smell of collective centers and of shel-ters is likely to be akin to the smell of concentration camps (that paradigm of modern power[55]): it is *the political* smell.

On the other hand, the sovereign attempt to make human life indistinct from the naked/bare life is never fully complete. The space of this failure of the biopolitical sovereign order is the space in which to resist depoliticizing strategies of modern power and its illusionary struggle to somehow heal the biopolitical fracture in question by turning and then eliminating that which is seen or constituted as politically non-relevant life. Therefore, the smell of collective centers cannot be described as emanating from absolute political powerlessness or victimization, for it is not experienced as completely or only defeating. There is always-already a degree in which a person feels active and non-powerless with regard to the (smell of) imposed political irrelevance and forced depoliticization even in the camp, although she is enveloped in it. The realization of always having been a part of the quotidian biopolitical manifestations in spite of their suffocating effect is complemented by resisting and traversing the political vicissitudes entailed. Thus, the smell where politically qualified life and politically made irrelevant life[56] become indistinct from each other and where the exception becomes the rule is where and when one starts to feel and act upon the fact that this very indistinction and its depoliticization are the purpose, target, and result of official 'politics.' These powerful 'feelings,' 'impressions,' 'hunches' that the grassroots activists have gone through during the biopolitical sovereign of our lives[57] often failed to foster articulate, reflective, or critical discourses and visions. However, they have been highly productive of practices traversing this siege more often than is commonly believed. The urge to resist and go beyond has been genuinely passionate, affective, and practically productive. Biopolitical siege is inextricable from the heightening of political passions, and these passions were also, even if less frequently, channeled toward emancipatory politics, and not solely toward new biopolitical, ethnonationalist enactments. Such recapturing of the political passion proper by the leftist political leanings is extremely important in the 'post-political,' 'post-ideological' times.

Those directing their affective urges toward alternative political acts and projects grabbed the moment, binding them together in a peculiar collectivity of those excluded with respect to the depoliticizations and technologizations of lives and deaths—inherent to both ('local') ethno-nationalist and ('international') liberal-multiculturalist politics.[58] Hence, the emergence of a solidarity-infused *communitas* or an anti-structure with regard to the instituted biopolitical structures could be discerned within the Bosnian NGO sector that sprang fleetingly during and after the war. A forced, but all the firmer and more committed, choice was exercised by the activist networks, which were disproportionately dominated by women and refugees (and/or activity related to them), a choice of not allowing their bodies and souls to be chained by sovereign biopolitics, and not to be brought in the position of mere depoliticized life. Although not that frequently as one would have liked, these very particular congealments of personal choices and experiences led to emancipatory resistances and transformations. This is why the women- and refugee-related civil sector (including grassroots activism and NGOs based upon it) is one of the critical agencies that have acted upon liminality/exception and have brought about openings fostered by biopolitical fractures toward the post-fantasmatic and post-conventional politics.[59]

MEDICA Zenica: Women-Oriented Civil Society Sector in Bosnia and Emancipatory Promise

When such insights are based in the larger context of war and post-war grassroots activism in Bosnia, they turn out to largely agree with one of the rare prominent studies of women-oriented and women-dominated civil societies and NGO sectors in Bosnia, conducted by Cynthia Cockburn.[60] Cockburn's investigation of how gender and national identities are negotiated in conflict includes the example of the MEDICA Women's Therapy Centre in Zenica, Bosnia, and the particular ways in which MEDICA's women activists responded to what Cockburn sees as their 'identity hurt' due to the disjunction between one's sense of self and the identities associated with it instigated by the war.[61] In the midst of these identity-related hurts, frictions, and contradictions, through their NGO MEDICA's activists enmeshed into the everyday praxis of "knitting, unravelling, texturing and tearing of the space between them," in other words, into 'the identity work.'[62] According to Cockburn, 'the space between us' stands for those social, physical, and political spaces between these women (including the researcher) within which they were working and communicating. 'Identity hurt' and 'identity work,' then, could be seen as something grassroots activists in 'ethnically mixed' NGOs have had to undergo because their own activities were clashing with the official political space in which identities with particular and rigid delimitations were the axial point.

Also, political language and discourses available to these activists were conventional ones, linked to the modern sovereign power nexuses and thus inextricable from identitarian problematics. Creative alternative practice could not gain a voice within such discursive arrangements; it required new imaginary and symbolic frames. This lack of words, and not just solitude in the midst of identity hurts and paradoxes, is perhaps one of the main reasons why acting out in the grassroots required a permanent link and deciding in between silence and speech, as one MEDICA activist expressed in Cockburn's research.[63] Although solitude was being, at least partly, countered by company in a new and hazy sense of community that MEDICA both created and stumbled upon through its work, it was much harder finding speech as a remedy for one's silence in the midst of overpowering and debilitating sovereign/ biopolitical clamor. However, the balance was being continuously sought. Although tied in these knots, the inspiration and drive behind this grassroots activism were not related to identity conundrums *per se* (in other words, activism was not simply one's remedy for identity crisis). Activism sprang from the shared and profound experience of exposure to biopolitics in the form of ethnic or gender chauvinism and exclusion, identity turmoil being only one facet of it (perhaps a more fitting description is the search for a politically relevant form of life that escapes the sovereign/biopolitical logic/fantasy).

These activists, similar to many Bosnian citizens, have been subject to a peculiar collusion of denial and offer, or a false choice with regard to their political identity and/or life. On the one hand, they were denied a meaningful political and social form-of-life, and on the other, they were offered the option of a specific identity that actually only inscribed their naked life (or mere birth) into the sovereign order, either as Muslim or Serb or Croat women with particular (biopolitical) functions. Activism, then, could be viewed as the refusal to succumb to this false choice structured as simultaneous denial and offer, and to give in to the fear that it engenders. It was a rejection of the security dilemmas imposed by ethno-nationalist biopolitics as the only framework for the enactments of one's politicality.

This grassroots activism resisting the ethno-nationalist (and gender-exclusionary) imaginaries and practices was not confined only to urban intelligentsia circles. Cockburn's ground-breaking research in Bosnia over the last several years extended its scope onto other regions and organizations throughout the country that were seen as having a potential to foster the integration of a deeply fragmented post-conflict society (both on ethnic and gender bases) and its further democratization and pluralization. The product of this research is *Women Organizing for Change*, a study of seven women's organizations in three distinct localities with different war and post-war histories, which explores the contradictory effects of war and post-war contexts in terms of simultaneous victimization and empowerment of women involved in various efforts toward an ethnically inclusive, women-friendly, and active democracy.[64] Cockburn's analysis is rather appropriate when it comes to the question of the promises and failures of these organizations, as well as the impediments they face, in their struggle to form an alternative movement within Bosnian civil society and to reinvigorate it. However, it remains unclear as to how activists who acted against the biopolitical regime in Bosnia can continue to be successful in the traversal of this regime. In other words, how can emancipatory openings that this activism might have produced or strengthened be sustained and not systematically foreclosed as it seems to have been predominantly the case? This is an all-important issue considering the consolidation of neo-liberal principles in Bosnian civil society after the Dayton Peace Accords.

BOSPO Tuzla: Political Collectivity, Liminal Communitas, and Doing the Impossible

Perhaps one answer to the earlier question is the strengthening of alternative political collectivities emerging from the experience of communitas in the state of liminality/exception. Shane Phelan's insights into feminist politics concentrate on the ways in which political practice progresses or might progress beyond the conventional visions and desires for mutual belonging and recognition, and call for alternative genealogies of community as a location of political action.[65] In Phelan's view, neither identitarian nor deconstructive approaches to community and to the vision/desire for collectivity and recognition are satisfactory bases for politics, but some other specific genealogies of community or specific communities can and may provide a way out of this identitarian versus deconstructive aporia. It is more than likely that various instances of *communitas* within grassroots activist scene in war and post-war Bosnia have represented an enactment of such non-conventional, non-statist, non-sovereign, and non-biopolitical, and yet political mode of community. Such communities are much closer to Phelan's advancement of Jean-Luc Nancy's thesis of community as compearance, as "simply the real position of existence," or as a matter of 'being-in-common' as the very ground of being itself.[66]

Grassroots activism in Bosnia, which underpins the work of MEDICA Zenica and other organizations featured in Cockburn's studies, as well as the work BOSPO Tuzla,[67] was related to the reinvigoration of this art of being-in-common in an almost impossible context. One of BOSPO's recent campaign slogans succinctly captures their long-term ethos: 'Let Us Be Real(istic), Let Us Do the Impossible.'[68] Indeed, they were continuously doing what was only a 'few minutes ago' deemed as impossible (for instance, the ground-breaking grassroots-based cross-ethnic, cross-entity work on human rights, return issues, and democratization in early 1997). Such repoliticizations instigated, and reinforced by the *communitas* BOSPO activists created and/or partook in, have not been about pursuing a substantial identity linked to an empirical or ideal place. What constituted/ performed their being-in-common, in other words, their community, was precisely their sharing of acute anxiety and instability of human experience, as well as of a lack of identity within instituted biopolitical frameworks.[69] However, through their identification with the excluded remainder of the social edifice (refugee, returnee, and/or woman) in the context of war, they formed an alternative political collectivity based on the experience of liminal *communitas*.

Therefore, community is a fact of everyday living, but such community is suppressed by modern/sovereign/biopolitical searches for 'Community' or for 'People' with all their exclusionary pitfalls. This pitfall was avoided by grassroots activism engaged by BOSPO and MEDICA, whose political mode of 'being-in-common' resisted the depoliticizing suppressions of ethno-national biopolitical orders. A community of this kind may be unstable and shifting, but it is the basis of all possibilities, as Nancy maintains.[70] This is why BOSPO could claim that it is possible for them to do what is 'impossible' in the instituted contexts. Considering BOSPO's record on encouraging and facilitating the return of refugees to highly sensitive areas in Bosnia (including both entities) and Croatia, and using creative and informal social ties and venues to achieve this,[71] whilst maintaining a low profile publicity-wise (away from the sovereign eyes), they quite practically challenged the (biopolitical/sovereign) 'impossibilities.' The first returnee to Srebrenica area, the site of the biggest atrocity of the Bosnian war (and of post-war Europe), was using alternative paths laid out discreetly and subtly by BOSPO-coordinated networks forming a fluid and shifting liminal *communitas* within the Bosnian society that enacted political 'impossibilities.'[72] My own investigations and experiences confirm that the very possibility of emancipatory political practices is grounded in these alternative spaces of collectivity, belonging, and recognition. Spaces inhabited or created by grassroots activists seeking traversals of conventional biopolitical destinies imposed upon them and their surrounding are not always and necessarily based only on some specific well-articulated bond between certain subjects or agencies. Their being-in-common was due to the phenomenon of appearing together, or the appearance of the *between* as such (expressed by Nancy's term 'compearance'[73]). However, negotiation and expansion of collectivity and solidarity are crucial in terms of emancipatory political agency. Thus, Cockburn's study of organizations negotiating the space *between* us in critical liminal situations engages precisely with the political and emancipatory possibilities that were not conventional and were therefore easily obscured.

Grassroots activist *communitas* in the state of liminality in war and post-war Bosnia has been lived out and thought of in terms of the following four processes that Phelan describes:

- as providers of a nongeographical space/place of support, of taken-for-grantedness, and of insulation from hostility;
- as a beacon of possibility of being a member and of certain ways of being;
- as a site for the modeling and interpretation processes with regard to members' lives; and
- as the base for or result of political mobilization where challenges to the hegemonic (dis)orders sprang from.[74]

All this implies positive political visions and subjectivizations, whose emergence was both inextricable from and highly needed in the context of the radical negativity caused by war traumas. The aim behind these modalities of *communitas* as alternative spaces/places of support and insulation opposed to biopolitics, of other possibilities of being (and being-in-common), of peculiar self-fashioning of political subjectivities, and of potent political positionings and actions has been to transgress or traverse the instituted social and political frameworks. Phelan's call for a community that surpasses both communitarian and deconstructive views on identity and political position and action is right in insisting that such alternative genealogies of community and communities should be the very basis of common action.[75]

Grassroots activism in Bosnia is a classic example of the simultaneity of two aspects immanent to identity, subjectivity, and collectivity: the ultimate provisionality of identities and yet their daily solidity within the relations of power under challenge. In the grassroots action by organizations such as BOSPO and MEDICA, as well as in the wider political and cultural contexts, the dynamics of exclusion and inclusion (which is the originary political distinction and/or category both for Agamben and Žižek) is always already there. Moreover, through this activism, the inclusion–exclusion dynamics is a quotidian experience that is not suppressed but permanently reflected upon, negotiated, and rendered as a solidarity-infused emancipatory drive. Both grassroots activism and the alternative *communitas* it is embedded in can be genuinely emancipatory forces, as they are not simply a refuge from the pain of liminality, but seek a peculiar coming together as the site of both love and pain, confusion and acceptance, anxiety and security.[76] Thus they engender emancipatory praxis based on oxymoronic (im)possibilities of being-in-common in a situation when the exclusion–inclusion dynamics along ethnic and gender lines is rampant. They do this through resistant and transformative political subjectivizations, and properly repoliticized forms-of-life (for instance, women experiencing violence, refugees and returnees . . .), whose predicament of exclusion is univerzalised and binds them together.

The activism of organizations such as BOSPO and MEDICA in Bosnia has avoided many aporias by focusing on ethico-political commitments inherent to the 'being-in-common' form of political community, rather than on identities. Although they needed a form of community/collectivity as a location for the production of meaning and values with which to underpin their activities and gestures, they negotiated and questioned what they had and would have in common, and what and how they shared or would share it. By being neither fully ascriptive nor voluntarist in terms of one's membership regarding this dynamic inclusive/exclusive recasting of collectivity through their own *communitas,* and by founding their inclusivity on political and subjective rather than fixed grounds,[77] these Bosnian NGOs have managed to embark on profoundly repoliticizing and transformative practices in their work. They did this from a space that gave them breathing space away from the biopolitics that surrounded them in the instituted indistinct public/private sphere, and which tried to victimize but inadvertently empowered them. Perhaps, to some observers, these gestures were minuscule in their scope, but this is not the case considering the depth and the impact of these subtle repoliticizations. Within the instituted symbolic (dis)orders and biopolitical regimes, they have been the forces and avenues enacting change, by drilling and chipping, huffing and puffing, at the points where breaks and cracks within the dominant instituted edifices appeared.[78] Becoming specific about communities, collectivities, discourses, and spaces by and from which we resist and transform is the way toward the traversal of fantasmatic politics underpinning the modern (nation-) state through tangible political gestures.

Pitfalls of Emancipatory Politics: Voiceless Grassroots/NGO Activism in the Shadows of Political Economy

But have such openings been sustained, fostered, and reinforced on the civil society scene in Bosnia? Moreover, what were the main features of the closure of potentialities for emancipatory politics at grassroots and NGO levels? Strategies for reinvigorating discourse, practice, and research related to emancipatory goals have been seriously lacking in Bosnia for a variety of reasons.[79] However, the main reason for this scarcity of discourse, practice, and research seems to be that the praxis of gender-related civic activism, although energetic in one sense, is not accompanied by powerful repoliticizing imaginaries. Practices by various women-oriented organizations and also more generally, for instance, youth or refugee initiatives, are not matched and empowered by the voices that challenge fantasmatic or real political and symbolic regimes in radical ways (or at least equally to gestures belonging to quotidian, ordinary, human praxis). The voices themselves tend to be weak, inarticulate, cacophonic, fragmented, and dissonant due to the lack or suppression of liberating new/old languages, discourses, and discursivities pertaining to refugee, youth, gender, poverty, and other issues. This debilitating state of affairs stems from the weakness of both research and dialogue on poignant issues in Bosnia, including biopolitical ethnonationalist and/or liberal multuculturalist problematics, which are both inherited from the pre-war period and also left intact in (post-)war period despite the significant presence of donors seemingly supporting and funding a so-called long-term democratization and strengthening of civil society. The international assistance is more often than not led by short-term fashions of the day,[80] issue-based, and problem-managing, following the logic of the market in a paradigmatic neoliberal manner: related projects revolve around service delivery and provision, creating a vicious and depoliticizing circle to which many NGOs have wittingly or unwittingly succumbed.[81]

Despite admirable grassroots practices,[82] the phenomenon of acute silence in public and/or political discourses amounts to a 'practice without language.'[83] Grassroots civic political practice is in danger of being petrified itself within donor guidelines, requests for project proposals, and other 'logical' frameworks required from 'mere' service providers. The diagnosis is as follows: firstly, the inability to articulate the position from which existing exclusionary arrangements, the sovereign, liberal-multiculturalist or ethno-nationalist, biopolitical projects, as well as the political economy of neoliberal global capital behind them can be challenged if not transformed, and secondly, the disarray in emancipatory visions, imaginaries and voices/discourses/languages. Both clearly indicate that the potential for the grassroots activism with an emancipatory potential to become a movement of profound social/political change is largely foregone. This is a consequence of the deep crisis of emancipatory projects within civil society and grassroots activism that can be countered only by a fundamental reinvigoration of the dynamics between discursive and praxeological visions/imaginaries, spaces, and agencies that could challenge both the sovereign biopolitics and the political economies underpinning it.

Perhaps it is best to illustrate both this crisis and the potential venues for overcoming it through the example of BOSPO Tuzla.[84] BOSPO could rightly be called a grassroots organization due to its genesis, activities, and the embeddedness of its programs in the refugee community, and to the motivations and backgrounds of its workers and activists.[85] Its practices often verged on the emancipatory, considering their ground-breaking character. For example, they were the first indigenous Bosnian NGO working in both entities (Federation of Bosnia and Herzegovina and the Republika Srpska) when any such activity was considered 'impossible.' Moreover, the nature of this activity was the hottest bit of news around—the issue of return and the refugee and returnee rights—and had to be handled in a highly creative and resourceful manner.[86] Thus, this purposefully low-profile grassroots activism pursued by BOSPO was not only crossing over but also traversing the inter-entity boundary line between Republika Srpska and Federation of Bosnia and Herzegovina, which was heavily fetishized by the sovereign ethnonationalist (biopolitical) regimes. It was an innovative creation of the 'space-between' that refuted the logic and fantasy the nation-state(s) fought for and over the issue of the two entities in Bosnia.

Admirable as they are, BOSPO's practices and many similar ones often hit the boundary of the neoliberal political economy pervading the conduct of the international donor community, upon whose financial aid the impoverished Bosnian NGO sector has been totally dependent. Little has been done in the post-war period related to the genuine empowerment of this sector as a whole. No effort was aimed at redirecting the processes of transformation of grassroots activism into NGOs (NGOization), which marks the shift from the emergency to the development phase, toward the creation of powerful civic/social movements enacting an emancipatory ethos.[87] The consequences of the increased professionalisation of activism according to neoliberal frameworks, which structure the competition for donor funding and the struggle for sustainability, have been enormous.

This, together with a failure to achieve clarity of vision and to articulate strategies of change, has led to the fragmentation and weakening of the potentialities that the newly formed civic activist *communitas* embodied. One form of this weakening is the gradual co-option of these latent or actual forces of change by the neoliberal and state project and actors (both national and international).

The edges of the very initiatives and civic networks that emerged in the state of liminality and exception in order to resist and traverse the sovereign biopolitical regimes have been frequently blunted. This is what happened with the project of legal and information aid that BOSPO envisioned and implemented through its grassroots activism within the marginalized communities of refugees and returnees, and that was funded, after initial reluctance (during which time USAID financed it), by UNHCR. In December 2000, UNHCR decided to continue funding the project only if it was given or moved (with its staff) to an international organization, Mercy Corps, which offered lower overhead costs if assigned to run the project. In other words, due to 'cost efficiency,' the project was taken away from BOSPO despite its genuine ownership of the program in terms of the ethos and commitments it entailed. Not only has UNHCR showed its preference for the principles of donor (global capitalist) logic over the empowerment of local civil society in Bosnia by failing to continue its support to BOSPO but it has also blackmailed its activists in a 'take it or leave it style,' leaving no room for a genuine dialogue, debate, or negotiation.[88] On the other hand, 'dialogue, debate, and negotiation' would have just been a camouflaging, in liberal clothing, the political and ideological workings of the UNHCR and other donor systems. But ever more discouraging is the fact that, although BOSPO protested against this far from democratic or just decision both in its verbal and written correspondence with UNHCR, there was no larger public protest over this affair. Such events surely deserve a solidarity voice from the NGO network to be raised against such power practices exercised by the 'supra-state protectors' of refugees. The lack of such protests in Bosnia shows that there is no larger civic movement bound by a clear and powerful vision of resistance and change in the face of gestures by the neoliberal, neocolonial, and sovereign regimes that debilitate radical, creative, non-institutional, non-state initiatives and agencies.

At the same time (2000), and because of the diversifying program, BOSPO underwent a major transformation by dividing itself into two organizations: MI-BOSPO, dealing with the microcrediting program, and BOSPO. The latter retained its focus on the development of civil society and NGO sector and on the problem of empowerment of socially marginalized groups (refugees, returnees, women, youth) and their rights, through a program including education, training, advocacy, awareness-raising, encouraging of return, mental health, and so forth. Thus, BOSPO proceeded to work actively on "a deepening and an expansion of the democratic principles by disaggregating elements in the democratic imaginary (e.g., human rights, freedom, equality, dissent) from the territorial state form."[89] Perhaps, it is more accurate to say that they were disaggregating their political imaginary more from the biopolitical than the territorial state form, the biopolitical being a more important factor in their struggle than the territorial axis of state project. Through its work, it opened up the possibility of accessing radical democratic imaginary in those spaces that, through specific discursive economies characterizing sovereign biopolitical order, kept this imaginary obscured and at bay.[90] BOSPO's practices thus often fell under the banner of radical democracy (or emancipatory politics) outside the institutional, governmental and/or state realms, and reinforced the symbolic potential of radical democratic acts in a manner that bypasses territorialization, biopoliticization, ethnonationalization, govermentalization, and so on. In this light, it can be claimed that, despite the UNHCR blow, and regardless of the scope of their projects, BOSPO has been rather successful in its attempt to remain faithful to a deeper emancipatory ethos in the domain of non-statist civic and more radical action (even if seemingly less ambitious or less productive). Hence, the experience and results of BOSPO's division exemplify both the closures and the openings that the initiatives and grassroots organization underwent, with a significant potential in traversing sovereign biopolitics.

What Bosnian war and post-war grassroots activism does demonstrate is the existence of the subversive gestures of political subjectivisation and free praxis that refigure the spaces constituted by sovereign biopolitics through new and imaginative forms of human thought and action. In their insistence on potentiality over actuality and in their redefinition of what is (im)possible, they have managed to find words and company in the uncertain terrains where the zones of indistinctions, exceptions as rules, and liminality have spread over the entire contemporary political space. These new subjects and subjectivities emerged from the negative void of the political trauma of war, and were then filled with positive contents of subjectivization through alternative metaphoric spaces, visions, and acts. Metaphoric elevations of a universal wrong and identification with the fate of the excluded, longings for the non-statist, metaphoric, emerging community in the form of *communitas*, refusals to be gentrified by instituted ideological orders, voluntary exodus, and a search for a refuge away from the logic/fantasy of the nation-state—all directed and shaped in the direction of resistance, change and transformation—were the emancipatory political gestures *par excellence*. Moreover, all this created non-ideological grounds from which to launch further emancipatory political practices that subvert and traverse the sovereign biopolitical project in a radical, democratic manner. Agencies engaged in this project have demonstrated a promising potential in enacting and empowering forms-of-life that repoliticize the petrified symbolic/ideological edifices in inspiring and creative ways, but have also shown failures, weaknesses, and closures in their efforts, especially when faced with the shadows of political economy looming over them.

On the Question of Agency and Action: Some Concluding Remarks on Emancipatory Political Practice

The problem of emancipatory political practice in the light cast by the earlier considerations indicates that the urgent questions to focus upon with regard to emancipatory politics are as follows:

- How does one ground the search for emancipatory politics in (and thus reinforce) a creative and imaginative substrate to individual and collective action and agency in the condition of ontological anxiety, Unsicherheit,[91] and/or liminality?
- Are such actions and agencies traversing the sovereign biopolitical matrices and the related instituted symbolic/ideological regimes effectively?

Such interrogations lead to a necessary dialogue with the theories of agency that have often been dominated by the symbolic versus material and the voluntarist versus determinist divide. The most productive in overcoming this split and reconfiguring the agency question in a manner that provides inspiring answers to the two questions above seems to be the latest work by Lois McNay arguing for a generative and dynamic theory of subject formation and autonomous agency.[92] Accounting for the ways in which subjects or social agents act in an active, unanticipated, creative manner in the conditions of uncertainty and in differentiated social edifices, McNay's theorizing does more than just going beyond the symbolic/material, and psyche/social dichotomies. It offers a less determinist, or generative and dialogical understanding of the temporal aspects of subject and agency formation, and thus emphasizes and reinforces "the protensive or future-oriented dimension of praxis as the living through of embodied potentialities, and as the anticipatory aspects inherent within subject formation."[93]

In this way, the emergence of agency that can instigate creative action and emancipatory politics in the situation of dislocation and liminality can be better accounted for. In Patricia Mann's words, "it is necessary to expand the vocabulary of political actions in order to make sense of individual agency in moments of discursive uncertainty and political change."[94] This necessity is directly and successfully addressed by McNay's introduction of Pierre Bourdieu's, Paul Riceour's, and Cornelius Castoriadis's insights into her revival of the emancipatorily creative substrate to action and agency. BOSPO and MEDICA exemplify McNay's claims relating to the formation of a promising political subjectivity as a result of a lived relationship between embodied potentiality and material relations, and to the capacity of such a political agency to resist, manage, and transform actively the discontinuous and conflicting relations of sovereign/biopolitical power.[95]

At times, grassroots activism of BOSPO and MEDICA affirms an emancipatory reconfiguring of political practice and agency through a creative and imaginative substrate that their actions entail. The reason for this is that they sometimes strive to posit themselves as the symbolic/material embodiments of the radical imaginary that they free from the petrifying and violent effects of the instituted/social imaginary as the underlying matrix of sovereign biopolitics. Because these activities/organizations exist or emerge as a disjunction between the *habitus* and the field (Bourdieu-inspired view) or between the radical and the socio-historical imaginary (Castoriadis-inspired view), they, through this very dislocation/disjunction enact their embodied potentialities in creative, reflexive, and autonomous ways, being both freed and constrained by the experience of the zone of indistinction. However, the uncovering of a creative or imaginative substrate to action that traverses the conventional sovereign politics is not sufficient to valorize agency or practice as emancipatory (although it is a condition of the possibility of an autonomous agency able to act unexpectedly and to institute the new and unanticipated forms-of-life).[96] Although these forms of agency do underlie the transformations of power relations and practices immanent to sovereign biopolitical project, the structural, institutional, and intersubjective constraints remain the context within which they have to be viewed[97] and which suffocates their potential. Indeed, any search for emancipatory agency or political practice must insist on creativity and imagination in the face of the trauma of the political and must also be done under the umbrella of a very Žižekian exclamation 'It's the political economy, stupid!'

Notes

1. To Edina Husanović, for her unreserved support. The chapter plays with themes explored in my doctoral thesis "Emancipatory Politics and Political Community: Lessons from Bosnia," Department of International Politics, University of Wales Aberystwyth.
2. Semezdin Mehmedinović, *Sarajevo Blues: Rje nik termina opkoljenog grada / Sarajevo Blues: Dictionary of Concepts from a Besieged City* (Sarajevo: Svjetlost, 1992), p. 19.
3. There is no absolute coincidence between people and People since the very remainder of 'people' that has not become part of People is bare life or politically irrelevant life. Therefore, there is always the fracture between people and People that the sovereign biopolitical power

tries to eliminate or hide, by eliminating or excluding the very embodiment of the fracture in question (bare life, Jew, refugee . . .). For further explication on this and other features of indistinct terrains of sovereign biopolitics, see, for instance:Giorgio Agamben, *Homo Sacer: Sovereign Power and Bare Life*, trans. by Daniel Heller-Roazen (Stanford, California: Stanford University Press, 1998); Giorgio Agamben, *Means without End. Notes on Politics*, trans. by Vincenzo Binetti and Cesare Cesarino (Minneapolis, London: University of Minnesota Press, 2000), Giorgio Agamben, *Potentialities. Collected Essays in Philosophy*, edited by Daniel Heller-Roazen, trans. by Daniel Heller-Roazen (Stanford, California: Stanford University Press, 1999), Giorgio Agamben, *Remnants of Auschwitz: The Witness and the Archive*, trans. by Daniel Heller-Roazen (New York: Zone Books, 1999).

4. Another notable area of relevance in this regard are some recent literary voices.

5. Agamben, *Homo Sacer: Sovereign Power and Bare Life*, p. 38.

6. The common remark by Bosnian folks is that "the Top List of Surrealists is now everyday life." The Top List of Surrealists (Top lista nadrealista) was the most popular socio-political satire in the former Yugoslavia (and Bosnia) in the 1980s and 1990s. It has emerged from the 1980s Sarajevo urban subculture created by the (then) youth generation born in the 1960s and 1970s. The epitome of this cult alternative subculture was the artistic/social movement *New Primitivism*, which, in terms of its importance and message, can be likened to punk in Western cultures. It is famous for its unique, creative, ironic, and burlesque-like pushing of the limits of social and political realities to their extremes. In subtle ways, it has also predicted and explored what was once thought to be the 'unimaginable' or the 'impossible,' namely both the war and post-war period in Bosnia.

7. Agamben, *Homo Sacer: Sovereign Power and Bare Life*, p. 122.

8. Agamben, *Homo Sacer*, p. 133. That Western humanitarianism was another name for the absolute political desubjectivization of Bosnians was blatantly clear in the obvious policy of continuing to expose the people to rampant ethnic nationalism 'fed and sheltered' to a survivable minimum. Humanitarian organizations and all those inspired to act for 'purely' humanitarian causes have thus been in secret solidarity with the state and ethno-national powers that were the cause of suffering in the first instance, and in order to operate, they all have relied on the cipher of bare life.

9. This was commonly stated on the banners during the 1993–1995 demonstrations in Srebrenica where Srebrenicans were protesting against the UN's inability to secure and impose Srebrenica's safe haven status.

10. Agamben, *Homo Sacer: Sovereign Power and Bare Life*, p. 148.

11. This is an opinion shared by many, both nationally and internationally (the film was awarded the Oscar for best foreign film in 2002, the Golden Globe Award for the best foreign film in 2002, and the Golden Palm for the screenplay, written by the film's director, at Cannes Film Festival 2001).

12. See Agamben, *Homo Sacer: Sovereign Power and Bare Life*, pp. 174–175.

13. Agamben, *Homo Sacer*.

14. Agamben, *Homo Sacer*, p. 175.

15. Agamben, *Homo Sacer*.

16. Agamben, *Homo Sacer*.

17. I am paraphrasing Agamben here - see Agamben, *Homo Sacer*.

18. Agamben, *Homo Sacer*, pp. 175–176.

19. Agamben, *Homo Sacer*, p. 176.

20. See Agamben, *Homo Sacer*, and Agamben, *Means without End. Notes on Politics*, pp. 42–43. I use the terms naked life and bare life interchangeably, although Agamben maintains that naked life is a more accurate translation of his concept.

21. It is the work of Pierre Bourdieu on the economy of symbolic practices that inspires this search for gestures that resist, transform, and/or traverse the instituted symbolic (dis)order, for transformative congealments of *habitus* and field that nurture these gestures, and/or for new forms of subjectivities that are behind them and that emerge in such constellations, hence my own identification of those *habitus*/field nexuses with the potentiality to traverse the biopolitical order in the field of non-state civil society. Here, one may also find, as Cornelius Castoriadis would put it, those embodiments of the radical imaginary and radical imagination that resist and go beyond the instituting/instituted social-historic imaginary underpinning the practices of sovereignty. See Pierre Bourdieu, *The Logic of Practice*, trans.

by Richard Nice (Cambridge: Polity Press, 1990), and Cornelius Castoriadis, *The Imaginary Institution of Society* (Cambridge: Polity Press, 1987).

22. Gaston Bachelard, *The Poetics of Space*, trans. by Maria Jolas (Boston: Beacon Press, 1994), p. xxvii.

23. For instance, one such palpable fracture where such practices emerged can be centered around the phenomenon of the collective center for displaced people, which Bosnia witnessed in hundreds, if not thousands.

24. See Yannis Stavrakakis, *Lacan and the Political* (London: Routledge, 1999).

25. Grassroots activism is situated in the space of 'civil society,' or 'non-governmental sector' (these are not considered as synonymous).

26. The trope 'liminality' relates to the betwixt–between margins of experience that emerge, together with the fracturing of sovereign biopolitics and related (de/re)politicizations of bare life.

27. These practices and agencies of interest can be seen as engaging in 'post-fantasmatic' or 'post-conventional' politics (thereby recasting the political) in the zone of indistinction characterized by practices of biopower whose operation renders liminal experiences a norm rather than an exception. See Chapter 4 'Beyond the Fantasy of Utopia: The Aporia of Politics and the Challenge of Democracy' in Stavrakakis, *Lacan and the Political*, pp. 99–121. Post-fantasmatic or less-fantasmatic politics—such as Laclau and Mouffe's project of radical democracy—goes beyond the fantasmatic cores of utopian/conventional politics concerned with change. In other words, whilst the centrality of the principle of hope in any radical political project is retained (overcoming the aporia of political paralysis), the fantasmatic ethics of harmony and the traditional ethics of the good are transgressed by an ethics of psychoanalysis. See also Chapter 5 'Ambiguous Democracy and the Ethics of Psychoanalysis' in Stavrakakis, *Lacan and the Political*, pp. 122–140.

28. My insights are predominantly based on the following works: Agamben, *Homo Sacer: Sovereign Power and Bare Life*, Agamben, *Means without End. Notes on Politics*, Agamben, *Potentialities. Collected Essays in Philosophy*, Agamben, *Remnants of Auschwitz: The Witness and the Archive*, Slavoj Žižek, *Did Somebody Say Totalitarianism? Five Interventions in the (Mis)Use of a Notion* (London and New York: Verso, 2001); Slavoj Žižek, "Enjoy Your Nation as Yourself!." In *Tarrying with the Negative: Kant, Hegel, and the Critique of Ideology*, edited by Slavoj Žižek (Durham, USA: Duke University Press, 1993); Slavoj Žižek, *The Fragile Absolute—or, Why Is the Christian Legacy Worth Fighting For* (London and New York: Verso, 2000), Slavoj Žižek, "An Interview with Slavoj Žižek," *Historical Materialism. Research in Critical Marxist Theory*, 7, Winter (2000); Slavoj Žižek, *Manje ljubavi - više mržnje!*, trans. by Ranko Mastilovic´ (Belgrade: Beogradski krug, 2001); Slavoj Žižek, *On Belief* (London, New York: Routledge, 2001); Slavoj Žižek, *The Ticklish Subject: The Absent Centre of Political Ontology* (London: Verso, 2000).

29. An explicit encounter between these two thinkers is to be found in the second chapter of Žižek's *Did Somebody Say Totalitarianism?* (where he engages with the central theme of Agamben's *Remnants of Auschwitz*, the key figure of the Nazi extermination camp, that of *der Muselmann* or the living dead), and, rather extensively, in the final two chapters of Žižek's book on September 11th, *Welcome to the Desert of the Real*, which lends an inspiring Žižekian twist to the Homo Sacer problematics of today. See, Žižek, *Did Somebody Say Totalitarianism? Five Interventions in the (Mis)Use of a Notion*, pp. 73–88; Agamben, *Remnants of Auschwitz: The Witness and the Archive*, pp. 41–86; Slavoj Žižek, *Welcome to the Desert of the Real* (London: Verso, 2002).

30. Žižek, *Welcome to the Desert of the Real*, pp. 91–93.

31. Žižek essentially views this subject through Lacanian lenses: there is an inhuman traumatic kernel or gap within the key figure of sovereignty-as-enactment (Homo Sacer), and it is this which is in the very midst of humanity itself. In this figure, we face pure negativity, a slate wiped off its positive human features, a Hegelian night of the world, the withdrawal from the symbolic that opens up the space for specifically human symbolic engagement, and the subject. Žižek, *Did Somebody Say Totalitarianism? Five Interventions in the (Mis)Use of a Notion*, p. 77.

32. Agamben, *Homo Sacer: Sovereign Power and Bare Life*, p. 11.

33. Žižek, *The Ticklish Subject: The Absent Centre of Political Ontology*, pp. 199–200.

34. Although the typical political categories lose their intelligibility in the zones of indistinction, it is only "on the basis of these uncertain and nameless terrains . . . that the ways and the forms of a new politics must be thought." The experience of Bosnian war is one such terrain where gestures of new politics emerged. See Agamben, *Homo Sacer: Sovereign Power and Bare Life*, p. 187.

35. As he elaborates it in Žižek, *The Ticklish Subject: The Absent Centre of Political Ontology.*
36. Following Antonio Negri's footsteps, quoted in Agamben, *Homo Sacer: Sovereign Power and Bare Life*, p. 43.
37. Žižek, *The Ticklish Subject: The Absent Centre of Political Ontology*, pp. 228–232.
38. Consider that the modern subject is both the negative Void, and the gesture of subjectivization that fills it with a positive content; hence the potency for 'new' subjects/agents when facing the traumatic Void or Beyond, perhaps in one of many forms of bare life, during limit experiences such as war or any other type of (political) trauma. Žižek, *The Ticklish Subject*, pp. 159–160.
39. Žižek, *The Ticklish Subject*, pp. 204–208.
40. Žižek, *The Ticklish Subject*, p. 185.
41. Agamben, *Means without End. Notes on Politics*, pp. 8–9.
42. Rather than with Yannis Stavrakakis's critique of utopian function as necessarily founded in the ideology/fantasy/arch-enemy triad, I agree with Bruce Fink's reading of late Lacan, which retains a utopian element through the reinvigoration of non-fantasmatic utopia. See Footnote 21. in Stavrakakis, *Lacan and the Political*, pp. 160–161.
43. This agrees with Foucault's view that the modern state is both a territorial state and a population state, where the accent is shifted toward the populational aspect (in terms of objectives, problems, mechanisms, and techniques with regard to the notion of population and its regulation). See, Michel Foucault, "Security, Territory, and Population." In *Essential Works of Foucault. Ethics: Subjectivity and Truth*, edited by Paul Rabinow (New York: The New Press, 1997), p. 63.
44. See Chapter 6 'Passages, Margins, and Poverty: Religious Symbols of Communitas' in Victor Turner, *Dramas, Fields, and Metaphors: Symbolic Action in Human Society* (Ithaca and London: Cornell University Press, 1974), pp. 231–271.
45. Liminality (*limen* being the threshold in Latin) stands for the betwixt-and-between ambiguous state between two symbolic domains in which the subject of *rites de passage* finds herself after separation from the old positive order of Being and before reaggregation into the new one. Turner, *Dramas, Fields, and Metaphors*, p. 231.
46. Turner, *Dramas, Fields, and Metaphors*, p. 232.
47. Marginals within the social fabric are closely related to outsiders, for they do not await new reinscription into a positive order of Being in order to resolve the ambiguity and antagonism inherent to their position (unlike ritual liminars who do). Turner, *Dramas, Fields, and Metaphors*, p. 233.
48. Turner, *Dramas, Fields, and Metaphors*, p. 234.
49. See Chapter 7 'Metaphors of Anti-structure in Religious Communitas' in Ibid, pp. 272–299.
50. Ibid, p. 50.
51. Agamben, *Means without End. Notes on Politics*, pp. 138–139. Italics mine.
52. An appropriate example in this respect is that, under the umbrella of such ethos towards the sovereign biopolitical practice, one has witnessed the repoliticization of the depoliticizing and depoliticized boundary between the so-called 'locals' (Bosnian NGO activists) and the 'internationals' (foreign governmental and non-governmental workers). This boundary was produced by the neo-colonial regime of humanitarian and development aid inextricable from the sovereign project. However, it seemed to dissipate and open the alternative space for alternative political gestures once this kind of a bond beyond the logic/fantasy of the sovereign biopolitical predominated, in other words, when shared solidarity and outsiderhood of the governed raised against the very governmentality principle. This is a rather Foucauldian insight. See Michel Foucault, "Governmentality." In *The Foucault Effect: Studies in Governmentality*, edited by Colin Gordon and Peter Miller Graham Burchill (Chicago: The University of Chicago Press, 1991). Clearly, there were two sides to this political bond—those partaking and those not partaking in it (those who were in solidarity of the governed and those oblivious to it, those ready to repoliticize their experience and surroundings and those considering identity politics and the state project as the only game in town). In this sense, there was a politically productive and potent Us-Them opposition (to follow Žižek here with his insistence on the potency and importance of duality and opposition) in emancipatory politics never static but dynamic in itself, and possibly emancipatory with respect to the instituted ideological regime. Personal notes from Slavoj Žižek's talk on Lenin's legacy held at LSE, January 2002.
53. These 'againsts' and 'beyonds' have not necessarily been followed by an articulate 'towards'—in other words, by a clear positive End to the political/social project or action that was being undertaken. However, they were instituting political form to life that was being stripped of it.

Avoiding narrow or grand articulations of positive political ends was most likely a conscious choice to eschew, at least for a while, new conventional/fantasmatic politic linked to the sovereign project. However, this discursive vagueness underpinning the emerging political yet non-conventional political praxis has had both a productive and a counter-productive effect. This is because open-endedness does not ipso facto lead to political emancipations, and can also be a catchword for the lack of direction, whereas vagueness and flexibility with respect to positive ends can also be nothing more than a shirking away from assuming political commitments fully and properly. With respect to practical political gestures, a weak or non-existent 'towards' is paradoxically both simultaneously liberating and debilitating—there is freedom and creativity in one respect, and a lack of clear strategy and powerfully defined vision in the other. This is the general diagnosis of the state of civil society (or NGO) sector in Bosnia and its predicaments at the moment, which few seem to deal with in a critical, reflective, and politically effective manner.

54. Perhaps it was the smell of naked/bare life, or even better—the smell of politically qualified and relevant life being effaced, depoliticized, and ushered away by sovereign politics—that was never totally achieved.

55. Agamben, *Homo Sacer: Sovereign Power and Bare Life*.

56. This irrelevance is only attempted at, but never accomplished fully.

57. Based on my formal and informal conversations with activists from the non-governmental sector in Bosnia and its wider region.

58. One might even say that they were being bound in and through solidarity of the governed: a concept coined by Michel Foucault in a Geneva press conference, following protesting activities organized by Medecins du Monde and Terres des Hommes against the violence of piracy against Vietnamese boat refugees, quoted in David Campbell, "Deterritorialised Loyalty: Multiculturalism and Bosnia" (paper presented at the Loyalty and the Post-national State, Keele University, 5-6 June 1998), 19.

59. See Chapters 4 and 5 in Stavrakakis, *Lacan and the Political*.

60. Cynthia Cockburn, *The Space between Us: Negotiating Gender and National Identities in Conflict* (London and New York: Zed Books, 1998), with Rada Stakić-Domuz. Cynthia Cockburn, and Meliha Hubić, *Women Organising for Change. A Study of Women's Local Integrative Organisations and the Pursuit of Democracy in Bosnia-Herzegovina* (Zenica: Medica, Infoteka, 2001).

61. See Introduction and Chapter 7 in Cockburn, *The Space between Us: Negotiating Gender and National Identities in Conflict*.

62. Cockburn, *The Space between Us*, p. 10.

63. Cockburn, *The Space between Us*, pp. 202–203. This is something that I explored in the article Jasmina Husanović, "Practice with No Language: A Reflection of the 'Gender Scene' in a Sarajevo Workshop," *International Feminist Journal of Politics*, 3(1) 2001.

64. Cynthia Cockburn, *Women Organising for Change. A Study of Women's Local Integrative Organisations and the Pursuit of Democracy in Bosnia-Herzegovina*.

65. Shane Phelan, "All the Comforts of Home: The Genealogy of Community." In *Revisioning the Political. Feminist Reconstructions of Traditional Concepts in Western Political Theory*, edited by Nancy J. Hirschmann and Christine Di Stefano (Boulder, Colorado and Oxford: Westview Press, 1996), p. 235.

66. Jan-Luc Nancy, *The Inoperative Community* (Minneapolis: University of Minnesota Press, 1991) quoted in Ibid, p. 239. In this view, community appeals to what is 'in common,' and to the process of being-in-common, which is always characterized by insecurity and instability, whereas the insistence on the common or the same is a push for identity, for essence, and as such is actually a denial of community. For Nancy, essentializing and fixing identities and locations through the creation of stable and secure community is the closure of the political because it eliminates politics as the art of being-in-common.

67. A prominent NGO operative in the northeast regions of Bosnia over the last seven years, which also sprang from a network of grassroots actors and activities.

68. BOSPO web-site (*www.bospo.ba*) accessed on February 15, 2002, and BOSPO's propaganda posters.

69. This is based on my own work with BOSPO in 1996 and 1997, as well as on the extensive cooperation and interviews in the period 1997–2002. It also agrees with Nancy's point of view—see Phelan, "All the Comforts of Home: The Genealogy of Community," 240.

70. Phelan, "All the Comforts of Home: The Genealogy of Community," 240.

71. These insights are based on my own work in BOSPO, as well as on my conversations with BOSPO activists, Nejira Nalić and Slavica Bradvić.

72. From a conversation with BOSPO director, Nejira Nalić, summer 2001.

73. Phelan, "All the Comforts of Home: The Genealogy of Community," 240.

74. Phelan, "All the Comforts of Home: The Genealogy of Community," 243-244.

75. It is important to be aware of the identitarian hubris but in this (deconstructive) avoidance of rigid identification(s), the political necessity of collectivity and commonality, which requires creative and flexible forms of identification, must never be sacrificed. A Phelan-informed genealogical specific approach to a particular community, such as the anti-state anti-biopolitical *communitas* of Bosnian grassroots activism, goes beyond the traditional approaches to political community and action because it focuses on specificities with regard to provisional political subjects and subjectivizations, and overlapping sites of group struggle in a Bosnian social space.

76. A simple test put to NGO activists on why they do what they do often results in love being placed first, followed by solidarity, friendship, 'never again' to the experience of fear, etc. For theoretical reflections, see Phelan, "All the Comforts of Home: The Genealogy of Community," 246-247.

77. Here, I echo some of Phelan's concerns. See Phelan, "All the Comforts of Home: The Genealogy of Community," 248.

78. I am again playing with some Phelan's thoughts—see Phelan, "All the Comforts of Home: The Genealogy of Community," 249.

79. An appropriate example is a Sarajevo gender workshop that took place in 2000 under the umbrella of International Forum Bosnia, which I have analyzed as a case study elsewhere. See Husanovic, "Practice with No Language: A Reflection of the 'Gender Scene' in a Sarajevo Workshop."

80. Aida Bagić, *International Assistance to Women's Movement: From Initiatives and Groups to Ngos* (International OSI Policy Fellowship Research Report, October 2001 2001 [cited 16 February 2002]); available on http://www.policy.hu/~bagic/.

81. This is a common tendency that many analysts have observed and criticized. See, for instance, in addition to Cockburn quoted earlier the following: Ibid.([cited), Ian Smillie, "Service Delivery or Civil Society? Ngos in Bosnia and Herzegovina," (Zagreb: CARE International, 1996), Martha Walsh, "Aftermath: The Role of Women's Organisation in Post-Conflict Bosnia and Herzegovina," (Washington: Centre for Development Information and Evaluation, U.S. Agency for International Development, 2000).

82. I refer here to a significant number of innovative grassroots organizations and the inspiring versatility of their activities ranging from humanitarian work to political empowerment of women.

83. Husanovic, "Practice with No Language: A Reflection of the 'Gender Scene' in a Sarajevo Workshop."

84. My knowledge of BOSPO's work comes from both professional and informal involvement and links with the organization.

85. This non-governmental organization was established in 1995 as a spin-off of Danish Refugee Council, with the aim of addressing the problems faced by displaced people. In the first two year this aim was pursued through a psycho-social program covering the Tuzla Canton; then, it broadened with the microcredit project and the legal/information aid project in 1996. These three projects were funded, by DANIDA, the World Bank, and UNHCR (USAID for a short time)respectively.

86. Witness the example of the first return of a Bosniac refugee to Srebrenica after the 1995 massacre that was supported and facilitated by BOSPO in a manner 'invisible' to the sovereign power and instituted order. This very first returnee to Srebrenica was one of BOSPO's activist's father, a citizen of Srebrenica before the exodus.

87. Prominent studies by Ian Smillie, Paul Stubbs, and Aida Bagić attest to this verdict in varying ways. See Aida Bagić, "International Assistance for Women's Organizing in South Eastern Europe: From Groups and Initiatives to Ngos," (OSI International Policy Fellowship 2001-2002, 2002), Ian Smillie, "Service Delivery or Civil Society? Ngos in Bosnia and Herzegovina," (Zagreb: CARE International, 1996), Aida Bagić and Paul Stubbs, "Civil Society Development Programme. An Independent Evaluation," (Zagreb, Croatia: CARE International. Bosnia-Herzegovina and Croatia, 2000).

88. Private conversation with Nejira Nalić, BOSPO's director at the time and currently the head of its Board of Directors.

89. Marc G. Doucet, "The Possibility of Deterritorializing Democracy: Agonistic Democratic Politics and the Apec Ngo Forums," *Alternatives: Global, Local, Political,* 26(3), 2001: 294.

90. Doucet, "The Possibility of Deterritorializing Democracy", p. 293.

91. The term *Unsicherheit* combines the meanings of three English terms—insecurity, uncertainty, and lack of safety.

92. Lois McNay, *Gender and Agency. Reconfiguring the Subject in Feminist and Social Theory* (Cambridge: Polity Press, 2000).

93. McNay, *Gender and Agency,* pp. 4–5.

94. Patricia Mann, Micropolitics: Agency in a Postfeminst Era (Minneapolis: University of Minnesota Press, 1994), p. 17, quoted in McNay, *Gender and Agency,* p. 11.

95. That McNay's views powerfully resonate with my Bosnian examples is obvious in her analysis of the concepts of identity and identification, and reflexivity and autonomy regarding the 'marginal' and the 'excluded' who negotiate spaces between them, establish a *communitas* on the basis of the solidarity of the governed, and engage in creative civic/political action. McNay, *Gender and Agency,* p. 16.

96. McNay, *Gender and Agency,* p. 22.

97. I echo McNay's thoughts here. See McNay, *Gender and Agency,* p. 23.

CHAPTER 12

Conclusion
Sovereignties, Exceptions, Worlds

R.B.J. WALKER

Contemporary transformations in the ordering of human societies are open to analysis and evaluation in many challenging ways. In this respect, we have become used to a flood of literatures and diagnoses from every scholarly direction. The volume has long ago become indigestible. Moreover, any conceptual innovations that might emerge to make better sense of what is going on are in constant danger of being smothered in powerful cliches or recaptured within the established practices of disciplinary reproduction. Most seriously, as the volume and diversity of literatures and diagnoses increase, discussions of the specifically political character and implications of contemporary transformations circulate within discourses about stasis and change that rarely shift their orbit. Claims about change are especially sucked into a familiar debate about the continuing presence or impending disappearance of the modern state. Continuing presence is marked by claims to political realism, supplemented by affirmations of the continuing appeal of nationalism or the entrenched capacities of statist institutions. Impending disappearance is marked less by old-fashioned claims to idealism or utopianism than by an updated combination of appeals to a cosmopolitan ethics and/or empirical evidence of something that might be known, however incoherently, under the names of globalization or empire. Few people now seem to be much convinced by the claim to political realism, but skepticism about the way claims about cosmopolitanism, globalization, or empire offer any clearer alternative is equally widespread.

The consequence in a fairly broad sense is that while we may be capable of impressively rich descriptions of contemporary transformations, and even of plausible stories about their economic, sociological, and cultural dynamics and causalities, our ability to think about them in political terms is rather thin, even embarrassing. At most, we might want to claim that the fad for utilitarian accounts of economic rationality has led to some understanding of new forms of quasi-international forms of regime formation and so on. Yet, utilitarian forms of rationality have rarely offered convincing grounds for thinking about the much harder questions of political authority under law and the place of violence in the delimitation of that authority, questions that the utilitarians and economists already tried to leave behind sometime in the eighteenth century and have resolutely ignored as the condition of much of their own authority ever since.

For the last decade at least, however, in response to claims about the discrepancy between the articulation of political authority and the distribution of material force, and the crises engendered by unilateralist attempts to trump multilateral responses to mass violence, questions about politics, even about the very possibility of what some cannot resist calling the political, have been increasingly unavoidable. They are questions about which those who have become accustomed to thinking of themselves as specialists in political analysis have become distinctly queasy. Assuming the horizons of statist community, they have become as bemused as any blinkered racehorse when told that they must trot off in many different new directions at once. Assuming the place of war and peace in the proper, if tragic, working of a system of sovereign states, they dutifully work through a familiar story of hopes for the gradual transformation of the international from probable war to possible peace only to confront patterns of violence that arise from many places other than the territorial edges of sovereign states. Assuming the priority of the economic, the sociocultural, or the ethical, they predict, or hope for, a profound change in the conditions under which we might be able to imagine a different form of political life, but then fight shy of thinking about what might be involved in thinking about a political life that is somehow different from the one they assume to be in place within and between modern states.

At least, this is a significant part of the context in which so many scholars have rediscovered the need to think much more seriously about that strange and ever more obscure phenomenon we have come to call sovereignty. The primary weakness of so much of the literature on the political character and implications of contemporary transformations is that it is premised on grossly simplified assumptions about what sovereignty must be. They are especially constrained by the assumption that sovereignty refers to something that is somehow real and yet without life, which is both concrete and simply present in the world rather than a complex process that works as a reality precisely as a claim about what must be rather than as an experience of what is involved in the enabling and enactment of sovereign lives. I have argued elsewhere that the entire Anglo-American discipline of international relations is premised on such assumptions, and consequently, it has had little to say except as an illuminating expression of the normative aspirations expressed in their simplifications, and of the discursive procedures through which idealizations have been converted into enormously influential claims about political realities and the limits of political possibility.[1]

Nevertheless, this situation is itself also clearly changing. This is partly a consequence of pervasive debates about how it is now possible to make claims about realities of any kind, and about ontologies that resist congealed understandings of the being of beings. It is more immediately the consequence of increasing sensitivities to the difficulty of making claims about change in the world in which we have come to live, and thus to the intensely problematic character of spatiotemporalities, becomings, and possibilities. Indeed, one of the most striking characteristics of contemporary critical analysis in many contexts, and now even of some of those more conventional traditions that have managed to resist the more obvious fallacies of naturalistic reification, is an increasing awareness of sovereignty as an extraordinarily complex site or event.

In opening up the sequence of meditations and conversations expressed in this book, Bill Connolly immediately and rightly insists that "sovereignty persists," but "does so amidst an intensification of ambiguities and uncertainties that have inhabited it all along."[2] Subsequent papers elaborate the theme, paying attention especially to the fluidities, reciprocities, and sometimes frozen paradoxes of relations, powers, and subjectivities. These papers offer a testimony not to the death or disappearance of sovereignty, thereby reproducing the conventional story once again, but to the collapsing authority of any account of authority that does not learn to speak in the languages of complexities and reciprocities, of the fluidities and productions of powers, agencies, and resistances. Sovereignty lives, has life, and enables lives.

At the same time, however, we surely recall enough about the historical capacity of some states at some times to freeze all fluids, to reify all temporalities, to effect the most awful discriminations, and to draw the sharpest of all lines. Carl Schmitt still speaks to us, insisting that we should remember to keep our politics within clear lines, under the law. Even more worryingly, we surely cannot help but reflect on the sovereign powers that have recently been declared and deployed in the name of a global order: on the expression of a sovereign supremacy that has profoundly destabilized another order of sovereign supremacies, or at least of a mutually agreed pretense to sovereign supremacies within an order that makes the very notion of sovereign supremacy possible in a world of similar but different human beings. In this context, these essays can be read as multiple expressions of a political as well as a scholarly ambition. They affirm that sovereignties might be engaged on terms other than those given by the tight logic of contradictions expressed in and around the line between norm and exception, between the exercise of sovereignty under state law, and the exercise of sovereignty to suspend that law, whether also under law as Schmitt insisted, or beyond the law as many others have come to suspect is increasingly the case. For what is ultimately at stake in all these discussions, of course, is the place of violence in political life, the constitutive role of violence in constituting an order that might be free of violence, and the deployments of violence in the name of securing an order that is supposedly free of violence. The correlate of an exploration of sovereign lives is inevitably the memory and apprehension of sovereign deaths.

Sovereignty, we have come to remember, can be understood simultaneously as a principle, an institution, and a practice, and, indeed, has to be understood historically as a complex site/event in which it is quite difficult, and perhaps necessarily impossible, to distinguish with much analytical clarity between principle, institution, and practice. We now speak about sovereignty less like an it, a thing, or achieved condition than as an act that works by producing a presence, a state of being, exactly where there is and can be no such thing. Whatever condition has been achieved in the name of sovereignty needs to be continually re-achieved, to be constantly affirmed as some kind of necessity rather than as a contingency, to be constantly fixed as spatialized presence/absence and constantly enacted/resisted as temporal activity and possibility.

We have also come to remember that while the problem of sovereignty may be found in many, most or perhaps even all societies, sovereignties work in relation to, and express, the cultural practices of specific societies. When we speak about sovereignty now, we speak almost entirely about specifically modern forms of sovereignty, recognizing both a common sense that modernity is indeed a distinguishable condition and a highly contested sense of what that condition is or ought to be in relation to the claims of sovereign authorization. Thus, to say that sovereignty is in some trouble is a kind of shorthand for saying that accounts of politics premised on specifically modern forms of human experience are also in trouble, although we might also wish to remember that modernity has often been identified as a condition in which the claims of sovereign authorization have always been in trouble.

In some places, at least, we have learnt to become critical of the habit of using the term sovereignty as a synonym for state sovereignty, a habit that has maintained its most tenacious grip on the disciplinary practices of political science and international relations. This is a habit that has enabled a pervasive forgetting about sovereignty as a problem, a problem that can be posed in spatiotemporally specific ways, as well as about the spatiotemporally specific principles, institutionalizations, and practices through which the problem of sovereignty has been declared solved under specific conditions and specific forms of authority have become authorized. Sovereignty has most obviously arisen as a problem in relation to both the violence of creation, of founding, of beginning, and to the violence of limitation, to the establishment of boundaries and horizons and to the possibility of their transgression; and thus to the ways in which specifically modern forms of sovereignty express spatiotemporally specific accounts of creation and limitation, and spatiotemporally specific accounts of spatiotemporality.

Even when thinking about the sovereignty of the modern state, we have begun to re-engage with the ways in which claims about state sovereignty are inseparable from claims in what seem to be three quite distinctive spheres of action. First, they have come to appear inseparable from the production of modern subjectivities in the world within states so as to constitute the standard problems of modern political theory in general, and of claims about "liberty" within modern liberal-democratic traditions in particular. Second, they have come to appear inseparable from the production of subjectivities in the world beyond states so as to constitute the standard problems of theories of international relations as an array of (anarchical) spatial structures, on the one hand, and of theories of history and anthropology as an array of (teleological) temporal structures, on the other, and thus from claims about "security" and "development" in particular. Third, they have come to seem inseparable from claims about the world as such, and thus from the relation between the production of sovereignty and the production of modern self-authorizing subjectivities, the relation between the problem of the legitimate authority in the world and the problem of legitimate knowledge about the world, and thus the practices of authorization that have been constituted as the principles, institutions, and practices of "politics" under specifically modern conditions of sovereign power/authority.

While appearing to seem distinctive spheres of action, however, the appearance of separation merely effaces the conditions under which the world of modern sovereignties and subjectivities, of liberties, securities, developments, and authorities/authorizations, has been a world of mutual productions. Moreover, we have come to see that the conditions that once enabled us to be satisfied with the semblances of separation are no longer as they once could be made to work in so many times and places. The site of separation, the line marking the limits of (domestic) liberty, the point at which the necessities of (international) security/development kick in, the outer edges of a modern politics that secures its liberties in an abstract yet massively embodied affirmation of the (original and final, authorized and authorizing) necessity of violence, marks the site of our murkiest conceptualizations, and our most dramatic apprehensions. If we start messing with sovereignty, and start suggesting that the principles, institutions, and practices of sovereign states and the forms of politics that have been enabled in their name are not up to the task of ordering and authorizing a world of politics under contemporary conditions, we are inevitably troubled by renewed thoughts about origins and limits, about the contingency of all foundations, and about the spaces and times of violence in the constitution of modern liberties/securities.

It is here, most of all, that the dominant modes of knowledge of our time are completely out of their depth, so to speak, and where the need to re-engage with those theologies and ontologies that the dominant forms of knowledge of our age have authorized themselves against has appeared most pressing. Start messing with the problem of sovereignty, with the violent inscription of authorization and the authorization of violence, and any simple assertion of authority or the method of authorization demands a careful humility, or risks acute embarrassment. Once sovereignty is understood to be a problem rather than a solution, as the site/event demanding engagements with the authorization of authority rather than the necessary ground of all authority, whether in politics or in scholarship about politics, knowledge must also be understood to be a problem. This problem can only be deferred, with serious consequences, by the desperate declaration of foundations and methods, usually by invoking visions of evil and relativity that serve to re-authorize the authority of those who assume a sovereign voice. Parodies of sovereignty offer little scope for a critical engagement with the practices that have been articulated in its name. Considerable energy has been mobilized and wasted by facile accounts of some loss of foundations as a consequence of a condition or era that is now somehow other than modern. These accounts may have brought bemused smiles to the Cartesians, Hobbesians, Humeans, Kantians, and other canonical authorities of modern skepticism, of those traditions that understand modernity as precisely a condition that is at least sometimes capable of critique rather than dogma, of thinking for one's never quite self-conscious self under conditions that can never be fully known, or at least can be known only through some leap of faith in the language of God/Geometry/Nature/Reason/Liberalism. This is a leap that is always susceptible to articulation as the garden path of common sense or collective interest.

It is hardly surprising, therefore, that thinking about sovereignty is now beset with some quite profound analytical difficulties, some involving a re-engagement with the complexities of modern sovereignty as a spatiotemporally specific achievement, and some concerning the frailty of that achievement in the context of contemporary spatiotemporal transformations.

Some have to do with the ways in which sovereignty appears to be a mystery, or at least a mere epiphenomenon, an abstraction, something that we should not take seriously despite all its claims to reality. In this way, we are led to think either about "theory," about sovereignty as unreal precisely because it is abstract or as abstract precisely because it expresses the most fundamental reality, or about "sociology," about the need to get at the material social practices that produce sovereignty as an abstract effect. By going either way, of course, we miss precisely what is of interest about sovereignty as a principle, institution, and practice that always works both as abstraction and as a material social form. Here, we may become acquainted with what used to be called the mysteries of state, the sacrifice of war, the pomp and circumstance of state occasions, the interpolation of statist necessities into the discourses of national belonging, and the fine line between rationality and the deadliest of irrationalities that have made the modern state such a centered and delimited site of both power and authority. Now, perhaps, we have to come to terms with new mysteries in new material forms as states and nations are recast under new spatiotemporal conditions that they are also working to rearticulate.

Some have to do with the ways in which analyses of sovereignty are usually carried out on terms given by modern sovereignty, especially those given by both a specific framing of the relation between immanence and transcendence, the legacy of both classical and Christian dualisms that have been reworked into the construction of modern subjectivities, and by a specific framing of spatiotemporal relations that seeks to encompass temporal contingency within a spatialized order. This leads, most crucially, to the difficulty of interpreting the rearticulation of those spatiotemporal conditions that have enabled the achievement of modern sovereignty on terms given by spatiotemporally specific practices of spatiotemporality. Thus, attempts to analyze "change" in or alternatives to modern sovereignty run up against the ways in which both temporal contingency and the possibility of alternatives are already scripted in terms given by modern sovereignty. This problem can be seen in the discourses of necessity and impossibility that structure modern discourses about political realism and in the recourse to claims about the need for a new hierarchy of levels, reminiscent of a return to some Great Chain of Being, that enable so many contemporary claims about cosmopolitanism and so on. It can also be seen in the ways in which alternatives to the present are scripted as an attempt to get outside a structure of insides and outsides, to find something other than a structure of selves and others, to somehow transcend a structure of immanence and transcendence, or, in the terms that have recently re-entered into circulation with some force, to somehow break out of a structure of norms and exceptions without reproducing the violent inscription of violence at the boundary of norm and exception.

At the least, these are some of the considerations that one might want to begin pondering over in order to make sense of a variety of recent claims that the crucial shift at work in the contemporary world involves neither a perpetual continuation of state sovereignties nor the disappearance or subsumption of state sovereignty into some kind of global or cosmopolitan authority, but a proliferation, differentiation, and mobilization of sovereignties. This shift, it is said, is expressed most vividly in attempts to shift the capacity to decide exceptions to the norm, to invoke Carl Schmitt's elegant and disturbing formulation, from the territorial edges of the modern state to somewhere else, wherever that somewhere else might be.[3] The sovereignty of the specifically modern state, the preceding considerations suggest, works so as to constitute and authorize specific forms of discrimination: between here and there, spatially; between past, present, and future, temporally; and between a world of norms and exceptions, politically. Far from seeing the continuing presence or imminent absence of this capacity, it may be that what is at stake in many claims about contemporary transformations, especially in relation to notions of globalization and empire, is that we have become caught up in radically novel forms of norm, as normativity and as normalization, and in radically novel, and dangerous, forms of exceptionalism.

Many contemporary debates about sovereignty have been forced to return to Carl Schmitt, usually with some trepidation. There are perhaps three primary and closely related reasons for this, all having much more to do with the critical possibilities that may be read into Schmitt's analysis, although with some difficulty, than with the ambitions that led Schmitt to articulate an account of sovereignty that has weighed so heavily on the conscience of modern political thought ever since.

The first is that Schmitt's formulation of sovereignty as a capacity to decide exceptions offers such an elegant and pithy account of what we might, unwisely, call the essence of modern sovereignty (unwise because modern sovereignty mobilizes the full force of the nominalist critique of essentialism, although Schmitt himself tended to lean heavily toward an essentialist account of a sovereigntist politics). It is an elegance that has something of the same force as Weber's account of the state as a monopoly of power/authority within a territorial state,[4] an elegance that at once expresses and represses the spatiotemporal specificities of a form of political existence that can both celebrate and regret the sharpest of discriminations between a norm and an exception.

The second is that it permits an engagement with the mutually constitutive duality of the principle/institution/practice of norm and exception, a duality that nevertheless becomes expressed as the most dualistic framing of mutually exclusive realms: as friend and enemy; as inside and outside, as, in Schmitt's terms, the norm that explains nothing and the exception that explains everything. Schmitt hardly ranks as a dialectical thinker, but one way of thinking about Schmitt as both a danger and an opportunity is to try to see how the declaration of an absolute rift masks the historical construction of a mutually constitutive duality.

The third is that it points to the radical instability of the distinction between democratic and authoritarian rule, to a realm of indetermination between law and the suspension of law in the declaration of emergency powers. Two quite different lines of analysis might be developed here, lines that are both at work, rather confusingly, in much of the literature that has sought to re-engage with the Schmittean problematic.

One harks back to Walter Benjamin's suspicions about a generalized or permanent exceptionalism as the emerging fate of capitalist modernity as he understood it in the 1920s, and/or looks aghast at the unilateralist decisionism of the millennial American regime of George W. Bush to postulate not so much a loss of (state) sovereignty as a profound rearticulation of a sovereign exceptionalism as indeed generalized or permanent, as now somehow global.[5] This line of analysis plays on a kind of reversal of the highly unstable relation between norm and exception that Schmitt sought to fix at the territorial edge of the sovereign state, so that the normal condition is understood as having become a constant state of exceptionalism. The influential reading of contemporary trends given by Hardt and Negri, for example, rests on an underlying claim about a shift from a world torn between immanence and transcendence to a world that has now become entirely immanent, a world of Empire that is at once a world of sovereignty and sovereignties.[6]

The other works less with the possibility of reversing polarities across a line that is radically unstable than with the indeterminacy that is always inherent in the relation between norm and exception. Moreover, this indeterminacy is seen less as a moment of decision or a sharp rift between the spaces of law and of their suspension than as a potentially widening zone of indeterminacy, both spatial and temporal, between a realm of norm and law and the arbitrary assertion of force and violence. This seems to be important for at least some moments in Giorgio Agamben's critique of Schmitt.[7] In Agamben's reading, Schmitt is to be understood precisely as a response to the dangers of the apocalyptic universalism expressed by Benjamin, as an attempt to ensure that the violence of modernity be brought under law. According to Schmitt, the state of exception involves a suspension of the legal order, but this suspension remains rooted in law; the sovereign remains exterior to the normally valid legal order while nevertheless belonging to that legal order. In Agamben's view, this tight contradiction or dialectic seems to be breaking apart. There is a growing rift between the law and what Derrida has popularized as the "force of law," between the law and its application.[8] It seems to be important to distinguish between the kind of dictatorship that arises from the suspension of limits to the exercise of power and the contemporary exercise of emergency powers that have increasingly escaped from legal constraint. What is of increasing interest, therefore, is the effort to construct the appearance of a relationship between the sphere of legal validity and an increasingly dissociated sphere of exceptionalism; a relationship that one might predict will require a much more acute understanding of the changing relationship between liberty, security/development, and authority/authorization. Agamben does not seem to go very far in this direction. To him, Benjamin's apocalyptic vision has now returned as a threat of global civil war, a threat that seems to lead Agamben to want to escape from the problem of sovereignty as fast as possible. The problem that nevertheless remains to be confronted concerns the changing relation between violence and law, that is, of the political under conditions that cannot be fixed now by the capacities of the sovereign state, no matter how authoritarian.

There are nevertheless some dangers in framing any analysis of modern sovereignty in terms given by Schmitt (and leaving aside the historical connection between Schmitt himself and fascist regimes of the interwar era). Two in particular seem likely to be of increasing concern.

First, Schmitt focuses on the singular exceptionalism of the sovereign state. Yet the sovereign state is not a singularity despite all the claims that it might make to a monopoly of power and authority. At the very least, to think about sovereignty as a capacity to decide exceptions ought to lead to an examination of the triple exceptionalism that marks modern accounts of the political, the exceptionalism that marks the limits of the modern individual, the exceptionalism that marks the modern state, and the exceptionalism that marks the modern system of states. Each of these exceptionalisms is different, although related.

To recover some of the complexity that is obscured in Schmitt's sharp formulations, we might recall the ways in which Hobbes sets out an understanding of sovereignty that opens up a space of ambivalence between the sovereign as a collective abstraction and sovereignty as an expression of somehow sovereign individuals. Perhaps more crucially under contemporary conditions, Hobbes set out a complex spatiotemporal exceptionalism under which both a past and a spatial distance was set out at the furthest edges of an imagined here and now, the idealized world of free and equal individuals. Hobbes contractarian account of the founding of modern sovereignties effectively relates a story about a constitutive exceptionalism, one that sets out a world spatiotemporally both within and beyond any possible system of states. The international is not the world, contrary to the easy synonym, and contrary to the even easier but increasingly troublesome assumption that we know what and where "the world" is. The modern world sketched by Hobbes is always within and beyond the system of states in which Hobbesian humans can live, although that world of absolute exceptions, the barbaric point of origin, and the almost, but not quite, barbaric empirical world of alterities spatially over there "in America", can always be brought back in as the exception that affirms our rules, and legitimizes still more violence. The modern world of sovereign politics is a world of constitutive exceptions, and the most important exception has not been the one that Schmitt identifies at the edge of the state. It is the one between the modern and its others/negations that has enabled the construction of a modern politics of sovereign states and subjectivities. To come to terms with the life and lives of sovereignties now is to think less about a shift from a state of exception to a generalized exceptionalism or a shift from a world of immanence/transcendence to a new condition of globalized immanence than about the increasing difficulty of keeping the world both in and out of the constitution of the political.

Second, Schmitt's world is a condition of absolute spatialities. Modern sovereignties were enabled by a capacity to fix exceptions on a territorial terrain and to imagine a world of spatialized subjectivities in a world of spatialized communities. This was an extraordinary achievement, although not one that can sustain itself forever. As we seek to recover the problem of sovereignty from the demands of a modern sovereignty of spatialized states, we may indeed come to see that sovereignty does have more to do with life, with being in time, than it does with the freezing of human life in territorial space. But it will take some imagination to rethink the origin of origins and the constitution of limits in temporal terms, to imagine sovereignties as mobile and temporally contingent, and to enable a politics of many worlds without including/excluding the world so as to affirm modern subjectivities through absolute negations, as the condition under which politics—plural as well as singular, the verb even more than the noun—can be imagined at all.

Notes

1. R.B.J. Walker, *Inside/Outside: International Relations as Political Theory* (Cambridge: Cambridge University Press, 1993).
2. William E. Connolly, "The Complexity of Sovereignty," this volume, pp. 23–24.
3. Carl Schmitt, *Political Theology: Four Chapters on the Concept of Sovereignty*, trans. by George Schwab (Cambridge, Massachusetts: MIT Press, 1985).
4. Max Weber (1918), "The Profession and Vocation of Politics." In Weber, *Political Writings* (Cambridge: Cambridge University Press, 1994).
5. Benjamin, Walter, "Critique of Violence"
6. Michael Hardt and Antonio Negri (2000), *Empire* (Cambridge, Massachusetts: Harvard University Press, 2000).
7. Giorgio, Agamben, *L'etat d'exception* (Paris: Editions du Seuil, 2003); see also Giorgio, Agamben, *Means Without End: Notes on Politics* (Minneapolis: University of Minnesota Press, 2000) and *Homo Sacer: Sovereign Power and Bare Life* (Stanford: Stanford University Press, 1998).
8. Jacques, Derrida, "Force of Law: The "Mystical Foundations of Authority"." In *Deconstruction and the Possibility of Justice*, edited by Drucilla Cornell, Michael Rosenfeld and David Gray Carlson, (New York: Routledge, 1992).

Selected Bibliography

Giorgio Agamben, "Security and Terror." *Theory and Event* 5(4), 2002.

Giorgio Agamben, *Homo Sacer: Sovereign Power and Bare Life*, trans. by Daniel Heller-Roazen (Stanford, California: Stanford University Press, 1998).

Giorgio Agamben, *L'etat d'exception* (Paris: Editions du Seuil, 2003).

Giorgio Agamben, *Means Without End: Notes on Politics*, trans. by Vincenzo Binetti and Cesare Casarino (Minneapolis: University of Minnesota Press, 2000).

Giorgio Agamben, *Potentialities. Collected Essays in Philosophy.* trans. by Daniel Heller-Roazen, edited by Daniel Heller-Roazen (Stanford, California: Stanford University Press, 1999).

Giorgio Agamben, *Remnants of Auschwitz: The Witness and the Archive.* trans. by Daniel Heller-Roazen (New York: Zone Books, 1999).

Giorgio Agamben, *The End of the Poem. Studies in Poetics* (Stanford: Stanford University Press, 1999).

Sara Ahmed, *Strange Encounters: Embodying Others in Post-Coloniality* (London: Routledge, 2000).

Gerald Alfred, *Heeding the Voices of our Ancestors* (Toronto: Oxford University Press, 1995).

Gerald Alfred, *Peace, Power, Righteousness: An Indigenous Manifesto* (Toronto: Oxford University Press, 1999).

Karen Anderson, *Chain Her By One Foot: The subjugation of native women in 17th Century New France* (London: Routledge, 1993).

Kim Anderson, *A Recognition of Being: Reconstructing Native Womanhood* (Toronto: Sumach Press, 2000).

Peter Andreas, and Richard Price, "From War Fighting to Crime Fighting: Transforming the American national Security State," *International Studies Review*, 3(3), Fall, 2001; 31.

Peter Andreas, *Border Games* (Ithaca: Cornell University Press).

Gaston Bachelard, *The Poetics of Space*, trans. by Maria Jolas, (Boston: Beacon Press, 1994).

Etienne Balibar, "Ambiguous Universality," *Differences: Journal of Feminist Cultural Studies*, 7(1), 1995:48–74.

Tarak Barkawi and Mark Laffey, "Retrieving the Imperial: Empire and International Relations," *Millennium: Journal of International Studies*, 31(1), 2002: 109–127.

Marie Battiste, editor *Reclaiming Indigenous Voice and Vision* (Vancouver: UBC Press, 2000).

Jean Baudrillard, "The Seismic Order," (1991). URL http://www.uta.edu/english/apt/collab/texts/sedismic.html

Walter Benjamin, "Critique of Violence"

Walter Benjamin, *The Origin of German Tragic Drama* (London: Verso, 1998).

Geoffrey Bennington, *Interrupting Derrida* (London: Routledge, 2000).

Lauren Berlant, "Live Sex Acts [Parental Advisory: Explicit Material." In *In near Ruins: Cultural Theory at the End of the Century*, edited by Nicholas B. Dirks . Minneapolis: University of Minnesota Press, 1998), pp. 173–197.

Steven M. Block, "The Growing Threat of Biological Weapons," *American Scientist*, 89(1), 2001: 28–40.

Menno Boldt and J. Anthony Long. *The Quest for Justice: Aboriginal Peoples and Aboriginal Rights* (Toronto: University of Toronto Press, 1985), Part 1.

Menno Boldt, *Surviving as Indians: The Challenge of Self-Government* (Toronto: University of Toronto Press, 1993).

Menno Boldt, *The Dispossessed: Life and Death in Native Canada* (Toronto: McArthur & Company, 1999).

Katherine Boo, "What Mother Teresa Could Learn in a Leather Bar." *The Washington Monthly*, June 1991, pp. 34–40.

Ken Booth and Tim Dunne, editors *Worlds in Collision: Terror and the Future of Global Order* (London: Palgrave Macmillan, 2002).

Jorge Luis Borges, *The Aleph and Other Stories, 1933–1969*, trans. by Norman Thomas di Giovanni (New York: Dutton: 1970).

John Borrows, *Recovering Canada: The Resurgence of Indigenous Law* (Toronto: University of Toronto Press, 2002).

Pierre Bourdieu, *Distinction : A Social Critique of the Judgement of Taste* (Cambridge, Massachusetts: Harvard University Press, 1984).

Pierre Bourdieu, *The Logic of Practice*, trans. by Richard Nice (Cambridge: Polity Press, 1990).

Curtis C. Breight, *Surveillance, Militarism and Drama in the Elizabethan Era* (New York: St. Martins, 1996), pp. 15–17.

Hedley Bull, *The Anarchical Society: A Study of Order in World Politics*, Second edition (London: Macmillan, 1995).

Robert Burgoyne, *Film Nation: Hollywood Looks at U.S. History* (Minneapolis: University of Minnesota Press, 1997).

Chandler Burr, "The Aids Exception: Privacy Vs. Public Health." *The Atlantic Monthly*, June 1997, pp. 57–67.

Catherine Bush, *The Rules of Engagement* (Toronto: Harper Flamingo Canada, 2000).

Richard L. Bushman, and Claudia L. Bushman. "The Early History of Cleanliness in America." *Journal of American History*, 74, 1988: 1213–1238.

Judith Butler, Ernesto Laclau and Slavoj Zizek, *Contingency, Hegemony, Universality* (London: Verso, 2000).

Alan C. Cairns, *Citizens Plus, Aboriginal Peoples and the Canadian State* (Vancouver: UBC Press, 2000).

Donald L. Carveth, "The Borderland Dilemma in Paris Texas: Psychoanalytic Approaches to Shepard, Sam, *Psyart: A Hyperlink Journal for Psychological Study of Arts* at: http:www.clas.ufl.edu/ipsa/journal/articles/psyart1997/ carvet01.htm.

Cornelius Castoriadis, *The Imaginary Institution of Society* (Cambridge: Polity Press, 1987).

I. J. Catanach, "The 'Globalization' of Disease? India and the Plague." *Journal of World History*, 12(1), 2001: 131–153.

John Cawelti, *The Six-Gun Mystique Sequel* (Bowling Green, Ohio: Bowling Green University Popular Press, 1999).

Dipesh Chakrabarty, *Provincializing Europe: Postcolonial Thought and Historical Difference* (Princeton: Princeton University Press, 2000).

James Chapman, *The British at War: Cinema State and Propaganda, 1939–1945*.

Partha Chatterjee, "Colonialism, Nationalism and Colonialized Women: The Contest in India," *American Ethnologist*, 16(4), 1989: 622–633.

Partha Chatterjee, *Nationalist Thought and the Colonial World: A Derivative Discourse?* (London: Zed Books, 1986).

Katherine Beaty Chiste, "Aboriginal Women and Self-Government: Challenging Leviathan" in *American Indian Culture and Research Journal*, 18(3), 1994: 19–43.

Rey Chow, *Women and Chinese Modernity: The Politics of Reading Between West and East* (Minneapolis: University of Minnesota Press, 1990).

Cynthia Cockburn, with Rada Stakić-Domuz, and Meliha Hubić. *Women Organising for Change. A Study of Women's Local Integrative Organisations and the Pursuit of Democracy in Bosnia-Herzegovina* (Zenica: Medica, Infoteka, 2001).

Cynthia Cockburn, *The Space between Us: Negotiating Gender and National Identities in Conflict* (London and New York: Zed Books, 1998).

Evan Connell, *Son of the Morning Star: Custer and the Little Bighorn* (New York: Harper Collins, 1984).

William E. Connolly, *Identity\Difference: Democratic Negotiations of Political Paradox* (Ithaca and London: Cornell University Press, 1991).

William E. Connolly, *The Ethos of Pluralization* (Minneapolis: University of Minnesota Press, 1995).

William E. Connolly, *Why I Am Not A Secularist* (Minneapolis: University of Minnesota Press, 1999).

Costas Constantinou, "Hippopolis/Cynopolis," *Millennium: Journal of International Studies*, 30(3), 2001: 788.

Robert Cooper, *The Postmodern State and the World Order* (London: Demos, 2000).

Mike Davis, *City of Quartz : Excavating the Future in Los Angeles* (London: Verso, 1990).

Mike Davis, *Ecology of Fear : Los Angeles and the Imagination of Disaster* (New York: Metropolitan Books, 1998).

Jodi Dean, editor Cultural Studies and Political Theory (Ithaca: Cornell University Press, 2000).

Gilles Deleuze, and Felix Guattari, *A Thousand Plateaus*, trans. by Brian Massumi (Minneapolis: University of Minnesota Press, 1987).

Don DeLillo, *Libra* (New York: Viking, 1988).

D. T. Dennis, "Plague in India: Lessons for Public Health Everywhere." *British Medical Journal*, 309(6959), 1994: 893–895.

Jacques Derrida, "Declarations of Independence," *New Political Science*, 15, 1986.

Jacques Derrida, "Force of Law: The "Mystical Foundations of Authority"." In *Deconstruction and the Possibility of Justice*, edited by Drucilla Cornell, Michael Rosenfeld and David Gray Carlson (New York: Routledge, 1992).

Jacques Derrida, "Violence and Metaphysics," in *Writing and Difference*, trans. by A. Bass (Chicago: Chicago UP, 1978).

Jacques Derrida, *Margins of Philosophy*, trans. by Alan Bass (Chicago: University of Chicago Press, 1982).

G.M. Dillon, and J. Everard, "Stat(e)ing Australia: Squid Jigging and the Masque of State," *Alternatives*, 17, 1992: 281–312.

Michael Dillon, and Julian Reid. "Global Governance, Liberal Peace, and Complex Emergency." *Alternatives*, 25, 2000: 117–143.

Marc G. Doucet, "The Possibility of Deterritorializing Democracy: Agonistic Democratic Politics and the Apec Ngo Forums," *Alternatives: Global, Local, Political*, 26(3), 2001: 283–316.

Ann Douglas, *Terrible Honesty: Mongrel Manhattan in the 1920s* (New York: The Noonday Press, 1995).

Jenny Edkins, "Sovereign Power, Zones of Indistinction, and the Camp," *Alternatives*, 25, 2000: 3–25.

Jenny Edkins, *Poststructuralism and International Relations* (Boulder, Colorado: Lynne Rienner, 1999).

John Ellis, *The Social History of the Machine Gun* (Baltimore: Johns Hopkins University Press, 1975).

Tom Englehardt, *The End of Victory Culture* (New York: Basic Books, 1995).

Cynthia Enloe, *Bananas Beaches and Bases: Making Feminist Sense of International Politics* (Berkeley: University of California Press, 1990).

Escobar Arturo, *Encountering Development* (Princeton: Princeton University Press, 1994).

Richard Falk, *On Humane Governance: Toward a New Global Politics* (Cambridge: Polity Press, 1995).

Richard Falk, *The Great Terror War* (New York: Arris Publishing, 2003).

Jo-Anne Fiske, "Child of the State, Mother of the Nation: Aboriginal Women and the Ideology of Motherhood" in *Culture*, 13(1), 1993: 17–35.

Michel Foucault, "Two Lectures," trans. by Leo Marshall Colin Gordon, John Mepham and Kate Soper. *Power/Knowledge: Selected Interviews and Other Writings 1972–1977*, edited by Colin Gordon (Brighton: Harvester, 1980), pp. 78–108.

Michel Foucault, *Discipline and Punish: The Birth of the Prison*, trans. by Alan Sheridan (London: Allen Lane, 1991).

Michel Foucault, *Power/Knowledge: Selected Interviews and Other Writings 1972–1977*, trans. by Colin Gordon (Brighton: Harvester Press, 1980).

Michel Foucault, "Of Other Spaces." *Diacritics*, 16(1), 1986: 22–27.

Michel Foucault, "Governmentality." In *The Foucault Effect: Studies in Governmentality*, edited by Colin Gordon and Peter Miller Graham Burchill (Chicago: The University of Chicago Press, 1991), pp. 87–104.

Michel Foucault, "Security, Territory, and Population." In *Essential Works of Foucault. Ethics: Subjectivity and Truth*, edited by Paul Rabinow (New York: The New Press, 1997), pp. 67–71.

Michel Foucault, "The Subject and Power." *Michel Foucault: Power*, Vol. 3, Essential Works of Foucault 1954–1984, edited by James D Faubion (New York: The New Press, 1994), pp. 326–348.

Michel Foucault, "Life, Experience and Science," *Revue de Métaphysique et de Morale*, January–March 1985.

Michel Foucault, *Discipline and Punish: The Birth of the Prison* (London, Allen Lane 1977).

Michel Foucault, *Power/Knowledge: Selected Interviews and Other Writings 1972–1977* (Brighton: Harvester Press, 1980).

Michel Foucault, *Society Must be Defended. Lectures at the Collège de France, 1975–1976* (New York: Picador, 2003).

Michel Foucault, *The History of Sexuality: Volume 1: An Introduction*, trans. by Robert Hurley (Harmondsworth: Penguin Books, 1990).

Johann Peter Frank, *A System of Complete Medical Police: Selections from Johann Peter Frank* (Baltimore: Johns Hopkins University Press, 1976).

Michael Fumento, *The Myth of Heterosexual Aids* (Washington, District Columbia: Regnery Publishing, Inc., 1993).

Tag Gallagher, "Angels Gambol Where They Will: *John Ford's Indians*. In *The Western Reader*, edited by Jim Kitses and Greg Rickman (New York: Limelight, 1998).

Andre Gardies, *Le Cinema de Robbe-Grillet: Essai semiocritique* (Paris: Albatross, 1983).

Laurie Garrett, "The Nightmare of Bioterrorism," *Foreign Affairs*, 80(1), 2000: 76–89.

Laurie Garrett, "The Return of Infectious Disease," *Foreign Affairs*, 74(1), 1996: 66–80.

Laurie Garrett, *Betrayal of Trust: The Collapse of Global Public Health* (New York: Hyperion, 2000).

Laurie Garrett, *The Coming Plague: Newly Emerging Diseases in a World out of Balance* (New York: Penguin Books, 1995).

Rodolphe Gasché, *Of Minimal Things. Studies on the Notion of Relation* (Stanford: Stanford University Press, 1999).

Larry George, "9-11: Pharmacotic War," *Theory and Event*, 5(4) http://www.muse.jhu.edu/journals/theory_and_event/v005.4

William Gibson, *Count Zero* (New York: Ace Books, 1987).

Anthony Giddens, *The Nation-State and Violence* (Berkeley: University of California Press, 1985).

William H. Goetzmann, and William N. Goetzmann, *The West of the Imagination* (New York: W. W. Norton, 1986).

Joyce Green, "Sexual Equality and Indian Government: An Analysis of Bill C-31 Amendments to the Indian Act," in *Native Studies Review*, 1(2), 1985: 81–95.

Mirko D. Grmek, *History of AIDS: Emergence and Origin of a Modern Pandemic*. trans. by Russel C. Maulitz and Jacalyn Duffin (Princeton: Princeton University Press, 1990).

Marianne Gronemeyer, "Helping." In *The Development Dictionary: A Guide to Knowledge as Power*, edited by Wolfgang Sachs (London: Zed Books, 1992), pp. 53–69.

Siba Grovogui, "Regimes of Sovereignty: International Morality and the African Condition," *European Journal of International Relations*, 8(3), 2002: 215–238.

Ian Hacking, *The Taming of Chance* (Cambridge: Cambridge University Press, 1990).

Peter Handke, "The Long Way Around." In *Slow Homecoming* (New York: Farrar/Straus/Giroux, 1985).

Michael Hardt, "Sovereignty" *Theory & Event*, 5(4), 2001.

Michael Hardt and Antonio Negri, *Empire* (Cambridge, Massachusetts: Harvard University Press, 2000).

Dona Harraway, *Simians, Cyborgs, and Women: The Reinvention of Nature* (New York: Routledge, 1991).

Stephen Hawking, *A Brief History of Time* (New York: Bantam, 1988).

Martin Heidegger, "What is Metaphysics?" In *Martin Heidegger: Basic Writings* (New York: Harper and Row, 1977).

Mary W. Helms, *Ulysses' Sail: An Ethnographic Odyssey of Power, Knowledge, and Geographic Distance* (Princeton: Princeton University Press, 1988).

Barry Hindess, *Discourses of Power: From Hobbes to Foucault* (Oxford: Blackwell, 1996).

Christopher Hitchens, *Blood, Class, and Nostalgia: Anglo-American Ironies* (New York: Farrar, Straus & Giroux,1990).

Douglas Hofstadter, *Metamagical Themas: Questing for the Essence of Mind and Pattern* (Basic Books, Harper Collins Publishers, 1985).

Bonnie Honig, "Declarations of Independence: Arendt and Derrida on the Problem of Founding a Republic," *American Political Science Review*, Winter, 1991: 97–113.

Edward Hooper, *The River: A Journey to the Source of HIV and AIDS* (New York: Little, Brown & Company, 2000).

Christine Howells, *Derrida: Deconstruction from Phenomenology to Ethics* (Cambridge, UK: Polity Press, 1999).

Aida Hozic, "Forbidden Places, Tempting Spaces, and Politics of Desire: On Stalker and Beyond." In *To Seek Out the New Worlds: Science Fiction and International Relations*, edited by Jutta Weldes (London and New York: Palgrave Macmillan, 2003).

Aida Hozic, "Zoning, or How to Govern (Cultural) Violence?" *Cultural Values*, 6(1), 2002: 183–195.

Samuel P. Huntington, Fouad Ajami, Robert L. Bartley, Liu Binyan, Jeane J. Kirkpatrick, Kishore Mahbubani, Gerard Piel and Albert L. Weeks. *The Clash of Civilizations?: The Debate* (New York: Foreign Affairs, 1996).

Jasmina Husanović, "Practice with No Language: A Reflection of the 'Gender Scene' in a Sarajevo Workshop," *International Feminist Journal of Politics* 3(1), 2001: 124–130.

John G Ikenberry, *After Victory: Institutions, Strategic Restraint, and the Rebuilding of Order After Major Wars* (Princeton, New Jersey: Princeton University Press, 2000).

Jason F. Isaacson, "Preface." In *Seeking the Truth : The AMIA Bombing Goes to Trial*, edited by Sergio Kiernan (New York: American Jewish Committee, 2001).

Matthew Frye. Jacobson, *Barbarian Virtues: The United States Encounters Foreign People at Home and Abroad, 1876–1917* (New York: Hill and Wang, 2000).

M. Annette Jaimes, editor *The State of Native America: Genocide, Colonization and Resistance* (Boston: South End Press, 1992).

C.L.R. James, *Mariners, Renegades, Castaways: The Story of Hermann Melville and the World We Live In* (Dartmouth: University Press of New England, 2001).

Kathleen Jamieson, "Sex Discrimination and the Indian Act." In *The Arduous Journey: Canadian Indians and Decolonization*, edited by J. Rick Ponting (Toronto: McLelland and Stewart, 1986).

Kathleen Jamieson, *Indian Women and the Law in Canada: Citizens Minus* (Ottawa: Minister of Supply and Services, 1978).

Chalmers A. Johnson, *Blowback: The Costs and Consequences of American Empire* (New York: Owl Books, 2003).

Steven Johnston, *Encountering Tragedy: Rousseau and the Project of Democratic Order* (Ithaca: Cornell University Press, 1999).

Robert D. Kaplan, *The Coming Anarchy: Shattering the Dreams of the Post Cold War* (New York: Vintage Books, 2001).

Robert D. Kaplan, "The Coming Anarchy." *The Atlantic Monthly*, February 1994, pp. 44–76.

Lily E. Kay, *The Molecular Vision of Life* (Oxford: Oxford University Press, 1993).

Lily E. Kay, *Who Wrote the Book of Life. A History of the Genetic Code* (Stanford: Stanford University Press, 2000).

Alan Keenan, "Promises, Promises: The Work of Arendt," *Political Theory* (May 1994), pp. 297–322.

Sergio Kiernan, *Atrocity in Buenos Aires : The AMIA Bombing, One Year Later* (New York: American Jewish Committee, 1995).

Kem Kilpatrick, "Canada's Ebola Scare over but Questions Just Beginning," *Canadian Medical Association Journal*, 164(7), 2001.

Alexander Kluge, "On Film and the Public Sphere," trans. by Thomas Y. Levin and Miriam B Hansen. *New German Critique* 24–25, Fall/Winter, 1981–1982: 21.

Phillip Kolker, and Peter Beicken, *The Films of Wim Wenders: Cinema as Vision and Desire* (New York: Cambridge University Press, 1993).

R. Koselleck, *Critique and Crisis. Enlightenment and the Pathogenesis of Modern Society* (Oxford: Berg 1988).

Charles A Kupchan, *The End of the American Era: US Foreign Policy and the Geopolitics of the Twenty-first Century* (New York: Alfred A Knopf, 2002).

Judith Walzer Leavitt, *Typhoid Mary: Captive to the Public's Health* (Boston: Beacon Press, 1996).

Primo Levi, *If This Is a Man and the Truce*, trans. by Stuart Woolf (London: Abacus, 1979).

Primo Levi, *The Drowned and the Saved*, trans. by Raymond Rosenthal (London: Abacus, 1989).

Debbie Lisle, "Consuming Danger: Re-Imagining the War-Tourism Divide'", *Alternatives*, 25, 2000: 91–116.

Patrick Macklem, *Indigenous Difference and the Constitution of Canada* (Toronto: University of Toronto Press, 2001).

Joseph B. McCormick, and Susan Fisher-Hoch, *Level 4: Virus Hunters of the C.D.C* (New York: Barnes & Nobles, 1999).

Lois McNay, *Gender and Agency. Reconfiguring the Subject in Feminist and Social Theory* (Cambridge: Polity Press, 2000).

John J. Mearscheimer, *The Tragedy of Great Power Politics* (New York: W W Norton, 2001).

Semezdin Mehmedinović, *Sarajevo Blues: Rjecnik Termina Opkoljenog Grada / Sarajevo Blues: Dictionary of Concepts from a Besieged City* (Sarajevo: Svjetlost, 1992).

Chandra Mohanty, Ann Russo and Lourdes Torres, editors. *Third World Women and the Politics of Feminism* (Bloomington: Indiana University Press, 1991).

Patricia Molloy, "Moral Spaces and Moral Panics. High Schools, War Zones and Other Dangerous Places." URL http://culturemachine.tees.ac.uk/Cmach/Backissues/j004/Articles/molloy.htm. Accessed October 27, 2003.

Gail Stacey Moore, "Statement on the Canada Package," Position Paper: Native Women's Association of Canada (February 2, 1992).

Wendy Moss, "The Canadian State and Indian Women: The Struggle for Sex Equality Under the Indian Act." In Women and the Canadian State/Les Femmes et l'Etat Canadien, edited by Caroline Andrew and Sandra Rodgers (Montreal & Kingston: McGill-Queen's University Press, 1997).

Teressa Anne Nahanee, "Indian Women, Sex Equality and the Charter." In Women and the Canadian State/Les Femmes et l'Etat Canadien, edited by Caroline Andrew and Sandra Rodgers (Montreal & Kingston: McGill-Queen's University Press, 1997).

Ashis Nandy, The Illegitimacy of Nationalism (Delhi: Oxford University Press, 1994).

Ashis Nandy, The Intimate Enemy: Loss and Recovery of Self under Colonialism (Delhi: Oxford University Press, 1983).

Uma Narayan, Dislocating Culture: Identities, Traditions, and Third World Feminism (New York: Routledge, 1997).

Tor Norretranders, The User Illusion, trans. by Jonathan Syndenham (New York: Viking Press, 1998).

Sekai Nzenza-Shand, Songs to an African Sunset: A Zimbabwean Story (Melbourne: Lonely Planet Publications, 1997).

Louiza Odysseos, "Laughing Matters: Peace, Democracy and the Challenge of the Comic Narrative," Millennium: Journal of International Studies, 30(3), 2001: 710.

Andrew Parker, Mary Russo, Doris Sommer and Patricia Yaeger, editors Nationalisms and Sexualities (New York: Routledge, 1992).

Jane Parpart, "Deconstructing the Development 'Expert': Gender, Development and the 'Vulnerable Groups.'" In Feminism/Postmodernism/Development, edited by Marianne Marchand and Jane Parpart (London: Routledge, 1995), pp. 221–243.

Maurice Pearton, The Knowledgeable State. Diplomacy War and Technology Since 1890 (London: Burnett Books, 1982).

Ralph Peters, "Our Soldiers, Their Cities," Parameters, 26(1), Spring, 1996: 43–50.

Shane Phelan, "All the Comforts of Home: The Genealogy of Community." In Revisioning the Political Feminist Reconstructions of Traditional Concepts in Western Political Theory, edited by Nancy J. Hirschmann and Christine Di Stefano (Boulder, Colorado and Oxford: Westview Press, 1996), pp. 235–250.

Jan Nederveen Pieterse, "My Paradigm or Yours: Alternative Development, Post-Development, Reflexive Development," Development and Change, 29, 1998: 343–373.

Mary Louise Pratt, Imperial Eyes: Travel Writing and Transculturation (New York: Routledge, 1992).

Richard Preston, The Hot Zone (New York: Random House, 1994).

Thomas Pynchon, Gravity's Rainbow (New York: Viking, 1973).

Jacques Rancière, "Politics, Identification, and Subjectivization," in October. vol. 61, summer 1992.

Jacques Rancière, Disagreements: Politics and Philosophy, trans. by J. Rose (Minneapolis: Minnesota UP, 1999).

Karen Rasmussen, and Sharon D. Downey, "Dialectical Disorientation in Vietnam War Films: Subversion of the Mythology of War," Quarterly Journal of Speech 77(2), May 1991: 176–195.

Robert Redeker, "In Place of Politics: Humanitarianism and War." In Masters of the Universe? NATO's Balkan Crusade, edited by Tariq Ali (New York: Verso, 2000).

Lewis Frye Richardson, Statistics of Deadly Quarrels (Pittsburgh: Boxwood Press, 1960).

Michael Rogin, Ronald Reagan, the Movie and Other Episodes in Political Demonology (Berkeley: University of California Press, 1987).

Theodore Roosevelt, The Winning of the West (New York: G. Putnam, 1889).

Gabriel Rotello, Sexual Ecology: AIDS and the Destiny of Gay Men (New York: Dutton, 1997).

Jean Jacques Rousseau, On the Social Contract: With Geneva Manuscript and Political Economy, trans. by Judith Masters (New York: St. Martin's, 1978).

Fiona Sampson, "History Train," Alternatives, 25(3), 2000: 285.

Kumkum Sangari and Sudesh Vaid, editors Recasting Women: Essays in Indian Colonial History (New Brunswick: Rutgers University Press, 1990).

Heather Schell, "Outbursts! A Chilling True Story About Emerging-Virus Narratives and Pandemic Social Change," Configurations, 5(1), 1997: 93–133.

Carl Schmitt, *Political Theology: Four Chapters on the Concept of Sovereignty*, trans. by George Schwab (Cambridge, Massachusetts: MIT Press, 1985).

Karen Schneider, "With Violence If Necessary," *Journal of Popular Film and Television* 27(1), 1999: 2–13.

Kam Shapiro, "From Dream to Desire: At the Threshold of Old and New Utopias," *Theory & Event*, http://muse.jhu.edu/journals/theory_and_event/v004/4.4r_kam.html

Michael Shapiro, "National Times and Other Times: Re-thinking Citizenship," *Cultural Studies*,1, January 2000.

Karena Shaw, *Leviathan's Angels: Indigenous Politics and the Limits of the Political* (PhD Dissertation, The Johns Hopkins University, 1999).

Randy Shilts, *And the Band Played On: Politics, People and the AIDS Epidemic* (New York: St. Martin's Press, 2000).

Chris Sievernich, editor. *Wim Wenders-Sam Shepard: Paris Texas* (Nordlinger, Germany: Greno, 1984).

Janet Silman, *Enough is Enough: Aboriginal Women Speak Out* (Toronto: The Women's Press, 1987).

Richard Slotkin, *Gunfighter Nation* (New York: Atheneum, 1992).

Ian Smillie, "Service Delivery or Civil Society? Ngos in Bosnia and Herzegovina." Zagreb: CARE International, 1996.

Claire Smith, and Graeme K. Ward, editors. *Indigenous Cultures in an Interconnected World* (Vancouver, UBC Press, 2000).

Dan Smith, *The Seventh Fire: The Struggle for Aboriginal Government* (Toronto: Key Porter Books, Ltd, 1993).

Neil Smith, "The Satanic Geographies of Globalization: Uneven Development in the 1990s," *Public Culture*, 10(1), 1997: 169–189.

Nevzat Soguk, *States and Strangers: Refugees and Displacements of Statecraft* (Minneapolis and London: University of Minnesota Press, 1999).

Gayatri Spivak, *In Other Worlds: Essays in Cultural Politics* (New York: Routledge, 1988).

Peter Stallybrass and Allon White, *The Politics and Poetics of Transgression* (Ithaca, New York: Cornell UP, 1986).

Yannis Stavrakakis, *Lacan and the Political* (London: Routledge, 1999).

Manfred Steger, Review of Hardt and Negri's Empire. *American Political Science Review*, 96(1), 2002: 264–265.

Mira Stout, *One Thousand Chestnut Trees* (London: Flamingo, 1997).

Aida Bagiæ Stubbs, and Paul, "Civil Society Development Programme. An Independent Evaluation." Zagreb, Croatia: CARE International. Bosnia-Herzegovina and Croatia, 2000.

Christine Sylvester, "African and Western Feminisms: World-Traveling the Tendencies and Possibilities," *Signs: Journal of Women in Culture and Society*, 20(4) 1995:941–969.

Christine Sylvester, "Development Poetics," *Alternatives*, 25(13), 2000: 335–351.

Christine Sylvester, *Feminist International Relations: An Unfinished Journey* (Cambridge: Cambridge University Press, 2002).

Peter Szondi, *An Essay on the Tragic* (Stanford: Stanford University Press, 2002).

Alexis de Tocqueville, *Democracy in America*, 2 vols., trans. by George Lawrence (New York: Harper and Row, 1969).

Alexis de Tocqueville, *Democracy in America: Vol. 1* (New York: Vintage Books, 1990 [1835]).

Victor Turner, *Dramas, Fields, and Metaphors: Symbolic Action in Human Society* (Ithaca and London: Cornell University Press, 1974).

Ellen Turpel, "Aboriginal Peoples and the Canadian Charter of Rights and Freedom." *Canadian Womens Studies/les cahiers de la femme* 10(2&3), 1989: 149–157.

Mary Ellen Turpel-Lafond, "Patriarchy and Paternalism: The Legacy of the Canadian State for First Nations Women". In *Women and the Canadian State/Les Femmes et l'Etat Canadien*, edited by Caroline Andrew and Sandra Rodgers (Montreal & Kingston: McGill-Queen's University Press, 1997).

Paul Virilio, *War and Cinema: The Logistics of Perception*, trans. by Patrick Camiller (New York: Verso, 1989).

Priscilla Wald, "Cultures and Carriers: 'Typhoid Mary' and the Science of Social Control," *Social Text* 15(3 and 4), 1997: 181–214.

Catherine Waldby, *AIDS and the Body Politics: Biomedicine and Sexual Difference* (New York: Routledge, 1996).

R.B.J. Walker, *Inside/Outside: International Relations as Political Theory* (Cambridge: Cambridge University Press, 1993).

Max Weber, "The Profession and Vocation of Politics." In Weber, *Political Writings* (Cambridge: Cambridge University Press, 1994).

Wim Wenders, *Written in the West* (Munich: Shirmer, 1987).

C.R. Whittaker, *Frontiers of the Roman Empire: A Social and Economic Study* (London: John Hopkins, 1994).

John Edgar Wideman, *Fever: Twelve Stories* (New York: Penguin, 1990).

Owen Wister, "The Evolution of the Cow-Puncher." In *Owen Wister's West*, edited by Robert Murray Davis (Albuquerque: University of New Mexico Press, 1987), pp. 33–53.

Geoffrey York, *People of the Pines: The Warriors and the Legacy of Oka* (Boston/Toronto: Little Brown, 1991).

Slavoj Žižek, "An Interview with Slavoj Žižek," *Historical Materialism. Research in Critical Marxist Theory*, 7, Winter 2000: 181–197.

Slavoj Žižek, "Enjoy Your Nation as Yourself!" In *Tarrying with the Negative: Kant, Hegel, and the Critique of Ideology*, edited by Slavoj Žižek (Durham, USA: Duke University Press, 1993), pp. 200–237.

Slavoj Žižek, *Manje ljubavi - više mržnje!* trans. by Ranko Mastilovic (Belgrade: Beogradski krug, 2001).

Slavoj Žižek, *On Belief* (London, New York: Routledge, 2001).

Slavoj Žižek, *The Fragile Absolute—or, Why Is the Christian Legacy Worth Fighting For* (London and New York: Verso, 2000).

Slavoj Žižek, *The Ticklish Subject: The Absent Centre of Political Ontology* (London: Verso, 2000).

Slavoj. Žižek, *Welcome to the Desert of the Real* (London: Verso, 2002).

Slavoj Žižek, *Did Somebody Say Totalitarianism? Five Interventions in the (Mis)Use of a Notion* (London and New York: Verso, 2001).

Index